Digitalization as a Driver for Smart Economy in the Post-COVID-19 Era

Leonilde Reis
Instituto Politécnico de Setúbal, Portugal

Luísa Cagica Carvalho
Instituto Politécnico de Setúbal, Portugal & CEFAGE, Universidade de Évora, Portugal

Clara Silveira
Polytechnic Institute of Guarda, Portugal

Duarte Xara Brasil
Instituto Politécnico de Setúbal, Portugal

IGI Global
PUBLISHER of TIMELY KNOWLEDGE

A volume in the Advances in Finance, Accounting, and Economics (AFAE) Book Series

Published in the United States of America by
IGI Global
Business Science Reference (an imprint of IGI Global)
701 E. Chocolate Avenue
Hershey PA, USA 17033
Tel: 717-533-8845
Fax: 717-533-8661
E-mail: cust@igi-global.com
Web site: http://www.igi-global.com

Library of Congress Cataloging-in-Publication Data

Names: Reis, Leonilde, 1962- editor. | Carvalho, Luísa Cagica, 1970- editor. | Silveira, Clara, 1964- editor. | Xara-Brasil, Duarte, 1970- editor.
Title: Digitalization as a driver for smart economy in the post-COVID-19 era / Leonilde Reis, Luísa Carvalho, Clara Silveira, and Duarte Xara-Brasil, editor.
Description: Hershey, PA : Business Science Reference, [2022] | Includes bibliographical references and index. | Summary: "This book presents a global and multidisciplinary approach that can contribute to a better understanding of the relationship and mutual influence of digital, entrepreneurship, marketing, sustainability, customer relationship management and innovation scientific areas"-- Provided by publisher.
Identifiers: LCCN 2021035403 (print) | LCCN 2021035404 (ebook) | ISBN 9781799892274 (hardcover) | ISBN 9781799892298 (ebook)
Subjects: LCSH: COVID-19 Pandemic, 2020---Economic aspects. | Entrepreneurship--Technological innovations. | Sustainable development--Technological innovations.
Classification: LCC HC59.3 .D54 2022 (print) | LCC HC59.3 (ebook) | DDC 330.9/052--dc23
LC record available at https://lccn.loc.gov/2021035403
LC ebook record available at https://lccn.loc.gov/2021035404

This book is published in the IGI Global book series Advances in Finance, Accounting, and Economics (AFAE) (ISSN: 2327-5677; eISSN: 2327-5685)

British Cataloguing in Publication Data
A Cataloguing in Publication record for this book is available from the British Library.

For electronic access to this publication, please contact: eresources@igi-global.com.

Advances in Finance, Accounting, and Economics (AFAE) Book Series

Ahmed Driouchi
Al Akhawayn University, Morocco

ISSN:2327-5677
EISSN:2327-5685

Mission

In our changing economic and business environment, it is important to consider the financial changes occurring internationally as well as within individual organizations and business environments. Understanding these changes as well as the factors that influence them is crucial in preparing for our financial future and ensuring economic sustainability and growth.

The **Advances in Finance, Accounting, and Economics (AFAE)** book series aims to publish comprehensive and informative titles in all areas of economics and economic theory, finance, and accounting to assist in advancing the available knowledge and providing for further research development in these dynamic fields.

Coverage

- Microeconomics
- Environmental and Social Accounting
- Economics of Intellectual Property Rights
- Bankruptcy
- Economics Geography
- Economics of Agriculture and Biotechnology
- Economics of Innovation and Knowledge
- Accounting information systems
- Economic Downturn
- Statistical Analysis

The Advances in Finance, Accounting, and Economics (AFAE) Book Series (ISSN 2327-5677) is published by IGI Global, 701 E. Chocolate Avenue, Hershey, PA 17033-1240, USA, www.igi-global.com. This series is composed of titles available for purchase individually; each title is edited to be contextually exclusive from any other title within the series. For pricing and ordering information please visit http://www.igi-global.com/book-series/advances-finance-accounting-economics/73685. Postmaster: Send all address changes to above address.

Titles in this Series

For a list of additional titles in this series, please visit: http://www.igi-global.com/book-series/advances-finance-accounting-economics/73685

Building the High-Performance Finance Function
André de Waal (Finance Function Research and Development Center BV, The Netherlands & HPO Center BV, The Netherlands) Eelco Bilstra (Finance Function Research and Development Center BV, The Netherlands) and Jacques Bootsman (Finance Function Research and Development Center BV, The Netherlands)
Business Science Reference • © 2022 • 375pp • H/C (ISBN: 9781799869290) • US $215.00

Strategic Cooperation and Partnerships Between Australia and South Asia Economic Development, Trade, and Investment Opportunities Post COVID-19
Anita Medhekar (Central Queensland University, Australia) Sreeparna Saha (Central Queensland University, Australia) and Farooq Haq (Canadian University Dubai, UAE)
Business Science Reference • © 2022 • 403pp • H/C (ISBN: 9781799886570) • US $195.00

Handbook of Research on Changing World Economic Order in the Post-Pandemic Period
Sushanta Kumar Mahapatra (IBS Hyderabad, The ICFAI Foundation for Higher Education, India) and Vishal Sarin (Lovely Professional University, India)
Business Science Reference • © 2022 • 470pp • H/C (ISBN: 9781799868965) • US $295.00

Cases on Applying Knowledge Economy Principles for Economic Growth in Developing Nations
Danilo Piaggesi (Knowledge for Development (K4D), USA) Helena Landazuri (Knowledge for Development (K4D), USA) and Bo Jia (Tsinghua University, China)
Business Science Reference • © 2022 • 327pp • H/C (ISBN: 9781799884170) • US $215.00

Economic Impact and Recovery Following a Global Health Crisis
Brian W. Sloboda (University of Maryland Global Campus, USA) and Yaya Sissoko (Indiana University of Pennsylvania, USA)
Business Science Reference • © 2022 • 253pp • H/C (ISBN: 9781799869009) • US $225.00

Handbook of Research on New Challenges and Global Outlooks in Financial Risk Management
Mara Madaleno (GOVCOPP, University of Aveiro, Portugal) Elisabete Vieira (GOVCOPP, University of Aveiro, Portugal) and Nicoleta Bărbuță-Mișu (University of Galati, Romania)
Business Science Reference • © 2022 • 470pp • H/C (ISBN: 9781799886099) • US $285.00

IGI Global
PUBLISHER of TIMELY KNOWLEDGE

701 East Chocolate Avenue, Hershey, PA 17033, USA
Tel: 717-533-8845 x100 • Fax: 717-533-8661
E-Mail: cust@igi-global.com • www.igi-global.com

Table of Contents

Section 2
New Trends on Management and Digital Marketing

Section 3
New Trends on Information and Communication Technology

Detailed Table of Contents

with a revolutionary, simple, and universal language based on the concept of adding colors, to ensure that there is an accurate understanding of communication whenever color is an identification factor, guidance, or choice, reducing the limitations felt by color-blind people. This tool is used in metro maps, clothing labels, hospitals, catalogs, nutritional traffic lights, medicines, games, computer systems, among many others. As a color identification system, the target audience is people with difficulty in interpreting colors, mostly color-blind people, which are near 350 million individuals.

The purpose of this research is to highlight innovative excellence of the United Arab Emirates (UAE). Currently, the nation serves as a digital economy exemplar to the rest of the world due to its futuristic thinking, planning, and strategies. In this chapter, the author and her research assistants summarize various United Arab Emirates (UAE) government strategies related to the development of an economy that is based on innovation and technological solutions to address the 21st century challenges. Furthermore, it presents innovative business solutions that are in practice and are lucrative outcomes of these strategies. These ventures are an answer to our post-pandemic world because they are resilient and sustainable. Additionally, these solutions may serve as exemplars of 'thinking differently'. The research further discusses lessons on innovations that may be teachable to the rest of the world for improving the human living experience and the power of innovation, technology, and digitalization in building profitable smart economies in the post-pandemic era.

The traditional food distribution channel has enjoyed a primary position in Italy, largely because the proximity service offered to the customer plays a fundamental role in the choice of store, understood in terms of the distance and effort that the consumer is willing to endure for obtaining supplies from a given point of sale. The characteristics of the Italian small retailers, strongly appreciated by customers, are however facing the evolutions and changes of the habits and demands of the reference buyers, encouraged and favoured by the pandemic events. In the light of these considerations, the aim of this work is to obtain information for underlining and arguing the changes that Italian small grocery retailers will have to implement in order to consolidate and develop their position in the market.

This chapter discusses the outcomes of online browsing for consumers, a behavior that is on the rise as social media and online content increased exponentially in the last year. An extensive literature review about browsing and its outcomes to consumer behavior, together with empirical data collected from 10 in-depth interviews with Generation Z consumers from Portugal, showcased that online browsing mainly produces positive outcomes, such as discovering new brands and products, increasing product knowledge and therefore improving consumer confidence in their purchase decision. Gen Z consumers from Portugal behave as expected, except that because they live in a more conservative and traditional context, they still have some barriers to online shopping and experience more traditional retail in their daily lives. However, the positive outcomes for online browsing remain the same, as consumers from this generation are digital natives.

In this chapter, the authors discuss the impact that the uses of digital marketing tools had on the performance of small food retailers in a municipal market in Portugal as a result of the challenges imposed by the pandemic situation of COVID-19. They developed a case study with the use of quantitative and qualitative methodologies seeking a more holistic view of the situation given the scarcity of research on this type of retail format. It is concluded that the experience and resilience of these retailers allowed them to quickly adapt to the requirements of the most basic digital marketing tools, namely social networks, and that these had some impact on their business in terms of sales and reputation. However, the small size of these retailers and their limited academic training has in many cases reduced the possibility of a systemic view of their marketing management and digital social networks.

This study investigates the changes that took place in the consumption patterns of art and artistic products during the coronavirus pandemic events in 2020 in Brazil. Data from a sample of 615 respondents indicated that, isolated in their homes, people reported an increase in the consumption of this type of offer, motivated by the need for entertainment and of "spending time." The audiovisual content mediated by technology (music, movies, series and television programs) showed a significant growth in consumption, with a decrease of modalities normally associated with live experiences, such as dance, theatrical performances, and exhibitions of visual arts and photographs. Evidence was also found that certain sociodemographic profiles (women and younger people) present greater intensity level of consumption of artistic and cultural products, as well as that some dimensions of involvement with art and culture, "assuredness in choice" and " relevance," may also be associated with changes in the consumption behavior.

To summarize the content and provide readers with an overview, the purpose of this chapter is stated as investigating digitalization and the drivers of individual innovative behavior (IIB) for a smart economy in the post-COVID-19 era in terms of the effects of information and communication technology (ICT) students' course design characteristics (CDCs) in developing their IIB. Modelling of the mediating effects of knowledge sharing behavior (KSB) and self-regulated learning (SRL) on ICT students' individual and contextual antecedents is also considered.

In a world where sustainability is increasingly important, we must look for ways to promote it; the Sustainable Development Goals (SDGs) fulfill this function. In software engineering, one of the main challenges for the success of a software solution is to achieve sustainability. This chapter introduces the development of two mobile applications on Android: Diabetes Tracker and Volunteer+ that are inspired by the SDGs, incorporating the principles and dimensions of the Karlskrona Manifesto in relation to the software development phases. In this investigation, a customized adaptation of the Scrum agile methodology was used, with a concern to promote software engineering for sustainability. To achieve this end, an iterative approach is used, allowing the principles of the manifesto to be crossed to emphasize the various dimensions of sustainability. The main results can be seen in the applications developed, specifically to facilitate the control of the diabetes disease and promote quality health, as well as enhance the participation of citizens by promoting volunteering.

There has been increased interest among researchers and industry to generate insights from user-generated data and ratings on account of valuable information such as data carry and its authenticity. Numerous studies offer insight into how traditional hotel classification ratings are influenced by the information and communication technology. However, no such studies that explore the relationship between traditional hotel ratings and the largest online hotel review website, TripAdvisor, could be found. To bridge the gap, the study uses the TripAdvisor hotel rating data from Greek hotels to explore this relationship using Kruskal-Wallis H test. The results show that mean TripAdvisor ratings of hotels are in proportion to the traditional hotel classification ratings.

Preface

The COVID-19 pandemic has accelerated globally the implementation of strategies underlying digital transformation as a way of responding assertively to the problem that institutions and citizens have faced. In this way, there has been an exponential increase in the demand for intelligent and reliable communications solutions.

The Pandemic brings huge challenges for all economic agents. Resilience and the capacity to adapt to new risks and challenges will be fundamental elements in our societies. In this field, recover demands could attend to new business models, new marketing channels and new markets that may be are reached using ICT, but also for innovative proposals and flexibility to capture value in a digital world. The Pandemic is a driver daily support and, many times, a way to develop creativity and innovation and will be expected that remains with a re-efforted effort in the post pandemic era.

It is consensual that digital technologies played was a crucial role during Pandemic to keep society functioning, new vocabulary comes for our daily life, such as, remote working, remote learning, digital marketing, e-business, etc. In this context it is fundamental that digitalization bring opportunities to a transition for a smarter economy based on innovation, sustainability, and wellbeing. Using the potential of technology for a sustainable recovery of COVID-19.

There is extensive literature can address the main topics on digitalization, ICTs, marketing, entrepreneurship, and innovation in an organizational context in the post-pandemic times. The purpose of this book is to present chapters describing research work in an organizational context to optimize the practices established in the most diverse domains of knowledge attending to the relation between digitalization and sustainability in a post pandemic era. Emphasizing the importance of digitization as an organizational support, guaranteeing long-term economic competition, and enhancing in times of recovering the new 5G systems and the nature of the impact of changes in stakeholders.

This book presents a global and multidisciplinary approach that could contribute to a better understanding of the relationship and mutual influence of digital, entrepreneurship, marketing, sustainability, customer relationship management and innovation scientific areas. The publication of studies of innovation in this context of recover emphasizing the capacities of ICT for inclusion towards the rapid training of decision-makers open to entrepreneurial solutions based on multi-stakeholder governance, guaranteeing fair and equal access to new opportunities created by digitization. It is important to research, studying and disseminating studies in various contexts from a perspective of innovation and entrepreneurships is emphasized.

The content of this book covers research topics that include new trends on digitalization and smart economies, ICTs and management and digital marketing in the post-pandemic times. And is ideal for professionals, executives, managers, policymakers, government officials, industry professionals, researchers, students, and academicians in the fields of ICTs, management, marketing, and communications. In this context what means, but the complex world, the requisites of a well succeed recover includes and the huge challenges concerning sustainability, climate change, ageing, social conflicts and a multipolarized world highlight the relevance of a multidisciplinary approach that mix and complement these topics and contributes to the organizations.

The book consists of thirteen chapters which the editors decided to organize in three sections: "New Trends on Digitalization for Smart Economy"; "New Trends on Management and Digital Marketing"; and "New Trends on Information and Communication Technology." It can be said that the boundaries between each of these sections are rather blurred as the chapters are to a greater or lesser extent interrelated. It is considered, however, that this structure will render the book's consultation more effective insofar as the first section on new trends promoted Digitalization and Smart Economy present some more general studies that discuss these issues in a macro perspective. The second section discuss the opportunities created for management and digital marketing. The last part, discuss a set of research that involves ICTs and new technologies as tools and strategies in the digitalization contexts around the world.

The first chapter, "Financial Literacy for Families: Perspectives in Portugal and Brazil as a Driver to Promote the Smart Economy in the Post-COVID Era," authored by Reis et al, analyzes the situation in Portugal and Brazil regarding actual Financial Literacy for families and initiatives to raise the awareness regarding this problem. In this research, authors used the Design Science Research methodology.

The second chapter, "Digital Innovation With Social Impact: The Case of ColorAdd," authored by Carvalho et al, discusses major concepts of digital innovation that may bring social impacts. In this case study, authors used the case of case of a color identification system "ColorAdd" that is targeted to people with difficulty in interpreting colors.

The third chapter, "A Case Study on the United Arab Emirates (UAE) as a Digital Economy Exemplar," authored by Chakravarti, summarizes various UAE national strategies focused on innovation and technological solutions, that may be useful to other nations that trust in innovation, technology, and digitalization as major competitive divers.

The fourth chapter, "Fast Digitalization in the Pandemic Era and the Urgency to Discover New Business Model Opportunities for Italian Small Grocery Retailers," authored by Tongiani, Ferrari & Alaimo, analyses the Italian food retailing industry, focusing on the competitive challenges that small retailers face and the changes that they will have to develop to improve their performance and consolidate their position in the market.

The fifth chapter, "The Outcomes of Online Browsing in Consumers: Insights From Portugal's Gen Z Consumers," authored by Sandes, discusses the outcomes of online browsing for consumers, using a data guttered from ten in-depth interviews with generation Z consumers. Results highlighted the online browsing impacts on their attitudes and perceptions.

The sixth chapter, "Digitalization and Small Retailers: New Opportunities – Case Study: Livramento Municipal Market," authored by Xara-Brasil and Vacas de Carvalho, discusses the impact of the uses of digital marketing tools on the performance of small food retailers in a municipal market in Portugal during the pandemic period, particularly in 2020 and 2021. In this research they used quantitative and qualitative methodologies.

The seventh chapter, "Consumption of Artistic and Cultural Products in the Pandemic and the Influence of Technology: Evidence From Brazil," authored by Andrade, Ramos, and Boava, analyzes the consumption of artistic and cultural products during the COVID lockdown. This is exploratory research with a quantitative methodology focused on the cultural pandemic consumption behaviors in that period.

The eighth chapter, "A Survey on the Deployment of Smart Factory in the Post-COVID-19 Era: The Role of 5G, Deployment Options, Benefits, and Business Models," authored by Psyrris, Kargas, and Varoutas, aims to describe the concept of Smart Factory as a key factor of the 4th industrial revolution and to deliver its most important factors for a successful implementation. Moreover, smart factory is interrelated with 5th generation of mobile communication systems (5G), which seems to offer the capabilities needed for the advanced industrial digitalization.

The ninth chapter, "ICT Process Optimization Framework: A Systematic Literature Review," submitted by Marchão, Reis, and Martins, presents a systematic literature review related to relationship management, optimization, and alignment of business processes between Information and Communication Technology areas and other organizational business units in a multidisciplinary way. The proposed Framework pretends to contribute to creating strategies and indicators that allow optimized risk management, resources management, cost control, and streamlining of the defined processes in a continual improvement cycle.

The tenth chapter is "Digitalization and Drivers of Innovative Behavior for a Smart Economy in the Post-COVID-19 Era: Technology Student Course Design Characteristics," authored by Ngugi and Goosen. The purpose of this chapter is stated as investigating digitalization and the drivers of Individual Innovative Behavior (IIB) for a smart economy in the post-COVID-19 era in terms of the effects of Information and Communication Technology (ICT) students' Course Design Characteristics in developing their IIB. Modelling of the mediating effects of Knowledge Sharing Behavior and Self-Regulated Learning on ICT students' individual and contextual antecedents are also considered.

The eleventh chapter, "Diabetes Tracker and Volunteer+ Software Engineering for Sustainability," authored by Torres, Júlio, Silveira, and Reis, presents the development of two mobile applications on Android: Diabetes Tracker and Volunteer+ that are inspired by the Sustainable Development Goals, incorporating the principles and dimensions of the Karlskrona Manifesto in relation to the software development phases. In this investigation, a customized adaptation of the Scrum agile methodology was used, with a concern to promote software engineering for sustainability.

The twelfth chapter is "The Impact of Information and Communication Technology (ICT) on Hotel Classification Ratings," submitted by Sufi and Vagena. This chapter explores the relationship between traditional hotel ratings and the largest Online Hotel Review website, TripAdvisor, could be found. The study uses the TripAdvisor Hotel Rating data from Greek Hotels to explore this relationship using Kruskal-Wallis H test. The results show that mean TripAdvisor ratings of hotels are in proportion to the traditional hotel classification ratings.

The thirteenth chapter is "ICT Pandemic Time Adoption and Immersive Technologies: A Comprehensive Review," submitted by Ali Yuce. This chapter presents comprehensive reviews about the impact of COVID-19 on the tourism industry through conceptualizing and contextualizing the remarkable aspects of innovation, digitalization, and digital transformation using immersive technologies.

To conclude, we would like to thank the authors whose collaboration has made this project possible and express our hope that readers will find this publication inspiring and useful.

Leonilde Reis
Luísa Cagica Carvalho

Clara Silveira
Duarte Xara Brasil

Section 1
New Trends on Digitalization for Smart Economy

Chapter 1
Financial Literacy for Families: Perspectives in Portugal and Brazil as a Driver to Promote the Smart Economy in the Post-COVID Era

Leonilde Reis
https://orcid.org/0000-0002-4398-8384
Instituto Politécnico de Setúbal, Portugal

Clara Silveira
Polytechnic Institute of Guarda, Portugal

Luisa C. Carvalho
https://orcid.org/0000-0002-9804-7813
Instituto Politécnico de Setúbal, Portugal

Conceição Aleixo
Instituto Politécnico de Setúbal, Portugal

Anabela Marques
Instituto Politécnico de Setúbal, Portugal

Geraldo Alemandro Leite Filho
University Estadual de Montes Claros, Brazil

Ismael Mendes dos Santos Junior
https://orcid.org/0000-0001-9412-6023
IFNMG, Brazil

ABSTRACT

Balanced development requires the involvement of all stakeholders. In this context, the smart economy will also create innovative mechanisms, especially digital mechanisms that allow optimizing solutions. The chapter aims to analyze the situation in Portugal and Brazil regarding initiatives to raise awareness of the problem by the fact that they are two countries in which families have a high level of indebtedness. The methodology adopted is the design science research because it is a methodology of wide use to allow several iterations during the construction and development of the artifact. The main results are pressing to present a systematization of financial literacy initiatives to list them and interconnect them with the legal framework at the European level in Portugal and Brazil.

DOI: 10.4018/978-1-7998-9227-4.ch001

INTRODUCTION

Presently families faced enticing proposals to obtain increments to their family level and are strongly motivated to use credit for the most varied purposes. On the supply side, liberalization, and gaps in the regulation in the financial system enhance the definition of strategies for betting on the credit segment to individuals, traditionally with low levels of indebtedness. On the other hand, the desire to change living standards, the fall in interest rates, the increase in disposable income and the containment of unemployment have also favored the increasing indebtedness of households.

In this sense, family indebtedness can be seen as the ability of families to be able to repay their loans. They have assertively allowing them to implement a particular family strategy. However, unforeseen factors or situations may occur such as unemployment, prolonged illness, divorce, and bad investments leading the family to the situation of over-indebtedness.

The financial literacy of families is particularly relevant because the rationalization of consumer´s financial decisions will allow the allocation of financial resources in a more appropriate and effective way. In addition, the level of financial literacy of families helps them to make more conscious financial decisions. In the European Union and OECD countries Financial Education must be assumed as a lifelong education, starting with school-age children and young people.

The motivation for the development of the chapter follows a research project that is being developed between Portugal and Brazil. Given the importance of the theme, it was considered pressing to proceed with scientific dissemination. The chapter aims to analyze the situation in Portugal and Brazil concerning initiatives to raise awareness of the problem of household indebtedness. For this purpose, good practices established in both countries are presented to emphasize the role of Information Systems and information and communication technologies. The dimension of the smart economy is also highlighted as an important factor for families, considering the impact of this context on human capital and the community.

This chapter is organized into six sections, where the problem is formulated, the methodology for carrying out the study is presented, the state of the art is characterized in the context of financial literacy for families in Portugal and Brazil. Solutions and recommendations, as well as future work, are also presented. Finally, the conclusion reflects the concerns in the domain of the subject in Portugal and in Brazil.

METHODOLOGY

The methodology adopted focuses on the literature review in the area under study. Based on the characteristics of the topic addressed, a methodology was selected that would allow conducting the analysis of the characterization of the population based on their specificities. The Design Science Research (DSR) methodology was chosen as the theoretical basis to support scientific validity (Peffers, Tuunanen, Rothenberger, & Chatterjee, 2007) for the preparation of this work.

As it is a research methodology indicated for research projects in information technologies and systems, system architectures (Ferreira et al, 2012) inherent to the activity of artifact design, it thus ensures discipline, rigor, and transparency. The DSR methodology (Roquete, 2018) is a research method that suits the area of information systems with connection to issues originating in organizations, contributing to the resolution of specific and complex problems (Bianchi & Dinis de Sousa, 2015; Hevner, March, Park, & Ram, 2004).

Figure 1. Design science research methodology
Source: adapted from (Peffers, Tuunanen, Rothenberger, & Chatterjee, 2007)

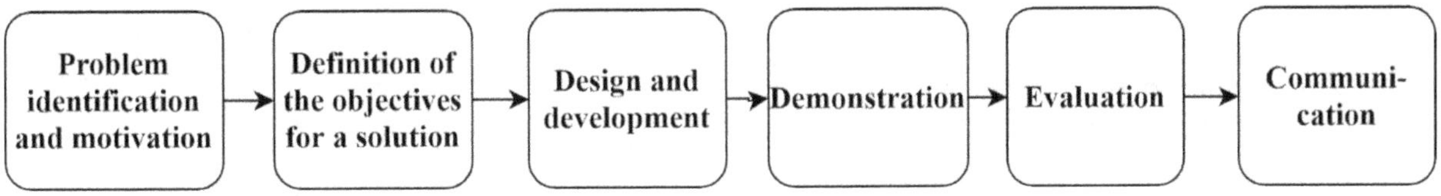

The steps of the DSR methodology are shown in Figure 1, allowing the characterization of the current situation of financial literacy. This methodology allows the study to be conducted based on the identification of the problem, definition of objectives, design and development, demonstration, evaluation, and communication of results.

FINANCIAL LITERACY

Financial literacy is a recent topic that has attracted the attention of governments around the world and financial institutions, especially after the financial crisis that began in 2008, (Alves, 2014). According to Van Rooij, Lusardi, & Alessie (2011), financial literacy influences the financial behavior of individuals. Analyzing student behavior in the field of financial information can be added value in view of their perception of aspects such as money management, savings, credit and debt, and investment (Walstad & Rebeck, K., 2010). The dissemination of tools is pressing to allow more and more citizens to interact with platforms that allow them to simulate and reflect on their level of indebtedness.

According to Orton (2007) financial literacy consists of specific knowledge related to monetary, economic, or financial matters and in the decisions that the individual be able to make about these matters. Financial literacy is thus linked to the ability to read, analyze, manage and a communicate about personal financial condition and how it affects your material well-being. It also includes ability to decide between financial choices, discuss financial and monetary matters without discomfort, planning the future and responding competently to everyday situations that involve financial decisions. This problem must be seen in a broad perspective, that influence families and society in general, where innovation and smart solutions are part of an aimed smart economy based on technology, that could bring technological solutions, mainly in the field of ICT (Information and Communication Technologies) allowing the identification of solutions to support families and enhance financial literacy through the dissemination of the relevant information. The next section provides a perspective about the Innovation and Smart Economy and how these trends could influence the day life of families and support better decisions.

Innovation and Smart Economy

Nowadays everything is label as smart: cities, tourism, apps, innovation, etc. The concept of the smart coming as a transversal approach for all society. In the fact this trend coming for the evolution of the society mainly based on the Industry 4.0, Education 4.0, innovation networks, high technology production (Carvalho and Paiva, 2021), high comfort level of mankind and environment is a key criterion for sustainable development (Galperina et al, 2016). Figure 2, provide a landscape about the evolution of the technologies among the centuries and highlight the importance of information, communication and computation and nanotechnologies in twenty-one century.

Figure 2. Evolution of the technology
Source: Carvalho and Paiva, 2021

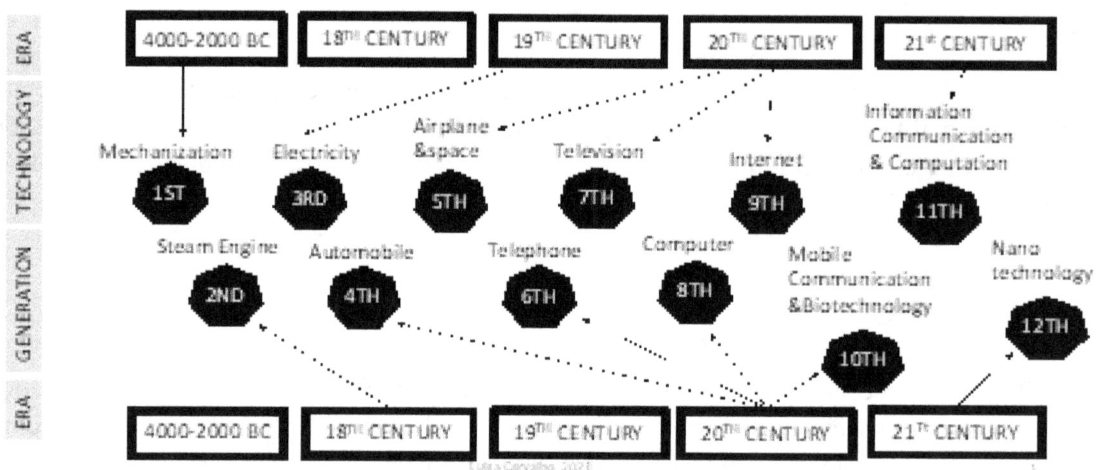

The concept of smart economy is applied as a synonym of sustainable development, and also linked to "green economy" that is defined by UNEP (2011) as a result of an improvement of well-being and social equity.

Bruneckiene and Sinkiene (2014) point out a set of common characteristics of the smart economy:

- Innovation and knowledge economy: Implementation of innovation, increasing productivity and reducing costs, in all sectors of the economy.
- Learning economy: considered as one of the most important processes in all domains of economy.
- Digital economy: disclosure information and telecommunication technologies in the economy.
- Competitive economy: The faculty to compete globally in an open economy. Using knowledge and innovation to get competitive advantages.
- Green economy: Application of the sustainable development principles, emphasis on generating a free of pollution "clean" economy and the efficient consumption of energy resources.
- Network economy: Expansion of the competencies networking between universities, business and government.
- Socially responsible economy: Enterprises and organizations are considered by economic, ethical, legal and philanthropic responsibility.

This concept of smart economy is linked with the smart city and allows a multidimensional vision including several areas such as firms, public sector, infrastructures, and citizens (Figure 3).

Figure 3. Smart city: an overview
Source: Carvalho, 2017

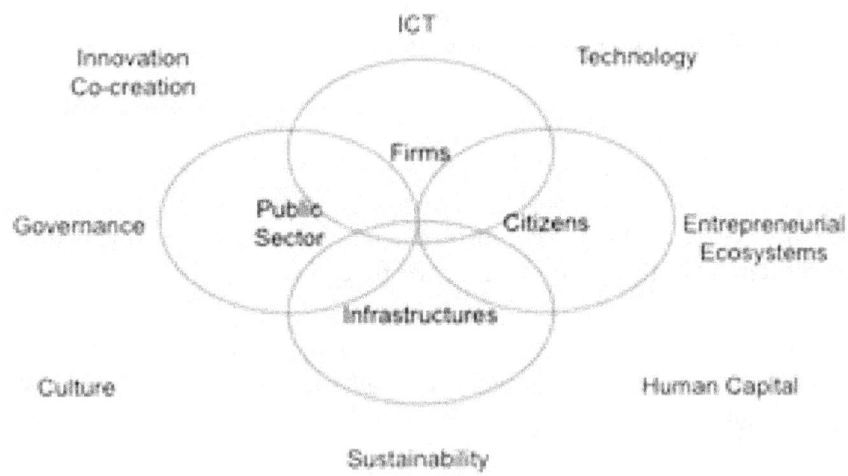

According to Carvalho (2017) a smart city is a smart regional ecosystem, that includes several interconnected stakeholders that develop collaborative networks (firms, citizens, public organizations, cultural, economic, and social infrastructures) to create an open and creative environment useful to improve the population's life quality and to develop smart and innovative businesses and social projects. These regions present high standards respecting some indicators associated with innovation, creativity, environment, life quality, entrepreneurial activities, and support facilities (Table 1).

Table 1. Smart cities dimensions

Dimension	Authors
ICT (use and availability)	Bakici et al., 2013; Caragliu et al., 2011; Hollands, 2008; Komninos, 2002; Thite, 2011; Tranos and Gertner, 2012.
Entrepreneurial ecosystems (entrepreneurial activities and business creation)	Carvalho, 2016; Gottdiener, 2001; Klein, 2000; Monbiot, 2000; Hollands, 2008; Lombardi et al., 2012; Thite, 2011.
e-government and resident inclusion	Bakici et al., 2013; Caragliu et al., 2011; Hollands, 2008; Schaffers et al., 2011.
Creative industries and high tech	Hollands, 2008; Florida, 2002; Winters, 2011
Human capital and community	Bolisani and Scarso, 2000; Kourtit et al., 2012.
Social capital and relationships	Coe et al., 2001; Kourtit et al., 2012.
Social and environmental sustainability	Caragliu et al., 2011; Nathan, 2013; Sen et al., 2012; Shafiullah et al., 2013; Sivaram et al., 2013.

Source: Carvalho, 2017

This dimension of the smart economy (and smart city) is also important for families considering the impact of this context in human capital and community. The topic of financial literacy can be considered as an important element in a micro perspective of the smart economy. The next section approach this topic attending to the propose of a framework to discuss financial literacy for families.

Financial Literacy Framework for Families

The underlying theme of financial literacy for families is of particular interest in terms of enhancing the optimization of decision-making to contribute to the definition of strategies to reduce the level of indebtedness. Financial literacy is part of our daily lives and plays a decisive role not only for a healthier economy, but also for a society that is more informed about the impact of its financial decisions, whether it concerns the management of the family budget, the perception of savings, the investments, credit, or consumption.

The promotion of financial literacy involves improving knowledge and changing financial attitudes and behaviour, contributing to raise the population's level of knowledge, to promote the adoption of adequate financial behaviour, contributing to increase the population's well-being and for the stability of the financial system.

The belief is implausible, given the speed of change in the financial market and the abyss between consumers' current competencies and those that are needed to understand the financial products that are marketed today. Furthermore, there is a disparity between educators and financial product companies in terms of resources to reach consumers (Willis, 2008). According to the author we can find ourselves with the concepts of financial literacy and financial education in which some authors advocate that financial education as formal in the context of teaching and financial literacy as being more comprehensive and including the various means of knowledge acquisition in the field of theme, although it is consensual for the authors the same objectives for individuals and families.

The author (Huston, 2010), presents concepts underlying financial literacy, financial knowledge and financial education are generally used in the thematic literature and in the media. Another valence is related to health literacy, in which standardized metrics are usually used, contrary to the lack of consensus of standardized instruments to measure the valences inherent in financial literacy.

According to Alves (2014), financial education has been the strategy used by governments to increase individuals' level of financial knowledge. However, its real effectiveness also depends on the behaviour of individuals, being conditioned by cognitive and emotional biases (overconfidence, risk aversion, etc.) that distance them from the complete rationality defended by Traditional Finance, thus emerging a new area of study, Behavioural Finance.

Individuals with a higher level of financial education can have a more stable financial life, whether through planning their family budget, or through planning their retirement, or even by actively participating in the stock market, obtaining in the medium-long term, take advantage of it. They also manage to have higher investment/savings income than those with a lower level of financial literacy and realize that the diversification of their assets helps to mitigate the risk of their investments (Carita, 2016).

Financial education is just one of the elements that contribute to the financial well-being of individuals. However, other factors such as employment, income, health, age and socioeconomic background also influence it. The study also alerts to the existence of some limitations that compromise the effectiveness of financial education. Nevertheless, he argues that all kinds of initiatives that promote the improvement of financial literacy are an asset for consumers (Fernandes, 2011).

Thus, it is considered that financial education can provide a more rational and sustainable use of resources, prevent situations of over-indebtedness, and contribute to a greater awareness of the personal financial situation by consumers. It is also important to mention that financial education is a continuous process that presupposes a continuous lifelong learning activity, given the pace of technological innovations and the emergence of new financial products (Fernandes, 2011).

Financial education is considered to enhance financial literacy or personal financial outcomes. In this sense, it is advocated that the metrics underlying financial literacy should encompass how we analyze existing literature in the face of a competitive market that encourages companies to educate their consumers, (Hastings, Madrian, & Skimmyhorn, 2013).

The studies revealed essentially three main obstacles to the development of a standardized approach to make it possible to use metrics to study issues in the field of financial literacy: the lack of conceptualization and definition of the construction of financial literacy, the content underlying the instruments and the interpretation of the instruments used in various contexts (Huston, 2010).

In view of the study, which shows that low scores of financial literacy in terms of assessing respondents about the taking of relevant courses in the field under study can be partially explained by the fact that the majority of students simply express their lack of motivation in defining strategies in the field of personal finance (Mandell & Klein, 2007) . The results of the study suggest an approach to teaching that places emphasis on the lack of motivation of students about financial literacy.

In this sense, it is considered crucial to initiate a set of strategies so that secondary school students are motivated to be interested in financial instructors. One of the ways of fostering the level of personal financial literacy may be to develop playful activities or other simulations in order to motivate students to the importance of the theme, (Mandell & Klein, 2007).

According to the model proposed by Kempson, Collard, & Moore (2005), cited by (Santos, 2015) the knowledge components includes; attitude; and behaviour. They also identified five areas of personal finance: 1. Balancing the budget 2. Maintaining control; 3. Choose products; 4. Plan the future; 5. Stay informed and get help. Each of these domains is composed of knowledge, financial attitudes, and financial practices that, together, increase individual financial capacity. However, (Kempson, Collard, & Moore, 2005) suggest that it is the element of behaviour that may be most important.

Most consumers around the world have in recent times taken on greater responsibility for their personal financial well-being. In this sense, changes in some levels of depth are considered to have markedly marked the area of consumer autonomy, as the adoption of financial decisions, including savings, consumer investment is an element of supervision and control, (Stolper & Walter, 2017).

Some studies present indicators that include in a cross-sectional assessment of the overall levels of consumer financial literacy in different countries compared to the different levels of development of each country. However, it should be noted that one of the limitations of the data underlying these indicators is the inevitability of comparing identical literacy measures that have been applied in studies conducted in several countries (Stolper & Walter, 2017).

Financial Literacy in Europe

The importance of financial literacy is increasingly recognized internationally, being considered essential to provide adequate management of the family budget and planning their personal finances in the medium and long term.

The number of countries adopting national financial education strategies and carrying out studies to assess the financial literacy of populations has been growing. These studies make it possible, on the one hand, to identify the deficits in financial literacy and, one the other hand, to make international comparisons of the results obtained that promote new financial education policies.

The Recommendation on Financial Literacy was adopted by the OECD Council during the 2020 OECD Ministerial Council Meeting. It presents a single, comprehensive, instrument on financial literacy to assist governments, other public authorities, and relevant stakeholders in their efforts to design, implement and evaluate financial literacy policies. It is part of a holistic approach to financial-consumer issues, where financial literacy, together with improved financial access, adequate consumer protection, and regulatory frameworks, are expected to support financial resilience and well-being (OECD, 2020). The Recommendation covers three main areas:

- National strategies for financial literacy;
- Financial literacy and the various sectors of the financial landscape;
- Effective delivery of financial literacy programs.

It also looks at how to address the needs of vulnerable groups, considers the increased digitalization of finance and draws on recent research and evidence. The Recommendation was developed initially in the OECD International Network on Financial Education (INFE) to consolidate four existing OECD Council Recommendations on financial literacy and to consider recent OECD work on financial literacy recognized in global as such as the G20 and APEC. It was then refined through a comprehensive and iterative process involving OECD Committees and a public consultation, reflecting a whole-of-government consensus in OECD countries.

The INFE (2020) mentions that the OECD governments officially recognized the importance of financial literacy in 2002 with the launch of a unique and comprehensive project. In 2008 the project was further enhanced through the creation of the International Network on Financial Education (OECD/INFE) to:

- Collect cross-comparable data and evidence;
- Develop methodologies to measure impact;
- Share experience and good practices;
- Develop research and comparative analysis;
- Design policy tools;
- Promote effective implementation and monitoring.

Ergun (2018) conducted a study to analyze the level of financial literacy among university students in Estonia, Germany, Italy, Netherlands, Poland, Romania, Russian Federation and Turkey. The purpose of the study was to determine the level of financial literacy among university students, and to find out the relationship between financial knowledge and demographic characteristics of students. In online survey 409 questionnaires were accepted for analysis. The results represent a medium level of financial literacy about personal finance and refers the importance of having financial courses should be provided in university education programs, which could help more students handle their finances better and improve their financial wellbeing. The study refers to the importance, in recent years, of environmental and technological influences in financial literacy.

Erner et al. (2016) conducted a survey in 2010 in a midsize German city among high school students and found similarly weak performances on standard financial literacy measures. The authors find that literacy scores vary as a function of sociodemographic characteristics and additionally, lower mathematical skills are related to lower levels of basic financial literacy, while worse general cognitive aptitude and foreign language skills are related to lower levels of sophisticated financial literacy. They refer the importance of financial literacy for an individual's life and defend a particular attention in targeted financial literacy programs.

Amagir et al. (2020) examined levels of financial literacy such as knowledge, attitudes, self-efficacy, and self-reported behavior among 15-year-old high school students in the Netherlands and investigated which factors are associated with the different financial literacy components. Their findings that there are significant differences in the level of financial literacy of students in the various high school groups:

- The higher the level of education, the higher the level of student´s financial literacy;
- Students with a lower level of math skills have lower levels of financial literacy;
- The level of education of parents is also directly related to the level of financial literacy;
- Students who do not discuss financial matters with classmates and family have less financial literacy.

The results show a large gap in financial knowledge levels between the lowest and highest high-school tracks in the Netherlands and support the need for financial education in high school to ensure more equal opportunities and demand a targeted approach.

Other study in Spain had the purpose to study the effect of family ownership and family generation on financial literacy. García et al. (2020) analyzed a sample of 195 Spanish family businesses, during the period October to December 2016, reaching the conclusion that the level of family ownership exerts a negative influence on financial literacy. On the other hand, as family generations advance, financial literacy is favored.

Hauff et al. (2020) analyze survey data from a representative sample of 551 Swedish citizens, a new 16-question measure of fact-based financial literacy is developed and validated. The results show a significant impact of fact-based and subjective financial literacy are found on three time-ordered stages of individuals' retirement behavior: planning, saving, and investment management. This study concluded that policies increasing final literacy are important in different phases of the life cycle.

The themes underlying financial literacy include a variety of approaches. In this sense, Table 2 was elaborated to systematize the themes addressed.

Table 2. Financial literacy

Dimension	Authors
Financial Education	(Alves, 2014); (Carita, 2016); (Fernandes, 2011); (Hastings, Madrian, & Skimmyhorn, 2013).
Recommendation on Financial Literacy	(OECD, 2020); (INFE, 2020).
Financial Literacy	(Ergun, 2018); (Amagir, Groot, & Maassen van den Brinkc, 2020); (Alves, 2014); (BdP, 2020); (Huston, 2010); (Mandell & Klein, 2007).

The authors present approaches to the problem to reflect on the lines of investigation given their importance in the context under study and social relevance.

Financial Literacy in Portugal - Framework

In Portugal, two surveys have been conducted on the financial literacy of the Portuguese population. The first was carried out in 2010 by Banco de Portugal and the second was carried out in 2015 by the National Council of Financial Supervisors, an entity that integrates Banco de Portugal, the Securities market Commission and the Insurance and Pension Funds Supervisory Authority, within the scope of the National Financial Education Plan. In 2015 the survey was more comprehensive as it included a set of questions, developed by INFE, which are fundamental for measuring and comparing the degree of financial literacy at the international level.

The results obtained in 2015 revealed improvements in the financial inclusion of the Portuguese population compared to 2010. The attitudes and behaviors in terms of the management of the family budget showed signs of prudence in the control of personal finances. However, the result of the survey still shows some gaps regarding the financial knowledge of the population and reinforce the need to promote financial education, so that the population can understand, analyze and decide when making financial decisions.

In Portugal, a few initiatives have been delineated in the field under study in view of the relevance of the theme and the fact that there are more and more families with a worrying level of indebtedness. The Banco de Portugal (BdP), as a central bank of Portugal, has defined as a strategy initiative linking international concerns (BdP, 2020) in which it mentions that the Organization for Economic Cooperation and Development (OECD) approved, on October 29, the Recommendation on Financial Literacy, which aims to support governments, public authorities and other relevant stakeholders in the definition, implementation, and evaluation of national financial literacy strategies.

The document "OECD Recommendation of the Council on Financial Literacy" presents principles and recommendations in three major areas (BdP, 2020):

- Design of national financial education strategies;
- Development of financial education programs in specific areas such as savings, investment, pension plans, credit and insurance;
- Implementation of national strategies and financial education programs;
- In the Recommendation, the OECD considers that financial literacy and inclusion, combined with adequate regulation and consumer protection, are key to increasing the financial resilience and well-being of the population.

The document giving rise to this Recommendation was prepared by the Working Group on Standards, Implementation and Evaluation of the OECD's International Network on Financial Education (INFE), which is attended by Banco de Portugal. It was based on the OECD recommendations on financial education and other policy instruments developed by the OECD for the G20 and the APEC (Asia-Pacific Economic Cooperation Forum). The recommendation was submitted to public consultation in February 2019 and resulted from a consensus among OECD members, (BdP, 2020).

In Portugal, (BdP, 2020) the National Council of Financial Supervisors (which integrates Banco de Portugal and the other two financial supervisors) has been supporting the National Financial Training Plan since 2011, a strategy that recognizes the importance of inclusion and financial training and that frames and supports initiatives at national level. The Plan follows the best practices of the OECD/INFE and the Portuguese experience was one of those that served as the basis for the recommendation now approved. Under the National Financial Training Plan, several initiatives were developed, namely the creation of the portal, as well as the e-learning platform with support material.

The Plan follows the best practices of the OECD/INFE, recognizing the importance of financial inclusion and training and that it frames and supports the implementation of initiatives at the national level. One of the first steps in the introduction of financial education in schools was the publication of the "Financial Education Benchmark for Pre-School Education, Basic Education, Secondary Education and Adult Education and Training", prepared by the financial supervisors and the Ministry of Education and approved in May 2013 by the Secretary of State for Basic and Secondary Education.

Following the OECD recommendation on Financial Literacy, the National Council of Financial Supervisors – composed of Banco de Portugal (BdP), the Portuguese Securities Market Commission (CMVM) and the Supervisory Authority for Insurance and Pension Funds (ASF) established in 2011 the lines of action of the National Plan for Financial Education (Plan) with a first-time horizon of five years.

The Financial Education Benchmark was prepared by the Ministry of Education, through the Directorate-General for Education and the National Agency for Qualification and Vocational Education, in partnership with the National Council of Financial Supervisors - Banco de Portugal, Market Commission Securities and Insurance Institute of Portugal (currently Supervisory Authority for Insurance and Pension Funds) - with the objective of promoting the financial education of children, young people and adults in the school and training context (Dias-DGE, et al., 2013).

The Financial Education Benchmark can be used by teachers in the context of teaching any subject or non-disciplinary area, at all levels of schooling and teaching modalities. Financial Education is included in Education for Citizenship (DL 139/2012 of 5 July) and is transversal to several disciplines. The referential is not a prescribed guide or program, it is a support instrument that, within the autonomy of each educational establishment, can be used and adapted according to the options to be defined in each context, framing the practices to be developed. There is no obligation to implement it in a school context (Santiago, 2015). In this sense, Portugal has already traveled a long way, following international trends, in the context of Promoting Financial Education. However, teacher training covers a very limited number of teachers, teaching materials for use in the classroom are still very scarce and are not specific for each of the subject areas (Santiago, 2015).

In the international survey that sought to assess the degree of financial literacy of adults 2020 promoted by the International Network o Financial Education of the Organization for Economic Cooperation and Development for Economic (OECD/INFE) in twenty-six countries, Portugal ranks seventh position, being that among the European countries it occupies the fifth position. The results show that the Portuguese have a better degree of financial literacy in terms of behavior and attitudes than in terms of financial Knowledge.

Financial Literacy in Brazil - Framework

In Brazil, several organizations and researchers investigated the profiles of Brazilians regarding investments, financial profile, financial education situation and national financial education strategy. Earlier studies about the financial literacy of Brazilians, proposed by Costa and Miranda (2013) investigated the influence of the level of financial education on the choice of the savings rate of individuals, once the individual characteristics of Brazilians were taken into account. They found that although schooling plays a fundamental role in determining income, as pointed out in human capital theories and empirical studies, schooling influences or little the determination of the savings rate, but the financial literacy of the person played a fundamental role in determining the savings rate. Hence the importance of studying and investing (having public policies) in the financial literacy of the Brazilian population.

According to Goeking (2020), in a survey conducted by Valor Investee with 2,071 Brazilians, he concluded that almost all respondents (97%) said they had difficulty dealing with their own money and half (49%) avoids even thinking about money so as not to be sad. In this sense, the researchers concluded that the root of the problem lies much more in the psychological issues that Brazilians have with their finances than with the information available on the subject, mainly due to the low financial literacy of the Brazilian population, turning the theme into a taboo. In the same vein, a study by Greencred (2021) conducted with 1,428 interviewees revealed that 73% of Brazilians do not keep money and, in general, find it difficult to maintain a healthy financial life, due to low income (expenses greater than revenues) and due to the low financial and educational literacy of people. The study also showed that 75% of respondents reported having difficulties in paying the bills in recent months, creating situations of financial penury, indebtedness and default.

There is a monthly survey conducted in Brazil by the National Confederation of Trade in Goods, Services and Tourism (CNC, 2021) in which it showed that the year 2021 began with more indebted families in Brazil, and the percentage of Brazilians with debts reached a level of 66.5% in January 2021, an increase of 0.2% compared to the previous month and 1.2% compared to January 2020. Over time, the trend is to increase indebtedness and people's defaults. In this sense, it is observed that only a part of Brazilians can save money for applications. A study by ANBIMA (2020) showed that of the total sample investigated, 38% managed to save in 2019, most (42% of this universe) invested money in financial products, for example, fixed income, government bonds, savings or stock market. This percentage is in line with 2017 levels and indicates a drop of six percentage points compared to 2018 (48%) which evidences the worsening scenario in the financial conditions of Brazilians.

Based on the fall of Brazilian investors evidenced by the research of ANBIMA (2020) and with an increase in indebted and defaulting from the CNC research (2021) it is inferable that the scenario of the Brazilian population in relation to personal finances is an increase in indebtedness and a reduction in savings capacity. These observations have been given the results of the Capital Research survey, evidenced by Rodrigues (2020) who interviewed virtually 43,152 investors and potential investors. The results showed that 70% of respondents would invest more if they had more money, and 63% if they had more knowledge, pointing out that the main problems in terms of personal finances in Brazil are the low average income per capita of the population as well as the low financial and educational literacy in terms of finance.

In this sense, Cordeiro, Costa e Silva (2018) in their study about panoramic perspective of financial education in Brazil concluded that Financial Education is a relatively new theme, little addressed in the school context of Brazil, but of extreme importance in the construction of a society more prepared to face possible situations of day to day. They highlight that textbook need to improve a lot to provide greater support to teachers, providing better financial guidance to students. Financial Education still has much to contribute within the school environment and consequently in building future generations more responsible for finances and increasing people's financial literacy. According to Cunha (2020), when it comes to Brazil, he argues that financial education should be a state policy, observing the contents to be addressed, seeking to solve real financial problems identified in specialized readings, in daily life and in reality. It also advocates actions of financial inclusion and financial literacy of population as a public policy.

From the point of view of actions for financial education, Brazil has a program called National Financial Education Strategy – ENEF that is a mobilization around the promotion of financial, security, social security and fiscal education actions in Brazil. The objective of ENEF, created through Federal Decree 7,397/2010, and renewed by Federal Decree No. 10,393 of June 9, 2020, is to contribute to the strengthening of citizenship by providing and supporting actions that help the population to make more autonomous and conscious financial decisions and foster the financial literacy of the population. ENEF brings together representatives of government agencies and entities, which together are part of the Brazilian Financial Education Forum (FBEF).

Another important action of the Brazilian Government through the Ministry of Education was the inclusion of financial education in the BNCC (National Common Curriculum Base) being approached in a transversal way by schools, that is, in the various classes and projects. Previews that education networks appropriate early childhood and primary education curricula, including this and other teaching skills, by 2020. In this sense, according to Tokarnia (2019), the results of financial education at school can bring immediate results because in a survey in made in partnership with Serasa Consumidor and Serasa Experian, showed that one in three students said they had learned the importance of saving money after participating in financial education projects. Another 24% started talking to parents about financial education and 21% learned more about how to use money better.

Good Practices in Portugal and Brazil

The problematic is of particular interest given the relevance and social relevance. The theme under study and its foreseeable impact on both countries, with reference to the conditions. It is intended to present the good practices established in the two countries to emphasize the role of Information Systems and Information and Communication Technologies.

ICT as a Support for the Dissemination of Financial Literacy Initiatives to Families

ICT enhances the dissemination of knowledge. In this sense, the initiatives that are called in Portugal are presented to contribute to the dissemination of a vast set of information. The National Financial Training Plan (NFTP) mentions that Financial Literacy and Consumer Education enable young people to acquire and develop fundamental knowledge and skills for decisions that, now and in the future, must make about their personal finances, enabling them as consumers, and specifically as consumers of financial products and services, to deal with the increasing complexity of financial contexts and instruments. In a broader perspective, it is intended to provide information that sustains individual choices of more judicious choice, contributing to solidarity and responsible behavior of the student as a consumer, in the context of the socio-economic and cultural system where the rights of the individual and their responsibilities in the face of sustainable development and the common good are articulated, (MCE, 2016a).

Another initiative that also presents a set of guidelines is the National Financial Training Plan 2016 – 2020, (MCE, 2016a), in which the Financial Education notebooks are intended to support students and teachers in addressing Financial Education Reference (FER) themes and can, as support material for Financial Education, be worked on in the various curricular contexts of learning. Its publication results from the partnership, under the National Financial Training Plan, between the Ministry of Education (through the Directorate-General for Education), financial supervisors (Banco de Portugal, Securities

Market Commission and Insurance and Pension Funds Supervisory Authority) and four associations of the financial sector (Portuguese Association of Banks, Portuguese Association of Insurers, Portuguese Association of Investment Funds, Pensions and Assets and Association of Specialized Credit Institutions).

The document (MCE, 2016b) has a wide range of information with concerns about the various age levels of students. Financial Literacy and Consumer Education enable young people to acquire and develop fundamental knowledge and skills for decisions they now and in the future must make about their personal finances, enabling them as consumers, and specifically as consumers of financial products and services, to deal with the increasing complexity of financial contexts and instruments. In a broader perspective, it is intended to provide information that sustains individual choices of more judicious choice, contributing to the student's supportive and responsible behaviors as a consumer, in the context of the socio-economic and cultural system where the rights of the individual and their responsibilities in the face of sustainable development and the common good are articulated.

The International Family Day 15 May is of particular interest. This date was elected by the UN General Assembly in 1993 but was first celebrated in 1994. With this global and annual ephemeris, the United Nations seeks, (DECO, 2020):

- Disseminate the importance of the family in society;
- Underline the basic nature of the family in the education of children;
- Elevate love, respect and unity as essential elements for the relationship of all family members;
- Alert society to the rights and responsibilities of families;
- Raise citizens' awareness of the social, economic and demographic problems that influence the family;
- Raise awareness among citizens about the different types of families around the world.

Characterization of Initiatives and Platforms in Portugal

The instrument presented have as technical characteristics be websites with informative content referencing also for national and European legal framework. In this sense, it is of particular interest to create a mobile application to simulate a set of indicators enhancing the optimization of family debit management.

In Portugal (DECO, 2020), there are about 4 million families that are important economic agents, have income and make financial decisions. However, most families have financial difficulties and many of them lack financial literacy skills. This is essential that everyone contributes to the financial balance of domestic budgets and that they talk about money and finance, that they know where and how the money is being spent. It is essential that everyone knows how to save and multiply incomes. By discussing the topic of money, the family will be contributing to the financial education of all its elements, even creating a good time to explain to the younger ones the value and how to manage the money. The Portuguese still need financial advice to face a process of renegotiation of credit agreements. As December 31, 2019, we have received more than 29,000 requests for help from families in financial difficulties. The number of cases with our intervention increased slightly compared to the previous year.

The public bank of Portugal Caixa Geral de Depósitos (CGD), mentions on its website the European Money Wanted in which the game of financial literacy in digital format, available for computer and smartphone, which puts in direct competition thousands of students at European level and tests their knowledge in areas such as savings and credit, risk, indebtedness, online security and personal finance management. The competition is intended for students between 13 and 15 years and is accessible to all schools in the country (limited to the number of vacancies available), (CGD, 2020).

Novo Banco's Financial Literacy Programme, (Novobanco, 2020) mentions that the challenges facing the banking sector are to contribute to increasing financial knowledge levels and promoting the adoption of appropriate behavior to foster the well-being of the population and the stability of the financial system. With the creation of the Financial Literacy Program, Novo Banco assumes its role as an institution that guides its positioning and management by principles of sustainability and corporate citizenship, contributing to the formation of a new generation of consumers of financial services increasingly informed and with greater power of analysis and decision. In this context, the Bank's performance in financial literacy is based on an architecture based on three pillars: Pedagogical Process (Portuguese Mathematical Olympiads); Commercial Offer (Micro Savings and Junior Scheduled Savings Account) and Personal Finance (Family Budget).

The University of Porto, through its Faculty of Economics and in partnership with the Museum of Paper Currency of the Dr. António Cupertino de Miranda Foundation, FEP Finance Club and the EXUP - Experience Upgrade Program FEP, structured a program to promote education and training financial literacy among young students in order to raise awareness of the importance of financial literacy at a crucial time of personal and professional development such as entering Higher Education (FEP, 2019).

"Ori€nta-te" is a social responsibility initiative, in the form of a contest, promoted by the Ageas Foundation and by the Entrepreneurial Minds, which aims to familiarize, in a practical way, the youngsters of the 3rd Cycle of Basic Education with Financial Literacy concepts. This is the 3rd edition of the "Ori€nta-te" Contest to take place during the 2020/2021 school year. The objectives of the contest 1- Train teachers of the 3rd Cycle of Basic Education in the schools covered, providing them with tools for replicating financial literacy workshops in the classroom through non-formal education methodologies. 2- provide young people from the 3rd cycle of basic education, from the schools covered, with tools and fundamental knowledge related to financial literacy, contributing to:

- The creation of saving habits;
- The development of young people aware of the impact and need for good financial self-management;
- The consolidation of skills that promote sustainable family economic management;
- The sharing of learning with the local community, promoting the application of better financial management (Fundação Ageas, 2020).

The National Plan for Financial Education (NPFF), whose initiative is called "Todos Contam", presents a wide range of information structured by areas of interest to citizens, such as: Planning the family budget; Make payments; Save and invest; Create a company; Get credit; Take out insurance; Prevent Fraud and Information/News. The NPFF, is an instrument that recognizes the importance of inclusion and financial education, defines the general guiding principles for its promotion and frames and supports the implementation of initiatives at national level. It is a medium and long-term project, in which the guidelines defined for 2016-2020 continue and reinforce the strategy pursued in the first five years of implementation, between 2011 and 2015. The NPFF has an integrated and coordinated vision of initiatives for financial education, recognizing that improving knowledge and influencing the population's attitudes and behavior in this area is only possible with the involvement of a wide range of partners. Partnerships established with ministries and public bodies, business and financial sector associations, consumer associations, trade union centers and universities allow for the adaptation of financial education to the needs of specific target audiences and provide the necessary territorial capillarity.

The (NPFF, 2021) aims to contribute to improving the knowledge and financial behavior of the population in general, considering the specific needs of different segments of the population. Aiming also to raise the level of financial knowledge of the population and promote the adoption of adequate financial behavior, through an integrated vision of financial education projects and by joining the efforts of interested parties, contributing to increase the well-being of the population and for the stability of the financial system.

It is observed that in Portugal, there are a wide range of initiatives to raise public awareness in the various age groups in order to disseminate a set of instruments to enhance the passage of information in order to sensitize families and their elements to the assertive management of money, thus contributing to the reduction of in datedness (CGD, 2020); (BdP, 2020); (DECO, 2020); (Novobanco, 2020); (FEP, 2019); (Fundação Ageas, 2020); (NPFF, 2021).

Characterization of Initiatives and Platforms in Brazil

In 2018, the National Council of Education (CNE) approved the inclusion of financial education in the BNCC, a reference for the preparation of school curricula and pedagogical proposals in Brazil. The inclusion of financial education in school curricula is adherent to the public initiatives of the National Financial Education Strategy (ENEF), which articulates dozens of sectoral and cross-cutting programs conducted by several entities of the National Financial System (SFN). The Central Bank of Brazil (Bacen) develops some programs in this direction, including: the "Learning Value"; "It's your business"; Registration; the My Financial Life page; the Citizen Calculator; in addition to the content on financial education produced for social networks. Bacen created the "Learn Value!" program that supports public elementary schools and education networks across the country to develop financial education and consumer education skills and skills. The proposal is to prepare the student to better deal with money in their day-to-day life, before even entering the job market. To this end, the program includes the training of school managers and teachers, provides a set of tools and for management and monitoring, provides educational resources for teachers and also provides mechanisms for evaluating learning and the impact of actions, including awarding the best results achieved (Learning Value, 2021); (Brazil, 2021).

The actions are oriented in three pillars: (i) planning the use of financial resources; (ii) actively save; and (iii) manage credit usage. The program follows the guidelines of the BNCC, dealing with these themes in a transversal and integrative way in school curricula. Started in the experimental phase in 2020, it is financed with funds from the Diffuse Rights Defense Fund of the Ministry of Justice and Public Security and entered the phase of national expansion in 2021 (Aprender Valor, 2021). So far it has served 429 schools in 257 municipalities, benefiting 14,000 students and more than 1,200 professionals, including managers and teachers, who are training themselves or have already completed the training offered. The expectation is to serve 22 million elementary school students from public schools across the country. The program benefits not only students, but also families. In addition to teachers, principals, school technicians and education departments, parents will also benefit, since students will bring knowledge indoors (Brasil, 2021a).

Another program developed by Bacen, "It's your business" is a set of sixteen free online courses that aim to better inform the consumer of financial services and were designed for those who work with the consumer protection of financial services. The program was created by Bacen with the support of the

National Consumer Secretariat (Senacon) and the courses are certified by the University of Brasilia (UnB). The courses work from financial planning, through behavioral aspects of consumption, on contractual protection mechanisms, to crimes against consumer relations (Brasil, 2021b; ENDC, 2021). The program contributes to maintaining education for the consumption and financial education of Brazilian citizens.

In a move towards transparency in financial information and for fraud prevention, Bacen developed the registration. It is a financial monitoring tool that allows citizens to consult free of charge which and how many current accounts, loans, Pix keys, foreign exchange transactions and international transfers are linked in their CPF (Bacen, 2021a). The My Financial Life page has a similar proposal: it allows citizens to ask questions and obtain information about various banking operations. In addition to access to Registration, you can also obtain information about unpaid checks and debts to the federal public sector (Brasil, 2021b). Another tool made available by Bacen is the "Citizen Calculator". The tool is available online and through a mobile app. Free, it allows simulates daily financial operations, such as applications with regular deposits, financing operations with fixed installments, future values, and correction of values through some indexer (Bacen, 2021b).

In the portal "Financial Citizenship", the Central Bank of Brazil (Bacen) brings together all programs in addition to allowing access to the virtual library, accessing material on consumer rights and duties, in addition to bringing data on citizenship and financial inclusion that can be useful to researchers and decision makers of public policies. In addition to the portal, social media is also an important channel for disseminating information about financial education used by Bacen. The Brazilian Securities and Exchange Commission (CVM), which is responsible for standardizing and supervising Brazilian stock exchanges and investors, also develops financial education programs. CVM since 1998 has been applying resources in the implementation of financial education projects, publications, and activities through the Investor Orientation Program (PRODIN). The program aims to stimulate the formation of savings and its conscious application and the adequate dissemination of information about the capital market in compliance with art. 4, item I, of Law No 6,385/76. To strengthen the actions in this direction, the CVM Educational Center was created in 2015, which brings adequate facilities capable of offering education and training actions to investors, civil servants, regulators, market professionals and the general public (CVM, 2021).

The CVM Educational Center, based on its operation, begins to have as main objectives: (i) To promote the financial education of the population; (ii) Strengthen the fundamental right of access to information and sets of documents of a permanent nature and historical or cultural value; (iii) Promote historical research on capital markets, organizing, preserving and disseminating the memory of CVM and its servers. The center has an educational nucleus, a memory core and a library nucleus (CVM, 2021). In addition to the creation of the center, CVM develops several financial education programs for children, adolescents, and young people (EF for children and Global Money Week) professionals (Financial Welfare Program) and researchers (Behavioral Sciences and Investor Protection Network). CVM also offers several online courses through the CVM Educational [REMOVED HYPERLINK FIELD](https://cursos.cvm.gov.br/). The entity through the Investor Portal (https://www.investidor.gov.br/) provides basic information for those interested in starting investments, provides information about the structure and functioning of the financial market, provides bibliography and gathers websites of cvm itself and other financial market entities that are of interest to the investor.

In 2018 the Center for Behavioral Studies and Research (CECOP) of CVM started the project "We need to talk about money", which disseminates information about financial education through lists of transmission to people who express interest in the subject through the Whatsapp application. The goal is to foster the culture of savings and investment and the content of the messages is directed to the newest audience in matters related to financial education and personal finance (CVM, 2018). The Superintendence of Private Insurance (SUSEP), responsible for the supervision of private/supplementary pension entities and insurers, also develops programs aimed at financial education. In the Portal My Future Insurance (https://www.meufuturoseguro.gov.br/), Susep provides a series of guidelines for each phase of the citizen's life, from birth to death, so that you know the options of credit and financial protection exist and brings relevant tips and guidance.

Another action still of the federal government is carried out by the Ministry of Citizenship. The ministry provides training and material for the realization of financial education workshops within the scope of the Service of Protection and Integral Family Care (PAIF). The methodology aims to contribute to improve the management of the budget of families through the reorganization of financial habits and planning strategies to achieve their individual and family objectives. The Financial Education System of the Future in Hand (EducFin) is a tool developed to request and monitor requests for material for the realization of financial education workshops under the PAIF. It is used by the managers of social assistance of the municipalities and by the managers of Social Assistance Reference Centers (CRAS) (Brasil, 2021c).

In addition to the actions of government entities, there are also actions developed by private banks. The National Federation of Banks (FEBRABAN) maintains the portal "Meu Bolso em Dia" (https://meubolsoemdia.com.br/) that brings news, educational articles, tools, and a platform that brings various materials, courses and videos on financial education. The next, Bradesco's digital bank, launched the nextJoy digital account (https://next.me/nextjoy) in the second half of 2020.[REMOVED HYPERLINK FIELD] It is a free bank account for minors, which promises to assist parents, guardians, and dependents in financial learning processes from an early age. A new app has been developed integrated into the next account of parents or legal guardians to allow them to have full management. The app offers services such as debit card, transfers, and financial education material. The Brazilian stock exchange (B3) also develops actions focused on financial education. On the B3 Education portal (https://edu.b3.com.br/) content and courses are available for personal finance, the financial market, and investments.

SOLUTIONS AND RECOMMENDATIONS

It has been assumed that the implementation of ict measures, which address sustainability concerns, is crucial. Thus, it was possible to identify and quantify options to optimize established practices, thus contributing assertively to sustainability (landum, moura, & reis, 2021).

The mobile application will use the simulation model for the purpose of predicting the level of personal indebtedness. It is understood that there is a need for people to monitor their propensity to debt to assess and, if necessary, take corrective measures to avoid over indebtedness that is a social problem, mental health and generates problems for and economy of the country. In this way, promoting financial literacy in families and stimulating more conscious attitudes and behaviors will encourage the economy in the post-COVID era.

As financial literacy is a lifelong learning activity, its development should be fostered right from childhood, through family examples and teachings. Include financial topics in academic curricula, from the 1st cycle of schooling to university education. In the workplace, financial literacy could be part of induction and professional development programs. For employees over fifty, create specialized programs for retirement planning. Public awareness campaigns in the media should also be promoted, highlighting why financial literacy is essential. Many stakeholders have a role to play if a successful outcome is to be achieved, including government, schools, employers, product suppliers and community organizations in general.

FUTURE RESEARCH DIRECTIONS

As a future work, the research is to validate with a focus group in Portugal and another in Brazil to measure the usability of the prototype in a broad sense. After this phase, the contributions will be incorporated to optimize the developed prototype and thus enhance its use in fulfilling its design. This focus group is of particular interest given the relevance of content validation and usability since it is intended an intuitive application of multipurpose characteristics to captivate a huge diversity of audiences.

The prototype of mobile app can promote financial literacy in post-pandemic times. The mobile application that allows families and individual users to simulate expenditure and their budget to instill the concern of definition spending and savings strategies. It is also considered that the mobile application prototype to be developed can be validated in both countries to become a pedagogical tool to promote the optimization of family management. It will be important to create a focus group in Portugal and another in Brazil to validate the research and to measure the usability of the prototype in a broad sense.

CONCLUSION

Sustainability is multidimensional and should be analyzed in view of the specificity of each theme under study and in this context, it is of particular interest to consider especially the economic, environmental, and social valences. Given the need to enhance the financial level of families, the chapter presents a characterization of the current state of the art in Portugal and Brazil.

In this sense, the use of ICT is advocated as support for the development of strategies of innovation and entrepreneurship to enhance the dissemination of information related to family indebtedness. It is considered that the mobile application could provide added value to enhance the use by numerous users to carry out simulations about their financial status and thus enhance the development of measures to combat family indebtedness.

The main results of the project are to characterize the theme by raising some initiatives that aim to implement awareness strategies of various audiences so that each family has access to diversified information adapted to each age group. It was also possible to reflect on European initiatives to develop a fundamental framework for the problem.

The analysis of the situation regarding the indebtedness or over-indebtedness of households in Portugal and Brazil was an extremely relevant exercise in view of the current situation of the two countries. The development of joint work in a spirit of collaboration to create added value allowing the development of a mobile application to be used in both countries.

Thus, it appears that there are several initiatives to raise awareness of families and citizens in different age groups, to promote a set of instruments to enhance communication to families and their members for an assertive management of money. In this way, the theme of financial literacy is an important element in a micro perspective of the smart economy.

REFERENCES

Alves, A. (2014). *Literacia financeira e comportamento na tomada de decisões financeiras.* Dissertação de Mestrado, Universidade de Aveiro, Departamentode Economia, Gestão e Engenharia Industrial, Obtido de Engenharia Industrial, Aveiro. https://ria.ua.pt/bitstream/10773/15756/1/Literacia%20financeira%20e%20comportamento%20na%20tomada%20de%20decis%C3%B5es%20financeiras.pdf

Amagir, A., Groot, W., & Maassen van den Brinkc, H. (2020). Financial literacy of high school students in the Netherlands: Knowledge, attitudes, self-efficacy, and behavior. *International Review of Economics Education, 34*(100185), 100185. doi:10.1016/j.iree.2020.100185

Anbima - Associação Brasileira das Entidades dos Mercados Financeiro e de Capitais. (2020). *Raio X do investidor Brasileiro.* https://www.anbima.com.br/pt_br/especial/raio-x-do-investidor-2020.htm

Aprender Valor. (2021). *O que é o programa aprender valor?* https://aprendervalor.caeddigital.net/#!/programa

Bacen. (2021a). *Banco Central do Brasil. Registrato.* https://www.bcb.gov.br/cidadaniafinanceira/registrato

Bacen. (2021b). *Banco Central do Brasil. Calculadora do Cidadão.* https://www.bcb.gov.br/acessoinformacao/calculadoradocidadao

Banco de Portugal. (2010). *Relatório do Inquérito à Literacia Financeira da População Portuguesa.* https://www.bportugal.pt/sites/default/files/relatorio_do_ inquerito_a_literacia_financeira_da_populacao_portuguesa_2010.pdf

BdP. (2020). *OCDE emite recomendação sobre literacia financeira.* Obtido de Banco de Portugal: https://clientebancario.bportugal.pt/pt-pt/noticias/ocde-emite-recomendacao-sobre-literacia-financeira

Bianchi, I., & Dinis de Sousa, R. (2015). *Governança de TI em universidades públicas: Proposta de um modelo.* Instituto Universitário de Lisboa (ISCTE-IUL).

Brasil (2021a). *Projeto de educação financeira nas escolas públicas é expandido para todo o país.* Portal Gov.br. Publicado em 31 mai. 2021. https://www.gov.br/pt-br/noticias/financas-impostos-e-gestao-publica/2021/05/projeto-de-educacao-financeira-nas-escolas-publicas-e-expandido-para-todo-o-pais

Brasil. (2021b). *Banco Central oferece ferramentas gratuitas de educação financeira.* Publicado em 15 de março de 2021. https://www.gov.br/pt-br/noticias/financas-impostos-e-gestao-publica/2021/03/banco-central-oferece-ferramentas-gratuitas-de-educacao-financeira

Brasil. (2021c). *Solicitar kits de Educação Financeira do Futuro na Mão* (Educfin). https://www.gov.br/pt-br/servicos/solicitar-kits-de-educacao-financeira-do-futuro-na-mao

Bruneckiene, J., & Sinkiene, J. (2014), Critical Analysis of Approaches to Smart Economy. *International Scientific Conference Business and Management.* http://www.dx.doi.org/10.3846/bm.2014.106

Carita, P. (2016). *A importância da literacia financeira nas decisões de investimento.* Dissertação de Mestrado, ISCTE. Obtido de http://hdl.handle.net/10071/13428

Carvalho, L. (2017). Entrepreneurial Ecosystems. Lisbon as a Smart Start-up City. In L. Carvalho (Ed.), *Handbook of Research On Entrepreneurial Development and Innovation within Smart Cities* (pp. 1–24). IGI Global. doi:10.4018/978-1-5225-1978-2.ch001

Carvalho, L., & Paiva, T. (2021). Education 4.0 - drivers, challenges, and opportunities. *Journal Advances in Higher Education, 13*(1), 5–16.

CGD. (2020). *European Money Quiz*. Obtido de CGD: https://www.cgd.pt/Sustentabilidade/Responsabilidade-Social/Pages/European-Money-Quiz.aspx

Conselho Nacional Supervisores Financeiros Banco de Portugal. (2016). *Relatório do Inquérito à Literacia Financeira da População Portuguesa*. https://www.todoscontam.pt/sites/default/files/SiteCollectionDocuments/Relatorio2InqueritoLiteraciaFinanceira.pdf

Cordeiro, N. J. N., Costa, M. G. V., & da Silva, M. N. (2018). Educação financeira no Brasil: uma perspectiva panorâmica. *Ensino da Matemática em Debate, 5*(1), 69 – 84.

Costa, C. M., & Miranda, C. J. de. (2013). Educação financeira e taxa de poupança no Brasil. *Revista de Gestão, Finanças e Contabilidade, 3*(3), 57-74.

Cunha, M. P. (2020). O mercado financeiro chega à sala de aula: Educação financeira como política pública no Brasil. *Educação e Sociedade, 41*.

CVM. (2018). *CVM lança projeto Precisamos Falar Sobre Dinheiro*. https://www.investidor.gov.br/noticias/2018_11_12.html

CVM. (2021). *Centro CVM de Educação e Letramento Financeiro para a América Latina e Caribe*. https://www.investidor.gov.br/menu/atividades/CentroEducacional/CentroEducacionalCVM_OCDE.html

DECO. (2020). *Em risco de sobre-endividamento? Peça ajuda à DECO*. https://www.deco.proteste.pt/familia-consumo/orcamento-familiar/dossies/como-travar-o-sobre-endividamento-com-a-deco

ENDC. (2021). *Escola Nacional de Defesa do Consumidor*. https://www.defesadoconsumidor.gov.br/escolanacional

Ergun, K. (2018). Financial literacy among university students: A study in eight European countries. *International Journal of Consumer Studies, 42*(1), 2–15. doi:10.1111/ijcs.12408

Erner, C., Goedde-Menke, M., & Oberste, M. (2016). Financial literacy of high school students: Evidence from Germany. *The Journal of Economic Education, 47*(2), 95–105. doi:10.1080/00220485.2016.1146102

FEP. (2019). *€DUCAR na U.Porto*. Obtido em 17 de 05 de 2021, de Programa de Promoção da Literacia Financeira da U.Porto: https://literaciafinanceira.fep.up.pt/

Fernandes, D. (2011). *Acerca da Literacia Financeira*. Dissertação de Mestrado, ISCTE - Instituto Universitário de Lisboa. https://repositorio.iscte-iul.pt/bitstream/10071/4382/1/Tese%20Acerca%20da%20LF%2

Ferreira, I., Ferreira, S., Silva, C., & Carvalho, J. (2012). Dilemas iniciais na investigação em TSI design science e design research, uma clarificação de conceitos. *Conferência Ibérica de Sistemas y Tecnologias de Informação*. https://repositorium.sdum.uminho.pt/bitstream/1822/21696/1/CISTI 2012.pdf

Fundação Ageas. (2020). *Ori€nta-te*. https://www.concursorientate.pt/

Galperina, L., Girenko, A., & Mazurenko, V. (2016). The Concept of Smart Economy as the Basis for Sustainable Development of Ukraine. *International Journal of Economics and Financial Issues*, *6*(S8), 307–314.

Goeking, V. (2020). *Brasileiros ligam finanças pessoais a sentimentos ruins e perpetuam tabu sobre dinheiro*. Valor Investe. https://valorinveste.globo.com/educacao-financeira/noticia/2020/11/10/brasileiros-ligam-financas-pessoais-a-sentimentos-ruins-e-perpetuam-tabu-sobre-dinheiro.ghtml

Greencred. (2021). *Finanças Pessoais: pesquisa revela que 73% dos brasileiros não guardam dinheiro*. https://greencred.com.br/financas-pessoais-brasileiros-nao-guardam-dinheiro/

Hastings, J., Madrian, B., & Skimmyhorn, W. (2013). Financial literacy, financial education, and economic outcomes. *Annual Review of Economics*, *5*(1), 347–373. doi:10.1146/annurev-economics-082312-125807 PMID:23991248

Hauff, J. C., Carlander, A., Garling, T., & Nicolini, G. (2020). Retirement Financial Behaviour: How Important Is Being Financially Literature? *Journal of Consumer Policy*, *43*(3), 543–564. doi:10.100710603-019-09444-x

Hevner, A., March, S., Park, J., & Ram, S. (2004). Design Science in Information Systems Research. *Management Information Systems Quarterly*, *28*(1), 75–105. doi:10.2307/25148625

Huston, S. (2010). Measuring financial literacy. *The Journal of Consumer Affairs*, *44*(2), 296–316. doi:10.1111/j.1745-6606.2010.01170.x

INFE. (2020). *Oecd.Org. International Gateway For Financial Education - Organisation For Economic Co-Operation And Development*. Https://Www.Oecd.Org/Financial/Education/Oecd-International-Network-On-Financial-Education.Html

Kempson, E., Collard, S., & Moore, N. (2005). *Financial capability: An exploratory study. Consumer research report 37*. Financial Services Authority.

Landum, M., Moura, M., & Reis, L. (2021). A framework for the alignment of ICT with Green IT. *Advances in Science, Technology and Engineering Systems Journal, 6*(2).

Mandell, L., & Klein, L. (2007). Motivation and financial literacy. *Financial Services Review*, *16*, 105–116.

MCE. (2013). *Referencial de Educação Financeira para a Educação Pré-Escolar, o Ensino Básico, o Ensino Secundário e a Educação e Formação de Adultos*. https://dge.mec.pt/sites/default/files/ficheiros/referencial_de_educacao_financeira_final_versao_port.pdf

MCE. (2016a). *Plano Nacional de Formação Financeira 2016-2020*. https://cidadania.dge.mec.pt/literacia-financeira-e-educacao-para-o-consumo/plano-nacional-de-formacao-financeira apresenta os pressupostos no âmbito do Plano supracitado

MCE. (2016b). *Educação para a Cidadania. Literacia Financeira e Educação para o Consumo*. https://cidadania.dge.mec.pt/literacia-financeira-e-educacao-para-o-consumo

Molina-García, A., Florido-Ruiz, B., Valenzuela, M. C. & Diéguez-Soto, J. (2020). The effect of family ownership and generation on financial literacy. *Small Business International Review*, *4*(1), 1-15.

Novobanco. (2020). *Programa de Literacia Financeira*. https://www.novobanco.pt/site/cms.aspx?labelid=literaciafinanceira

OECD. (2015). *OECD / INFE Toolkit for measuring financial literacy and financial inclusion*. OECD.

OECD. (2020). *OECD/INFE 2020 International Survey of Adult Financial Literacy*. www.oecd.org/financial/education/launchoftheoecdinfeglobalfinancialliteracysurveyreport.htm

OECD. (2020). *OECD Recommendation on Financial Literacy*. Obtido de OECD: https://www.oecd.org/finance/OECD-Recommendation-on-Financial-Literacy.html

Orton, L. (2007). *Financial Literacy: Lessons from International Experience*. http://cprn3.library.carleton.ca/documents/48647_EN.pdf

Peffers, K., Tuunanen, T., Rothenberger, M., & Chatterjee, S., (2007). A Design Science Research Methodology for Information Systems Research. *Journal of Management Information Systems*, *24*(3), 45-78.

Rodrigues, E. (2020). *63% dos brasileiros não investem por falta de conhecimento*. Capital Research. https://cantarinobrasileiro.com.br/blog/63-dos-brasileiros-nao-investem-por-falta-de-conhecimento/

Santiago, A. (2015). A Educação Financeira Escolar Em Portugal. *Boletim GEPEM*, 20-30.

Santos, A. (2015). *Literacia Financeira: O caso dos alunos dos cursos da área financeira da Escola Superior de Ciências Empresariais (ESCE) do Instituto Politécnico de Setúbal (IPS)*. Dissertação de Mestrado.

Stolper, O., & Walter, A. (2017). Financial literacy, financial advice, and financial behavior. *Journal of Business Economics*, *87*(5), 581–643. doi:10.100711573-017-0853-9

UNEP. (2011). *Towards a Green Economy: Pathways to Sustainable Development and Poverty Eradication. A Synthesis for Policy Makers*. UNEP.

Van Rooij, M., Lusardi, A., & Alessie, R. (2011). Financial Literacy and Stock Market Participation. *Journal of Financial Economics*, *101*(2), 449–472. doi:10.1016/j.jfineco.2011.03.006

Walstad, W., Rebeck, K. K., & MacDonald, R. A. (2010). The Effects of Financial Education on the Financial Knowledge of High School Students. *The Journal of Consumer Affairs*, *44*(2), 336–357. doi:10.1111/j.1745-6606.2010.01172.x

Willis, L. (2008). Against Financial Literacy Education. *Iowa Law Review*.

KEY TERMS AND DEFINITIONS

Financial Literacy: Consists of specific knowledge related to monetary, economic, or financial issues and decisions that individuals and families can outline as strategies for financial decision-making.

Information and Communication Technologies: A technological resource set used to process information and ensure communication. When used in an integrated way it enhances information transmission and communication processes.

Information Systems: Is the organized set of components such as people, processes of collection and transmission of data and material resources, automated or manual. The interaction of components enhances the processing and dissemination of information.

Software Systems Development: Set of activities involved in the production of software. These activities are related to each other in an iterative and incremental process.

Sustainability: Ability to sustain life on the planet, considering the five dimensions: individual, social, economic, technical, and environmental.

Chapter 2
Digital Innovation With Social Impact:
The Case of ColorAdd

Luisa Margarida Cagica Carvalho
https://orcid.org/0000-0002-9804-7813
Instituto Politécnico de Setúbal, Portugal & CEFAGE, Universidade de Évora, Portugal

Bianca Marques Barreto
Instituto Politécnico de Setúbal, Portugal

Margarida Cristina
Instituto Politécnico de Setúbal, Portugal

Margarida Martins
Instituto Politécnico de Setúbal, Portugal

Sofia Cristina
Instituto Politécnico de Setúbal, Portugal

ABSTRACT

This chapter aims to discuss the concepts of digital innovation that bring social impacts. In order to develop this approach, this chapter presents a literature review with the main topics and a case study. The case fits in with digitalization with social impact and reports the case of ColorAdd, which is a tool with a revolutionary, simple, and universal language based on the concept of adding colors, to ensure that there is an accurate understanding of communication whenever color is an identification factor, guidance, or choice, reducing the limitations felt by color-blind people. This tool is used in metro maps, clothing labels, hospitals, catalogs, nutritional traffic lights, medicines, games, computer systems, among many others. As a color identification system, the target audience is people with difficulty in interpreting colors, mostly color-blind people, which are near 350 million individuals.

DOI: 10.4018/978-1-7998-9227-4.ch002

LITERATURE REVIEW

Innovation

According to Drucker innovation is the specific tool of entrepreneurs, the means by which they exploit change as an opportunity for a different business or a different service (Drucker, 1985).

This means that innovation is an organized process and is something structured, and that leads to systematic innovation, which is a purposeful and organized pursuit to create changes and are based in the analysis of opportunities.

In other perspective innovation can be seem as a manifestation of its creative capacity and as the result of humanity's efforts to propose responses to its needs and improve its quality of life (Cajaiba-Santana, 2014).

According to Manual de Oslo innovation can be defined as a new or improved product or process (or a combination of them) that differs significantly from the organization's previous products or processes, available to potential users (product) or put into use by the organization (process) (OECD/Eurostat, 2018). Innovations can be radical or incremental depends on the adjustments introduced during innovative process. It's also possible to find other definitions for types of innovation, such as marketing innovation that happens when a new marketing strategy that leads to changes in the package or design of the product, or price and promotion (Kylliäinen, 2019).

SOCIAL INNOVATION

The *Bureau of European Policy Advisors* (BEPA) outlines Social Innovation (SI) as "innovations that are social both in their ends and in their means" and claims that they stipulate an effective mode to "empower people" and "drive societal change" (BEPA, 2010). Howaldt and Kopp (2012:47) outline SI as "a new combination and/or new configuration of social practices in certain areas of action or social contexts". A marginally different approach is suggested by Moulaert (2013: 2), who state SI as "innovation in social relations (…) not just particular actions but also (…) outcome of actions which lead to improvements in social relations, structures of governance, greater collective empowerment, and so on".

Nevertheless, Franz et al. (2012:4), question if all social innovation are "really intended as social and/or using social means", and suggest examples of SIs, such as fast food restaurants and the internet, which were not planned as being social, neither in their ends nor in their means. In this perspective, the 'social' in SI reflects that the *object* of innovation is fundamentally a social phenomenon (i.e. a social practice or relation, as opposed to e.g. a new technology or product).

The Young Foundation (2012) identified eight aspects of social innovation that differentiate it from other types of innovations:

1. Intersectoral. Social innovation can encompass and occur in all sectors and move between sectors as they development.
2. Open and collaborative. Social innovation has to be inclusive and capable of adding a higher number of actors in their development and implementation.
3. Bottom-up. The communities and beneficiaries are who develop these initiatives, fostering empowerment processes and increasing the efficiency of the solution.

4. Pro-sumption and co-production. There is no explicit limit between who produces and who consumes. Users become producers or suppliers. Change in the vision of who receives the benefit for one where it is co-responsible of producers and consumers for the solution and its maintenance in the long term.
5. Mutualism. It starts with the idea that individual and collective well-being can be obtained only through mutual dependence.
6. Create new roles and relationships. They are developed "with" and "by" users and are not delivered "to" and "to" them—social innovations differentiate by the type of relationships they create.
7. Better use of assets.
8. Develop assets and capabilities.

It is important to distinguish four perspectives of change and innovation: 1) social innovation, (2) system innovation, (3) game-changers and (4) narratives of change. A linked concept of Transformative Social Innovation TSI could be seem as a resulting interactive, co-evolutionary process between distinct but intertwined dimensions of innovation and change. Behind relational understandings of transformation processes (Jørgensen, 2012, Garud and Gehman, 2012, Hargreaves et al., 2013). (Table 1).

Table 1. Four shades of change and innovation: working definitions

4 Shades of Change & Innovation	Working Definition
Social innovation	Change in social relations, involving new ways of doing, organising, knowing and framing.
System innovation	Change at the level of societal sub-systems, including institutions, social structures and physical infrastructures.
Game-changers	Macro-developments that are perceived to change the (rules, fields and players in the) 'game' of societal interaction.

Source: Avelino et al, 2019

Impact of Social Innovation

It's important to note that social innovation (digital or not) impact on society. Mulgan (2010) recapitulated a number of the key models in an analysis that determined strongly on learning from well-established practice in government and from theory within welfare economics.

Nevertheless, the same author noted some problems with these measures. Part of them coming from conventional accounting practices and are not planned to capture social impact (Nicholls 2009).

Nevertheless it is consensual that measuring the social impacts of social innovation is not an easygoing task and is usually related to its level of maturity. Epstein and Yuthas (2014) suggested five levels:

1. Emergent. The information or measurement supports internal decisions by tracking revenues and expenses. It focuses on maintaining the operation and survival of the organization.
2. Established. It focuses on evaluating the quantity and quality of the products and services delivered to the market and beneficiaries. The information helps to make decisions about the value generated by the product or service in a specific market niche and how is exploited.

3. Driven by objectives. It seeks to measure, directly or indirectly, the social impact created in the beneficiary, mainly at the level of direct effects. It begins to be a strategy to acquire more investments that allow the model to scale.
4. Integrated. They incorporate performance metrics in the company's processes, from a social and economic perspective. The measurement becomes a key aspect of decision making.
5. Evolutionary. Performance results are used to promote the allocation of resources and to review strategies to ensure the continuous improvement of social impacts.

Maree and Martens (2012) argued that existing 'economic' measures for non-market production are supported on an optimization approach, more linked to the value of production such as, the application of cost-effectiveness analysis (CEA - indicators for the measurement of non-market goods) and cost-benefit analysis (CBA - based on monetary valorization). These authors suggested that while traditional methods used to calculate economic value creation can be useful sometimes in particular cases, they frequently fail to reflect the full range of the social impacts.

Another indicator proposed in the literature is Social Return on Investment (SROI) approach (Emerson et al. 1999, Nicholls 2009, Arvidson et al. 2010) focus the economics cost benefit calculation created around establishing the materiality to stakeholders of key outcomes and then developing financial proxies for each. SROI involves 'reviewing the inputs, outputs, outcomes and impacts made and experienced by stakeholders of an organization in relation to the activities of an organization, and putting a monetary value on the social, economic and environmental benefits and costs created by an organization' (Arvidson et al. 2010, p. 6).

DIGITALIZATION

Nowadays digitalization is not a trend is an imperative and consequently digital innovation is fundamental for organizations. Digital innovation could be defined as the use of digital technology to improve workforce efficiency, as well as enhance customer experience and improve existing business processes, among many other aspects (Mendix Technology, 2021).

Digital technologies enable most innovations, in the sense that they allow the creation of new digital products and business models, such as social media. They also facilitate innovation in production and distribution processes, allowing better efficiency and lesser margin for error in these business processes (OECD, 2019).

Due to digital innovation and its involvement in today's business practices and processes, we are witnessing four changes in innovation dynamics across all sectors, according to OECD's Digital Innovation Report (OECD, 2019):

1. The first change is the fact that data is becoming a key input for innovation. This means that – because there has been an exponential growth in the generation of different types, such as business and personal, and more people than ever are connected digitally – data became crucial, since this data offers opportunities for research and stimulate innovation.
2. Innovation in services is being enabled by digital technologies. Digital transformation provides opportunities, such as the creation of new digitally enabled services since data and software are replacing numerous physical components and products. Due to the growing competitive pressures

caused by the entry of digital players and customer demands, organizations feel the need to offer digitally enabled services, while current service providers make use of digital technologies to improve what they already offer.

3. The third change is related to the acceleration of innovation cycles. The very existence of digital technologies allows accelerating innovation cycles since it significantly reduces R&D costs and the time it takes for a product or a service to reach a market. Some digital technologies contribute to faster innovation cycles, such as virtual simulation and 3D printing, making the entire process of creating the design, prototype and testing a certain product easier.
4. The last change consists of collaborative innovation. The innovation ecosystem is becoming increasingly open and diverse due to organizations interacting more and more with, for example, research institutions and firms. This is due to three different reasons; the first is because it allows them to acquire access and exposure to a better and more complete pool of expertise, that complement their own skill. Then, these collaborations grant sharing the cost and risk of investments that are not as stable or certain in digital innovation. The last reason is the reduced cost of communication, that permits a better interaction between organizations, firms or institutions that are engaged in innovation.

In this context this phenomenon can be understood not only pose as changes, but also as the new characteristics of innovation in the digital age, that can and should be taken into consideration in the future. In a nutshell, digital innovation not only accelerates the innovation cycles, as well as reduces cost of production and time-to-market.

DIGITAL SOCIAL INNOVATION

Digital Social Innovation (DSI) associate social innovation with technology, mainly with Information and Communication Technologies (ICT), Nowadays Internet allows the use of the platforms and digital information processing tools that allow create value through collaboration between several stakeholders cheaply and rapidly. This innovation initiatives are not simply product or service innovation, but also includes social relationships that distinguish a social group and a solid community structure (Murray, Caulier-Grice and Mulgan, 2010).

According to Bria (2014, p.5) social innovation can be defined as "a type of social and collaborative innovation in which final users and communities collaborate through digital platforms to produce solutions for a wide range of social needs and at a scale that was unimaginable before the rise of Internet-enabled networking platforms".

Digital social innovation facilitates people to collaborate using digital technologies to co-create knowledge and solutions for a wide range of social needs, and at a scale that was unimaginable before the rise of internet-enabled platforms (Bria, 2015, p. 6). Some literature report DSI as an angle of digital innovation—understood as the welfare of human beings as members of society—under the umbrella of specific subthemes, such as social inclusion (Trauth, et al, 2018), societal challenges (Majchrzak et al., 2016), or IS innovation in emerging economies (Srivastava & Shainesh, 2015).

In the fact DSI attends as an emerging umbrella definition to define a nascent field where digital technologies are applied to tackle societal challenges and encourage alternative models to the centralization of information, data and resources in the hands of a few big players in the tech industry (Cangiano et al, 2017).

Within the stream of IT innovation, the studies of information and communication technologies for development (ICT4D) have highlighted aspects related to social welfare, where scholars highlight dimensions of the process of IT innovation such as national culture or global politics, which are normally absent in mainstream IS (Avgerou, 2008, 2017). In the IS literature, the global practice of sourcing IT services from less developed contexts has recently turned into an analysis that accounts for their engagement with social development and impact (Babin & Nicholson, 2012; Khan et al., 2018). Referred to as social sourcing (Madon & Sharanappa, 2013) or impact sourcing (Heeks, 2013), the idea behind this new practice of global IT sourcing is to incorporate social and developmental goals within business practices (Sandeep & Ravishankar, 2016).

Social Purpose of Business Models

Several times the social impact of the companies is oriented for Corporate Social Responsibility (CSR). This orientation is associated to a conceptual simplicity of what is the contribution of each company to the society and how innovative is (Brown, de Jong, & Levy, 2009). Nevertheless this simplicity sometimes comes as a difficulty due the necessity to establish some criteria of differentiation between social initiatives developed by companies and social purpose of the business (Portales, 2017).
Portales (2019) established a set of criteria to do this differentiation:

1. The degree of social impact that each of them seeks.
2. The interest of the social initiative to align itself organically with the company's strategy, as well as the business model and the activities that have led it to consolidate.
3. The ability of the initiative, to take advantage of a market opportunity to generate economic income for the company, while at the same time addressing problems and needs that a specific vulnerable group presents.
4. The potential that the company has to consolidate as an alternate business unit to those already existing by the company, in such a way that in the long term it can operate independently.
5. The definition of the attributes that a purposeful business model must contain is in the rupture that it represents regarding the traditional CSR practices of on the part of the companies.

In this umbrella appear the concept of inclusive businesses that allows attending groups that are in a situation of vulnerability or poverty. This type of business model is an economically profitable business initiative, environmentally and socially responsible, that under a logic of mutual benefit contribute to improving the quality of life of low-income or vulnerable communities, through their participation in the value chain of a business (Márquez et al., 2010). This kind of business permits the inclusion in risk of poverty or social exclusion or other situations of vulnerability.

CASE STUDY

Brief Description of the Problem

About 350 million people and about 10% of the entire male population are colorblind (Neiva, ColorADD, 2020). Color blindness is a genetic and recessive disease that is linked to the X chromosome. Those who suffer from this disease have difficulty in distinguishing colors, others cannot see certain colors and in extreme cases there is the possibility that the person unable to distinguish or identify any color and see shades of gray. There is still no type of cure and in terms of treatment for color blindness, just the use of filters on glasses or contact lenses can increase the ability to distinguish some colors, but it is not totally effective (Pereira, 2018).

The Entrepreneur

Miguel Neiva, the creator of ColorADD, together with several universities, eye surgeons and ophthalmologists collected the following statistics: 64% of individuals consider color confusion to be their biggest problem; 59% identify only a few colors; 22% do not see some colors; 51% are unable to "see" the colors; 42% feel that it is difficult to be fully socially integrated (Neiva, ColorADD, 2020).

Normally color blindness is diagnosed accurately from 10 years of age, but it can show signs in children from preschool age, that is, it is a disease that affects the individual's whole life. A colorblind person can live a so-called normal life but is faced with many limitations and still depends on others to make certain simple decisions such as choosing a set of clothes. Being necessary to wear clothes every day this proves to be a constant challenge for those who cannot distinguish or see colors at all and 88% of those affected admit having to ask for help to choose their sets and 90% need help to buy clothes (Neiva, ColorADD, 2020). But there are other situations that are much more uncomfortable for people suffering from color blindness. Since the disease is usually diagnosed at school age this can lead to learning difficulties since graphs, images, tables, and maps are used to teach different subjects (Pereira, 2018). From that time onwards, color blind people feel that they are not socially integrated, and although the limitations are not visible to other people, it greatly affects the individual's self-esteem and perception of himself.

In 2010, to promote the integration of color-blind people, Miguel Neiva created the ColorADD code, which is a color identification system and aims to be a tool that guarantees the full integration of the color-blind public.

The Social Innovation

The code is based on the three primary colors, blue, red, and yellow, which are represented by symbols, as well as white and black.

Mixing two primary colors gives rise to secondary colors, for example, green, orange, and purple. This means that the code gives rise to secondary symbols. Mixing secondary colors gives rise to tertiary colors and composite symbols. Black and white help to distinguish dark from light colors.

Gray is represented by two symbols, dark gray and light gray. Golden and silver tones are represented by adding parentheses.

The code has already been implemented in various areas of activity, the most important of which are health, education, and public transport. Since education can be so limited for color blind people and here the implementation of the code can prove to be fundamental to school success, education is included in ColorADD's pro-Bono licensing regime. In educational terms, this code can be found in colored pencils, maps, school manuals and is part of the national exams referencing since 2013, since that color can affect choices made by the student. For the implementation of Color ADD code by partners, a license is assigned, and these partners contribute to the ColorADD Social project whose mission is to avoid social exclusion in the school path. ColorADD Social is an offshoot of the project and was created in 2014 and is a non-profit organization. It has already organized 260 municipal and school libraries, has already carried out about 32,500 color blindness screenings in the 1st Cycle and has already promoted 3,000 awareness and training actions (ColorADD, 2015).

This code is already recognized internationally, more specifically by the organization Color Blind Awareness, founded in the United Kingdom in order to support in particular parents and teachers of color blind children; by the president of the association Daltónicos No Anónimos, and was featured on ICOGRADA, which is an international reference in graphic design, which considered that with this idea the "color wheel was reinvented". ColorADD is also a highly awarded project and has several relevant distinctions: it was a finalist project in the European competition Zermatt Summit in 2014; it was one of the best projects recognized by the Zero Project in disabilities and accessibility; came first in the European Mobile for Good Europe Awards; was elected the best application at the World Summit Award in 2014 in the Inclusion & Empowerment category; is a project certified by BCorporation.

The Digital Social Innovation

The ColorADD code is already present in more than 90 countries and has helped 100,000 people through schools alone. It is already associated with more than 300 companies and entities. Around the world it is spread on about five million colored pencils and more than 100 million clothing labels.

Digital innovation is the process in which companies use digital technologies to solve traditional problems. Digital transformation is leading to a debate between policy-makers, economists and industry leaders about its social impact. There is a big concern in regards to its growth and how it´s affecting jobs, wages, inequality, health, resource efficiency and security. There is an estimate of global job losses due to digitalization from 2 million to 2 billion by 2030 because many jobs can be easily replaced by automation. Employees need to consider upgrading their skills to keep up with the demands of the market in order to maintain their job. (World Economic Forum, 2021)

However digital transformation has the potential to make a positive contribution and has most definitely made many positive contributions to society.

The International Labor Organization projects 24 million new jobs generated globally by 2030 in logistics and electricity industries. Automation will replace many human beings, but new forms and patterns of work have emerged because of digital technology.

Digital initiatives in the industries could estimate 26 billion tons of net avoided CO_2 emissions from 2016 to 2025, almost the equivalent to the CO_2 emitted by all of Europe across that period of time. This means overcoming hurdles relating to the acceptance of circular business models, customer adoption and the environmental impact of digital technology itself.

Through the web and the internet, the way people interact and communicate have changed radically with emails, conference calls, social media apps, among others.

Digital transformation has saved thousands of lives with advanced machinery and innovations that have been introduced to the health industry.

E-commerce is one of the most revolutionary services the Internet has provided because it removes the usual constraints of time, distance, and resources. It also saves entrepreneurs from the cost of having physical stores.

There is a digital future for everyone, digital technologies have progressed more rapidly than any technology in history, transforming societies radically. We will have to learn to adapt ourselves to these changes, because evolution is positive. (Ocampos, John, 2020)

In the case of ColorADD, we´re facing a digital innovation, as this is an innovation linked to technology, a growing trend and an innovation in the business model, since it allows the development of competitive advantages, which allows people who suffer from color blindness to live a better-quality of life.

The Pandemic Times

Recently, color blind people have faced yet another limitation. In a time of pandemic due to Covid-19, more situations were created in which individuals with color blindness do not feel socially integrated and may even be at risk. In an interview with Agência Lusa in October 2020, Miguel Neiva explains that color blind people who depend on others to identify certain colors are still having more problems in carrying out everyday tasks, whether it is asking for help to buy clothes or to understand all traffic light systems. that were implemented in certain control situations, better known as "covid traffic lights", as there is a need for social distance and little contact between individuals. To face this situation, Neiva has already presented the project to the Ministry of Health to implement the code in the "covid traffic lights" and to the European Commission to implement the code, for example, on the "Re-open Europe" website, among others.

An app is being developed, which is expected to be launched by the end of 2020, which will help color blind people in other limiting situations. All funds generated through the app will revert to ColorADD Social.

The Impact

ColorADD is a color identification system for color-blind people. The impact that this type of innovation has socially is to bring organizations closer to their customers and offer a more personal experience to each user, thus giving them a much more positive experience. Color blind people have access to this unique tool, which helps them to live a more autonomous life.

FUTURE RESEARCH DIRECTIONS

Digital Social innovation is now more than a trend it is a source of possibilities to solve social problems using technology. This chapter focused on a case study that use digital tools to support a huge number of persons around the world that have health problems in the recognition of the colors.

This topic is aligned with the topic of this book due the possibility to discuss real cases with social impact. Further research can explore and develop this topic mainly the access of the impact of this kind of innovation using a quantitative methodology to collect data with the users.

CONCLUSION

Digital social innovation is more than a trend is a reality in the organizations. This type of innovation could impact positively in the day life of numerous people around the world.

After analyzing this business model with a social impact, it was possible to conclude that the color code developed by Miguel Neiva was an innovation that had a great impact on the lives of color-blind people. This analysis proves that digitalization can produce relevant social impacts on societies. It can be concluded that the way in which a code was created was innovative, that there was still nothing identical, and a code based on primary colors was created, to go from there and create an extremely complete code that gives color-blind people the chance to live a more autonomous life, without the help of third parties to carry out normal daily tasks. This tool brought color blind patients a solution for their life and a better inclusion in society. Since this disease can be forgotten, since it is not perceived by those who do not have it, this color code was revolutionary and innovative in the sectors where it was applied. In addition, this innovation developed for this sector can be replicable for other sectors and may even be adopted by even more brands, to spread this tool further and further improve the autonomy of color-blind people. ColorADD fits perfectly into examples a innovation with social impacts using digital innovation.

ACKNOWLEDGMENT

The first author acknowledge the support to ERASMUS+ funds within the project number 612542-EPP-1-2019-1-LV-EPPKA2-KA, KABADA – Knowledge Alliance of Business idea Assessment: Digital Approach.

REFERENCES

Arvidson, M., Lyon, F., McKay, S., & Moro, D. (2010). *The ambitions and challenges of SROI.* Third Sector Research Centre. Available from: http://www.tsrc.ac.uk/LinkClick.aspx?fileticket1/4QwHhaC%2br88Y%3d&tabid1/4762

Avelino, F., Wittmayer, J., Pel, B., Weaver, P., Dumitru, A., Haxeltine, A., Kemp, R., Jørgensen, M., Bauler, T., Ruijsink, S., & O'Riordan, T. (2019). Transformative social innovation and (dis)empowerment. *Technological Forecasting and Social Change, 145*, 195–206. doi:10.1016/j.techfore.2017.05.002

BEPA (Bureau of European Policy Advisors). (2010). *Empowering people, driving change. Social Innovation in the European Union.* European Commission.

Bria, F. (2014). *Digital Social Innovation. Interim Report. A deliverable of the project "Digital Social Innovation.* European Commission, DG Connect.

Bria, F. (2015). *Growing a digital social ecosystem for Europe.* DSI report, EU Commission. https://www.nesta.org.uk/sites/default/files/dsireport.pdf

Brown, H. S., de Jong, M., & Levy, D. L. (2009). Building institutions based on information disclosure: Lessons from GRI's sustainability reporting. *Journal of Cleaner Production*, *17*(6), 571–580. doi:10.1016/j.jclepro.2008.12.009

Cajaiba-Santana, G. (2014). Social innovation: Moving the field forward: A conceptual framework. *Technological Forecasting and Social Change*, *82*, 42–51. doi:10.1016/j.techfore.2013.05.008

Cangiano, S.; Romano, Z. & Loglio, L. (2017). The growth of digital social innovation in Europe. An Open Design approach to support innovation for the societal good. *The Design Journal, 20*(sup1), 3546-3559.

ColorADD. (2015). *ColorADD*. Retrieved from http://www.coloradd.net/index.asp: http://www.coloradd.net/about.asp

Drucker, P. (1985). *Innovation and Entrepreneurship*. Harper Business.

Emerson, J., Wachowicz, J., & Chun, S. (1999). *Social return on investment: exploring aspects of value creation in the nonprofit sector. In REDF Box Set* (Vol. 2). Roberts Enterprise Development Foundation.

Epstein, M. J., & Yuthas, K. (2014). *Measuring and improving social impacts: A guide for nonprofits, companies, and impact investors*. Berrett-Koehler Publishers.

Franz, H. W., Hochgerner, J., & Howaldt, J. (2012). *Challenge Social Innovation: Potentials for Business, Social Entrepreneurship, Welfare and Civil Society*. Springer. doi:10.1007/978-3-642-32879-4

Hargreaves, T., Longhurst, N., & Seyfang, G. (2013). Up, down, round and round: Connecting regimes and practices in innovation for sustainability. *Environment & Planning*, *45*(2), 402–420. doi:10.1068/a45124

Howaldt, J., & Kopp, R. (2012). Shaping social innovation by social research. In Challenge Social Innovation. Springer. doi:10.1007/978-3-642-32879-4_3

Jørgensen, U. (2012). Mapping and navigating transitions – the multi-level perspective compared with the arenas of development. *Research Policy*, *41*(6), 996–1010. doi:10.1016/j.respol.2012.03.001

Kylliäinen, J. (2019, october). *Types of Innovation – The Ultimate Guide with Definitions and Examples*. Retrieved from https://www.viima.com/blog/types-of-innovation

Majchrzak, A., Markus, M. L., & Wareham, J. (2016). Designing for digital transformation: Lessons for information systems research from the study of ICT and societal challenges. *Management Information Systems Quarterly*, *40*(2), 267–277. doi:10.25300/MISQ/2016/40:2.03

Maree, M., & Mertens, S. (2012). The limits of economic value in measuring the performance of social innovation. In A. Nicholls & A. Murdock (Eds.), *Social innovation: blurring boundaries to reconfigure markets* (pp. 114–136). Palgrave Macmillan. doi:10.1057/9780230367098_5

Márquez, P., Reficco, E., & Berger, G. (2010). *Socially inclusive business: Engaging the poor through market initiatives in Iberoamerica*. Harvard University Press.

Moulaert, F. (Ed.). (2013). *The International Handbook on Social Innovation; Collective Action, Social Learning and Transdisciplinary Research*. Edward Elgar.

Mulgan, G. (2010). Measuring social value. *Stanford Social Innovation Review*, *8*(3), 38–43.

Murray, R., Caulier-Grice, J., & Mulgar, G. (2010). *The open book of social innovation*. Young Foundation/NESTA.

Neiva, M. (2020, October). *Covid-19 numa pandemia de semáforos quem não distingue cores enfrenta desafios*. Retrieved from https://observador.pt/2020/10/26/covid-19- numa-pandemia-de-semaforos-quem-nao-distingue-cores-enfrenta-desafios/

Neiva, M. (2020). *ColorADD*. Retrieved from http://www.coloradd.net/index.asp: http://www.coloradd.net/why.asp

Nicholls, A. (2009). 'We do good things, don't we?': 'blended value accounting' in social entrepreneurship. *Accounting, Organizations and Society*, *34*(6–7), 755–769. doi:10.1016/j.aos.2009.04.008

OECD. (2019). *Digital Innovation: Seizing Policy Opportunities*. OECD Publishing. doi:10.1787/a298dc87-

OECD/Eurostat. (2018). Oslo Manual 2018: Guidelines for collecting, reporting and using data on innovation (4th ed.). OECD.

Pereira, D. S. (2018). *Instituto de Apoio e Desenvolvimento*. Retrieved from http://www.itad.pt/daltonismo/

Portales, L. (2017). De la RSE a la atención de problemas sociales por medio de modelos de negocio con propósito. In E. Raufflet, L. Portales, C. García de la Torre, J. F. Lozano Aguilar, & E. Barrera Duque (Eds.), Responsabilidad, ética y sostenibilidad empresarial (pp. 203–216). Cd. de México: Pearson.

Portales, L. (2019). *Social Innovation and Social Entrepreneurship Fundamentals, Concepts, and Tools*. Palgrave Macmillan. doi:10.1007/978-3-030-13456-3

Srivastava, S. C., & Shainesh, G. (2015). Bridging the service divide through digitally enabled service innovations: Evidence from Indian Healthcare Service Providers. *Management Information Systems Quarterly*, *39*(1), 245–268. doi:10.25300/MISQ/2015/39.1.11

The Young Foundation. (2012). Social innovation overview: A deliverable of the project. In J. Caulier-Grice, A. Davies, R. Patrick, & W. Norman (Eds.), *The theoretical, empirical and policy foundations for building social innovation in Europe*. European Commission.

Trauth, E., Joshi, K. D., & Yarger, L. K. (2018). ISJ editorial. *Information Systems Journal*, *28*(6), 989–994. doi:10.1111/isj.12201

World Economic Forum. (2021). *Understanding the impact of digitalization on society*. Retrieved from https://reports.weforum.org/digital-transformation/understanding-the-impact-of-digitalization-on-society/

ADDITIONAL READING

Carvalho, L., Jeleniewicz, M., Franczak, P., & Vanková, Z. (2021). Business Models for Digital Economy: Good Practices and Success Stories. In L. Carvalho, L. Reis, A. Prata, & R. Pereira (Eds.), *Handbook of Research on Multidisciplinary Approaches to Entrepreneurship, Innovation, and ICTs* (pp. 1–21). IGI Global. doi:10.4018/978-1-7998-4099-2.ch001

Carvalho, L., & Viana, A. (2019). Social Innovation as a Promoter of the Welfare: The Case of One Dollar Glasses in Brazil. In L. Carvalho & M. J. Madeira (Eds.), *Global Campaigning Initiatives for Socio-Economic Development* (pp. 1–10). IGI Global. doi:10.4018/978-1-5225-7937-3.ch001

de Sousa, E. G., & Júnior, V. M. V. (2013). Social Enterprises in Brazil: Socially Produced Knowledge Versus Social Innovation. *Journal of Technology Management & Innovation*, (8), 166–176.

European Commission DG REGIO. (2013). *Guide to social innovation.* Retrieved from: https://publications.europa.eu/en/publication-detail/-/publication/12d044fe-617a-4131- 93c2-5e0a951a095c

European Commission DG R&I. (2017). *Vision and Trends of Social Innovation for Europe*. Retrieved from: https://publications.europa.eu/en/publication-detail/-/publication/a97a2fbd-b7da-11e7- 837e-01aa75ed71a1/language-en

Reynolds, S., Gabriel, M., & Heales, C. (2017) *Social innovation policy in Europe: where next?* European Commission. Retrieved from: https://www.siceurope.eu/policy-portal/social-innovation-policy-europe-where-next

KEY TERMS AND DEFINITIONS

Collaborative Innovation: Process in which multiple participants jointly develop new products with customers and suppliers.

Color Blindness: The reduced capability to see colors or colors difference.

Color Palette: Color range or selection.

Digital Transformation: Integrate digital technology into all areas of the business.

Digitalization: Process of transforming analog in a digital format.

Innovation: Implementation of a new idea by introducing a new product or service.

Symbolic Language: A communication method that uses characters or images to express concepts.

Chapter 3
A Case Study on the United Arab Emirates (UAE) as a Digital Economy Exemplar

Sriya Chakravarti
https://orcid.org/0000-0002-5396-0318
Higher Colleges of Technology, Dubai, UAE

ABSTRACT

The purpose of this research is to highlight innovative excellence of the United Arab Emirates (UAE). Currently, the nation serves as a digital economy exemplar to the rest of the world due to its futuristic thinking, planning, and strategies. In this chapter, the author and her research assistants summarize various United Arab Emirates (UAE) government strategies related to the development of an economy that is based on innovation and technological solutions to address the 21st century challenges. Furthermore, it presents innovative business solutions that are in practice and are lucrative outcomes of these strategies. These ventures are an answer to our post-pandemic world because they are resilient and sustainable. Additionally, these solutions may serve as exemplars of 'thinking differently'. The research further discusses lessons on innovations that may be teachable to the rest of the world for improving the human living experience and the power of innovation, technology, and digitalization in building profitable smart economies in the post-pandemic era.

INTRODUCTION AND BACKGROUND TO THE STUDY

The global coronavirus pandemic has taken a huge toll on the world populace and catapulted it into gloom. The spread of the virus has changed not only the way we operate in our daily lives but also altered lofty government long-term goals worldwide. It has pointed out the stark inequalities between nations and the speed, priority of a government's response in a crisis. The pandemic has pushed third world countries further into poverty, while the first world nations wrestled with recession. The lockdown required people and governments to rethink a new way of being.

DOI: 10.4018/978-1-7998-9227-4.ch003

However, with strict protocols for the new normal and the rapid development of the mRNA vaccines, the year 2021 has started to beam with optimism (The Economist, 2021). Mckinsey Global Survey reports a positive momentum in the world economy. While the results on confidence vary by geography, the developed world economies anticipate recovering quickly from the mayhem of the pandemic (Mckinsey Global Survey, 2021). Unfortunately, emerging economies continue to face a barrage of health challenges, overwhelmed public health systems, lack of vaccine access or shortages, health frauds, along with higher inflation, education disruption, weak economic growth and high levels of unemployment. The Economist Newspaper (2021) states that the developing economies are the victim of and going through a period of fighting a long covid with low resources, less energy that are delaying its recovery process.

The virus disease has required us to broaden our thinking and to harness the creativity that exists to develop and adopt solutions to the many problems faced. Resilience and flexibility are fundamental elements to survive in our societies today. Innovative thinking, sustainable solutions, human welfare, creativity, new business models and markets are the need of the hour.

In this dark hour of human history, there are bright spots that shine like a light at the end of long black tunnel. Many researchers view the pandemic as a fast track revolution, as it unmasked untapped opportunities, while others are of the opinion that it is the start of a global golden age in innovation (Thompson, 2021). In Latin America, online shopping gained momentum and presented unique business growth opportunities as result of the contagious disease. In the Indian nation state, the pandemic is currently reshaping the automotive and public transportation industries.

The introduction of plant based protein in the United States of America (USA), Chinese youth leading the games of the future through esports, young entrepreneurs flourishing in South Korea against family owned conglomerates and consumers using their purchasing power to transform industries are some examples of positive and innovative outcomes from the contagion of the deadly virus (Knowledge@ Wharton, n.d.).

Innovation and technology are central and hold key roles in reconstructing, reimagining opportunities and resilient outcomes for the post COVID world society. In this book chapter, the researchers present the case of the United Arab Emirates (UAE) as a smart economy with sustainable cities that drives on the power of digitization and emerging, innovative technologies. The focus on digitalization enabled the country to minimize the economic impact of the coronavirus. The country not only addressed the pandemic with a superior strategy, planning, grit and diligence but has also prepared itself for the VUCA (Volatile, Uncertain, Complex, Ambiguous) challenges by turning itself into a smart resilient economy through its national strategies and policies before the corona crisis.

The 49-year-old country has taken an innovative approach to address the 21st century challenges. Moreover, it is in the process of successfully diversifying its economy. For its futuristic vision, efforts and approaches towards economy development, the United Arab Emirates (UAE) has won several awards in a variety of competitions worldwide. The nation has turned heads by emerging as one of the most productive and successful countries in terms of innovation.

The United Arab Emirates (UAE) government aspires to be one of the world's most innovative nations. To achieve this, the nation has launched a number of initiatives to drive and foster innovation in all fields and spread the culture of innovation in the country and consolidate its practices. The United Arab Emirates (UAE) National Innovation Strategy (2014) encouraged new thinking and groundbreaking solutions in seven priority sectors (Energy, Education, Health, Space, Technology, Transportation and Water) with the youth playing a leading role in driving innovation. Furthermore, every government entity appointed a Chief Innovation Officer, and the country provided various platforms and forums for future entrepreneurs to shape innovative solutions to global challenges. Abu Dhabi's Hub71 and Dubai's Area 2071 are centers to facilitate collaboration, boost startups in the technology field, diversify the economy away from oil and enrich the entrepreneurship ecosystem in the Arab region (UAE Embassy in USA, n.d).

In 2019, the Global Innovation Index (GII) announced that the United Arab Emirates (UAE) is the most innovative country in the Arab world. The Global Innovation Index (GII) report annually ranks countries based on their capacity to innovate. In 2020, it measured the performance of 131 countries and economies representing 99 percent of global Gross Domestic Product (GDP), with a focus on understanding 'who will finance innovation?'(Gulf Today, 2020). The United Arab Emirates (UAE) maintained its global high standing in the year 2020 of being the number one innovator in the Arab World for the fifth consecutive year and improved its ranking to 34 globally. This improvement in numbers and positive shift in world ranking for innovation indicate a significant development in the areas of research, technology, business sophistication and creative outputs of the country (Gulf Today, 2020).

Innovation occupies a colossal role in government strategies for building a competitive economy. The main objective behind the United Arab Emirates (UAE) government's encouragement for innovation lies upon enhancing the country's global competitiveness, launching corporate methodologies as well as a culture for innovation. The nation wants to diversify its economy from the oil sector, and execute a sustainable investment plan for the nation's human capital (Gulf Today, 2020).

Abdullah Bin Touq Al Marri, Minister of Economy, said that the United Arab Emirates (UAE) improving performance in the worldwide innovation index is a result of the government and leadership's long-term vision adopted by the country over the past years. Per the United Arab Emirates (UAE) Centennial 2071 plan (UAE-Centennial-2071, n.d) the country aspires to be a regional and international innovation hub. Furthermore, the "plan aims at investing in the future generations, by preparing them with the skills and knowledge needed to face rapid changes" and make the nation one of the best countries in the world by the next centennial in 2071.

In this chapter, the authors summarize various United Arab Emirates (UAE) government strategies related to the development of an economy that is based on innovation and technological solutions, to address the 21st century challenges. Furthermore, the author and the researcher assistants present innovative business solutions that are in practice and are lucrative outcomes of these strategies. These ventures are an answer to our post pandemic world because they are resilient and sustainable. Additionally, these solutions may serve as exemplars of 'thinking differently' to the rest of the world. The purpose of this research is to highlight innovative excellence of the United Arab Emirates (UAE). The research further discusses lessons on innovations that may be applicable to the rest of the world in improving the human living experience and highlighting the power of innovation, technology and digitalization in driving smart economies in the post pandemic era.

This study may interest researchers, members from the academic community, business managers, students and potential entrepreneurs who have an interest in learning about resilience, smart economy, sustainable cities and innovative business solutions.

SETTING THE STAGE AND MAIN FOCUS OF THE CHAPTER

The next section of the study gives a brief background on the United Arab Emirates (UAE). It then discusses the significance of innovation in addressing the VUCA (Volatile, Uncertain, Complex, and Ambiguous) challenges. The paper continues to discuss governmental strategies and policies to bolster innovation embedding across the nation for development. In conclusion, the research illustrates tangible outcomes (services and products) and lessons on innovation that are a byproduct of these government strategies.

Overview of United Arab Emirates (UAE)

The United Arab Emirates (UAE) is a constitutional federation of seven emirates. Abu Dhabi city is the capital of the UAE. It is bordered by Saudi Arabia and Oman. H. H. Sheikh Khalifa bin Zayed Al Nahyan is the President of the country. He is also the Ruler of Abu Dhabi. United Arab Emirates (UAE) is a stable nation with tolerant values. The 200 nationalities living, working, learning or touring the state are a testament to the nation's approach on harmonious living (Chakravarti, 2017). Residents enjoy freedom of civil rights and practice of religion (Encyclopædia Britannica, n.d.). In 2019, The World Economic Forum placed it on the 25th position globally for the display of overall competitiveness in the world.

The country follows a moderate foreign policy and believes in balanced relationships with the international community. It observes the principle of non-interference in the internal affairs of other countries and opts for a dialogue to reach peaceful resolution of disputes. It supports the mission of the United Nations and is an important regional and global partner in promotion of peace and stability, eradication of terrorism, humanitarian operations and responding to emerging crises (Fact Sheet, n.d). Furthermore, the United Nations (UN) and the United Arab Emirates (UAE) engage in interventions related to the natural sciences, biodiversity, and climate change (United Nations, n.d).

Islam is the official religion of the nation and Arabic is the formal language. However, English is widely spoken around the Emirates and literacy rate stands at 95% (Minhas, 2018). The country has a desert climate and the stable Arab Emirati Dirham (AED) is pegged to the US dollar (USD) at 3.67. Presently, the nation holds 6.7% of the world's oil reserves. Keeping the future in mind, the country has invested in several plans to diversify itself from an oil-based economy. Innovation is a key pillar in all strategies and policies of the nation.

By the end of 2030, the nation state aspires to achieve its various goals along with the meeting the Sustainable Development Goals of UN 2030 and agenda items like ending poverty, protecting the planet, economic and technological progress through collaboration (United Nations, n.d).

The next section of this paper presents the significance of innovation to address the multitude of challenges and opportunities we live with today:

Significance of Innovation to Address the VUCA (Volatile, Uncertain, Complex, Ambiguous) Challenges

Individuals, organizations and economies around the world need ways to sustain in this volatile, uncertain, complex and ambiguous (VUCA) environment due to changes in customer demands, technology, disruptions, and increasing market competition (Sushil,2017). If they do not adapt to the changing needs it will translate into missed opportunities for growth due to a limited mindset and lack of innovativeness. Therefore, it is imperative to nurture an entrepreneurial and innovative mindset to sustain in this competitive era (Bag et.al, 2018).

Innovation is important today more than ever because it helps us evolve and foster a culture of effective problem solving and ingenuity. It keeps us relevant and different. The key to innovation is creative thought expression.

Creativity is associated with generating new ideas, whereas innovation refers to their successful application. Therefore, innovation starts with creativity. Innovation is the creation of better or more effective products, processes, services, technologies, or ideas that are accepted by markets, governments, and society. However, as they are both separate constructs, creativity and innovation require different conditions in order to flourish (Pandya, 2014).

Innovation is the catalyst to growth and in an organizational context it may be linked to positive changes in efficiency, productivity, quality and competitiveness. Innovation is what gives life to a business in a market economy. Innovation drives growth and opportunity in new markets and breathes life into a mature industry (Pandya, 2014).

Damanpour (1996) calls innovation as a "means of changing an organization, either as a response to changes in the external environment or as a preemptive action to influence the environment." He further states that innovation can be "new products or services, new process technologies, new organizational structures or administrative systems, and new plans or programs pertaining to organizational members."

A sweep of the literature review indicates that there is no single characterization of innovation. However, the definition provided by (Baregheh, Rowley, and Sambrook, 2009) captures the aim and several aspects of innovation. According to (Baregheh, Rowley, and Sambrook, 2009), Innovation is the multi-stage process whereby organizations transform ideas into new/improved products, services or processes, in order to advance, compete and differentiate themselves successfully in their marketplace

However, innovation scholars categorize innovation as a minor or major improvement or change in processes (Bodlaj, M., & Čater, B. (2019). It is frequently point out that the external environment provides the primary stimulus for innovation (Damanpour and Schneider, 2006). Baregheh, Rowley, and Sambrook (2009) state that innovation's central role is in creating value and sustaining the firm's competitive advantage.

Competitive and innovative cultures are goal oriented and produce results. This mindset enables individuals, organizations and governments be the first to enter the market with innovative products and earn premium. In such environments, the focus is on the customer and any necessary changes are made in the process to satisfy the customers (Bag et.al, 2018).

The next segment covers the determinations of the federal and local governments of the United Arab Emirates (UAE) to turn the nation into a smart country through various approaches, policies and strategies.

Strategies in the United Arab Emirates (UAE) for Innovation and Digital UAE

UAE mGovernment Initiative

H. H. Sheikh Mohammed bin Rashid Al Maktoum, Vice-President and Prime Minister of the United Arab Emirates (UAE) and Ruler of Dubai, inaugurated the Mobile Government initiative on May 22, 2013, to make government services available to people wherever they are, 24 hours a day, seven days a week. Sheikh Mohammed's goal was to move customer service centers into every consumer device, believing that a successful government is one that goes to its customers wherever they are rather than waiting for them to come to it. The UAE mGovernment initiative is in line with Vision 2021 that foresees high quality of life built on world-class public infrastructure, government services and a rich recreational environment. (UAE mGovernment Initiative, n.d).

This strategy has improved the quality of life for the citizens and residents of the United Arab Emirates (UAE). Each initiative aims to empower the government organizations to deliver services via mobile phones and smart devices by utilizing intelligent service delivery approaches such as predictive analytics-based mobile applications. Some of the important projects and initiatives are as follows:

- UAE Government Apps have a comprehensive listing of the UAE government's applications, which number over 100 now, and is accessible on both the Apple Store and Google Play. Based on the user's location, the App Store offers distinct features and services. The UAE is the world's first government to offer services via the App Store.
- SmartPass is a system that allows users to log in to all government services with a single login and password for efficient management and quick access to federal and local government transaction within a secure electronic environment.
- One App is currently a work-in-progress application. Users can access over 4000 federal and local government services using the app. The app would be user-friendly and provide services and notifications based on the needs of the user. It will be available on a variety of platforms after its first release.

The Fourth Industrial Revolution Strategy

During the United Arab Emirates (UAE) Government's Annual Meetings in September 2017, the Government unveiled the strategy for the Fourth Industrial Revolution. The Fourth Industrial Revolution intends to strengthen the nation's position as a global center for the Fourth Industrial Revolution and boost its contribution to the national economy. The strategy also lays out a roadmap for achieving the future experience of government services by providing intelligent and interactive government services around the clock to ensure customer satisfaction and to position the United Arab Emirates (UAE) as an exemplar for interactive cities that use artificial intelligence to achieve sustainability. (The UAE Strategy for the Fourth Industrial Revolution, n.d). The Fourth Industrial Revolution Strategy focuses on a variety of crucial areas, like innovative education, artificial intelligence, intelligent genomic medicine, and robotic healthcare. The aims is to attain future security of water and food supply by using bioengineering sciences and sophisticated renewable energy technologies. Improve economic security by implementing digital economy and block chain technologies in financial transactions and services. Enhance the use of satellite data in city planning in the future and develop advanced defense industries by fostering national robotics and autonomous vehicle technology sectors.

National Strategy for Advanced Innovation

In February 2018, the government of the United Arab Emirates (UAE) approved the National Strategy for Advanced Innovation. The strategy is an updated version of the National Innovation Strategy launched in 2014. It encourages experimentation, and taking well thought out risks for the development of the nation and achieving the goals of UAE Centennial 2071. The new strategy aims to establish a national platform innovation and learning. It hopes to ignite the spirit of initiative taking within the community. The new strategy focusses on areas of exploration, quality of health, green power, technologies to serve humankind, innovative transport methods and futuristic skills. It expects that concentrating on the above areas and collaborating with international experts can help in achieving scientific breakthroughs that are for the welfare of all people (National Strategy for Advanced Innovation, n.d).

The UAE Digital Government Strategy 2025

The key objective of the digital strategy 2025 is to embed digital aspects into overall government strategies for efficient practices. Providing an excellent digital infrastructure, unified digital platform, customer need based seamless digital services, upgrading digital capabilities and skills are the key priorities of this strategy (The UAE Digital Government Strategy, n.d).

The National Digital Government Strategy is aligned to Vision 2021, to make United Arab Emirates (UAE) a competitive economy and one of the best countries to live in. Furthermore, it supports strategies of national importance, for example:

- Unified Digital Platform Policy for raising efficiency in providing digital services
- National Cybersecurity strategy for a strong cyber infrastructure and regulatory framework to protect the cybersecurity ecosystem
- UAE Centennial 2071 plan that is a roadmap for future government work. Strategy for Artificial Intelligence to achieve the objectives of UAE Centennial 2071 and boost government performance at all levels
- Emirates Blockchain Strategy 2021 to benefit from on the blockchain technology save time, effort and resources and facilitate people to process their transactions.
- Fourth Industrial Revolution (4IR) Strategy to transform the nation into a leading hub of innovation and excellence

The above strategies clearly indicate the serious intentions of the government to improve the quality of life by harnessing the power of available technologies. At the federal level, Telecommunications and Digital Government Regulatory Authority (TDRA) is the overarching figure accountable for providing infrastructure and developing strategies, which drive the process of digital transformation in the country based on the National Digital Government Strategy of the United Arab Emirates (UAE).

Each local government authority is further responsible for aligning to the vision and the on boarding of its resident entities. For example, according to Digital UAE - The Official Portal of the UAE Government, Dubai Digital Authority (DDA) is responsible for all matters related to digital transformation and information security. It is also responsible for developing, approving and managing policies and strategies for advancing the development of next level digitization. The aim is to enhance Dubai's smart and digital transformation, providing high-level digital services to customers while maintaining highest standards of cyber security. The DDA has its own judicial identity and legal authority. Dubai Data Establishment Center, Dubai Electronic Security Center, Dubai Statistics, Smart Dubai Department, Smart Dubai Government operate under the purview of the DDA. The DDA assigned to drive digital transformation of the government across government services, shared government solutions, data management, cybersecurity, and ecosystem and governance (Digital UAE, n.d).

The subsequent piece of this paper will discuss the innovative outcomes that have resulted as a by-product of the government strategies and policies.

Innovative Outcomes of the United Arab Emirates (UAE) Government Strategies

Due to its various governmental policies the United Arab Emirates (UAE) in 2020 was ranked first in the global competitive indices of Mobile broadband Internet subscriptions, Mobile broadband subscriptions, Mobile network coverage per population, Wireless broadband, Number of accredited health facilities, Healthcare coverage, Terms of trade, Employment rate, Absence of bureaucracy and Entrepreneurship (Digital UAE, UAE Gov, n.d). It. This data indicates that the strategies set in place by the wise leaders of the country have had a positive effect on the nation. The following section presents the major digital achievements of the nation:

Digital Economy, Sustainable Environment and Integrated Infrastructure (Digital UAE, UAE Gov, n.d)

According to the Digital Transformation Report of 2020, United Arab Emirates (UAE) achieved an increase of 300 per cent in eCommerce over 2019 (UAE government, n.d). It also launched the following initiatives to boost the economy:

- 3D printed government offices
- Basher - a digital platform to establish businesses within 15 minutes
- Emirates Blockchain Strategy 2021 to transform 50 per cent of federal government transactions into the blockchain platform by 2021 to cut cost and save the environment.
- Inaugurating the largest vertical farm in the country at the Al Maktoum International Airport to meet the internal needs of the populace, food sustainability sources and security. Appointing the Ministry of Climate Change and Environment to manage waste scientifically based on data analysis of the National Waste Database.
- Going solar with Noor Abu Dhabi, the world's largest single-site project that produces 1.2 GW of power to cover the demand for 90,000 people. The project reduces reliance on natural gas and enables increased production of renewable energy resulting in a carbon footprint reduction of 1 million metric tons per year, which is equivalent to taking 200,000 cars off the road.

Digital Health (Digital UAE, UAE Gov, n.d)

The Digital Health platform of the government provides services like the Virtual Doctor for COVID-19, International telemedicine service, Doctor for every citizen and The DOH RemoteCare app. The international telemedicine operates under the guidance of the Ministry of Health and Prevention (MoHaP). It assists patients and doctors get remote second opinion consultations from experts abroad. The service is available in 16 public hospitals and it covers all medical specialties. The smart robotic pharmacy in the emirate of Fujairah has robots dispense drugs within 8-12 seconds and works around the clock with hospitals.

The Doctor for Every Citizen is an initiative overseen by Dubai Health Authority (DHA). The consultation is free of charge and round the clock service through voice and video calls is available with DHA certified physicians. These physicians can issue electronic prescriptions and request e-copies of laboratory and radiology tests.

The DOH RemoteCare app is managed by Department of Health (DOH) Abu Dhabi. It enables people to receive healthcare at their own homes, without visiting a hospital or clinic physically. The app has several features like booking face-to-face appointments, tele-consultations and symptom diagnosis.

Digital Education (Digital UAE, UAE Gov, n.d)

The United Arab Emirates (UAE) has implemented distance learning on all educational entities as a precaution to protect students from COVID-19. It offered free satellite broadband services for students in areas lacking connectivity and free home internet connection for families who have no home internet connection. It conducted professional trainings for educators to implement the digital learning processes. Furthermore, it launched smart learning platforms and guidelines to manage teacher and student conduct during distance learning. eLearning, m-learning are part of curriculum from K through 12 and Higher Education Institutes (HEI). Expanding the creation of Higher e-Education Institutions such as the Hamdan Bin Mohammed Smart University has been given a significant boost to eLearning in the region for accredited bachelor and master's courses. Furthermore, Mohammed Bin Zayed University of Artificial Intelligence is the first university for postgraduate studies in Artificial Intelligence research worldwide.

Other digital education initiatives include Madrasa, a free eLearning platform that provides 5,000 free videos in Arabic language on topics of STEM topics. The platform is accessible online to over 50 million Arab students around the world. The Digital School an initiative of Mohammed bin Rashid Al Maktoum Global Initiatives (MBRGI) provides a certified online education to students who live in refugee camps or hail from deprived communities. These children do not have easy access to formal education particularly in the Arab region.

KidX is another innovative concept and a digital platform for children and adolescents. Through games and virtual reality technologies, children's awareness of the government is increased and they are encouraged to express their views on the services.

*Digital Justice, Cybersecurity and Robotic Service Providers*_(Digital UAE, UAE Gov, n.d)

With the goal of improving efficiency, accessibility of courts, speeding up proceedings and reduce delays in justice, the Ministry of Justice of the United Arab Emirates (UAE) has digitally transformed 95 per cent of its services. Some of these services include search of status of a case, eSessions, searching lawyers, remote hearings, eNotary public, eFiling, eMarriage.

In the field of cybersecurity, the aim is to create a safe and strong cyber infrastructure for the country. Advanced Mobile Location is service to help in identifying the caller's location. My Safe Society is an application that enables people to report a crime or suspicious activity to the Public Prosecutor. E-Police in your Mobile assists in completing transactions with police stations seamlessly. Hassantuk (fire protection system) is a smart system for protection from fire protection targeting 500,000 buildings and residences.

Dubai Police employed the world's first operational RoboCop who officially joined the line of duty in 2017. The RoboCop communicates in six languages, can interact with the public and respond to queries. It can detect emotions, hand signals and offer a military salute. Furthermore, the Road Transport Authority (RTA) uses robots to clean Dubai Metro stations. The robotic cleaners reduce consumption of water required for traditional cleaning and provide enhanced sterilization. Rashid chatbot uses artificial intelligence to offer reliable answers to customers' questions regarding the necessary procedures, documents, and requirements to conduct various transactions. Finally, robot Hamad provides exceptional service to the customers. His main job is happiness of the customers and is installed in all government centers across the country. The robot Hamad provides services, like receiving ID renewal applications, identifying ID card status, and updating personal information of customers.

Smart Cities (Digital UAE, UAE Gov, n.d)

Smart cities are sustainable, efficient, competitive and innovative. The government's goal is to preserve the environment and the same time achieve a perfect balance between economic and social development. Currently, Abu Dhabi and Dubai are planning and developing several smart sustainable cities.

These cities use information and communication technologies (ICTs) and other means to improve quality of life, while ensuring that it meets the needs of present and future generations with respect to economic, social and environmental aspects.

Masdar City is one such example of a smart utopian city in the emirate of Abu Dhabi with a heart for sustainable initiatives, being environment friendly and reducing wastage of energy and water. It is not just a city to live in, but also a city for research and development to enhance sustainable urban living. It has one of the best-ranked institutes in the world for science and technology. The city uses clean energy that is created onsite from the rooftop solar systems, which is considered one of the largest photovoltaic installations in the Middle East and North Africa (MENA) region. The city is home to a rapidly growing clean-tech cluster, business free zone and residential neighborhood with restaurants, shops, and public green spaces.

There is no place for traditional transportation system at the city. People living and working in Masdar City use unmanned electric cars, known as Personal Rapid Transport (PRT) pods. Most restaurants offer organic food and the city takes all aspects of sustainability into serious consideration. The goal of the city is to become the world's most sustainable and ecofriendly city.

The Silicon Park (SP) project in Dubai has transformed the emirate into a smart city. As of January 2016, it had succeeded in reducing cumulative energy consumption by 31 per cent exceeding the target set by Dubai Integrated Energy Strategy 2030 of 30 per cent. The Sustainable City is another such smart city intiative implemented in DubaiLand. The township has 10,000 trees, organic farms, car free and runs on solar energy produced indigenously. All properties are equipped with energy saving appliances. Dubai South District is the venue of Expo 2021. The electricity used by Expo will come from renewable sources that are generated on the site itself. Furthermore, the material used in construction will be used in building infrastructure.

CAFU

CAFU is a Dubai based company that supplies on demand fuel service, anywhere, anytime without delivery charges. The price of gasoline and diesel is the comparable to the petrol station. CAFU trucks operate 24 hours a day and it is extremely convenient, a contactless experience and saves a lot of user time. The delivery process is seamless using the CAFU app. An individual can use the application from the comfort of their home and they do not have to be present physically on site. They can simply pinpoint the location of the vehicle on the app, keep the fuel tank open for the refill and make payment.

CAFU has quickly grown as an organization and currently provides employment to 600 people that are able to deliver the CAFU experience. After the huge success of CAFU's services for delivering fuel, the company has decided to expand and widen their services to the extent of changing car batteries, car oil, car tires, and much more (CAFU, 2021).

DGrade

DGrade is Dubai based company that recycles plastic bottles into sustainable clothing using Greenspun technology. Through this technology, the bottles are processed, melted into fiber and then spun into yarn for clothing. The company is cognizant of its operational impact on the environment. It claims that not only the plastic diverted from landfills but also the process is energy efficient (DGrade, 2021).

Hyperloop

Virgin Hyperloop One is a futuristic transit system in the UAE and is in the process of connecting Gulf countries. Hyperloop is a transport system that works with the help of electric propulsion and electromagnetic levitation. It saves the environment from pollution and deforestation, and provides employment to people who work on the project. The nation invested millions of dollars in the research and development of the Hyperloop. This project aims at providing the fastest and safest technologies of transportation between the Emirates of UAE and Saudi Arabia. The new travel time from Dubai to Abu Dhabi will be 11 minutes. Moreover, Hyperloop system can propel passenger or cargo pods at speeds of over 1000 km/h. This means that it is 3 times faster than high-speed rail (Abbas, 2019). On November 8, 2020, the first passengers traveled safely on the transportation marvel and making history.

Tendered

Tendered is startup born in the Silicon Valley, USA but operates in UAE and KSA. Their goal is to combine the efficiencies of a marketplace with the latest technologies to assist contractors operate economically and effectively by accessing the equipment analytics system, and other sophisticated applications that enable them to increase equipment productivity, regulate emissions and run tools sustainably (TENDERED, 2021).

The next section of this chapter discusses key innovation lessons from the United Arab Emirates (UAE):

RECOMMENDATIONS AND SOLUTIONS ON INNOVATION

Innovate While Preserving the Social Fabric of the Society

The United Arab Emirates (UAE) believes in the mantra - survival of the fittest. They remain number one in the Arab region for their progressive policies and adapting to the rapidly changing global environment. They have embraced modernization in line with global trends to be competitive and successful in the world. The country has been able to transform while being sensitive to the need of preserving the traditions, values and fabric of its culture.

Innovate for Multiple Returns and Improved Quality of Life

The United Arab Emirates (UAE) has streamlined the process of doing business in the country. Favorable policies indoctrinated in service of Foreign Direct Investments. Investing in infrastructure, embracing latest technology to improve quality of life and giving local and global companies freedom of ownership and operations are reaping multiple revenue streams for the government, providing employment and giving customers a wide variety of product choice. This process has not only brought income and influence to the nation, but also it has turned it into a cultural junction of international trade. This validates the work of Baregheh, Rowley, and Sambrook (2009), as innovation is playing its central role of creating value and building competitive advantage for the nation.

The Department of Health (DOH) RemoteCare app in Abu Dhabi is an illustration of improving the lives of people in Emirates. It enables the public to receive healthcare at their own homes, without visiting a hospital or clinic physically. The app has several features like booking face-to-face appointments, tele-consultations and symptom diagnosis. In Dubai, Doctor for Every Citizen by Dubai Health Authority (DHA) is a round the clock service with free consultation from DHA certified physicians. These physicians can issue electronic prescriptions and request e-copies of laboratory and radiology tests. The above advances in medicine have radically improved the living experience of citizens and residents of the country.

Innovate to Address Pain Points, Increased Access and Improved Services

For food security, the largest vertical farm in the country has been developed and maintained at the Al Maktoum International Airport. This is an example of the country inventing to secure sustainable food supplies and procedures to cater to the population of the desert land.

To improve and modernize the justice system and speed up proceedings, the Ministry of Justice of the United Arab Emirates (UAE) has digitally transformed 95 per cent of its services. Some of these services include search of status of a case, eSessions, searching lawyers, remote hearings, eNotary public, eFiling, eMarriage. This is another example of improved access of services in the country.

DGrade a Dubai based company tackles the pain point of plastic bottles ending up in landfills. It recycles plastic bottles into sustainable clothing using Greenspun technology. Through this technology, the bottles are processed, melted into fiber and then spun into yarn for clothing. The company is cognizant of its operational impact on the environment. It claims that it uses an energy efficient process to convert and divert plastic from landfills.

The above cases demonstrate the importance of innovation in addressing the pain points of the United Arab Emirates (UAE) society.

Innovate for Philanthropy

The United Arab Emirates (UAE) generous nature is no secret. Their digital education initiative Madrasa provides 5,000 free videos in Arabic language on topics of STEM topics. The platform is accessible online to over 50 million Arab students around the world for building and improving their skillset. Furthermore, The Digital School by Mohammed bin Rashid Al Maktoum Global Initiatives (MBRGI) provides a certified online education to students who live in refugee camps or hail from deprived communities. These children do not have easy access to formal education particularly in the Arab region.

This is an example of how a creative philanthropic idea of educating the masses turns global through innovation. It builds on the research work of Pandya (2014) who states that innovation fosters a culture of problem solving and ingenuity, as observed above on the educational initiatives like Madrasa and The Digital School initiatives.

Innovate to Capitalize on an Opportunity

Pioneering companies like CAFU and TENDERED are both examples of capitalizing on new ideas and opportunities available due to advancement of technologies and changing world dynamics. Not only do these services provide ease of use but also are efficient and effective in improving the process. They also provide new business models and bring a fresh perspective on thinking differently. Furthermore, it corroborates the research of (Bag et.al, 2018) (Chakravarti, 2021), who state that companies and countries that have innovative cultures are goal oriented, and when they enter new markets or products, they earn a premium and in the process satisfy the customers and gain their loyalty.

Innovate for Sustainability and Futuristic Living

Smart cities like Masdar City and Silicon Park are examples of a futuristic living experience. Projects like Noor Abu Dhabi enable increased production of renewable energy resulting in a carbon footprint reduction of 1 million metric tons per year. These cases of sustainable innovations and futuristic living experiences highlight the nation's mindset of imagining a new reality and of protecting the planet and keeping it furbished for the next generation.

CONCLUSION

From the pandemic, the world has understood that decisive leadership is the need of the hour. It has realized that investment in the health care system, digital infrastructure; human resources and advanced technologies are key priorities for better quality of life and improved social experience of human beings.

In this chapter, the authors presented a backdrop of the United Arab Emirates (UAE) and briefly reviewed various government strategies related to the development of the country, the impact on the economy and quality of human living experience. The cornerstones for these strategies and policies were awareness and practice of innovation, embracing, and embedding of technological solutions, across the public and private sector and taking calculated risks for development of the nation. Additionally, the book chapter presented lessons on innovation from the United Arab Emirates (UAE) case study that may be relatable and teachable to the rest of the world.

Finally, the research displayed lucrative outcomes (innovative business solutions, services and practices) of the government strategies. These revolutionary outcomes, ventures are currently in practice and may serve as an answer to our post pandemic world because of their creative, resilience and sustainable approaches. Additionally, these solutions may aid as exemplars of 'thinking differently' to the rest of the world for improving the quality of human life experience. Moreover, it may drive nations to embrace the idea of smart economies through innovation, technology implementation and digitalization in the post pandemic era.

To conclude, we have to remember, one cannot solve problems with the same level of thinking, we have to dare and dream the impossible. In the words of Nelson Mandela, "It always seems impossible until it is done." Therefore, innovation will be the pillar that supports the imagination process while the enduring human spirit releases itself from the clutches of the pandemic.

REFERENCES

Abbas, W. (2019). *Vision to connect entire Gulf with Hyperloop, Abu Dhabi to Riyadh in 48 minutes.* Retrieved June 15, 2021, from https://www.khaleejtimes.com/news/transport/uae-hyperloop-to-reduce-travel-time-to-just-6-minutes--

Bag, S., Gupta, S., & Telukdarie, A. (2018). Importance of Innovation and Flexibility in Configuring Supply Network Sustainability. *Benchmarking*, *25*(9), 3951–3985. doi:10.1108/BIJ-06-2017-0132

Baregheh, A., Rowley, J., & Sambrook, S. (2009). Towards a Multidisciplinary Definition of Innovation. *Management Decision*, *47*(8), 1323–1339. doi:10.1108/00251740910984578

Bodlaj, M., & Čater, B. (2019). The Impact of Environmental Turbulence on the Perceived Importance of Innovation and Innovativeness in SMEs. *Journal of Small Business Management*, *57*(sup2), 417–435. doi:10.1111/jsbm.12482

CAFU. (n.d.). https://www.cafu.com

Chakravarti, S. (2017). Entrepreneurship in the Emirates. *International Journal of Management IT and Engineering*, *7*, 126–138.

Chakravarti, S. (2021). Ascertaining the Interest of Women to Drive Innovation Through Entrepreneurship Post-Pandemic: A Research Study in the United Arab Emirates (UAE). In Handbook of Research on Entrepreneurship, Innovation, Sustainability, and ICTs in the Post-COVID-19 Era (pp. 341–363). IGI Global.

Damanpour, F. (1996). Organizational Complexity and Innovation: Developing and Testing Multiple Contingency Models. *Management Science*, *42*(5), 693–716. doi:10.1287/mnsc.42.5.693

Damanpour, F., & Schneider, M. (2006). Phases of the Adoption of Innovation in Organizations: Effects of Environment, Organization and Top Managers. *British Journal of Management*, *17*(3), 215–236. doi:10.1111/j.1467-8551.2006.00498.x

Digital U. A. E. - The Official Portal of the UAE Government. (n.d.). https://u.ae/en/about-the-uae/digital-uae

DGrade. (n.d.). https://www.dgrade.com

Encyclopædia Britannica Inc. (n.d.). *Land of the United Arab Emirates*. Encyclopædia Britannica. https://www.britannica.com/place/United-Arab-Emirates/Land

Fact sheet - The Official Portal of the UAE Government. (n.d.). https://u.ae/en/about-the-uae/fact-sheet

Innovation - The Official Portal of the UAE Government. (n.d.). https://u.ae/en/about-the-uae/the-uae-government/government-of-future/innovation-in-the-uae

Innovation and Change During a Global Pandemic. (n.d.). *Knowledge*@Wharton. https://knowledge.wharton.upenn.edu/special-report/innovation-change-global-pandemic/

McKinsey & Company. (2021, June 29). *Economic conditions outlook, June 2021*. McKinsey & Company. https://www.mckinsey.com/business-functions/strategy-and-corporate-finance/our-insights/economic-conditions-outlook-june-2021

Minhas, W. A. (2018). *Advancing entrepreneurship in the united arab emirates: Start-up challenges and opportunities (1st* (2018 ed.). Palgrave Macmillan. doi:10.1007/978-3-319-76436-8

National Strategy for Advanced Innovation - The Official Portal of the UAE Government. (n.d.). https://u.ae/en/about-the-uae/strategies-initiatives-and-awards/federal-governments-strategies-and-plans/national-strategy-for-advanced-innovation

Pandya, J. (2014). Importance of emotional intelligence, creativity and innovation in vuca environment. *Sansmaran Research Journal, 4*(1), 14-17. http://ezproxy.hct.ac.ae/login?url=https://www-proquest-com.ezproxy.hct.ac.ae/scholarly-journals/importance-emotional-intelligence-creativityand/docview/1960232569/se-2?accountid=1215

Serkal, M. M. A. (2021, June 7). *Revealed: The top 25 tech innovations used in UAE government departments in 2021*. Government – Gulf News. https://gulfnews.com/uae/government/revealed-the-top-25-tech-innovations-used-in-uae-government-departments-in-2021-1.1616051339585

Sushil. (2017). Does flexibility mitigate or enhance risk? *Global Journal of Flexible Systems Management, 18*(3), 169-171.

Sustainability. (n.d.). Retrieved June 15, 2021, from https://masdar.ae/en/forasustainablefuture?utm_source=googleutm_medium

The UAE's Fourth Industrial Revolution (4IR) Strategy - The Official Portal of the UAE Government. (n.d.). https://u.ae/en/about-the-uae/strategies-initiatives-and-awards/federal-governments-strategies-and-plans/the-uae-strategy-for-the-fourth-industrial-revolution

The UAE Digital Government Strategy 2025 - The Official Portal of the UAE Government. (n.d.). https://u.ae/en/about-the-uae/digital-uae/uae-national-digital-government-strategy

Thompson, D. (2021, June 28). World War II's Lesson for After the Pandemic. *The Atlantic*. https://www.theatlantic.com/ideas/archive/2021/06/covid-19-pandemic-golden-age-innovation/619300/

UAE 1st among Arab countries in Global Innovation Index 2020. (n.d.). *Gulf Today*. https://www.gulftoday.ae/business/2020/09/03/uae-1st-among-arab-countries--in-global-innovation-index-2020

Centennial U. A. E. 2071 - The Official Portal of the UAE Government. (n.d.). https://u.ae/en/about-the-uae/strategies-initiatives-and-awards/federal-governments-strategies-and-plans/uae-centennial-2071

UAE. A Global Hub for Innovation. (2021, February 11). *UAE & USA: United for a Better Future*. https://www.uaeusaunited.com/story/uae-global-hub-innovation/

UAE mGovernment Initiative - The Official Portal of the UAE Government. (n.d.). https://u.ae/en/about-the-uae/digital-uae/uae-mgovernment-initiative

United Nations. (n.d.). *Transforming our world: the 2030 Agenda for Sustainable Development | Department of Economic and Social Affairs*. United Nations. https://sdgs.un.org/2030agenda

United Nations. (n.d.). *UNSDG | UN in Action - United Arab Emirates*. United Nations. https://unsdg.un.org/un-in-action/united-arab-emirates

Tenderd. (n.d.). https://www.tenderd.com/ae/about

The Economist Newspaper. (n.d.). *Our coverage of the coronavirus*. The Economist. https://www.economist.com/coronavirus-pandemic

The Economist Newspaper. (n.d.). *India's economy is suffering from long covid*. The Economist. https://www.economist.com/asia/2021/07/18/indias-economy-is-suffering-from-long-covid

Hyperloop, V. (n.d.). Retrieved June 15, 2021, from https://virginhyperloop.com/

KEY TERMS AND DEFINITIONS

3D Printing: 3Dprinting is a method of creating a three-dimensional object using a computer created design. 3D printing creates less material wastage.

Artificial Intelligence (AI): Artificial intelligence (AI) is the programmed simulation of human intelligence in machines. It mimics human action and applicable to any machine that exhibits traits linked to a human mind like problem solving.

Blockchain: Blockchain is a type of database that stores its information using blocks and then chains it together. Diverse types of data are stored through a blockchain but currently it used only for ledger transactions.

Carbon Footprint: A carbon footprint is the total amount of greenhouse gas emissions caused by our individual actions, events, services, products, and organizations.

Cybersecurity: Cybersecurity is the practice of protecting computer systems and programs from digital attacks.

Fourth Industrial Revolution: The Fourth Industrial Revolution represents imagination of a new way to live. It is a chapter in human development, enabled by extraordinary technology advances. The revolution is not merely about technology driven change but an opportunity to serve everyone in all nations. The movement is inclusive, human centric and hopes to make a positive influence on the world.

Gross Domestic Product (GDP): Gross domestic product (GDP) is the economic health card of any given nation. It measures the total monetary or market value of all the finished goods and services produced within a country's borders in a specific time period.

mRNA Vaccines: mRNA vaccines do not use a live virus but teaches the body to make a protein that will trigger an immune response. It creates antibodies that help fight the infection if a virus enters your body in the future.

Smart Cities: A smart city is a composed of Information and Communication Technologies (ICT), to create and implement sustainable development practices to address growing urbanization challenges.

VUCA World: It describes a world that is volatile, uncertain, complex, and ambiguous.

Section 2

New Trends on Management and Digital Marketing

Chapter 4
Fast Digitalization in the Pandemic Era and the Urgency to Discover New Business Model Opportunities for Italian Small Grocery Retailers

Maria Giovanna Tongiani
https://orcid.org/0000-0002-5988-3747
University of Pisa, Italy

Eva Ferrari
University of Pisa, Italy

Adriana Alaimo
University of Pisa, Italy

ABSTRACT

The traditional food distribution channel has enjoyed a primary position in Italy, largely because the proximity service offered to the customer plays a fundamental role in the choice of store, understood in terms of the distance and effort that the consumer is willing to endure for obtaining supplies from a given point of sale. The characteristics of the Italian small retailers, strongly appreciated by customers, are however facing the evolutions and changes of the habits and demands of the reference buyers, encouraged and favoured by the pandemic events. In the light of these considerations, the aim of this work is to obtain information for underlining and arguing the changes that Italian small grocery retailers will have to implement in order to consolidate and develop their position in the market.

DOI: 10.4018/978-1-7998-9227-4.ch004

INTRODUCTION

According to research data, digital sales channels have replaced and complemented physical sales mainly because of the obligatory closures enforced by the SARS-CoV-2 health emergency measures.

Initially, the onslaught of consumers concerned about possible product shortages sustained and sometimes increased the traditional small-scale retail trade, however, subsequently the market evolved in favour of virtual businesses. The latter have provided new users with the required safety, hygiene, and variety of choice.

The characteristics of the Italian small retailers, strongly appreciated by customers, are however facing the evolutions and changes of the habits and demands of the reference buyers, encouraged and favoured by the pandemic events. In the light of these considerations the aim of this work is to obtain information for underlining and arguing the changes that Italian small grocery retailers will have to implement in order to consolidate and develop their position in the market.

The information acquired through interviews with Italian food retail shoppers seeks to highlight the elements of the commercial service considered most significant by the target customers. The results of the survey allow for identifying opportunities for smaller Italian retailers to introduce changes in business models to adapt their offer in terms of useful and differentiated products and services, in line with the demands and needs of the target shopper.

BACKGROUND WITH LITERATURE REVIEW OF OMNICHANNEL GROCERY RETAILER: THE ROLE OF LOGISTICAL PROXIMITY AND URBAN DISTRIBUTION STRUCTURES

In this section we examine contributions made by literature to the three different areas of interest:

1. the first area examines contributions made by literature to omnichannel retailing in the grocery sector;
2. the second area concerns logistical proximity and urban consumers;
3. the third area addresses business models in the digital era and the role of the urban distribution structures.

Omnichannel Retailing in the Grocery Sector

The development of technology and its preponderant presence in society and the adoption of an internet connection in almost all Italian homes have led many people to turn to e-commerce to satisfy their purchasing needs, an activity that offers consumers numerous advantages in terms of greater convenience, therefore with time, and often also money savings (Seitz, C., Pokrivčák, J., Tóth, M., & Plevný, M.2017)

The Internet as a means of shopping makes it possible to overcome the limitations of physical stores, such as spatial gaps, when stores are physically distant from the consumer and the latter can therefore avoid travelling long distances; there may also be time gaps when the customer wishes to buy outside opening hours, needs which are once again met by online shopping; finally, there may be qualitative gaps, when the consumer in the physical store is only able to choose from a limited number of brands and product categories. These limitations are entirely overcome in the comfort of one's own home, so these advantages make the consumer a multi-channel buyer, i.e., a buyer who turns to both the offline and online markets to take advantage of the benefits that both channels offer. E-commerce offers a new way of approaching shopping, and whereas before the only way to buy was to go to a store and have physical contact with the products and the sales staff, today it is possible with a smartphone to search for the product with the desired characteristics, often at a convenient price, and that can be delivered to one's own home as soon as possible with just a click. (Klepek, M., & Bauerová, R. 2020)

This is a new way of virtually linking supply and demand throughout the sales process. It should also be emphasised that often the virtual link is not used to purchase a product, but it turns out to be useful in gaining information about the products, the components, where they come from or how they are used, becoming in fact a valid substitute for the assistance offered in offline stores, but also for sharing one's own opinions with other users. (Tongiani, M. G., Carfora, J. & Reut, A.2019)

The introduction of online channels leads retailers towards multi-channelling which refers to the management of multiple sales channels and contact points that co-exist but are not coherently linked. When we talk about multi-channels, the operation of proximity and Last Mile activities are reduced and exclusive for each of the sales channels used by the same retailer, the supply therefore differs according to the attributes and availability of each type. (Cai, Y. J., & Lo, C. K., 2020)

Consequently, in this case buyers of the different channels receive an offer with different levels of service that can lead to conflict and customer dissatisfaction; consequently, the strategy that should be of reference for the future of companies is the omnichannel strategy, i.e., one in which the relationship between retailer and buyer takes place through different channels, both physical and non-physical, which are in total integration and without any differentiation of treatment or offer among them. Omnichannel marketing has become an increasingly important concept over the last few years, even more prominent in recent times. (Verhoef, P. C. 2021)

In fact, the term omnichannel strategy means the ability to both follow customer behaviour and manage communication in real time in different contact points which allows buyers to use them in an interchangeable manner. (Verhoef, P. C. (2021)

Omnichannel retailing on the retailer's side involves providing a shopping experience that appropriately guides the nodes of the distribution network to efficiently meet the demands of customers across different sales channels. (Lim, S. F. W., & Srai, J. S. 2018) Moreover, retailers must be able to create trade-offs between the product inventories they offer, while ensuring the speed of delivery and the convenience of their service. The Last Mile logistics activity is at the heart of omnichannel strategies as it allows for coordinating and organising activities close to the consumer for the purpose of defining processes and technologies that are valid across all channels, thus providing continuous, consistent, and reliable services for consumers. (Saghiri, S., Wilding, R., Mena, C., & Bourlakis, M. 2017)

Omnichannel management is defined as the synergistic management of customer contact points in such a way as to optimise the customer's experience through the services offered on the different sales channels. It is aimed at offering an appropriate and identical experience regardless of the moment in the purchasing process or the location of the customer, and regardless of the purchasing channel they use. (Alonso-Garcia, J., Pablo-Martí, F., & Nunez-Barriopedro, E. 2021)

The omnichannel strategy is useful for retailers for incorporating the modern tools in their business that follow the digitisation process of their target markets, which has increased in recent years and developed even further following the SARS-CoV-2 crisis.

The basis for the creation of this strategy is the integrated management of the different sales channels which, by harmonising and cooperating in logistical activities, allow the company to offer a coherent and efficient offer on the various sales channels. (Payaro, A., & Papa, A. R. 2021).

According to a number of studies, omni-channelisation is the basis for the survival of retailing on the market of the future.

Compared to the year 2019, the information available on the population of Italian consumers over the age of 14 shows a 6% increase in the use of internet in at least one purchasing phase. It is clear how, especially for urban retailers, it is necessary for them to change their sales strategy in order to adapt to changes in the market and the new behaviour of consumers who use different purchasing channels according to the needs of the moment. (Nielsen e Politecnico di Milano (2020).

The offline sales channel is still the most widely used, but it needs to be properly integrated with digital tools that provide information and support in the pre- and post-sales phases. (Nault, B. R., & Rahman, M. S.2019)

Indeed, according to an Italian survey, respondents who said they were familiar with buying consumer goods online also said they buy up to 60 per cent of their groceries virtually. Along with this statement, they highlighted what they see as the benefits of an omnichannel strategy: flexibility and time savings during the shopping process, the ability to compare prices and save money, accessibility to a wider range of products and a wider range of services and information, together with the quality assurance defined by the physical presence of the retailer. (Nault, B. R., & Rahman, M. S.2019)

Studies on omnichannel retailing argue that the degree of trust placed in a retailer and the size of the retailer's store are the main factors of interest when consumers are shopping for groceries online.

The main motivations for consumers to shop online are convenience and time-savings, while the factors that drive customers away from the virtual service are related to their diffidence in entrusting the retailer with the selection of the products purchased. Food consumers are reluctant to entrust retailers with the selection of fresh produce such as fruit, vegetables, fish, meat, and dairy products, as they cannot evaluate them personally at the time of purchase. (Seitz, C., Pokrivčák, J., Tóth, M., & Plevný, M. (2017)

However, analyses have also shown that the retailer's ability to offer groceries on the digital channel allows end users to feel free of the physical commitment and time involved in the shopping process. Consumers who buy online are in fact willing to pay a premium for a home delivery service that provides assistance and convenience. According to the data, it is mainly working mothers, young people, and people aged 65 and over who show an interest in e-grocery shopping, however, a large proportion of consumers reject this channel, mainly due to habit and a lack of trust. (Seitz, C., Pokrivčák, J., Tóth, M., & Plevný, M.2017)

The willingness to buy food items on the virtual channel depends on the type of product required. Problematic foods, in other words, foods that require special handling, and frozen foods, are seen as unsuitable for online shopping which favours the sale of packaged products. The main reason why consumers are turning away from online shopping is confirmed to be the difficulty in assessing the freshness and quality of the products. Furthermore, according to literature survey data, the elements that have the greatest negative impact on the growth of grocery e-commerce include the lack of control over the transaction, the insecurity resulting from the virtual channel, and the lack of contact with the goods themselves. (Seitz, C., Pokrivčák, J., Tóth, M., & Plevný, M.2017)

The surveys conducted suggest that in the aim of adopting a winning omnichannel strategy, companies should appropriately select their reference target audience, increase their awareness of the services on offer, and gain their trust without making any mistakes.

Some products are more likely to be sold on the web based on a number of features that also include after-sales service. In addition, some survey results show that the presence of a traditional store favours the latter and increases the consumers' willingness to stock up with e-grocery items from that particular retailer. Researchers argue that the likelihood of consumers buying from a sales point depends on the distance they are from the store, and for this reason an omnichannel retailer must ensure the logistical proximity of their service in order to reduce any costs of disutility that a customer could encounter during an online grocery purchase. (Nault, B. R., & Rahman, M. S.2019)

Logistical Proximity and Urban Consumers

The proximity service offered by a retailer consists of guaranteeing the reference customer the possibility of obtaining products quickly, thus eliminating their need to use transport means to reach the store. (Sbrana, R. & Gandolfo, A., 2007)

Logistics services encompass all organisational, managerial, and strategic activities within a company that relate to the movement of materials and information. The logistics include all the stages of the activities, starting from the purchase of products either physically or online, up to the delivery and availability of the products to the end users, also considering the after-sales service where it exists. (Cardenas, I., et al., 2017)

Logistics referring to e-commerce channels are supported by structures, delivery processes, and fulfilment activities that are grouped together and implemented in areas of high population concentration located in proximity to customers.

To be able to provide the best possible proximity services, companies need to organise all their logistics activities in such a way as to favour and prioritise the attributes related to the speed of the purchasing and delivery process, as well as the ability to meet the consumer's requirements. (De Silva, C. K., Sano, K., & Hatoyama, K.2020)

The proximity logistics implemented within urban centres consist of the activities of actors, systems, and rules that are established within a well-defined territorial jurisdiction, namely, the urban centres. (Cardenas, I., et al., 2017)

Proximity distribution activities have assumed an important role in the modern development of retail trade, their relevance being mainly due to the recent evolution of the phenomenon of Proximity Commerce involving businesses, the commercial form of which defines a retailer's sales activity in favour of final consumers located in geographically close proximity to the place where the sales outlet is located. (Roberto Liscia, Consorzio Netcomm. 2020)

The use of this Proximity Commerce strategy concerns the new logistics organisation in which the e-commerce manager involves the traditional retail outlet in order to decrease the disutility of e-commerce purchases.

According to literature studies, using distribution and logistics strategies linked to the concept of proximity enables retailers to reduce the disutility that online sales services cause to consumers for both food and non-food goods. (Nault, B. R., & Rahman, M.S., 2019). Included among these disutility aspects, above all in the case of foodstuffs, are the excessive cost of delivery, the loss of freshness and quality of the products during the delivery, the impossibility of personally observing and choosing the products, and the impossibility of turning to a physical store for any post-purchase problems and clarifications. (Nault, B. R., & Rahman, M S.2019).

The interest that businesses place in the proximity service is represented by the "Last Mile" activities implemented. These lead entrepreneurs to deal with the costs of carrying out orders, with the customers' sensitivity to the price levels of the service, with the pressure of competitors, and with the increased expectations of consumers with regard to the scheduling and timing of the delivery and supply of the service. (Janjevic, M., & Winkenbach, M.2020).

According to academic research in the field of retailing, to ensure that trust exists between the retailer and the consumer, the latter must believe the retailer has the ability and willingness to offer a quality service and reliable delivery. Studies show that it is usually the traditional channel that earns the highest margins of consumer trust, while the online channel is instead more likely to meet with more distrust the marked problems linked to the non-physical nature of the service. (Janjevic, M., & Winkenbach, M.2020)

Academic research also shows that a dual-channel grocery retailer (having both a traditional and an e-commerce sales channel), can provide superior and well-defined benefits for the consumer and appears able to mitigate the costs of disutility arising from the online part of the sales channel. The benefits associated with carrying out correct proximity logistics activities depend on the ability to effectively reduce the elements of dissatisfaction that consumers face when they choose to buy online. And consequently, they depend on the ability to overcome these discrepancies through the correct implementation of dual-channel commerce. (Nault, B. R., & Rahman, M S.2019).

The possibility of dealing with any defects, returns, problems, or assemblies within a traditional retail shop is what gives the consumer the security of the sales process and consequently, it is what compensates the cost to the consumer of using online purchasing service. (Nault, B. R., & Rahman, M S.2019).

Previous surveys shed light on the fact that the probability that a consumer has of visiting a store depends on their distance from the store, which is why many retailers consider and invest in activities that help gain proximity to their business and thus reduce the distance of the logistics centre from the user. The importance of providing an adequate and close logistics service can be deduced by considering the weight of the total transport costs that consumers have to bear to get supplies from a traditional physical store and then comparing it with what is called the disutility cost deriving from online shopping. The disutility costs tend to drop in proportion to the reduction in distance from the point of purchase. (Nault, B. R., & Rahman, M S.2019).

The operations that are implemented during the distribution process between the order assembly point where the stock is located, and the preferred delivery location chosen by the consumer, are therefore called Last Mile activities. (Janjevic, M. & Winkenbach, M.2020)

Last Mile and logistics management, and the related travel components are the first elements affecting the changes linked to the reorganisation of sales points in line with the prerequisites of Proximity Commerce. The challenges faced by retailers wishing to establish a Last Mile service and, in this way, manage the phase where the customer is geographically closest to the business, are mainly related to their ability to minimise service costs and environmental impact, as well as the capacity to increase the overall efficiency of their infrastructures. (Mazareanu, E.,2020).

In order to understand the management of proximity service activities, it is necessary to know in advance the characteristics and requirements of consumers belonging to the market segment to which one refers. (Lim, S. F. W., Jin, X., & Srai, J. S.2018) Research shows that proximity and exercising of neighbourhood activities represent varying levels of importance for consumers depending on their specific geographical provenance. (Sousa, R., Horta, C., Ribeiro, R., & Rabinovich, E.2020)

Customers living in urban areas have significantly different characteristics and needs compared to customers in rural areas. In general, rural areas are defined as areas where more than 50% of the population resides in rural municipalities, which are defined as those municipalities the population density of which is less than 150 inhabitants per km^2. (Istat, 2020)

Urban areas, on the other hand, are intense built-up areas that extend beyond the boundaries of the municipality and form real cities. To be able to identify an urban centre, it is necessary to combine the geographic continuity of a city and its minimum population threshold. When the population density of an area is high, we can speak of an urban centre, and when the population intensity is low, we speak of rural cells. (Istat, 2020)

The literature quantifies that in 73% of cases, rural consumers show a greater willingness to wait for delivery and retrieval of the product or service for longer periods than the willingness reported by consumers living in urban areas. From the analyses it can be observed how the challenge of the last mile and same-day delivery is prioritised in more populated areas, where delivery close to the end user becomes an essential element for customer satisfaction and completion of the sales transaction. Furthermore, it is evident that urban consumers spend less time on the shopping process and require faster order delivery, showing a low level of willingness to wait for delivery services. (Sousa, R., Horta, C., Ribeiro, R., & Rabinovich, E.2020)

In the aim of meeting the needs of urban consumers, therefore, it is important for companies to locate their delivery and storage points in areas that are geographically close to their final destinations for offering quick pick-up of products from inventories that are both easily accessible and sufficiently complete.

This situation is even more significant for the online grocery sector where several studies report that 92% of consumers require home delivery services to be provided on the same day as placing the order, and 65% of these consumers consider changing their choice of retailer from which to purchase when this service is not offered. (Deloitte 2020).

According to consumers, the main obstacles that businesses face in offering adequate logistics services include the ability to increase their volume of business, compliance with sustainability criteria in their logistics activities, the ability to offer low delivery costs and handle requests quickly, and finally, the ability to recruit the appropriate workforce to improve not only their business but also the social environment in which the business is embedded.(Boysen, N., Fedtke, S., & Schwerdfeger, S. 2021)

On the supply side, there is an emerging need for collaboration and partnership tools between multiple retailers for obtaining the capabilities to fulfil Proximity Commerce activities and offer fast and flexible sales processes. (Davis-Sramek, B. et al.2020).

In the order of importance that consumers attach to last-mile sales activities, first and foremost is the ability to select delivery and collection times, followed by the speed of order tracking services, reduced home delivery costs, flexibility in selecting the final destination of goods, and the environmental impact of the company's logistics chain. (Mazareanu, E. 2020a)

Business Models in the Digital Era and the Role of the Urban Distribution Structures

The business model of a company refers to the way in which it creates, delivers, and captures value (Wiener, M., Hoßbach, N., & Saunders, C. 2018). The key components include the value proposition, understood as the set of goods and services that make up the offer to customers, the value architecture which concerns the implementation and organisation of resources and capabilities in order to make the offer available in the market (Li, F. 2020), and the value finance (Jocevski, M. 2020) regarding the way of implementing an economically sustainable organisation capable of achieving adequate turnover to bear the costs necessary for the activity, and which refers to the set of internal and external stakeholders involved in the production and delivery of the offer. Furthermore, the development of digital technologies (Balaji, M. S., & Roy, S. K. 2017) has brought considerable change in business strategies and solicited business model innovation. (Carvalho, L. C., Jeleniewicz, M., Franczak, P., & Vanková, Ž. 2021)

In the retailing sector, in addition to the components, it is of fundamental importance to identify the business model, also and above all, how the offer is sold, and the collaborations and partnerships with players outside the company required to make the value proposition available to the reference target. (Jocevski, M. 2020) To this end, in the omnichannel activity in the grocery retailing sector, the urban distribution structures become indispensable.

Urban Distribution Strategies

The strategies and structure formats that urban retailers can implement to manage a proximity omnichannel system may be of different types. Retailers need to select the distribution format that suits the needs and demands of their target customers in order to offer products and services that are useful and ensure adequate differentiation. (Meza-Peralta, K., et al., 2020, October)

The exercising of the retail trade requires the existence of a warehouse for the storage of goods, irrespective of whether one's own or a third party's, which structurally becomes the basis of the commercial activity.

Warehouses are also defined as distribution centres and are classified according to their specific characteristics as follows:

- Dedicated distribution centres that manage the activities, goods, and sales strategies of a single retailer.
- Integrated distribution centres, which combine the inventories of several retailers. (Davis-Sramek, B. et al.2020)

The Dark Store

Retailers can offer the customer the possibility of ordering online and using the Home Delivery service.

They can also offer the use of the Click and Collect service, which allows customers to order the product online and pick it up themselves at the company's physical point of sale or station.

To ensure an adequate service, it is necessary for the pick-up point to be centrally and strategically located to reduce the time needed to reach it, and avoid queues, overcrowding and waiting at the pick-up point.

To this end, the retailer can resort to a particular method by using an active point of sale such as a Dark Store, Dark Supermarket, or Dotcom Centre, i.e., it can create a distribution centre out of retail outlets or open warehouses that are totally or partially closed to the customer and temporarily or permanently transformed into online order-processing centres accessible only to sales staff and designed exclusively for online shopping. (Thomas, S., Vatavwala, S., & Sinha, P. K. 2017)

The Dark Store has its origins in the UK when the well-known supermarket chain, Tesco, decided to use some stores and storage centres exclusively as warehouses for processing online purchases. (Bitterman, A., & Hess, D. B)

The model for this structure is based on the search for spaces that can be sales outlets, shopping centres, offices, or storage facilities already existing inside or outside the company, for transforming them into online order-processing centres. (Bitterman, A., & Hess, D. B)

Dark Stores can sometimes be accessible to the customer in a part of their structure, in which case they are only partially integrated with the warehouse. In the latter case, the Dark Store allows the company to reach and satisfy not only customers who appreciate and use the online food shopping experience and those who prefer to continue buying directly in the physical shop, but also consumers who use services integrating the two channels, such as Click and Collect. (Bitterman, A., & Hess, D. B)

RETAIL FOOD EXPENDITURE AND THE POST SARS2 PANDEMIC NEEDS OF ITALIAN CONSUMERS

Characteristics and Evolution of Food Retailing in Italy and the Repercussions of the Covid SARS2 Pandemic

According to the most up-to-date reports on the Italian domestic trade and services in the year 2018, Italian retail trade was characterised by 577,807 enterprises, mainly small and defined as micro enterprises, which had on average 3.2 employees each. Food retailing numbered 175,655 enterprises in the same year, with a total of 734,273 employees or an average of 4.2 employees each. Enterprises engaged in digital commercial activities or outside the physical point of sale amounted to 106,740 in 2018 with an average of 1.6 employees each.

There were 30,525 enterprises engaged in non-specialised food retail businesses with an average of 14 employees per enterprise, including 10,781 supermarkets, 3,263 department stores and 629 hypermarkets. The points of sale were distributed throughout Italy without any special distinctions or geographical concentrations.

In terms of sales, retail trade grew by 0.7% in 2019, and more specifically, by 1.4% for large-scale retail trade and 18.4% for e-commerce.

In contrast, trade carried out by micro enterprises fell by 0.7%. (Istat, 2020a)

The press releases about food retail sales during the following year 2020, however, highlighted the totally uncertain situation that characterised national trade compared to previous years.

During July 2020 and the months immediately preceding, there were declines of -1% in value, which then recovered and stabilised at the end of the year. This situation allowed businesses to close the period in the food retail sector with a slight growth of 0.1%.

The beginning of 2021 confirmed the growth in volumes of food products in general and maintained the trend that had emerged during the month of December 2020. (Istat, 2021)

According to the data, digital sales channels replaced and complemented physical sales, especially following the closures rendered compulsory by the SARS-CoV-2 health emergency. (Fruitbook Magazine, 2020).

Initially, the assault on supermarkets by consumers concerned about possible product shortages, allowed for sustaining and at times even increased traditional retailing, but subsequently the market evolved in favour of virtual commerce activities. The latter have provided new users of the online service with the safety, hygiene, and variety of choice they demand. As demonstrated by the surveys, offline retail activities recorded an exponential growth of 16.1% during the first phase of the pandemic, with most of this growth occurring in stores located close to the more populated centres; however, this growth fell to 3.2% in the immediate aftermath, confirming how digital was the solution. It is estimated that in the phase immediately following the first national lockdown that occurred indicatively between 09/03/2020 and 18/05/2020, 36% of Italian consumers maintained the habit, which had begun during the pandemic, of shopping for groceries online, and expressed a general increase in perceived satisfaction with the service compared to the previous months. (Netcomm Forum Live, 2020)

The Click and Collect service in Italy increased its sales share of 8.3% in 2019 to 15% during the first lockdown phase, settling at 13% in the following months. (Liscia, R. Consorzio Netcomm, 2020)

The Click and Collect service was favoured because it was considered by consumers to be more rapid and more convenient than home delivery, and therefore better in terms of efficiency. During the same months, large-scale retail distribution enterprises saw their share of online business increase by 96.4%. (Netcomm Forum Live, 2020)

The constant development of online processes of shopping for groceries, especially in the wake of the recent pandemic, has necessitated the emergence of forms of retail trade with characteristics and resources that are consistent with the evolution of the modern markets. (Bitterman, A., & Hess, D. B)

According to ISTAT data referring to Italy, compared to 2020, there was a large reduction in out-of-store sales and small stores in January 2021. The decline also occurred in sales by large-scale retail distribution enterprises, while the only distribution form characterised by a 38.4% growth was e-commerce. (Istat, 2021)

The information emerging above has therefore guided the research carried out in this paper, considering the current and future changes that retailing, and in particular, the small Italian grocery retailers are facing.

The survey conducted by the authors analyses the importance of certain attributes and services required by consumers during web purchases, for the purpose of verifying changes in interest and purchasing habits. In doing so, they highlight the possible dynamics of development of business models in retailing with specific reference to small Italian grocery retailers and the preferences of consumers.

Retail Food Expenditure Service Attributes Required, and Their Level of Importance for the Buyer

The aim of this paper is to assess the potential of the omnichannel business for food retailing in densely populated areas. It makes an assessment of the relevant consumers/buyers with respect to the characteristics and importance of the service attributes requested.

After defining the objectives of the research, the sample on which to carry out the analysis was selected. The interest in studying all subjects related to food shopping, both offline and online, determined this choice.

For consumer respondents, the prerequisite for inclusion in the sample was that they had developed sufficient shopping experience to be able to freely express opinions and preferences regarding the different methods of purchasing.

Respondents took part in the interview after having received or viewed a link on the social channels Facebook, Instagram, Twitter, and LinkedIn, as well as on instant messaging channels or direct emails.

The questionnaire used to collect the information was administered to a group of consumers/food buyers according to the following criteria:

minimum age 18 years;

the fact of being a decision-maker or exerting influence in decisions and methods of buying foodstuffs.

The respondents constituted a convenient sample of Italian consumers. In fact, small grocery retailers are numerically very relevant in the Italian territory, moreover, the greater presence of consumers from Northern Italy is linked to the presence of much more densely populated cities in this geographical area.

The analysis cohort was therefore represented by those subjects whose participation in food shopping was considered active and frequent. It involved a sample of 410 self-selected respondents, because after receiving a contact or viewing an online message they spontaneously chose to participate in the survey and therefore to be part of the sample.

The survey of the consumers was largely made up of respondents from Northern Italy (77%), 81.46% of whom stated that they shop for food once a week or more, 8.05% every day, whilst the remainder shop for food less frequently.

Initially, without distinguishing between the attributes offered on the different sales channels, the elements of the general food service were assessed, so the aim was to obtain data on those which, according to the research information, influence the consumers' choice from among the different sales points. For this reason, consumers were asked to evaluate just how much geographical proximity (Nault, B. R., & Rahman, M S.2019), variety (Sousa, R., Horta, C., Ribeiro, R., & Rabinovich, E.2020) and freshness of the products (Seitz, C., Pokrivčák, J., Tóth, M., & Plevný, M.2017) are relevant and indispensable when shopping for groceries.

In this way it was subsequently possible to consider distribution strategies that meet these needs and any problems related to this offer. The possibility of avoiding overcrowding and queues, the speed of the shopping process, and the assistance provided by the sales staff were the next questions to be asked, and in this case, they made it possible to indirectly assess the characteristics of the Dark Stores. The latter avoid the unpleasant inconveniences caused by the physical organisation of the different functions that a retailer performs, therefore, they must be equipped with the features that the consumer feels are a source of convenience. Precisely in the aim of understanding what preferences respondents have in their habits when developing an omnichannel retailing exercise such as the Dark Store, they were then asked to evaluate the provision of a service of an e-grocery sale. In this case, information was requested on Home Delivery, Click & Collect, digital payment services and after-sales support.

Finally, specific questions were asked about the products, frequency of online food purchases and the use of and satisfaction with the in-store cross selling and guarantee services, which, as explained above, make the Dark Store a winning solution for overcoming lack of trust in online food shopping.

The aim of this study was to find out what consumers want when buying food, in order to relate this with the e-grocery characteristics and assess their strengths and weaknesses.

The main items studied by this research included the speed of service that the literature judges necessary during online delivery, the coverage for purchases of all fresh products, and in particular, for urgent and last-minute purchases, the elimination of waiting times, and the degree of trust placed in the choice of products by retailers. (Seitz, C., Pokrivčák, J., Tóth, M., & Plevný, M.2017).

Following are the results (Figure.1) showing how consumers rate the importance of certain service elements when shopping for food, irrespective of the purchasing channel used, with a comparison of the average response with the score attributed to each item.

Figure 1. How important are these elements in choosing a grocery store? (Knowing that: 1=Not Important at All, and 5= Extremely Important)
Source: Author's own presentation.

	1 Not Important At All	2	3	4	5 Extremely Important	Total	Weighted Average
To be geographically close to the store	*2,20% 9*	*6,59% 27*	*27,56% 113*	*33,41% 137*	*30,24% 124*	*410*	*3,83*
The time taken to get to the store	*1,46% 6*	*8,05% 33*	*25,12% 103*	*35,61% 146*	*29,76% 122*	*410*	*3,84*
The variety of products and brands offered	*0,98% 4*	*2,20% 9*	*15,61% 64*	*32,44% 133*	*48,78% 200*	*410*	*4,26*
To be able to compare products	*2,93% 12*	*9,51% 39*	*25,37% 104*	*31,95% 131*	*30,24% 124*	*410*	*3,77*
The quality and freshness of the goods	*0,24% 1*	*0,49% 2*	*3,17% 13*	*17,56% 72*	*78,54% 322*	*410*	*4,74*
The prices level	*0,73% 3*	*3,66% 15*	*22,20% 91*	*34,15% 140*	*39,27% 161*	*410*	*4,08*
Familiar place and atmosphere	*13,66% 56*	*19,51% 80*	*26,59% 109*	*22,93% 94*	*17,32% 71*	*410*	*3,11*
To be able to avoid queues and overcrowding	*1,46% 6*	*7,07% 29*	*19,27% 79*	*30,24% 124*	*41,95% 172*	*410*	*4,04*
The presence of shop assistants	*9,51% 39*	*15,12% 62*	*28,78% 118*	*26,34% 108*	*20,24% 83*	*410*	*3,33*
To be able to buy on the e-commerce website	*42,68% 175*	*23,66% 97*	*17,80% 73*	*7,32% 30*	*8,54% 35*	*410*	*2,15*

The data obtained from the questionnaire show that for users, the choice of shop to buy food from depends on the quality and freshness of the goods on offer, which were considered important by 96,1% (Figure.1) of respondents, followed by the variety of brands and products on offer, which was supported by 81,22% (Figure.1) of respondents. The reasons underlying the preferences for these elements, as highlighted by the literature in question, derive from the great need of consumers to always have the quality and freshness of the products guaranteed, especially during the online purchase phases, in order to establish a relationship of authentic trust with the retailer. Less important were the presence of the sales staff (46,58% in Figure 1) and the familiar environment (40,25% in Figure 1). This is probably due to the speed required when making purchases in order to better organise the shopping process, which consequently lowers the interest of most consumers in the relational part of the sale. (Seitz, C., Pokrivčák, J., Tóth, M., & Plevný, M.2017).

Following, in order, 73,42% (Figure 1) chose the store based on the price level of the products offered, while 72,2% (Figure.1) of consumers wanted to avoid overcrowding and queues during the shopping process. In particular, more than 80% of users over 36 years of age considered this peace of mind during the shopping phase to be important, avoiding unpleasant delays that would reduce the feelings, described in the relevant literature, of enjoyment when shopping for grocery products. (Seitz, C., Pokrivčák, J., Tóth, M., & Plevný, M.2017).

Figure 2. Indicate the importance of the following components of online grocery shopping. (Knowing that:1= Not Important At All, and 5= Extremely Important)
Source: Author's own presentation.

	1 Not Important At All		2		3		4		5 Extremely Important		Total	Weighted Average
To be able to compare brands and prices	4,88%	20	5,85%	24	20,49%	84	34,15%	140	34,63%	142	410	3,88
To have more variety of goods	4,63%	19	3,41%	14	14,15%	58	37,07%	152	40,73%	167	410	4,06
To reduce the spending time	5,61%	23	8,54%	35	18,54%	76	30,49%	125	36,83%	151	410	3,84
Fast delivery of products	5,85%	24	8,29%	34	17,80%	73	26,83%	110	41,22%	169	410	3,89
Proximity to the storage warehouse	22,93%	94	20,24%	83	26,10%	107	20,49%	84	10,24%	42	410	2,75
To be able to select delivery time slots	10,73%	44	7,56%	31	15,85%	65	24,15%	99	41,71%	171	410	3,79
To be able to collect the order in a physical store	13,66%	56	12,68%	52	25,37%	104	28,78%	118	19,51%	80	410	3,28
Proximity to the pickup point	11,22%	46	8,78%	36	19,02%	78	31,46%	129	29,51%	121	410	3,59
Quick purchase of urgent products	4,63%	19	4,88%	20	11,22%	46	28,29%	116	50,98%	209	410	4,16
Selection of different payment methods	6,83%	28	5,12%	21	9,27%	38	28,78%	118	50,00%	205	410	4,1

This information confirms the literature data where younger consumers demand speed in a process considered a waste of time, geographical proximity of the store and the time taken to reach it were evaluated as important elements for more than 60% (Figure.1) of consumers, and convenience influenced the choice of food retailer. Consumers buy from retailers according to their distance from home. (Nault, B. R., & Rahman, M.S., 2019).

In a second phase, consumers were asked to rate the importance attributed to food sales variables specifically when shopping through the online channel. The elements considered important here represent what consumers believe the virtual channel must have and/or provide for effectively competing with the traditional physical store, regardless of whether consumers are currently using the e-grocery channel itself.

Also in this case, the results (Figure.2) required that consumers rate the importance of service attributes when shopping online.

Considering the possible decision to take advantage of an online food product offer, the services that are most in demand were for 67,32% (Figure.2) of consumers the ability to reduce the time allocated to the shopping process and, consequently, the possibility of rapidly purchasing any urgent products (voted for by 79,27% of respondents). 77,8% of respondents said that the variety of goods on offer is an important component of grocery services, especially when carried out online. In addition, 78,78% endorsed the possibility of using different payment methods in order to take advantage of the omnichannel offer and obtain greater convenience. The possibility offered by the virtual channel to buy urgent products more rapidly is important, especially for consumers under the age of 35, and confirms once again the literature that sees younger users as the least willing to spend time on shopping. (Seitz, C., Pokrivčák, J., Tóth, M., & Plevný, M.2017)

The proximity to the pick-up point which, according to theory, is directly correlated with the likelihood of obtaining supplies from a retailer (Nault, B. R., & Rahman, M.S., 2019) was also confirmed as important in the case of online grocery shopping by 60,97% of consumers. In fact, geographic proximity guarantees greater product freshness and less likelihood of problems during delivery to the final destination. (Seitz, C., Pokrivčák, J., Tóth, M., & Plevný, M.2017)

Similarly, 65,86% of respondents require the selection of delivery time slots in order not to lose the convenience typical of the online service, confirming the theoretical data on the importance of the functionality of the speed and organisation of e-grocery services for guaranteeing the consumer more control over the purchasing process and consequently, a higher level of satisfaction. (Hübner, A. H., et al., 2016)

Although lower in percentage than the data reported in the literature, (Seitz, C., Pokrivčák, J., Tóth, M., & Plevný, M.2017), 56,1% of respondents are still reluctant to entrust third parties with the choice of product in the belief that because they cannot physically touch it, this could give rise to a selection error. The fact that in the store there is the possibility for consumers to add further products to the purchases made online and picked up in this way exploiting both sales channels depending on the product categories to be selected, is relevant for 73,65% of respondents in the case of adding food products, and for 70,98% of respondents for other non-food products.

Consumers were then asked to rate which reasons discourage them from buying food products online (Figure.3)

Figure 3. Indicate the importance of the following reasons in choosing not to buy groceries online. (Knowing that: 1= Not Important At All and 5= Extremely Important)
Source: Author's own presentation

	1 Not Important At All		2		3		4		5 Extremely Important		Total	Weighted Average
Wrong choice of products	15,12%	62	13,90%	57	28,05%	115	20,49%	84	22,44%	92	410	3,21
Loss of products quality	11,22%	46	12,68%	52	23,17%	95	23,90%	98	29,02%	119	410	3,47
Prices too high	10,98%	45	16,34%	67	26,83%	110	21,95%	90	23,90%	98	410	3,31
Lack of habit	7,80%	32	9,76%	40	21,46%	88	19,51%	80	41,46%	170	410	3,77
Risk of theft of personal or banking data	26,34%	108	24,39%	100	18,78%	77	14,63%	60	15,85%	65	410	2,69
Having transport, delivery or return problems	9,02%	37	14,63%	60	21,22%	87	25,85%	106	29,27%	120	410	3,52

The results show that the reasons justifying the non-use of the e-grocery channel are for 60,97% (Fig.3) of all users the lack of habit that discourages awareness of the service, as also reported in literature (Seitz, C., Pokrivčák, J., Tóth, M., & Plevný, M.2017), and for 55,12%, the possibility of encountering problems with transport, delivery, or return of products. The reason for non-purchase is considered important by 52,11% of respondents, who attribute the possible loss of quality of the products during all phases through the online purchase. The possible wrong choice made by the retailer to whom the selection is delegated is the reason for the hesitancy expressed by 42,93% of respondents, which confirms the data collected in previous surveys regarding the lack of trust in selection by a third person.

In general, 58,54% of respondents were in favour of an omnichannel offer from retailers, and more than 70% considered it useful to have a service that would allow them to collect their online orders in-store, and therefore to offer a Click & Collect service that would also enable them to buy from several retailers via a single point of sale.

A minority of all the consumers who completed the questionnaire take advantage of the online sales service. 7,07% of respondents said that they buy their food online regularly while 77,31% buy traditionally from large-scale retail distribution enterprises.

In order to assess the reliability of the questionnaire scales and be able to make a reliable comparison with the theory, Cronbach's Alpha was used.

Compared to the items on the scales of the consumer survey, the average internal reliability derived is a Cronbach's Alpha of 0.8304, which is in line with the requirements of the literature. (Cortina, J. M.,1993)

In addition, the correlation existing between the variables analysed in the survey was assessed and in order to obtain this information on the qualitative variables of the questionnaires, Cramer's V index was measured, which normalises the value of the Chi square of the association between qualitative variables, varying between 0 and 1. When it is equal to 0, the two variables are mutually independent, while the closer it is to the value of 1, the greater the association between the variables and therefore, there is a direct relationship between the variation of the first and the behaviour of the second variable. (De Luca, A, .2006)

In the questionnaire submitted to consumers, irrespective of the use expressed by the latter of the online purchasing channel, they were asked to assess the benefits of using a Click and Collect service for products ordered online, which would allow them to add other products upon going to the physical store.

Figure 4. Results of the Cramer's V Index calculated on the variables present in the questionnaire addressed to grocery consumers
Source: Author's own presentation

VARIABLE 1	*VARIABLE 2*	*CRAMER'S V INDEX*
In-store, to be able to add other groceries to your online shopping	*In-store, to be able to add other non-food products to your online shopping*	*0,7856*
The time taken to get to the store	*Geographical proximity to the store*	*0,6473*
Products quality safety	*Products origin safety*	*0,5507*
Products quality safety	*Maintaining the freshness of the products during the delivery phase*	*0,5371*
Risk of not getting the same quality of products when buying online	*Risk of making the wrong choice of products when buying online*	*0,5025*
Variety of goods offered	*Timing of the spending process*	*0,3986*

With a Cramer's index of 0,7856 (Figure.4), the association between the possibility of withdrawing and adding more grocery products and the possibility of adding products from other product categories, confirms the relevance described by the surveys (Istat, 2021) of the use of the pick-up service and adds value to the importance of the services offered by the Dark Store. The possibility of purchasing some foods online and physically picking up others could help to maintain the high quality and freshness of goods that consumers demand. (Seitz, C., Pokrivčák, J., Tóth, M., & Plevný, M.2017). Similarly, the ability to purchase products, even from different retailers and through different channels, from a single point of sale, allows retailers to increase their customer base by offering a complete service to the end consumer.

The association index between the importance expressed regarding the time taken to reach the store where the shopping is being carried out and the geographical proximity of the same is 0,6473. The existence of a relationship between these two variables confirms, as reported in the literature, that the existence of a physically present store, located in areas close to the consumer is in fact useful to all consumers due to reducing the time they spend during the shopping process, irrespective of whether carried out online or offline. The combined importance of these variables shows that the consumer's choice of store to buy from is closely linked to the their place of residence and, therefore, their proximity to the retail outlet. (Nault, B. R., & Rahman, M. S., 2019)

Similarly, consumers require that the safety of the origin and quality of the products they buy be present at the same time, especially for food products selected online that are subject to greater perishability. The elements linked to the preservation of the healthiness of grocery products are the first to be related to online purchases, their importance makes them highly associated, so it is essential to devise a service that allows the specific characteristics of the goods to be maintained during the delivery and collection processes. Users for whom the risk of buying online is represented by the possible decline in product quality, also consider the risk of receiving the wrong product to be of great importance and therefore demonstrate a lack of confidence in their choice of retailer, preferring autonomous decision-making for certain product categories and instead benefiting from online purchasing for others. (Seitz, C., Pokrivčák, J., Tóth, M., & Plevný, M., 2017).

Finally, there is less association between the variety of goods required when buying online and the timing of the shopping process, as reported in the literature. In fact, consumers of a young age living in urban areas are willing to give up variety in their purchases if it means they can maintain high speed levels in receiving the products. (Sousa, R., Horta, C., Ribeiro, R., & Rabinovich, E., 2020)

OPPORTUNITIES AND ADVANTAGES OF A NEW BUSINESS MODEL IN OMNICHANNEL STRATEGIES FOR SMALL GROCERY RETAILER

Firms in The Post-Pandemic Era

Based on the information obtained from the analyses of the questionnaires administered, Italian consumers are characterised by a low propensity to buy food products online. Even though ISTAT data have made it possible to assess the exponential growth of this channel and all the related services such as Click & Collect and Home Delivery, only 7% of the respondents to our survey currently make online food purchases.

The reasons underlying this mistrust of the virtual channel are mainly related to the lack of security with respect to the quality of the service offered. What hinders the e-grocery purchase, as also highlighted by the literature, is first and foremost the possible loss of freshness and quality of the products, and secondly, the impossibility of controlling the sales transaction and having to entrust the choice to a stranger without being able to see or touch the products the purchase made. A further impediment to online grocery shopping relates to the time and cost of the service, which could create inconveniences during the delivery or collection process if not adequately efficient. (Seitz, C., Pokrivčák, J., Tóth, M., & Plevný, M., 2017).

Despite these assumptions, it can be observed how the survey sheds light on several elements that introduce possible solutions and development trajectories for grocery retailers interested in offering an appropriate proposition with value for their customers.

In fact, geographic proximity to the point of sale, pick-up point and/or storage point for online orders is of great importance for more than 60% (Figure.5) of respondents positively inclined towards omnichannel grocery services.

72,4% (Figure.5) of consumers who already buy food products online are interested in the amount of time it takes them to reach the point of sale and the same statement of importance is made by 66,06% (Figure.5) of consumers who do not currently use the e-grocery channel.

Geographical proximity of the shop is important to all consumers and in particular, to 65,54% (Figure.5) of those who do not currently buy online. The same service element is of great value to 65,8% (Figure.5) of users who place their trust in retailers offering different sales channels.

The hypothesis can be deemed as confirmed in which geographic proximity is considered an adequately compensation for part of the service disutility caused by the online distribution offer. This conclusion derives from the great importance expressed by all respondents regarding the physical proximity of the retailer and therefore of their physical and online Last Mile activities.

Figure 5. Association of the grocery consumers' responses relative to the importance of the different variables
Source: Author's own presentation

TYPE OF CONSUMER	*HIGH IMPORTANCE ATTRIBUTED TO SERVICE ELEMENTS*
Consumers for whom perceived satisfaction increases when the retailer offers omnichannel services: online + offline shopping	• *High importance attributed to the geographical proximity of the store 65,8%* • *High importance attributed to the time taken to get to the store 68,3%* • *High importance attributed to the proximity of the collection point of goods ordered online 66,6%*
Consumers who buy groceries online (always or almost always)	• *High importance attributed to the geographical proximity of the store 58,6%* • *High importance attributed to the time taken to get to the store 72,4%*
Consumers who do not buy groceries online (never or almost never)	• *High importance attributed to the geographical proximity of the store 64,54%* • *High importance attributed to the time taken to get to the store 66,06%*

These results confirm the importance for retailers intending to implement an omnichannel strategy of the need to activate partnerships with other operators in order to ensure adequate logistical proximity to customers. This situation seems to find a valid solution in the adopting of a format similar to the Dark Store with a hybrid formulation in partnership with other online retailers, and through collaboration with small traditional grocery retailers. (Endres, H., Stoiber, K., & Wenzl, N. M., 2019)

In fact, small grocery retailers, by innovating their business model, can create a value proposition for their customers that allows them to offer a proximity service in line with the needs expressed by consumers, as well as significantly reducing the disutility associated with online grocery shopping, instead of further implementing the utility elements.

FUTURE RESEARCH DIRECTIONS

Due to the limitations encountered during this research, in future it would be worthwhile to evaluate the commercial outcome of an omnichannel strategy based on Dark Stores in order to gain insight into the changes in traditional retailing and consequently obtain real evidence of the effectiveness of the format for the development of the online food channel.

The evaluation of the gratification of consumers purchasing online from a retailer, such as an Omnichannel retailer implementing a Dark Store, could be compared with that of those who still continue to buy traditionally from the same retailer, also in this case, in the aim of understanding the actual success of the format as a solution for online grocery stores.

An additional investigation in the future could assess the sustainability benefits of carrying out neighbourhood logistics distribution activities through resource sharing among multiple retailers and partnerships with small traditional grocery retailers.

It is also worth emphasising that the survey should be expanded to include consumers in other countries for the purpose of testing and evaluating the viability of this format at an international level.

CONCLUSION

During the recent pandemic phase, the use of the online sales channel made it possible to comply with safety regulations, avoiding queues and overcrowding at points of sale while still allowing consumers to replenish their supplies. The following measures, which emerged in a situation of extreme emergency, could be replicated, and maintained in the future to address the need for speed, convenience, and non-population at the point of sale that consumers require when shopping, irrespective of the presence of force majeure causes such as the Sars-CoV-2 virus.

From the analysis in this paper, it is evident that changes are occurring in shopping processes; the presence of sales staff, for example, is not a reason for consumers to prefer one retailer over another, nor is there the risk of data theft when shopping online.

On the other hand, the survey has highlighted the great significance that consumers attach to the proximity of the food pick-up and provisioning point and the possibility of completing their online shopping by choosing other food and/or non-food products at the pick-up point. This indicates how the proximity service that distinguishes small grocery retailers and fosters a valid relationship with the clientele, is a primary element in creating a viable omnichannel offer.

There is consequently an urgent need for small Italian grocery retailers to implement an innovative business model, (Carvalho, L.C., Jeleniewicz, M., Franczak, P., & Vanková, Ž. 2021), exploiting their entrepreneurial capacity, skills and abilities to engage customers, (Kajalo, S., & Lindblom, A. 2015),but also with reference to the Dark Store format in a hybrid form, which is integrated in the traditional point of sale activities in partnership and collaboration with other operators for the delivery of goods purchased online.

All in the aim of encouraging new trajectories of sustainable development for small Italian grocery retailers and omnichannel online sales activities in the grocery sector.

REFERENCES

Alonso-Garcia, J., Pablo-Martí, F., & Nunez-Barriopedro, E. (2021). *Omnichannel Management in B2B. Complexity-based model. Empirical evidence from a panel of experts based on Fuzzy Cognitive Maps.* Industrial Marketing Management.

Balaji, M. S., & Roy, S. K. (2017). Value co-creation with Internet of things technology in the retail industry. *Journal of Marketing Management*, *33*(1-2), 7–31. doi:10.1080/0267257X.2016.1217914

Bitterman, A., & Hess, D. B. (n.d.). *Going dark: The post-pandemic transformation of the metropolitan retail landscape.* Academic Press.

Boysen, N., Fedtke, S., & Schwerdfeger, S. (2021). Last-mile delivery concepts: A survey from an operational research perspective. *OR-Spektrum*, *43*(1), 1–58. doi:10.100700291-020-00607-8

Cai, Y. J., & Lo, C. K. (2020). Omni-channel management in the new retailing era: A systematic review and future research agenda. *International Journal of Production Economics*, *229*, 107729. doi:10.1016/j.ijpe.2020.107729

Cardenas, I., Borbon-Galvez, Y., Verlinden, T., Van de Voorde, E., Vanelslander, T., & Dewulf, W. (2017). City logistics, urban goods distribution and last mile delivery and collection. *Competition and Regulation in Network Industries, 18*(1-2).

Carvalho, L. C., Jeleniewicz, M., Franczak, P., & Vanková, Ž. (2021). Business Models for Digital Economy: Good Practices and Success Stories. Handbook of Research on Multidisciplinary Approaches to Entrepreneurship, Innovation, and ICTs, 1-21.

Davis-Sramek, B., Ishfaq, R., Gibson, B. J., & Defee, C. (2020). Examining retail business model transformation: A longitudinal study of the transition to omnichannel order fulfillment. *International Journal of Physical Distribution & Logistics Management*, *50*(5), 557–576. doi:10.1108/IJPDLM-02-2019-0055

De Luca, A. (2006). *Le ricerche di mercato. Guida pratica e teorica* (Vol. 622). FrancoAngeli.

De Silva, C. K., Sano, K., & Hatoyama, K. (2020). Exploring the relationship between urban form and spatial organisation of Amazon fulfilment facilities in the United Kingdom and Japan. *Transportation Research Procedia*, *46*, 46. doi:10.1016/j.trpro.2020.03.175

Deloitte. (2020). *Last Mile Logistics. Challenges and solutions in Spain.* Deloitte.

Endres, H., Stoiber, K., & Wenzl, N. M. (2019). Managing digital transformation through hybrid business models. *The Journal of Business Strategy, 41*(6), 49–56. doi:10.1108/JBS-07-2019-0142

Fruitbook Magazine. (2020). *Dopo il Covid-19, i dark store potranno davvero essere il futuro del retail?* Fruitbook Magazine Online.

Hübner, A. H., Kuhn, H., Wollenburg, J., Towers, N., & Kotzab, H. (2016). Last mile fulfilment and distribution in omni-channel grocery retailing: A strategic planning framework. *International Journal of Retail & Distribution Management, 44*(3). Advance online publication. doi:10.1108/IJRDM-11-2014-0154

Istat. (2020). *Rapporto sul territorio 2020. Appendice*. Le geografie e le classificazioni territoriali usate nel rapporto.

Istat. (2020a). *22 Commercio interno e altri servizi*. Istat, Annuario Statistico Italiano 2020.

Istat. (2021). *Notizie sul commercio al dettaglio*. Sito ufficiale Istat.

Janjevic, M., & Winkenbach, M. (2020). Characterizing urban last-mile distribution strategies in mature and emerging e-commerce markets. *Transportation Research Part A, Policy and Practice, 133*, 133. doi:10.1016/j.tra.2020.01.003

Jocevski, M. (2020). Blurring the lines between physical and digital spaces: Business model innovation in retailing. *California Management Review, 63*(1), 99–117. doi:10.1177/0008125620953639

Kajalo, S., & Lindblom, A. (2015). Market orientation, entrepreneurial orientation and business performance among small retailers. *International Journal of Retail & Distribution Management, 43*(7), 580–596. doi:10.1108/IJRDM-04-2014-0044

Klepek, M., & Bauerová, R. (2020). Why do retail customers hesitate for shopping grocery online? *Technological and Economic Development of Economy, 26*(6), 1444–1462. doi:10.3846/tede.2020.13970

Li, F. (2020). The digital transformation of business models in the creative industries: A holistic framework and emerging trends. *Technovation, 92*, 102012. doi:10.1016/j.technovation.2017.12.004

Lim, S. F. W., Jin, X., & Srai, J. S. (2018). Consumer-driven e-commerce: A literature review, design framework, and research agenda on last-mile logistics models. *International Journal of Physical Distribution & Logistics Management, 48*(3), 308–332. doi:10.1108/IJPDLM-02-2017-0081

Lim, S. F. W., & Srai, J. S. (2018). Examining the anatomy of last-mile distribution in e- commerce omnichannel retailing. *International Journal of Operations & Production Management, 38*(9), 1735–1764. doi:10.1108/IJOPM-12-2016-0733

Liscia, R. (2020). *Consorzio Netcomm. Il lockdown triplica i Nuovi Consumatori Online in Italia tra gennaio e maggio*. https://www.consorzionetcomm.it/il-lockdown-triplica-i-nuovi-consumatori-online-in-italia-tra-gennaio-e-maggio

Mazareanu, E. (2020). *Last-mile logistics worldwide: statistics & facts*. Statista.

Mazareanu, E. (2020a). *What are your costumers more important wishes when it comes to last mile delivery?* Statista.

Meza-Peralta, K., Gonzalez-Feliu, J., Montoya-Torres, J. R., & Khodadad-Saryazdi, A. (2020, October). A unified typology of urban logistics spaces as interfaces for freight transport: A Systematic Literature Review. In Supply Chain Forum. *International Journal (Toronto, Ont.)*, *21*(4), 274–289.

Nault, B. R., & Rahman, M. S. (2019). Proximity to a traditional physical store: The effects of mitigating online disutility costs. *Production and Operations Management*, *28*(4), 1033–1051. doi:10.1111/poms.12957

Netcomm Forum Live. (2020). *La spesa alimentare online si consolida come abitudine dei consumatori italiani. Consorzio Netcomm - Il Commercio Digitale Italiano Nielsen e Politecnico di Milano (2020). Osservatorio Multicanalità. Politecnico di Milano*. School of Management.

Payaro, A., & Papa, A. R. (2021). Online Grocery Brick and Mortar Retailers. State of the Art in Italy, But Is It a Profitable Strategy? *Management*, *9*(1), 14–23.

Saghiri, S., Wilding, R., Mena, C., & Bourlakis, M. (2017). Toward a three-dimensional framework for omni-channel. *Journal of Business Research*, *77*, 53–67. doi:10.1016/j.jbusres.2017.03.025

Sbrana, R., & Gandolfo, A. (2007). *Contemporary retailing. Il governo dell'impresa commerciale moderna* (Vol. 1). Giappichelli.

Seitz, C., Pokrivčák, J., Tóth, M., & Plevný, M. (2017). Online grocery retailing in Germany: An explorative analysis. *Journal of Business Economics and Management*, *18*(6), 1243–1263. doi:10.3846/16111699.2017.1410218

Sousa, R., Horta, C., Ribeiro, R., & Rabinovich, E. (2020). How to serve online consumers in rural markets: Evidence-based recommendations. *Business Horizons*, *63*(3), 351–362. doi:10.1016/j.bushor.2020.01.007

Thomas, S., Vatavwala, S., & Sinha, P. K. (2017). *BigBasket. com: Redefining the Business Model.* Indian Institute of Management Ahmedabad.

Tongiani, M. G., Carfora, J., & Reut, A. (2019). Digital Marketing and Grocery Retailing Evidence From a Large Retailer in Italy and Belarus. In *Global Campaigning Initiatives for Socio-Economic Development* (pp. 168–189). IGI Global. doi:10.4018/978-1-5225-7937-3.ch010

Verhoef, P. C. (2021). Omni-channel retailing: Some reflections. *Journal of Strategic Marketing*, *29*(7), 608–616. doi:10.1080/0965254X.2021.1892163

Wiener, M., Hoßbach, N., & Saunders, C. (2018). Omnichannel businesses in the publishing and retailing industries: Synergies and tensions between coexisting online and offline business models. *Decision Support Systems*, *109*, 15–26. doi:10.1016/j.dss.2018.01.008

ADDITIONAL READING

Bilińska-Reformat, K., Kucharska, B., Twardzik, M., & Dolega, L. (2019). Sustainable development concept and creation of innovative business models by retail chains. *International Journal of Retail & Distribution Management*, *47*(1), 2–18. doi:10.1108/IJRDM-04-2017-0071

Eriksson, E., Norrman, A., & Kembro, J. (2019). Contextual adaptation of omni-channel grocery retailers' online fulfilment centres. *International Journal of Retail & Distribution Management*, *47*(12), 1232–1250. doi:10.1108/IJRDM-08-2018-0182

Hood, N., Urquhart, R., Newing, A., & Heppenstall, A. (2020). Sociodemographic and spatial disaggregation of e-commerce channel use in the grocery market in Great Britain. *Journal of Retailing and Consumer Services*, *55*, 102076. doi:10.1016/j.jretconser.2020.102076

Kembro, J. H., & Norrman, A. (2019). Warehouse configuration in omni-channel retailing: A multiple case study. *International Journal of Physical Distribution & Logistics Management*, *50*(5), 509–533. doi:10.1108/IJPDLM-01-2019-0034

KEY TERMS AND DEFINITIONS

Click and Collect: The degree of satisfaction provided by a company's goods or services.

Customer Review: The propensity to disseminate opinions on the products, services, or personality of a company among other consumers.

E-Tailing: The application of electronic commerce to the retailing sector.

Home Delivery: When the products purchased are delivered directly to the customer's home.

Proximity Logistics: The activities of the actors, systems, and rules that are established within a well-defined territorial jurisdiction.

Spatial Gap: When stores are physically distant from the consumer and the latter therefore has to travel long distances.

Urban Distribution Structure: Warehouse that manage the activities, goods, and sales strategies of a single or several retailers.

Chapter 5
The Outcomes of Online Browsing in Consumers:
Insights From Portugal's GenZ Consumers

Fabio Shimabukuro Sandes
Universidade Lusófona, Portugal

ABSTRACT

This chapter discusses the outcomes of online browsing for consumers, a behavior that is on the rise as social media and online content increased exponentially in the last year. An extensive literature review about browsing and its outcomes to consumer behavior, together with empirical data collected from 10 in-depth interviews with Generation Z consumers from Portugal, showcased that online browsing mainly produces positive outcomes, such as discovering new brands and products, increasing product knowledge and therefore improving consumer confidence in their purchase decision. Gen Z consumers from Portugal behave as expected, except that because they live in a more conservative and traditional context, they still have some barriers to online shopping and experience more traditional retail in their daily lives. However, the positive outcomes for online browsing remain the same, as consumers from this generation are digital natives.

INTRODUCTION

Consumers do all sorts of things online: they work, read the news, stay connected to their friends and family, and browse through various products and services. The unique characteristics of the online experience have been discussed in the literature, exploring how online customer experience differs from the shopping experience in traditional retail (Trevinal and Stenger, 2014), how online advertising entails different strategies for brands when compared to traditional advertising (Morgan-Thomas and Veloutsou, 2013), and how online communities impact brand's presence in the market (Kozinets et al., 2010; Arvidsson and Caliandro, 2016; Dessart, Veloutsou, and Morgan-Thomas, 2016). and online browsing is different than offline browsing (Rowley, 2001; Moe, 2003; Sandes, Komarova, and Botelho, 2020).

DOI: 10.4018/978-1-7998-9227-4.ch005

Anecdotal evidence suggests that online browsing is on the rise: the number of time consumers spend connected online has been increasing year over year, reaching an average of 7.5 hours per day in the US (Kemp, 2021). Among the online behavior, we highlight the access of two social media platforms directly related to online browsing: Instagram and Pinterest. Instagram was ranked as the 4th most accessed social media website in 2020 (Kemp, 2021), with about 500 million consumers interacting actively every day on their platform. On average, a consumer spends more than thirty minutes per day scrolling their feed and watching stories. Furthermore, according to a survey Instagram conducted with 4,508 users in 2018, 58% of respondents affirmed they were more interested in a product or brand they came across on Instagram.

Previous literature has shown that browsing is defined as a product search with no purchase intention (Bloch, Sherrell, and Ridgway, 1986; Bloch, Ridgway, and Sherrell, 1989) that consumers engage in for fun, as a recreational activity, or as learning, activity to leverage their knowledge about specific products they have a particular interest in (Bloch and Richins, 1983; Bloch, Sherrell, and Ridgway, 1986). As online browsing does not need previous planning and does not need physical displacement to occur (as it is mandatory in offline browsing), it is expected that online browsing occurs more intensively than offline browsing, possibly leading to different outcomes for consumers. An excellent example of how online browsing may affect consumer behavior is the work of Kozinets, Patterson, and Ashman (2017), where they conducted an elaborated analysis of how the sharing of images in social media platforms, such as Instagram, incentives and contributes to the formation of desire in consumers.

Pinterest is a social media known as the browsing social media because it is a shared online space where consumers store and share images they find while online browsing (Youn and Jin, 2017). With more than 200 million consumers using the platform (Kemp, 2021), Pinterest seems to be engaging consumers to use their tools to keep track of their browsing activities. During the COVID-19, where consumers spend most of their time at home, Pinterest reported an increase of 6.2% in their users' database, and even a more robust growth in European countries such as Greece (49%), Belgium (21%), France (15%), Germany (14%), and Portugal (8%). Pinterest is the third most popular social media platform in Portugal, right after Facebook and Instagram (Kemp, 2021).

However, it is interesting to notice that the largest growth amongst Pinterest users happened in Europe, a continent where the population is older when compared to other Continents. This may suggest that online browsing behavior is also growing in European countries, even though the population of these countries is older and tends to have less intimacy with online behaviors. The impacts of online browsing on consumer behavior is indeed a field to be explored by researchers, as few researchers address the outcomes of such behavior (Johnson et al., 2004; Moe and Yang, 2009; Sandes, Komarova, and Botelho, 2020), and one matter that might be worthy of further investigation is the impacts of the growth of online browsing behavior amongst consumers from a more traditional, offline context as European consumers. Therefore, the objective of this chapter is to contribute to the literature by presenting a discussion of the impacts of online browsing on consumer behavior amongst consumers from Portugal, the third country with the oldest population in the world (Kemp, 2021) and where Pinterest is one of the main social media channel used by consumers (Kemp, 2021).

LITERATURE REVIEW

Browsing is a topic of interest in many areas of research. Browsing entails scanning through products or information in leisure and casual way, at random. (Chang and Rice, 1993) As I will discuss later, the terms "casual," "leisure," and "random" are relevant parts of the definition of browsing when thinking about consumer behavior literature.

The multidisciplinary approach to browsing is one of the key aspects of this concept. Hjørland (2011) used browsing as a context to discuss the importance of assessing multiple theories of knowledge when discussing a concept. The author juxtaposed the dimensions and characteristics of browsing proposed in information science literature with the main findings in other fields. In addition, Hjørland (2011) built on the conceptualization proposed by Bates (2007), which states that when individuals are browsing, they (1) get a glimpse of what they are looking for, (2) often select or sample this object, (3) examine what they have found, and (4) conceptually acquire or abandon it. Browsing is a cognitive and behavioral expression of exploratory behavior, motivated by curiosity (Bates, 2007). However, the focus in this research was on the exploratory aspect of browsing; Hjørland (2011) criticized this as he stated that browsing may not be completely random but can also be used strategically. He argued that various theories could be used to navigate the concept, browsing can be used as an orientation strategy. He argued that "different people browse in different ways because they have different purposes and schemata or theories" (Hjørland, 2011, p. 600) and that individuals use their previous knowledge to navigate a series of possible paths when they are not sure which direction they should go. Thus, browsing can also be an orienting strategy that guides individuals in their search.

For marketing researchers, browsing has been discussed both as a distinctive concept, such as in the form of offline browsing (Bloch & Richins, 1983), and as a dimension or part of related concepts, such as window shopping (Rowley, 2001), ongoing search (Bloch, Sherrell, & Ridgway, 1986), retail therapy (Atalay & Meloy, 2011), and thrift shopping (Bardhi & Arnould, 2005). In the online context, browsing has been researched as part of a search strategy that consumers engage in when they conduct an exploratory, non-directed search (Moe, 2003; Ono *et al.*, 2012)

BROWSING AS A MULTIDIMENSIONAL FRAMEWORK

Browsing has been studied in various research areas, and this has been demonstrated by Chang and Rice (1993). They developed an extensive literature review on browsing as a broader category of behaviors and listed studies on browsing activities in different disciplines, such as library and information science (related to the search for information behavior), end-user information retrieval, and system design (related to behavior when performing searches), mass media audience studies (related to search behavior on media or entertainment), organizational communication (related to social browsing, and browsing for information about companies or organizations), wayfinding and environmental design (related to discussions about cognitive, perceptual, social, and physical processes of search behavior), and consumer behavior. They proposed a general model for organizing research on browsing, where consumers' behavior influences browsing, motivation, cognition, and resources they have available to browse, which leads them to engage in browsing behavior that can result in positive (e.g., serendipity – that is related to unexpected, good things - and learning) or negative (e.g., disorientation, overload) consequences.

Thus, browsing is a human behavior studied from various angles and is an activity individuals engage in for a range of motivations or impulses, and for various reasons—rather than only when they need to search for information (Bates, 2007). Nevertheless, most research on browsing has been conducted within the information search field. According to this discussion, browsing is one stage of information search behavior and is usually related to the early stage of search where scanning information takes place (Wilson, 2002; Moorthy, Ratchford, & Talukdar, 1997). Wilson (2002) suggested that browsing is a stage of information search during which individuals start to differentiate information they have found after scanning available information. According to Bates (2007), browsing is an iterative process of exploratory activities that may or may not lead to a desirable result and usually follows four steps: glimpse a field of vision; select an object or information to explore further; examine that object or information; finally, keep it or discard it. Browsing then continues to other new glimpses or ceases.

Browsing has also been extensively studied in end-user information retrieval and system design, as this concept helps explain how consumers navigate websites and collect, exchange, and offer information (Dames, Hirschfeld, Sackmann, Thielsch, 2019). In this area, researchers have mainly discussed the characteristics of websites that users consider when they browse. Recently, Dames et al. (2019) specifically discussed that users with directed goals (searching) versus non-directed goals (browsing) might perceive the aesthetics and content of websites differently. Researchers agree that browsing incorporates scanning, accessing, or just looking through different information or products without a defined or specific goal.

BROWSING IN THE CONSUMER BEHAVIOR LITERATURE

In the consumer behavior literature, Bloch and Richins (1983) published a seminal article on browsing, referring to as "shopping without a purpose." The authors defined browsing as an activity where consumers look for products without the intention to buy, for two main reasons: (1) to entertain themselves and (2) to collect information about a product in which they have a special interest (to become an expert about that product). The authors then defined consumers as browsers (consumers willing to engage in browsing activities) or nonbrowsers. They noted that browsing is positively related to product interest, actively looking for information about a product, obtaining knowledge about it, and engaging in word-of-mouth about it. According to the discussion about prepurchase search by Bloch et al. (1986), the presence of a goal to fulfill a specific need drives consumers' information-seeking and -processing activities, which aids their decision-making during the buying process. The lack of purpose in browsing primarily differentiates it from the prepurchase search, where consumers have the objective of obtaining knowledge that will allow them to make better purchase decisions (Engel & Roger, 1978). Bloch et al. (1986) gave us an example of browsing consumers in a shopping mall, walking in and out of stores without looking at any specific products, looking through the options these stores have to offer. I refer to this activity as offline browsing, as it happens in a physical store.

In online browsing, some studies have considered the phenomenon mostly as part of the search behavior consumers engage in online and classify the behavior as browsing when consumers do not have a specific goal or are not intending to buy specific products. Moe (2003) discussed the three main behaviors consumers engage in online stores as buying, searching, or browsing, and evaluated in-store navigational behavior in consumers to propose a typology of shopping patterns to understand purchase behavior better using clickstream information. Moe divided search behavior into direct and exploratory, counterpointing with the immediate or future purchasing horizon. Based thereon, she proposed four types of search behavior for consumers online: direct buying (DB), when consumers are goal-directed and looking for immediate purchase; search deliberation (SD), when consumers are goal-directed and looking for future purchases; hedonic browsing (HD), when consumers are searching in an exploratory manner for immediate purchase; and knowledge building (KB), when consumers are searching in an exploratory manner for future purchase. Rowley (2001) proposed that browsing is a relevant behavior to observe in consumers online. It offers a possibility for firms to create product and relationship opportunities with existing and potential customers. However, later consumer behavior literature observed that browsing is part of search behavior and that the discussions were centered mainly on the pathways and clickstreams consumers follow online, and how these clickstreams can be used in models to understand and predict consumer behavior online, where browsing is conceptualized as exploratory, non-directed navigation (Huang, Lurie, and Mitra, 2009; Laing and Royle, 2013; Anderl, Schumann, and Kunz, 2016).

The concept of browsing has also evolved into various concepts within the consumer behavior literature. The entertainment dimension of shopping comprises two concepts that contain elements of browsing in their definitions: window shopping, which is browsing to collect information about a product that the consumer is considering buying in the immediate or long-term future (Rowley, 2001); and retail therapy (Atalay & Meloy, 2011; Rick, Pereira, & Burson, 2014), which is when consumers browse for products to buy to improve their mood. In both window shopping and retail therapy, consumers browse for buying things to satisfy their need to shop. Window shopping is an offline concept, as it includes looking at the window in a physical store. Retail therapy does not have this limitation, as a shopping spree can happen either online or offline. What differentiates these concepts from browsing is the intensity of purchase intention. While in browsing, the purchase intention may vary from low to high, the purchase intention can only be high in window shopping, and consumers are browsing what to buy. In retail therapy, the purchase intention is even higher because the thrill of buying drives purchasing behavior.

Consumer behavior literature has also discussed the thrill of getting a good deal (Schindler, 1989; Bardhi and Arnould, 2005; Kim and Kim, 2008). This is also part of the browsing concept, as consumers browse opportunities to find good deals. Instead of searching for a product or a service out of curiosity, consumers looking for a good deal seek good sale opportunities. Concepts related to the thrill of getting bargains have been referred to in consumer behavior literature as thrift shopping (Bardhi and Arnould, 2005). As mentioned above, the thrill of finding discounts has also been discussed as part of couponing (Bawa and Shoemaker, 1987) or e-couponing (Kang, Hahn, and Fortin, 2006; Dickinger and Kleinjnen, 2008), which is a form of compulsive behavior that comprises browsing for discount coupons either online or offline. The informational dimension of browsing can also be transformed into a specific behavior: ongoing search. Bloch, Sherrell, and Ridgway (1986) proposed that ongoing search is motivated by consumers' interest in a specific product or service, for which these consumers are constantly looking for information.

As online browsing is not necessarily related to the consumption of products and services, the outcome of browsing is not the purchase of a product. Instead, previous literature suggested the outcome of browsing to be an increase in product knowledge, the discovery of new brands and products, and desire for products (Moe, 2003; Johnson *et al.*, 2004; Kozinets *et al.*, 2010), but the literature is silent about the impacts of online browsing in consumer online shopping behavior: as online browsing increases consumers' product knowledge and their access to new brands and products, it is possible to expect that online browsing also influences consumers to increase their online shopping behavior, as they have more access to products and brands. This is one of the outcomes that is going to be discussed in this chapter.

THE ENTERTAINMENT ASPECT OF BROWSING

As Bloch and Richins (1983) noted, one of the reasons for browsing is to have fun; this can be divided into two categories: the fun of getting a bargain or a good deal; and the fun of shopping itself. The former addresses the drive to find a smart buy (Schindler, 1989) and obtain value for money; the latter addresses the need to shop (Holbrook & Hirschman, 1982). For each of these, related concepts have been discussed in the consumer behavior literature. For example, the search for good deals entails the concept of arousal from getting a bargain (Schindler, 1989), couponing (Bawa & Shoemaker, 1987), or electronic couponing (Dickinger & Kleinjnen, 2008), where consumers engage in searching for discounts—shopping conditions that lead them to find good deals in their shopping routine. These concepts incorporate browsing as a stage in the process of scanning for deals. What differentiates couponing from browsing is coupons' key role in browsing (offline or online) behavior. In couponing, consumers browse coupons to find deals and not the products available per se. A related concept discussed in the literature is thrift shopping (Bardhi & Arnould, 2005; Schindler, 1989), which pertains to the thrill consumers experience when they feel they have made a good purchase decision, or a smart buy. Here, consumers browse for opportunities to buy things that are on sale. This concept is similar to couponing, with the difference that in thrift shopping, consumers look for bargains in a more specific manner, focused on products of interest, and engaging more actively in browsing via stores, malls, or websites for the best options available at that time (Schindler, 1989), independent of whether they have coupons. In couponing, the search is more focused on the availability of promotional coupons (Bawa & Shoemaker, 1987; Ieva, De Canio, & Ziliani, 2016). Thrift shopping can happen either online or offline and differs from browsing (either online or offline) because what drives the browsing behavior is the possibility of finding good deals. In the offline context, instead of browsing an entire store, a thrift shopper will go straight to the sales rack. In the online context, they will do the same—that is, they will click to find sales and focus their browsing on that part of the online store.

The hedonic aspect of online browsing concerning consumers' perceptions of products and services is more prominent in products with which consumers are involved, seeking an experience from online shopping, rather than engaging in goal-directed online buying behavior (Wolfinbarger and Gilly, 2001). The classification of hedonic and utilitarian shopping has often been used in literature about browsing: a browsing experience is utilitarian when it is related to buying products where the search goal is directed (Park *et al.*, 2012), mission-oriented (Kesari and Atulkar, 2016), or focused on the search for specific information (Huang, Lurie and Mitra, 2009); it is classified as hedonic when the focus of the browsing is on products with which consumers are involved (Kesari and Atulkar, 2016), where information provided by experienced users is also relevant for browsing (Huang, Lurie and Mitra, 2009).

Mathwick and Rigdon (2004) proposed that online information search about a product can be transformed into a positive experience, bringing joy to consumers. This transformation is moderated by product involvement and is also related to the skill consumers have to browse information. If their skill to collect and process information is sufficient, and product involvement is present, they get a positive feeling from browsing; however, if skills are insufficient, it could lead to a negative perception of the browsing experience, creating feelings of anxiety.

THE INFORMATIONAL ASPECT OF BROWSING

One of the key aspects of browsing is product involvement, which has been defined as "an ongoing commitment on the part of the consumer concerning thoughts, feelings, and behavioral response to a product category" (Quester & Lin Lim, 2003, p. 24). As Bloch and Richins (1983) identified, consumers may browse to become better informed about products or topics, so information seeking is one of the motivators of browsing. Some years later, Bloch et al. (1986) proposed the concept of ongoing search; this is related to browsing and entails gathering more information about specific products, and was defined by Bloch et al. as "search activities that are independent of specific needs or decisions" (p. 120). Specifically, the concept refers to consumers' ongoing interest in searching for information about a product they are involved in. Consumers engage in ongoing browsing for such products, frequently looking for information about new releases and discussions about the product with specialists, in magazines, or at tradeshows. The search is constant, unrelated to the need to buy, but pertains to knowing more about the product. Bloch et al. (1986) acknowledged that the line that separates ongoing search and prepurchase search is blurred, as the decision to buy may arise during the ongoing search, but that the motives for the search differ. Rather than deciding to buy, consumers who engage in ongoing search do so for hedonic reasons. Because of their involvement with the product, they experience fun and pleasure from acquiring more information and retaining information for future use. What makes the ongoing search a distinct behavior from offline browsing is that the former is conceptualized as a browsing activity where product involvement "is enduring in character" (Bloch et al., 1986, p. 120), which is not part of the concept of offline browsing.

Consumers may also browse for information when they are uncertain about a specific brand or product characteristics so that their goal is to mitigate their uncertainty. Moorthy et al. (2016) argued that consumer browsing depends on whether there is relative brand uncertainty. The informational aspect of browsing may also relate to minimizing utilitarian, goal-directed browsing (Ozkara, Ozmen, and Kim, 2016).

THE EXPLORATORY ASPECT OF BROWSING

One characteristic that is central in browsing is its exploratory nature. Even in the definition of browsing in other disciplines, the exploratory nature of browsing is a key aspect, as consumers engage in it to understand what is being offered in a more experiential manner (Pace, 2004). Scanning is part of the exploratory behavior in browsing, where consumers peruse the available options to drive their navigation (Moorthy, Ratchford, and Talukdar, 1997; Sismeiro and Bucklin, 2004). Bates (2007) considered browsing as the cognitive and behavioral expression of an individual's exploratory behavior.

Browsing is an exploratory way of looking for something. It includes scanning behavior and mixing it with previous knowledge about a topic, the presence of a purpose or objective, and search criteria (Chang and Rice, 1993). COB is exploratory for both experiential and goal-directed consumers (Zheng *et al.*, 2019). For the former, the experience of visiting a website and exploring products is part of the browsing experience, while for the latter exploratory behavior focuses on finding ways to optimize the browsing experience.

METHODOLOGY

A qualitative methodological approach is proposed to explore the possible impacts of online browsing behavior in Portuguese consumers, composed of in-depth interviews with ten consumers from generation Z (born between 1995 and 2010) in Portugal, one of the countries with a more significant than average growth in Pinterest users. Generation Z consumers were chosen because they are considered social media natives (Gazzola et al., 2020), obliterating any technological knowledge issue regarding online browsing behavior.

The interviews started with a pre-defined script with the outcomes of offline browsing existing in literature, such as an increase in product knowledge, unplanned and impulsive buying, positive and negative emotions related to the browsing activities (Bloch and Richins, 1983; Bloch, Sherrell and Ridgway, 1986; Moe, 2003). The interviews used the iterative process suggested by Arsel (2017), where the script was constantly reviewed and adapted for each interviewee and included or excluded topics. These interviews followed a phenomenological approach (Thompson, Locander, and Pollio, 1989), where interviewees' perception is the center of the analysis. Table 1 presents the demographical information about interviewees. Interviewees were all Undergraduate students from Portugal, 23 years of age, on average.

Table 1. Demographic information about interviewees

Interviewee	Gender	Age	Profession	Country
Ana	Female	24	Undergraduate student	Portugal
Sofia	Female	21	Undergraduate student	Portugal
Bruno	Male	21	Undergraduate student	Portugal
Renato	Male	22	Undergraduate student	Portugal
Emanuel	Male	26	Undergraduate student	Portugal
Catarina	Female	25	Undergraduate student	Portugal
Margarida	Female	22	Undergraduate student	Portugal
Carlos	Male	22	Undergraduate student	Portugal
Melissa	Female	21	Undergraduate student	Portugal
Monica	Female	22	Undergraduate student	Portugal

RESULTS

After analyzing the content of all the ten interviews, it was possible to group them into ten main topics that are presented in this discussion:

- **Motivation for browsing**: Interviewees responded they mostly start online browsing unintentionally, usually prompted by social media, especially Instagram, where they are triggered to click through pages of products, stores, and brands to spend time online browsing unintentionally. Product interest drives their decision to click and start online browsing: the interviewees said they tend to click only on products they are interested in or are curious about. Some interviewees mentioned that they engage in online browsing intentionally as well. The interviewees said that they engage in it when they need to relax or distract themselves before starting an activity or right after a lunch break. Only a few respondents said they browse the apps or websites of specific stores daily, suggesting that online browsing occurs more incidentally than intentionally.

- **Offline browsing versus online browsing**: In this topic, interviewees discussed the characteristics of offline browsing behavior, such as the presence of salespeople, which inhibits browsing behavior as they reported feeling pressured by salespeople to buy things and do not feel comfortable browsing through products the way they want to. In addition, in offline browsing, it is necessary to plan the time needed to get to the mall (or store) and return home or to work. For that reason, offline browsing is mainly intentional. Generation Z consumers often rely on the internet for most – if not all – of their activities (Cooke and Zubcsek, 2017), but in the case of Gen Z consumers from Portugal interviewed, that is not always the case. Even though they reported to spend most of their days connected online, they still like going to the shops or malls to spend time with friends, and offline browsing is a planned activity that they keep on doing. As interviews were held during the lockdown imposed due to the COVID-19 pandemic, respondents showed some emotional connection to offline browsing as something they used to do before the pandemic and that they miss doing it, suggesting that offline browsing is a leisure and appreciated activity in Portugal, even for Gen Z consumers.
- **Online browsing characteristics**: The extensive selection of products and brands were mentioned as a key factor that leads interviewees to engage in online browsing, especially when considering the context of Portuguese consumers. Throughout the internet, these consumers access companies and brands from all over Europe that are not physically present in Portugal, and respondents say this is important. The convenience of online shopping is not viewed as a major advantage for some Portuguese consumers. Most respondents say that in most cases, they choose the option to collect in the store option, so they avoid the expensive shipping costs and do not need to worry if there will be people at home to receive the delivery. Only a few buildings have doorman services available in Portugal, and consumers must be home to receive their shipments.
- **The entertainment function of browsing**: Almost all interviewees agreed that browsing is fun, and it is an activity they tend to do so in their leisure time. Online browsing is often mentioned as something they do to pass the time, relax their minds, or between tasks.
- **Resistance to online shopping**: It was possible to see that even Gen Z Portuguese consumers (the consumers we interviewed) are resistant to shop for everything online, especially products they feel the need to try on, touch, and test. There is also the positive perception of physical retail stores and malls, seeing them as recreational areas. Indeed, in 2021, several large stores sell books, CDs, and DVDs (i.e., Bertrand and Fnac) all over Portugal, going in the opposite direction of complete digitalization of these types of stores in the rest of the world.
- **Impulsive buying and browsing**: An interesting characteristic that differentiates online from offline browsing pertains to impulsive buying (Sandes, Komarova, and Botelho, 2020). Interviewees reported that they conduct most impulsive buying offline because, in offline browsing, they have less control over the experience, undergo a multisensory experience in the store, feel pressured to buy by the presence of salespeople, and have only a short time in which to decide which product to buy. During online browsing, consumers have control over adding and excluding products from their shopping cart and have time to think about whether they will buy the product. Some interviewees mentioned that they have to stop and type in delivery and payment information gives them time to think about whether they want to buy the product, which is when they decide against the purchase.

Gen Z Portuguese consumers mentioned that they act impulsively on websites where they can purchase low-cost products. Almost all interviews mentioned three websites: Shein, Alibaba, and Vinted. On these websites, they can purchase products that cost up to five euros without thinking. Some mention that they even have a group of friends to buy this kind of product together to share the shipping costs.

- **Increase in Product knowledge**: This is the main positive outcome from browsing, whether online or offline. Interviewees mentioned learning about products through browsing. After browsing, they know more about the characteristics of products and can make better purchase decisions. Some mentioned feeling they become specialists in specific products they have browsed for. The interviewees appreciate this acquired knowledge and thus attribute positive feelings to the browsing experience.
- **Other positive outcomes of browsing**: Interviewees mentioned other positive outcomes of browsing. Discovering new brands or products is a very positive outcome from browsing, especially in online browsing, where interviewees say they found new products, services, and brands throughout browsing. Most identified they were triggered by social media ads or something that captured their attention when seeing posts from friends or digital influencers. And then started to research them. Two interviewees mentioned that browsing inspires them either for their professional careers, as they came across brands or products that helped them propose new things in their career.
- **Conscious consumption**: Interviewees mentioned the topic of conscious consumption spontaneously, without being prompted. This concern relates to buying too much. Interviewees often mentioned wanting to reduce their consumption because of the environment. One possible explanation for this is that the script made interviewees think about their browsing behavior and consumption patterns, raising the question of conscious consumption in their minds. Also, as we interviewed only Gen Z consumers, the relevance of environmental matters is always high (Giovannini, Xu, and Thomas, 2015).
- **Impacts of COVID-19 pandemic**: All interviewees mentioned they have completely changed their shopping and browsing habits due to the COVID-19 pandemic. As they could not go to physical stores for a long time, they had to start to find ways to buy everything they needed and most of the things they had to buy online. They also mention having experienced shopping at least one type of item online for the first time. Most of them were clothes and shoes. Gen Z consumers mentioned that most of these habits they learned during COVID-19 are likely to stay because they overcame their fears and prejudice against online shopping. Those who would not keep buying online prefer to do them offline (because they like the process, or they feel more confident in physical stores).

Altogether, it was possible to notice that Gen Z Portuguese consumers perceived online browsing as something positive. The main outcome from online browsing is that it empowers consumers as it offers them new perspectives of brands, products, and services, and it is an activity that allows consumers to understand the characteristics of a product or a brand, collecting information they recognize as valuable and relevant about the brands and products they browse for. This information help consumers make better purchase decisions and support them to monitor the brands' positioning on various matters such as diversity, inclusion, topics that this generation appreciate, and expect that brands and companies they use in their daily lives (Gazzola *et al.*, 2020), posit a positive attitude towards these matters.

Particularly in Portugal, it was interesting to notice that its Generation Z consumers live in a context where the population and its habits are more conservative and traditional. Portugal is one of the countries with the oldest population in the world (Kamp, 2021). This characteristic is reflected in more conservative consumer habits, where physical stores still play a prominent role in the retail market. Large chain stores such as Bertrand (who owns the world's oldest bookstore still running) and FNAC offer consumers the experience of traditional offline retail stores, which is rare to find in other non-conservative countries, such as The United States and Brazil. By living in this more traditional context, Gen Z consumers in Portugal still appreciate going to physical stores and rely on them much more, if compared to a Gen Z consumer from less conservative cultures.

MANAGEMENT IMPLICATIONS

The results of this study helps to better comprehend how browsing is a relevant part of online behavior as it allows consumers to gather information about products and services, discover new products and brands, and feel more confident of their choices as consumers. As our study focused on consumers from Portugal, a country where tradition is valued and consumers are expected to behave with more caution when browsing and buying online, it was interesting to notice that even for these consumers these positive outcomes of browsing are still valid, as consumers engage in online browsing to gather information and feel more confident in their roles as consumers. They do seem, however, to expect to find some kind of experience in their offline behavior, as they are used to go to stores as a leisure and familiar activity, which may help to understand why large bookstores and wholesalers like Fnac, Bertrand, and Worten were able to keep most of their stores open and running in Portugal, even after the COVID-19 pandemic.

LIMITATIONS OF THIS STUDY

As the methodology used in this study was an exploratory, qualitative study, and our empirical data was collected in a relative small sample, generalizations should be made with caution. The aim of this study was to explore the topic and offer some insights about anecdotal evidence and findings in the literature about the relevance of online behavior for GenZ consumers. As we chose to use Portugal, a small, traditional and conservative country from Europe, readers should also bare in mind that this context may have some characteristics that influence consumers´ perception, and should therefore be taken into account.

RECOMMENDATION FOR FUTURE STUDIES

This was an exploratory study about the impacts of browsing in consumers´ online behavior, and one of the most relevant outcomes of this study was to offer direction for future investigation on this topic. Three topics are highlighted as suggestions for future research. The first topic to be further explored by researchers is the role of browsing in helping consumers feel more confident as consumers: as the empirical data suggested, consumers acquire product knowledge, and thus feel more confident due to browsing, but it would be important to investigate to what extend this effect exists, and to which conditions they happen: would all type of browsing help consumers acquire product knowledge, or any specific condition is necessary? These are examples of research questions that will help managers and researchers better understand the extension of this positive outcome of online browsing. The second topic to be explored is how product interest is related to consumers´ pleasure in browsing: does the browsing need to be for specific products to have an entertainment effect to consumers, do they need to have a special interest for a product to feel pleasure to browse for this product? And the third topic that may offer a valuable contribution is how online browsing may help new brands to be discovered by consumers. As consumers seem to be engaging more actively in online browsing, and our empirical data - and anecdotal evidence - suggest that consumers do report to find new brands through intentional or incidental browsing, it is important to further investigate in which conditions consumers are more open to get in touch with information or publications from new brands and products, as it will be a valuable input for brand managers everywhere.

REFERENCES

Anderl, E., Schumann, J. H., & Kunz, W. (2016). Helping Firms Reduce Complexity in Multichannel Online Data: A New Taxonomy-Based Approach for Customer Journeys. *Journal of Retailing. New York University*, *92*(2), 185–203. doi:10.1016/j.jretai.2015.10.001

Arsel, Z. (2017). Asking questions with reflexive focus: Atutorial on designing and conducting interviews. *The Journal of Consumer Research*, *44*(4), 939–948. doi:10.1093/jcr/ucx096

Arvidsson, A., & Caliandro, A. (2016). Brand public. *The Journal of Consumer Research*, *42*(5), 727–748. doi:10.1093/jcr/ucv053

Atalay, A. S., & Meloy, M. G. (2011). Retail therapy: A strategic effort to improve mood. *Psychology and Marketing*, *28*(6), 638–659. doi:10.1002/mar.20404

Bardhi, F., & Arnould, E. J. (2005). Thrift shopping: Combining utilitarian thrift and hedonic treat benefits. *Journal of Consumer Behaviour*, *4*(4), 223–233. doi:10.1002/cb.12

Bates, M. J. (2007). What is browsing - Really? A model drawing from behavioural science research. *Information Research*, *12*(4).

Bawa, K., & Shoemaker, R. W. (1987). The Coupon-Prone Consumer: Some Findings Based on Purchase Behavior Across Product Classes. *Journal of Marketing*, *51*(4), 99–110. doi:10.1177/002224298705100409

Bloch, P. H., Ridgway, N. M., & Sherrell, D. L. (1989). Extending the concept of shopping: An investigation of browsing activity. *Journal of the Academy of Marketing Science*, *17*(1), 13–21. doi:10.1007/BF02726349

Bloch, P. H., Sherrell, D. L., & Ridgway, N. M. (1986). Consumer Search: An Extended Framework. *The Journal of Consumer Research*, *13*(1), 119. doi:10.1086/209052

Chang, S.-J. S. J., & Rice, R. E. (1993). *Browsing: A multidimensional framework*. Annual Reviews of Information Science and Technology.

Cooke, A. D. J., & Zubcsek, P. P. (2017). The Connected Consumer: Connected Devices and the Evolution of Customer Intelligence. *Journal of the Association for Consumer Research*, *2*(2), 164–178. doi:10.1086/690941

Dames, H., Hirschfeld, G., Sackmann, T., & Thielsch, M. T. (2019). Searching vs. Browsing—The Influence of Consumers' Goal Directedness on Website Evaluations. *Interacting with Computers*, *31*(1), 95–112. doi:10.1093/iwc/iwz006

Dessart, L., Veloutsou, C., & Morgan-Thomas, A. (2016). Capturing consumer engagement: Duality, dimensionality and measurement. *Journal of Marketing Management*, *32*(5-6), 399–426. doi:10.1080/0267257X.2015.1130738

Dickinger, A., & Kleinjnen, M. (2008). Coupons going wireless: Determinants of consumer intentions to redeem mobile coupons. *Journal of Interactive Marketing*, *22*(3), 23–39. doi:10.1002/dir.20115

Engel, J. F., & Roger, D. (1978). Consumer Behavior. The Dryden Press.

Gazzola, P., Pavione, E., Pezzetti, R., & Grechi, D. (2020). Trends in the fashion industry. The perception of sustainability and circular economy: A gender/generation quantitative approach. *Sustainability (Switzerland)*, *12*(7), 1–19. doi:10.3390u12072809

Hjørland, B. (2011). The importance of theories of knowledge: Browsing as an example. *Journal of the American Society for Information Science and Technology*, *62*(3), 594–603. doi:10.1002/asi.21480

Holbrook, M. B., & Hirschman, E. C. (1982). The experiential aspects of consumption: Consumer fantasies, feelings, and fun. *The Journal of Consumer Research*, *9*(2), 132–140. doi:10.1086/208906

Huang, P., Lurie, N. H., & Mitra, S. (2009). Searching for experience on the web: An empirical examination of consumer behavior for search and experience goods. *Journal of Marketing*, *73*(2), 55–69. doi:10.1509/jmkg.73.2.55

Ieva, M., De Canio, F., & Ziliani, C. (2018). Daily deal shoppers: What drives social couponing? *Journal of Retailing and Consumer Services*, *40*, 299–303. doi:10.1016/j.jretconser.2017.03.005

Johnson, E. J., Moe, W. W., Fader, P. S., Bellman, S., & Lohse, G. L. (2004). On the Depth and Dynamics of Online Search Behavior. *Management Science*, *50*(3), 299–308. doi:10.1287/mnsc.1040.0194

Kang, H., Hahn, M., Fortin, D. R., Hyun, Y. J., & Eom, Y. (2006). Effects of Perceived Behavioral Control on the Consumer Usage Intention of E-coupons. *Psychology and Marketing*, *23*(10), 841–864. doi:10.1002/mar.20136

Kemp, S. (2021). *Digital 2021: Global Overview Report*. Hootsuite. Available at: https://datareportal.com/reports/digital-2021-singapore

Kesari, B., & Atulkar, S. (2016). Satisfaction of mall shoppers: A study on perceived utilitarian and hedonic shopping values. *Journal of Retailing and Consumer Services. Elsevier*, *31*, 22–31. doi:10.1016/j.jretconser.2016.03.005

Kim, H. Y., & Kim, Y. K. (2008). Shopping enjoyment and store shopping modes: The moderating influence of chronic time pressure. *Journal of Retailing and Consumer Services*, *15*(5), 410–419. doi:10.1016/j.jretconser.2007.10.003

Kozinets, R., Patterson, A., & Ashman, R. (2017). Networks of desire: How technology increases our passion to consume. *The Journal of Consumer Research*, *43*(5), 659–682.

Kozinets, R. V., De Valck, K., Wojnicki, A. C., & Wilner, S. J. S. (2010). Networked narratives: Understanding word-of-mouth marketing in online communities. *Journal of Marketing*, *74*(2), 71–89. doi:10.1509/jm.74.2.71

Laing, A., & Royle, J. (2013). Bookselling online: An examination of consumer behaviour patterns. *Publishing Research Quarterly*, *29*(2), 110–127. doi:10.100712109-013-9318-3

Mathwick, C., & Rigdon, E. (2004). Play, Flow, and the Online Search Experience. *The Journal of Consumer Research*, *31*(2), 324–332. doi:10.1086/422111

Moe, W. W. (2003). Buying, Searching, or Browsing: Differentiating Between Online Shoppers Using In-Store Navigational Clickstream. *Journal of Consumer Psychology*, *13*(1–2), 29–39. doi:10.1207/153276603768344762

Moe, W. W., & Yang, S. (2009). Inertial disruption: The impact of a new competitive entrant on online consumer search. *Journal of Marketing*, *73*(1), 109–121. doi:10.1509/jmkg.73.1.109

Moorthy, S., Ratchford, B. T., & Talukdar, D. (1997). Consumer Information Search Revisited: Theory and Empirical Analysis. *The Journal of Consumer Research*, *23*(4), 263–277. doi:10.1086/209482

Morgan-Thomas, A., & Veloutsou, C. (2013). Beyond technology acceptance: Brand relationships and online brand experience. *Journal of Business Research*, *66*(1), 21–27. doi:10.1016/j.jbusres.2011.07.019

Ono, A., Nakamura, A., Okuno, A., & Sumikawa, M. (2012). Consumer Motivations in Browsing Online Stores with Mobile Devices. *International Journal of Electronic Commerce*, *16*(4), 153–178. doi:10.2753/JEC1086-4415160406

Ozkara, B. Y., Ozmen, M., & Kim, J. W. (2016). Exploring the relationship between information satisfaction and flow in the context of consumers' online search. Computers in Human Behavior, 63, 844–859. doi:10.1016/j.chb.2016.06.038

Pace, S. (2004). A grounded theory of the flow experiences of web users. *International Journal of Human-Computer Studies*, *60*(3), 327–363. doi:10.1016/j.ijhcs.2003.08.005

Park, E. J., Kim, E. Y., Funches, V. M., & Foxx, W. (2012). Apparel product attributes, web browsing, and e-impulse buying on shopping websites. *Journal of Business Research. Elsevier Inc.*, *65*(11), 1583–1589. doi:10.1016/j.jbusres.2011.02.043

Quester, P., & Lin Lim, A. (2003). Product involvement/brand loyalty: Is there a link? *Journal of Product and Brand Management*, *12*(1), 22–38. doi:10.1108/10610420310463117

Rick, S. I., Pereira, B., & Burson, K. A. (2014). The benefits of retail therapy: Making purchase decisions reduces residual sadness. *Journal of Consumer Psychology*, *24*(3), 373–380. doi:10.1016/j.jcps.2013.12.004

Rowley, J. (2001). "Window" shopping and browsing opportunities in cyberspace. *Journal of Consumer Behaviour*, *1*(4), 369–378. doi:10.1002/cb.81

Sandes, F. S., Komarova, Y., & Botelho, D. (2020). Consumer Online Browsing: distinctive consumer behavior in marketing literature. *American Marketing Association Summer Conference.*

Schindler, R. (1989). The excitement of getting a bargain: Some hypotheses concerning the origins and effects of smart-shopper feelings. *Advances in Consumer Research. Association for Consumer Research (U. S.), 16*(2), 447–453. doi:10.100710603-011-9158-5

Sismeiro, C., & Bucklin, R. E. (2004). Modeling purchase behavior at an E-commerce Web site: A task-completion approach. *JMR, Journal of Marketing Research, 41*(3), 306–323. doi:10.1509/jmkr.41.3.306.35985

Thompson, C. J., Locander, W. B., & Pollio, H. R. (1989). Putting consumer experience back into consumer research: The philosophy and method of existential-phenomenology. *The Journal of Consumer Research, 16*(2), 133–146. doi:10.1086/209203

Trevinal, A. M., & Stenger, T. (2014). Toward a conceptualization of the online shopping experience. *Journal of Retailing and Consumer Services, 21*(3), 314–326. doi:10.1016/j.jretconser.2014.02.009

Wilson, T. D. (2002). Information behaviour: An interdisciplinary perspective. *Information Processing & Management*. Advance online publication. doi:10.1016/S0306-4573(97)00028-9

Wolfinbarger, M., & Gilly, M. C. (2001). Shopping Online for Freedom, Control, and Fun. *California Management Review, 43*(2), 33–55. https://www.csulb.edu/~mwolfin. doi:10.2307/41166074

Youn, S., & Jin, S. V. (2017). Reconnecting with the past in social media: The moderating role of social influence in nostalgia marketing on Pinterest. *Journal of Consumer Behaviour, 16*(6), 565–576. doi:10.1002/cb.1655

Zheng, X., Men, J., Yang, F., & Gong, X. (2019). Understanding impulse buying in mobile commerce: An investigation into hedonic and utilitarian browsing. *International Journal of Information Management. Elsevier, 48*(February), 151–160. doi:10.1016/j.ijinfomgt.2019.02.010

Chapter 6
Digitalization and Small Retailers:
New Opportunities – Case Study: Livramento Municipal Market

Duarte Xara-Brasil
Instituto Politécnico de Setúbal, Portugal

Leonor Vacas de Carvalho
https://orcid.org/0000-0001-8065-0932
Universidade de Évora, Portugal

ABSTRACT

In this chapter, the authors discuss the impact that the uses of digital marketing tools had on the performance of small food retailers in a municipal market in Portugal as a result of the challenges imposed by the pandemic situation of COVID-19. They developed a case study with the use of quantitative and qualitative methodologies seeking a more holistic view of the situation given the scarcity of research on this type of retail format. It is concluded that the experience and resilience of these retailers allowed them to quickly adapt to the requirements of the most basic digital marketing tools, namely social networks, and that these had some impact on their business in terms of sales and reputation. However, the small size of these retailers and their limited academic training has in many cases reduced the possibility of a systemic view of their marketing management and digital social networks.

INTRODUCTION

Since March 2020, the Portuguese Governmental Authorities, declared several states of emergency and restrictions over coronavirus outbreak. As a result of the spread of COVID-19, measures were taken that severely restricted the movement of people and the economic activity of many companies. In the city centers that are more frequented by a fluctuating population that includes tourists, workers and visitors, the almost total absence of people meant that, at a glance, economic agents were forced

DOI: 10.4018/978-1-7998-9227-4.ch006

to consider alternative ways of interacting with their public that they greatly reduced their travel, due to legal impediments and fear of exposure to possible infection. It is becoming challenging for most businesses across the world to keep their financial wheels rolling, given reduced revenues and the high level of uncertain (Verma, 2020).

This situation that has been experienced since March 2020 has had a major impact on food retailers, regardless of their size. For smaller stores, the situation was particularly challenging: their physical conditions – reduced sales areas, few possibilities for sufficient distance between people and fewer financial resources – and the characteristics of most of its promoters – older and more vulnerable people, with less digital skills and often without great investment capacity – would make people fear devastating consequences. In fact, we observed innovative responses everywhere: many entrepreneurs quickly adapted their business practices, improving their retailing-mix, providing an adequate response to their client's expectation, and overlapping some very relevant constraints.

This study seeks to understand the changes implemented by small retailers in their way of communicating and interacting with customers due to the COVID-19 pandemic, in order to contribute to the improvement of these retailers' marketing strategies.

BACKGROUND

The retail food trade has changed significantly in recent decades: the large super and hypermarket brands have conquered a very considerable share of this market: in 2020, in Portugal the large hyper and supermarkets held 49.7% of the market and the small food outlets only 17.5% (NielsenIQ, 2021). Small businesses and municipal markets, often located in the centers of large cities, are exposed to very diverse challenges: (1) the emergence of new operators, with very competitive offers, greater convenience and variety of products and services (2) the physical expansion of cities and the removal of many inhabitants to new residential neighborhoods, far from historical urban centers and its local retailers, a situation that is aggravated in many cities with the constraints of access to the center, due to the intense traffic, the difficulties in parking and the growing pressure to reduce car traffic in many city centers (3) the aging and little education of shopkeepers and their difficulty in adapting to new technologies and management methods. The Municipal Markets have also been losing part of their relevance, due to the difficulty in competing with the big retail brands, the desertification of the city centers where they are usually located and the lack of innovation, communication and commercial aggressiveness (Xara-Brasil et al., 2021).

Many traditional retailers have been able to develop a successful economic activity, due to the existence of strong relationships with their customers, sometimes developed over decades, capable of accumulating great experience and know-how, creating very solid relationships of trust, loyalty and even affectivity (Mullis & Kim, 2014; Khan et al., 2020). Geographical proximity and the existence of a differentiated and authentic range of products are also highly valued aspects for many customers at these points of sale (Skallerud & Wien, 2019). There are also government programs to support small traders in city centers, which have contributed to improving management practices and the attractiveness of these points of sale.

MUNICIPAL MARKETS

Municipal Markets are commercial units located in the center of cities, generally implemented and managed by local governments (municipalities) that historically seek to put producers, traders and inhabitants of the regions in contact, functioning as an anchor space for the city, allowing the supply of populations and dynamization of economic activity in city centers and local producers (Barreta, 2012). They are generally owned by the municipalities and include a diverse number of small merchants who carry out their activity there, mainly selling fresh and local products. With the development of large retail networks and shopping centers and the changes introduced in cities and in the needs and behavior of consumers, these spaces lost part of their importance in supplying populations.

Many Municipal Markets have been losing part of their relevance, due to the difficulty in competing with the big retail brands, the desertification of the city centers where they are usually located and the lack of innovation, communication and commercial aggressiveness (Xara-Brasil et al, 2021). In other cases, the Municipal Markets have obtained good results, retaining local customers and attracting tourists, managing sometimes conflicting needs and expectations of very different audiences, such as proximity customers (usually older), younger audiences in search a the most exclusive range of products and tourists, who are looking for an authentic experience of the region, making contact with its traditions and productions. (Crespi-Vallbona, & Dimitrovski, 2016). Most of the players in these Markets are small retailers, often with a long experience in the area, usually are elderly people, with low academic education and business management training and limited digital proficiency. They own very small outlets, without specialized technical support to facilitate processes of change and innovation, namely regarding the use of new technologies or home delivery services.

THE LIVRAMENTO MARKET IN SETÚBAL

The Livramento Municipal Market in Setúbal is a place of great economic and social importance, supplying food products to all this region. Setúbal is a medium size city with 91000 inhabitants, located about 50 kilometers south of Lisbon and close to the sea and a very important fish harbor in Portugal. In addition to being one of the main Municipal Markets in Portugal, it is considered one of the main fish markets in the world and a central tourist spot in the region (USA TODAY, 2017).

Opened in 1876, the Livramento Municipal Market currently has 136 sales stands and 42 stores. The most relevant activities in this market are fish trade (52), fruits and vegetables (35) and butchers (15). We can also find bakeries, wine stores and a specific area for small local producers. (Pardal et al, 2021).

In a survey carried out in 2021 by the local municipality, it was found that more than 70% of traders in this market are over 50 years old, while the percentage of traders under 30 years old does not exceed 2%. In terms of education, 32% of merchants have up to fourth grade and that 37.7% have at least middle school. With regard to professional experience, most traders have been operating in this market for more than 20 years, and many of the businesses already belong to at least a second generation.

The age of many of the retailers, the low level of academic education and the small size of the businesses and teams make it difficult to introduce digital technologies, such as those related to digital marketing and social networks. For merchants, the use of digital media for the promotion or sale of products was an area of very little interest, but this situation may have changed after the first wave of COVID-19, during the year 2020.

The use of digital tools for the promotion and sale of products, services and activities related to the Livramento Market in Setúbal is historically reduced by operators and their management entity. This market does not use digital tools systematically: it does not have an official website, Facebook page, Instagram or other digital tools, which in this way has reduced its visibility, interaction and interactivity. Most of its retailers do not systematically plan their communication and interaction actions with current and potential customers, nor do they use digital marketing tools, such as websites or social networks.

COVID-19 IMPACT OF FOOD RETAIL ACTIVITY

The dissemination of COVID-19 led to a reduction in retail opening hours and the flow of people, and restrictions on the range of products they could sell. This situation implied severe changes in the retail industry that was felt in an asymmetric way by different operators. In general, retailers of non-essential goods felt a stronger negative due to the COVID-19 influence than food retailers (Zwanka, & Buff, 2021). In 2020 in Portugal, the retail industry turnover decreased 1.5%, but the food retail grew 8.1% (APED, 2021), During this period, many of the major food retail companies across the world increased their turnover during this period (Roggeveen & Sethuraman, 2020).

The COVID-19 pandemic caused the suspension or cessation of activity of retail stores or shortened their opening hours and, consequently, losing or limiting their main channel of communication and interaction with their customers. However, losing the face-to-face customer service, does not necessarily mean losing customers. Retailers need to learn how to reach their customers in different ways, namely using digital channels (Calle, 2020).

The COVID-19 pandemic also increased sensitivity towards the shopping environment, and increased the consumers search for online shopping and the possibility of using home delivery services (Eriksson,2020). This migration of customers to digital services, increased the importance of other channels, such as a website or social media pages (Calle, 2020).

Some traditional stores had to be closed because of stay-at-home policy. For the smaller stores, the situation was very challenging and would fear devastating consequences. In fact, the physical conditions of the points of sale, usually with reduced sales areas difficult the possibilities of distance between people, additionally the low financial resources limited the investments in the stores and finally the characteristics of most of its owners who are generally older and vulnerable people, with reduced digital skills who are usually not versed in Internet technologies (Bollweg et al., 2020).

Since March 2020, many economic agents have reinvented themselves, quickly adapting their business models and overcoming relevant constraints, such as the lack of digital skills. Their great knowledge of their economic activity and of their customers wants and the need for survival, in addition to careful management of points of sale, good communication skills, the focus on online commerce, telesales and home deliveries have contributed to overcome the main constraints. Despite the difficulties, situations of great dynamism in response to the challenges imposed by COVID-19 multiplied, online commerce and social media management have become more relevant aspects in the marketing management of many retailers.

With COVID-19 we also observed significant changes in consumption patterns. According to Eriksson (2020) the impacts related to the "Panic-buying" behavior stand out, caused by the fear that there might be supply disruptions occurred mainly in the first weeks of the pandemic. Changes in cooking behavior that corresponded to the new needs related to extended stays at home for the whole family and that made average purchases grow and many bankruptcies sought to return to old family traditions, such as family recipes, bread production, etc.

In the case of the Livramento Market, many adjustments were made to the operating model and the performance of retailers, with a globally positive balance, at least regarding the number of merchants who ceased their activity: Since the beginning of the pandemic and until June 2021, the number of retailers in the Livramento Market that ceased its activity was only of six, two of them of fish and the remaining four of fruit and vegetables.

DIGITALIZATION AS A MARKETING TOOL FOR SMALL RETAILERS

With public healthcare concerns and governmental COVID-19 pandemic mitigation policies, the role and impact of social media as a marketing tool stands to increase in importance because, at a time when social distancing is a common practice, social media offers avenues for consumers to interact with others without having physical contact. Therefore, businesses may find new opportunities to gain competitive advantage through their use of effective social media marketing strategies.

Calle (2020) argued that for small food retailers going digital is more important than ever and is indispensable to stay relevant during the pandemic. During the first wave of COVID-19, the internet became an essential tool to continue with "life as usual", and social media became the way to be social in a time when the recommendation was to stay at home. With numerous consumers migrating to use digital services, it is necessary to utilize these channels to reach them. Results show the importance of using digital channels to interact with customers. Therefore, it is recommended that small food retailers enhance their social media presence to maintain the level of intimacy with their customers and compensate for the lack of face-to-face interaction at the retail store.

Developments in technology have taken place worldwide and have changed the way business leaders communicate with their customers (Allan & Ali, 2017, Hofacker & Belanche, 2016). The use of social media marketing has become a component of businesses in the 21st century. According to Hudson et al. (2015) and Galati et al. (2017) social media is widespread, and companies are beginning to integrate social media in their communication strategies. During the last few years and specialty since COVID-19 pandemic begun, consumers have increased their utilization of social media as a tool for identifying products, collecting information on products, evaluating products, and making product purchases and many businesses adopted to changes in consumers' social media behaviors (Mason, Narcum & Mason 2021)

Social media has become not only a place for business leaders to market their products and services, but also an arena to interact directly with customers (Edosomwan et al., 2011). Kietzmann et al. (2011) and Coleman et al. (2013) argue that successful business owners realize the potential value of using social media to increase sales, improve their reputation, and extend their ability to survive in a competitive environment. Social media marketing is an effective means for business owners to reach new customers and improve their brand awareness in the marketplace. Furthermore, social media can be used as a tool for some small business to improve customer attention, interest, desire and action (Hassan, Nadzim & Shiratuddin, 2015).

For small business owners, social media is a means to respond to customer's comments, show a genuine interest in the customer, improve the customer's perception of the company, and build lasting relationships (Liu, Chou & Liao, 2015). Effective social media marketers recognize the value of customer loyalty, brand awareness, and building a long-term relationship with the customer to gain repeat business (Kasemsap, 2017).

Despite the advantages of social media marketing, many company leaders have not successfully implemented social media strategies to adjust to the increasing numbers of consumer-oriented communication via social media (Effing & Spil, 2016; Felix, Rauschnabel, & Hinsch, 2017).

Moreover, although social media marketing strategies are valuable tools for small business owners to reach new customers, increase sales and grow profitability, some lack the resources and expertise to implement effective strategies (Galati et al, 2017). Hassan, Nadzim & Shiratuddin (2015) emphasize that many of small business owners fail to make effective use of social media marketing. Bhatnagar and Papatla (2016) claim that small business owners may lack marketing knowledge intended for understanding specific marketing problems to increase sales and Hassan and Casaló Ariño (2016) noted that small business owners have a variety of inexpensive technological resources to engage in effective social media marketing campaigns.

With an increasing number of being left behind in this innovative marketing race has led to most businesses venturing into the social media world (Kim & Drumwright, 2016). After experiencing a decay in traditional marketing effectiveness, business leaders searched for new marketing mediums, resulting in the exponential growth in social media marketing, yet many small business owners lack the knowledge and experience to mount effective social media marketing campaigns (Naylor, Lamberton, & West, 2012). In agreement with Naylor et al. (2012), Rambe (2017) postulated that some small business owners lack the confidence and technological know-how to implement a successful social media marketing strategy. To harness the effectiveness of increasing networking with consumers and improving customer engagement, small business owners need the ability to implement social media marketing strategies.

Thota (2018) argues that businesses can use social media to activate consumers' product needs by triggering brand conversations that promote positive perceptions about products, services, or ideas and increases company message exposure. As such, social media provides businesses with virtual avenues to enhance consumers' product/brand awareness. Social media platforms are also used for consumer-to-consumer interactions to share their product/brand experiences (Thota, 2018). As such, social media offers businesses a means to generate brand awareness for their products or services.

RESEARCH METHODOLOGY

In view of the situation experienced by small food traders in Municipal Markets in the context of the COVID-19 pandemic, a case study was developed in the Livramento Market in Setúbal, seeking to understand the changes introduced by small retailers in their business model and in their way of communicating and interacting with customers due to the COVID-19 pandemic.

In addition to in-depth knowledge of the performance of these retailers, we aim to discuss the future implications that the practices implemented or deepened by retailers in this time of pandemic will have on their future performance. This study was carried out with retailers who are generally elderly and with little academic education, in a Municipal Market that is traditionally visited by locals, but also a major touristic attraction, and therefore, very threatened by reduction of the number of tourists in this region.

This case study included the application of a survey to retailers of the Livramento Market in order to assess the changes they have made, due the constraints imposed by COVID-19 pandemic. After that, we develop in-depth interviews with specific retailers that invested more in digital approaches, to better understand their practices, impacts and future expectations.

This survey was answered autonomously and anonymously. Respondents who wished could identify themselves and express their willingness to participate in the in-depth interviews that were subsequently carried out with a smaller number of retailers.

We delivered 160 questionnaires to the merchants of the Livramento Market, which corresponded to all the merchants present in those days. Of these, 140 self-completed questionnaires were obtained, and the fieldwork took place in June 2021.

The questionnaire has Tree parts. In the first one, a brief characterization of the respondents in terms of sociodemographic characteristics and identification of the business was carried out, in the second one we want to identify the principal channels of communication to consumers used by the retailers before the COVID-19 pandemic, the changes in communication and in their business due the COVID-19, the main influences for those modifications, the goals they want to achieve, and which ones they intend to maintain in the future. Finally, for those who use or start using the social media during the pandemic period, we want to know the impact on sales and who manage the social media.

All the questions, except one were closed questions and the options included in the were based in previous academic research, namely Calle (2020), Dean (2019), Oliveira et al. (2021) and Pinheiro and Macêdo (2021).

For small retailers, before the COVID-19 pandemic, face-to-face interaction with clients at the store was the principal or the unique mode of interaction and communication with consumers (Calle, 2020; Dean, 2019, Oliveira et al.,2021). With the "stay-at-home" measures, retailers need to adapt their business model. According to Calle (2020), Oliveira et al. (2021) and Pinheiro and Macêdo (2021) the main changes in retail companies was the growing use of digital media, including websites, Instagram, Facebook and WhatsApp. Among the changes made by small retailers, Calle (2020) also highlights the home deliveries services.

The in-depth interviews were carried out with 11merchants who indicated that they had recently developed a more significant digital presence, namely through websites and social networks. We sought to detail these practices, their strategic framework, impacts and expectations for continuity.

RESULTS

This survey was carried out with small food merchants from the Livramento Municipal Market and showed that most of them are over 60 years old and have limited academic qualifications. Most of these are micro-enterprises or independent traders that are not large enough to allow them specific support structures to design or manage a systematic communication policy - namely the management of social networks - or to carry out other activities, such as deliveries in clients' house.

Their retailing activity was never suspended during the COVID-19 Pandemic. Contrary to many other economic and retail trade activities, including restaurants, their operation was continuous, with peaks in demand being recorded in some cases, as a result of some buying behavior for storage (fearing that there would be supply difficulties, or because of the customers' desire to reduce their shopping travels) and by increased consumption at home, as a result of the closing of restaurants and the extra time that many people had to be at home.

For many of these small food retailers, the pandemic situation implied higher turnover, so their activity was not severely affected, and even more work was required due to the new public health rules and the contingencies of supply and interaction with customers. In other cases, there were downturns in activity, especially to those retailers whose sales were mainly concentrated in restaurants and other business customers, who suffered major shortfalls in turnover.

Consumers behaved very differently during this period. Many consumers, due to their advanced age - or even for health reasons - have reduced or eliminated their shopping trips, and many of them do not have the means or skills to shop online: many of these supplies were provided by local solidarity networks, neighbors, relatives, friends and small merchants where they usually shop. In other cases, the remote work at home, the increased available time, and the impossibility of attending restaurants and the decrease in social events, meant that other consumers – especially younger ones – have chosen to cook more sophisticated meals, increasing their purchases in these establishments.

From the survey is clear that it was clearly identified the need to innovate in the way they communicate and interact with their customers: Although with scarce resources, many retailers implemented a more systematic use of alternative interaction supports, like an extensive use of the smartphone as a contact tool, pressing on them to provide information, in particular about products, prices and schedules and combine ways of delivery, payment and ordering. Not fitting the "official" typology of digital social networks, smartphones are undoubtedly the most frequently used way of managing relationships with consumers by these small retailers.

WhatsApp was another of the main communication mechanisms with customers / consumers. The simplicity of use, the possibility of customizing the contents, low cost and its versatility – allows sending written information, photos, movies, video conversations – are pointed out as very strong points by many of the merchants who chose to use it.

Facebook is the oldest and most widespread actual digital social network. Its use is more complex than WhatsApp - normally with larger hardware requirements and a more sophisticated communication approach, with test and image - but it allows a more structured and permanent communication. In the case of the Livramento Market, there were retailers who took advantage of their personal Facebook pages to promote their business. Other retailers created or intensified the use of specific pages for their businesses. In one of the interviews, a retailer stated that "I started to post photos in my Facebook and some of my clients started to call me and to spread my pots to their families and friends"

Instagram is a more recent and very graphic social network, which, due to the profile of customers and merchants, was little used, as well as the creation / management of its own website.

Related to the use or intensification of the use of social networks, merchants referred to the need to implement electronic payment methods (PayPal type) and to structure a delivery process to the customers' homes

All digital social networks – WhatsApp, Facebook and Instagram – include some complexity, technological resources and costs – The use of these tolls involves handling a smartphone or a PC, internet, some specific know-how on Digital Marketing, the need to structure appealing and appropriate content and messages, the expenditure of time, etc. However, as shown in table 1, the use of these forms of interaction was intensified after the outbreak of the pandemic, in most of the 140 merchants who responded to the survey.

Table 1. The use of digital social networks before and after covid-19

Digital Social Networks	Before Covid-19	After Covid 19
Telephone	87	98
WhatsApp	25	30
Facebook	25	43
Instagram	7	10

Source: Survey

To manage their social networks, different methodologies were chosen: some retailers took their own photos and posted them in their Facebook page; In other situations, several retailers sent photos or establish live call in WhatsApp to help their customer to choose the exact products to send. In other cases, those posts were organized by an employee or to an external service provider. But in most situations, they stated that they used very elementary posts – even with their smartphones – and they got interesting results, in a very time-consuming task.

Of the 140 surveys analyzed, it was possible to verify not only the intensification of the use of digital social networks in the cases of merchants who already used them – WhatsApp, Facebook and Instagram – but also a greater integrated use of these instruments. Although more than 20 of the market's merchants have adhered to these practices at this stage, some of them choose to use more than one tool, making their approach more complex. As shown in Table 2, eight of the merchants use three of these tools in an integrated way, 20 use two social networks (more than 4 previously) and 19 use one of these digital tools

Table 2. Number of social networks used by each retailer

# Social Network	Before Covid-19	After Covid 19	Var
0 Social network	113	93	-20
1 Social network	4	19	15
2 Social network	16	20	4
3 Social network	7	8	1
Mean	0,41	0,59	0,18
St- Error	0,891	0,936	

Source: Survey

It is also observed the existence of a relationship between the respondent's level of academic education and the use of social networks, especially in the integrated use of more and a social network. Traders with lower qualifications generally use even a social network, while the rest are more apt to make an integrated management of this process, as shown in Table 3.

Table 3. The use of digital social networks and retailer academic education

Education	# Social Media (SM) After COVD-19			
	0 SM	1 SM	2 SM	3 SM
No instruction	3	0	0	0
Some elementary Education (less than 4th grade)	49	8	2	3
Some secondary Education (less than 9 years	22	4	6	1
High school	13	3	6	2
University	4	4	6	2

Source: Survey

Finally, there is a perception that the integrated use of these tools brings a better sales performance. Although they almost never reported a very important impact, as shown in table 4, these relationships are verified.

Despite their satisfaction with the results, in terms of sales and feedback, many operators comment on the difficulties that these additional tasks bring them, in terms of time consumed and even costs, in the case of home deliveries. Effectively, the lack of resources and skills of these little merchants makes the development and implementation of a systematized approach to social networks more complex.

RECOMMENDATIONS

The intensification of the use of alternative forms of interaction with customers, namely through digital tools, is identified as a relevant aspect for the future performance of these retailers, particularly with younger and more sophisticated targets. In this context, a greater focus on the acquisition of marketing skills and digital skills should be implemented, so that this action is more efficient and structured within a well-defined marketing strategy. Otherwise, there will be (only) a few retailers, usually that separately will develop specific efforts through some digital social networks.

With the renewal of retailers and a greater focus on developing the skills of current traders, it will be possible to deepen these practices, adding complexity and value to them. Digitization, digital interaction, and often online purchases are increasingly part of consumers' routine, which is why it is very important that small retailers deepen their performance in these vectors.

For local governments, the promotion of the municipal market must also be done in an increasingly sophisticated way, using digital tools that allow it to increase its attractiveness, attracting customers and generating business. These government entities and managers of these markets must also encourage, train and challenge the small retailers in these spaces to deepen their skills and practices, through incentive programs, training plans and specific monitoring.

FUTURE RESEARCH DIRECTIONS

The lack of academic research on Municipal Markets and their importance in the context of sustainable management of communities, their tourist interest and their central role in the social, commercial and cultural life of communities, add interest to the study of these Markets and their sustainability economic, namely in terms of Marketing.

Municipal Markets and small retailers are important players in supplying the population and in the flow and promotion of local products, so they need more research to be carried out in order to benefit from their outputs.

This theme has a very relevant international scope. All over the world there are markets and small retailers, perhaps sharing similar threats and constraints. The development of international research and comparative studies will allow for more robust conclusions and analysis tools and will lead to better knowledge and interventions with these retailers.

This research limitations are related with the fact that we are presenting exploratory research, centered in a very specific reality – local and historical market – exclusivity analyzed with a quantitative methodology and in a single lapse of time. The development of complementary research, using different methodologies and in other locations is s necessary step in this process.

It is important to thoroughly research the purchasing behavior of consumers in these commercial spaces, their expectations, and priorities. There are different types of customers in these spaces that should be studied, such as residents, younger consumers or more sensitive to sustainability issues, tourists.

The results of these retailers' marketing practices must be measured over time, to perceive their effective impact on consumers' perceptions and on the retailers' performance.

CONCLUSIONS

COVID-19 brought major changes to the performance of most retailers around the world, including to the operation of the Livramento Market, with occasional limitations on opening hours, on the number of visitors and a decrease in demand, due to restrictions on circulation, the fears of the inhabitants and the stoppage of tourist activity. Many food retailers were able to adapt their practices to the new reality, through several changes to their practices, namely using new technologies.

In the Livramento Market, we observed that many retailers made a substantial effort to adapt their practices to this specific situation, with the growing use of digital tools and even alternative forms of contact, such as the use of the telephone – in this case smartphone - . In general, this effort was made by the main manager / owner of the point of sale or by a family member, having obtained results that satisfied its proponents, through the retention and attraction of customers, namely through the word-of mouth.

The challenge of an integrated management of marketing and the use of technologies is particularly complex for many small marketers due to their age, lack of skills, resources and supporting organizational structures. In the case of many traders operating in Municipal Markets, many of them micro traders, the challenge was very big, and it was important to know and debate the practices and results, comparing them with the existing literature on digital marketing and social media management in the retail, contributed to a debate on the subject and the search for better future solutions.

Our research clear demonstrated the use of new technology and specially the use of social media directly affected the communication policy of these retailers and become a central component of their communication activities and businesses models to increase attention, awareness, sales, reputation, loyalty and gain competitive advantages. Those results are aligned with the literature and were accelerated with COVID-19 pandemic scenario.

Small retailers may use digital marketing tools as an inexpensive way to attract, interact and build long-term relationship with their customers, included in a systematic marketing strategy and promotional programs. Unfortunately, there are frequent handicaps on marketing and technological competences play a central paper in this process. Although these retailers have a large retail expertise a successful relational background with their customers, they have a lack of strategical and managerial skill that inhibits a systematic marketing approach with a planned activities and resources allocation.

In our case study, we could observe that many of those retailers used their social networks, to communicate with their existing clients, in a immediate response to their fear of being left behind. This unplanned action had some important benefits, at least for some of the retailers that started to include a more systematic approach, with more and planes contents and multiple channels of communication, that could include different tools (Facebook, Instagram, WhatsApp, etc) and services (ex: delivery, larger assortments options, etc.). In fact, we noticed that some "innovative retailers "are happy with their results, but many of them are not, due to the lack of time (resources to manage this complexity) and results.

Another obstacle related with the implementation of a digital marketing strategy is the frequent lack of managerial and marketing skills, that inhibits the development of a consistent business model linked with a systematic marketing approach and adequate operational plans

It is important for merchants and market management entities to develop programs aimed at strengthening the digital bet, enhancing the experience and knowledge gained in the meantime, through training, incentive and even technical support programs. This process could be gradual and integrative and constitute the first phase of a more integrated system of online sales and home delivery services.

REFERENCES

Allan, M., & Ali, N. N. (2017). Employing social media websites and its role in determining the target audience for marketing within cloth manufacturing in Jordan. *Innovative Marketing*, *13*(2), 47–55. doi:10.21511/im.13(2).2017.05

APED - Associação Portuguesa de Empresas de Distribuição. (2021). *Vendas no retalho com quebra de 1,5% em ano de pandemia Vendas no retalho com quebra de 1,5% em ano de pandemia*. http://aped.pt/2021/03/30/vendas-no-retalho-com-quebra-de-15-em-ano-de-pandemia/

Barreta, J. (2012). *O comércio de proximidade – fazer acontecer a regeneração urbana*. Confederação Empresarial de Portugal.

Bhatnagar, A., & Papatla, P. (2016). Increasing online sales by facilitating spillover shopping. *Journal of Retailing and Consumer Services*, *29*, 58–69. doi:10.1016/j.jretconser.2015.11.009

Bollweg, L., Lackes, R., Siepermann, M., & Weber, P. (2020). Drivers and barriers of the digitalization of local owner operated retail outlets. *Journal of Small Business and Entrepreneurship*, *32*(2), 173–201. doi:10.1080/08276331.2019.1616256

Calle, J. Y. (2020) *Understanding COVID-19's impact on small food retailers in Finland*. Master's Thesis of Master Programme in International Business Development. LAB University of Applied Sciences LTD.

Coleman, L. J., Chandler, K., & Gu, J. (2013). Social media: A moving target. *Journal of Marketing Development and Competitiveness*, *7*(1), 73–77. doi:10.100740139-013-0010-2

Crespi-Vallbona, M., & Dimitrovski, D. (2016). Food markets visitors: A typology proposal. *British Food Journal, 118*(4), 840–857. doi:10.1108/BFJ-11-2015-0420

Dean, C. (2019) *Social Media Strategies used by Owners of Small Retail Businesses.* PhD Thesis. Walden University

Edosomwan, S., Prakasan, S. K., Kouame, D., Watson, J., & Seymour, T. (2011). The history of social media and its impact on business. *The Journal of Applied Management and Entrepreneurship, 16*(3), 79–91. doi:10.1007/9781-4419-5725-2_9

Effing, R., & Spil, T. A. (2016). The social strategy cone: Towards a framework for evaluating social media strategies. *International Journal of Information Management, 36*(1), 1–8. doi:10.1016/j.ijinfomgt.2015.07.009

Eriksson, N., & Stenius, M. (2020). Changing Behavioral Patterns in Grocery Shopping in the Initial Phase of the Covid-19 Crisis—A Qualitative Study of News Articles. *Open Journal of Business and Management, 8*(05), 1946–1961. doi:10.4236/ojbm.2020.85119

Felix, R., Rauschnabel, P. A., & Hinsch, C. (2017). Elements of strategic social media marketing: A holistic framework. *Journal of Business Research, 70*, 118–126. doi:10.1016/j.jbusres.2016.05.001

Galati, A., Tinervia, S., Crescimanno, M., & Spezia, F. (2017). Social media as a strategic marketing tool in the Sicilian wine industry: Evidence from Facebook. *International Journal of Globalisation and Small Business, 6*(1), 40–47. doi:10.1016/j.wep.2017.03.003

Hassan, M., & Casaló Ariño, L. V. (2016). Consumer devotion to a different height: How consumers are defending the brand within Facebook brand communities. *Internet Research, 26*(4), 963–981. doi:10.1108/IntR-03-2015-0090

Hassan, S., Nadzim, S. Z. A., & Shiratuddin, N. (2015). Strategic use of social media for small business based on the AIDA model. *Procedia: Social and Behavioral Sciences, 172*, 262–269. doi:10.1016/j.sbspro.2015.01.363

Hofacker, C. F., & Belanche, D. (2016). Eight social media challenges for marketing managers. *Spanish Journal of Marketing-ESIC, 20*(2), 73–80. doi:10.1016/j.sjme.2016.07.003

Hudson, S., Huang, L., Roth, M. S., & Madden, T. J. (2015). The influence of social media interactions on consumer-brand relationships: A three-country study of branch perceptions and marketing behaviors. *International Journal of Research in Marketing, 33*(1), 27–41. doi:10.1016/j.ijresmar.2015.06.004

Kasemsap, K. (2017). *Professional and business applications of social media platforms. In Analyzing the strategic role of social networking in firm growth and productivity*. IGI Global. doi:10.4018/978-1-5225-0559-4.ch021

Khan, I., Hollebeek, L. D., Fatma, M., Islam, J. U., & Riivits-Arkonsuo, I. (2020). Customer experience and commitment in retailing: Does customer age matter? *Journal of Retailing and Consumer Services, 57*, 102219. doi:10.1016/j.jretconser.2020.102219

Kietzmann, J. H., Hermkens, K., McCarthy, I. P., & Silvestre, B. S. (2011). Social media? Get serious! Understanding the functional building blocks of social media. *Business Horizons*, *54*(3), 241–251. doi:10.1016/j.bushor.2011.01.005

Kim, E., & Drumwright, M. (2016). Engaging consumers and building relationships in social media: How social relatedness influences intrinsic vs. extrinsic consumer motivation. *Computers in Human Behavior*, *63*, 970–979. doi:10.1016/j.chb.2016.06.025

Liu, S., Chou, C., & Liao, H. (2015). An exploratory study of product placement in social media. *Internet Research*, *25*(2), 300–316. doi:10.1108/IntR-12-2013-0267

Mason, A. N., Narcum, J., & Mason, K. (2021). Social media marketing gains importance after Covid-19. *Cogent Business & Management*, *8*(1), 1–17. doi:10.1080/23311975.2020.1870797

Mullis, K., & Kim, M. (2011). Factors determining inshopping in rural US communities: Consumers' and retailers' perceptions. *International Journal of Retail & Distribution Management*, *39*(5), 326–345. doi:10.1108/09590551111130757

Naylor, R. W., Lamberton, C. P., & West, P. M. (2012). Beyond the "like" button: The impact of mere virtual presence on brand evaluations and purchase intentions in social media settings. *Journal of Marketing*, *76*(6), 105–120. doi:10.1509/jm.11.0105

NielsenIQ. (2021). *Evolução dos Canais de Retalho*. Author.

Oliveira, E., Cremonezi, G., Casagrande, J., & Souto, A. (2021). Marketing Strategies: Innovation in retail during the restriction and social measures caused by Covid-19 pandemic. *Brazilian Journal of Development*, *7*(7), 67155–67173. doi:10.34117/bjdv7n7-135

Pardal, P., Xara-Brasil, D., Carvalho, L., & Cordeiro, J. (2021). O uso da metodologia de focus group na construção de uma análise swot aplicada ao mercado do livramento - Setúbal. In *Book of Proceedings – Full Papers, V International Forum on Management (IFM) "Connected in a Multipolar World: Everything Becomes Smart and Digital"*. Setúbal: Instituto Politécnico de Setúbal.

Pinheiro, A., & Macêdo, M. E. (2021) Marketing Digital: Estratégias de Vendas com o Varejo Digital na Pandemia do Covid-19. *Revista Multidisciplinar e de Psicologia, 15*(55), 194-205. https://idonline.emnuvens.com.br/id

Rambe, P. (2017). Social media marketing and business competitiveness: Evidence from South African tourism. *Problems and Perspectives in Management*, *15*(2), 411–423. doi:10.21511/ppm.15(2-2).2017.10

Roggeveen, A. L., & Sethuraman, R. (2020). How the COVID-19 pandemic may change the world of retailing. *Journal of Retailing*, *96*(2), 169–171. doi:10.1016/j.jretai.2020.04.002

Skallerud, K., & Wien, A. H. (2019). Preference for local food as a matter of helping behaviour. *Insights from Norway*, *67*(January), 79–88. doi:10.1016/j.jrurstud.2019.02.020

Thota, S. (2018). Social media: A conceptual model of the why's, when's and how's of consumer usage of social media and implications on business strategies. *Academy of Marketing Studies Journal*, *22*(3), 1–12.

USA Today. (2017). *Seafood markets around the world.* https://eu.usatoday.com/picture-gallery/travel/experience/food-and-wine/2017/08/17/seafood-markets-around-the-world/104695964/

Verma, S., & Gustafsson, A. (2020). Investigating the emerging COVID-19 research trends in the field of business and management: A bibliometric analysis approach. *Journal of Business Research, 118*, 253–261. doi:10.1016/j.jbusres.2020.06.057 PMID:32834211

Xara-Brasil, D., Pardal, P., Cordeiro, J., & Carvalho, L. (2021). A compra de produtos locais: mercados municipais versus moderna distribuição. In *Book of Proceedings – Full Papers, V International Forum on Management (IFM) "Connected in a Multipolar World: Everything Becomes Smart and Digital"*. Setúbal: Instituto Politécnico de Setúbal.

Zwanka, R. J., & Buff, C. (2021). COVID-19 generation: A conceptual framework of the consumer behavioral shifts to be caused by the COVID-19 pandemic. *Journal of International Consumer Marketing, 33*(1), 58–67. doi:10.1080/08961530.2020.1771646

KEY TERMS AND DEFINITIONS

Digital Marketing: Marketing communication activities that include de use of electronic devices to interact with the target audience, such as websites, digital social networks, search engines, etc.

Digital Social Networks: Interaction tools that citizens may use through the internet. Simple a cheap way to send photos and messages, mainly using posts. Facebook, Instagram, Twitter, Tic-Toc are examples of digital social networks.

Municipal Markets: Commercial units located in the center of cities, generally implemented and managed by local governments (municipalities) that historically seek to put producers, traders and inhabitants of the regions in contact, through a large number of independent retailers.

Promotional Programs: Is a series of marketing activities that are link with the strategic marketing options that are operationalized and monetarized in order to archive the short- and long-term objectives.

Strategic Marketing: Marketing options that companies establish for their brand and or business that don't change for a large period and guide marketing operational plan and activities.

Telesales: The use of sales promotion using a telephone or a smartphone, with actual or potential customers.

Chapter 7
Consumption of Artistic and Cultural Products in the Pandemic and the Influence of Technology:
Evidence From Brazil

Josmar Andrade
Universidade de Sao Paulo, Brazil

Julia Aparecida Bibiano Ramos
Universidade de Sao Paulo, Brazil

Giovanna Bezerra Boava
Universidade de Sao Paulo, Brazil

ABSTRACT

This study investigates the changes that took place in the consumption patterns of art and artistic products during the coronavirus pandemic events in 2020 in Brazil. Data from a sample of 615 respondents indicated that, isolated in their homes, people reported an increase in the consumption of this type of offer, motivated by the need for entertainment and of "spending time." The audiovisual content mediated by technology (music, movies, series and television programs) showed a significant growth in consumption, with a decrease of modalities normally associated with live experiences, such as dance, theatrical performances, and exhibitions of visual arts and photographs. Evidence was also found that certain sociodemographic profiles (women and younger people) present greater intensity level of consumption of artistic and cultural products, as well as that some dimensions of involvement with art and culture, "assuredness in choice" and " relevance," may also be associated with changes in the consumption behavior.

DOI: 10.4018/978-1-7998-9227-4.ch007

INTRODUCTION

Among the various activities affected by restrictions determined by the sanitary measures to combat Coronavirus and prevent Covid-19, the consumption of artistic and cultural products was perhaps one of the most impacted, especially in the initial period of the sanitary programs determined by authorities in 2020 (FGV, 2020).

Some of these offers depend on consumption *in loco*, such as attending live musical concerts, dance events, exhibitions, museums and art galleries, activities that were restricted with the lockdown decree and social isolation in several countries around the world. Even activities of a more individualized nature, such as the consumption of literature and music, for example, did not escape this transformation either. With the quarantine period, the routines and the amount of time allotted to work, study and leisure have changed, as well as the new ways of living together and the number of people present at homes, which has not always contributed to creating the conditions of isolation necessary for more introspective activities.

On the other hand, the events of the pandemic brought about a huge transformation in the way of consuming artistic expressions through digital media. Isolated and without access to public spaces for leisure and entertainment and, at the same time, demanding mechanisms of well-being and psychological comfort that contribute to mental health, millions of people around the world searched online for content that could provide distraction, escape and spiritual elevation, structured by technologies that determine a new mode of availability and access to artistic and entertainment products. Music, literature, cinema, visual arts, various art expressions were adapted to a new context and alternative forms of artistic offer were created, such as virtual tours to collections, virtual music shows, dance and theater presentations, electronic seminars, debates and lectures. In short, forms that were incipient previously were accelerated and with the technology support, expanded consumption opportunities, even for audiences that did not have such habits before.

Having said that, the impacts must be assessed in positive and negative terms; there are winners and losers within the changes and new conditions imposed by health restrictions. Some types of offers were more suitable for isolated consumption, such as audio and video streaming services, as an example, while other services encountered insurmountable difficulties, such as the cinematographic exhibition sector and theatrical presentations.

Given the fragility of the sector in terms of jobs and income guarantees and the impacts involved in the cancellation of several events scheduled around the world, relief and assistance measures were taken by governments, both from economic nature (emergency funding, grants and financing) and non-economic (creation of new jobs opportunities, training and qualification of personnel and alternatives for presenting content mediated by technology). The book by Salvador, Navarrete and Srakar (2021) presents several European experiences and identifies three central issues in the policies implemented in different countries during the period: (i) the recognition of the non-essentiality of culture and art for society; (ii) the lack of data for monitoring the cultural sector at a critical moment; and (iii) the disruptive nature of the pandemic in the culture and art sector.

This specific historical moment is important as a milestone for understanding the process that involves the accelerated incorporation of technology by art, considering the technical apparatus as a process enhancer, both in terms of production, communication and exhibition of works, as well as serving as a facilitator for engaging consumers with artistic themes, cultural institutions, specialists and with the artists themselves. Increasingly facilitated, this connection between the artists, the event/content/work they produce and want to disseminate, and their audience frees the artistic experience from the imperative of physical spaces and moves towards digital spaces (Dowbor, 2018; Fossati, Gemetto 2011). In addition, the expansion of technological tools domain for production and the ease of connection provided by digital means of communication have created new opportunities outside the mainstream giving voice to independent artists, who united art and entertainment, setting up a new condition for the artistic offer and for the status of the cultural producer (Sogabe, 2016).

Situated within the discussions on the creative economy and the interface with the evolution of technological means, the purpose of the study presented in this chapter was to investigate the changes that took place in the consumption patterns of art and artistic products during the coronavirus pandemic events in 2020. Therefore, exploratory research was carried out, with a sample obtained by convenience, with a quantitative approach, with a total of 615 respondents.

It was intended to answer the following question: what are the differences in the consumption of products of artistic nature, comparing the periods, before and after social isolation? The study also tried to assess whether the respondents' sociodemographic characteristics and attitudinal profiles explain the value and importance attributed to these offers, with differences in the declared degrees of intensity of change.

The perspective offered is from the Brazilian market, but certainly its findings can contribute to establishing benchmarks for comparison, providing a picture of a moment in the evolution of the production of the artistic product, its access and consumption, conditions that will certainly impact the future dynamics of the sector and that, ultimately, affects tastes and preferences and ways of attributing value to the artistic experience.

Despite the temporal sanitary specificity, it is necessary to recognize the circumstances as a momentum in a process that has been accelerating over time: the increase in the consumption of digital cultural products. The pandemic can be understood, then, as an inflection point, due to the financial impacts it has had on the sustainability of various businesses and sectors and the perspectives it has opened up in several others. The implications are of great interest for the management of the creative economy, in every link of the value network that connects creators, producers, distributors and consumers, but also for the planning of public policies related to this important sector, which employs and generates income for millions of people in the world.

The chapter is organized as follows: initially, the literature review will be presented in three topics: (i) the consumption of cultural products related to the creative economy; (ii) aspects related to technology in the production and consumption of cultural products and services; and (iii) the impacts of the pandemic on the Brazilian market. Following it will be presented the research methodology, and the results organized by the sample profiling, comprising conditions to internet access, data on art consumption during the lockdown, the degree of declared change organized firstly by sociodemographic and then by attitudinal profiling. The chapter ends with a discussion about the results and implications for management and consumption.

BACKGROUND

The Consumption of the Cultural Product Related to the Creative Economy

There are several discussions and controversies about the scope of what is conventionally called the creative economy. Markusen et. al. (2008) developed an important review on the range of products and services related to creative activity and cultural occupations, dialoguing with authors who even discuss whether activities related to religion, sports and games can be included within the limits of this industry.

A report produced by a sectorial institution (Firjan, 2014) divides the creative industry into several dimensions: activities directly related to business and consumption (advertising, architecture, design and fashion); activities related to cultural expression (crafts, folklore and gastronomy; heritage and arts; music and performing arts); activities related to the media (editing and audiovisual); activities related to technology (research and development; biotechnology and information and communication technologies). In addition, this vision encompasses activities for the industrial realization of events and materials related to its creation, as well as the necessary services and support activities.

Conceptually, the creative economy can be defined as a set of activities in which "creativity and intellectual capital are the raw material for the creation, production and distribution of goods and services" (Howkins, 2002).

Within the scope of this chapter, the idea of an "artistic and cultural goods" offer is accepted which, following the proposals of Hesmondhalgh (2002), involves audiovisual products and services, printed materials such as newspapers, magazines and books, recording and distribution of music and other materials of an editorial nature, in addition to performing arts experiences in spaces for the presentation of cultural and artistic works, such as museums and art galleries. All of these activities involve the creation and availability of culturally significant content, products and services that offer intellectual, entertainment or evasion experiences, which elevate the spiritual state of individuals. Coman (2020) proposes that this type of experience increases the feeling of fulfilment in life, being the value that the cultural product provides to its audiences and consumers. For Radermecker (2020) art and culture are consumed for several reasons, including the positive results they bring to individuals; the impact on mental health and well-being has been shown by studies to reduce tension, stress and anxiety.

From an economic point of view, there are a series of implications for the creation, production, distribution and consumption of art, aspects ranging from intellectual property associated with reproduction and access, revenue obtained from the sale of tickets to events, licensing, in addition to the commercialization of the tangible artistic product (buying and selling books, paintings, sculptures, among other tangible goods). These activities taken together constitute a relevant occupation chain and generate income and wealth. For this reason, the "cultural industry", located at the heart of the "creative economy", is increasingly deserving the attention of scholars and being the object of discussions that lead to the planning of public policies.

Globally, the creative economy, taken comprehensively, contributes with an annual revenue of 2.25 trillion dollars, and exports over 250 billion dollars. This is a sector that employs around 30 million people across the world, being the sector that most employs young people between 15 and 29 years old (UNESCO, 2021).

In Brazil, there are estimates that the creative economy (including the set of all activities described above) is responsible for 2.6% of the National GDP, accounting for about 840.000 formal jobs (Firjan, 2017, apud FGV, 2020) with aggregate impacts on the order of US$ 30 billion on the economy (El Pais, 2021).

Technology in the Production and Consumption of Cultural Products and Services

The digitization processes in the art sector dates from many years before the COVID-19 pandemic. The use of computers to help organize, catalogue and coordinate collections of cultural institutions has started in the early years of 1960s, when the primary goal was to have an efficient and clear method to sort their expanding collections, as to not rely only on physical records (Dahlgren, Wasielewski, 2021). According to Bianconi (2017), these processes were developed initially for the recovery, restoration, documentation and conservation of cultural heritage, but a lot of opportunities have been explored since then.

The initial focus on preservation and repository management changed pace by the adoption of computers as a tool to produce and consume art and culture, especially since the 1980s, as the computers became more affordable and accessible for individual creators and consumers of art (Dahlgren, Wasielewski, 2021). Respini (2018) provides an overview of the impact of the internet on artistic creation and production and on the forms of consumption of these contents from the 1990s onwards, materials "made on and for the internet", recognizing that from the outset there was a complex relationship with the traditional art world. The new information highways have transformed the circulation of artistic work while opening up perspectives that are still being explored.

In a broader sense, the impact of technology on the culture and arts sector can be analyzed from two points-of-view: production and consumption. On the production side, cultural institutions, such as museums, had invested in technological augmentation (Noehrer et. al, 2021), given access to devices and programs for editing and processing images and text, transforming the ability to carry out art and democratizing the number of people involved in creative processes (Ebrahimi et. al, 2020). The aimed augmentation can be achieved through a process called dematerialization, which consists of "the opportunities to transform a physical product into a service" (Willard, Halder, 2003). Nobre (2020) exemplifies transforming a physical facility, such as a museum, through a service, as can be seen by the virtual tours and contents many institutions promote.

Pennington and Eltham (2021) emphasize how this process has become a global trend among cultural institutions in the lockdown period, resulting in many cultural producers being overwhelmed with the sensation of insecurity, as many of them didn't have experience with technology required by institutions to integrate a digital staff.

As for the other side, that of consumption, explored by Rademecker (2020), in which more people are able to access content that was previously only available through physical means, face-to-face experiences, or that involved access costs (including price, time and place), which restricted the profile and the number of people able to consume such an offer. As an example of this evolution, Ryder (2020) shows how a person located in a small town in Latin America is able, through digital devices, to make a virtual visit to important European museums, a situation that can be considered less rich than a face-to-face experience, but that would not even be possible without the evolution of information and telecommunications technologies.

There is still, according to Ryder (2020), a mutual and beneficial exchange between the production and the consumption. As fans and other engaged audiences participate in events, share content, donations and discussions occur, thus data is generated and stored for the cultural institutions to analyze. Another important point is the creation of support communities, as a secondary effect of the interactions provided by technology. This facilitates measuring the effectiveness of actions and planning content and other communication and product strategies.

The Impacts of the Pandemic on the Brazilian Market

During the period of the pandemic, especially in the years 2020 and 2021, the Brazilian market was impacted by several interventions implemented by the government in order to reduce the evolution of the transmission of the disease caused by the coronavirus. Among these measures, Aquino et. al. (2020) highlights the lockdown, the reinforcement of adequate health behavior, social distancing, procedures that involve closing schools and universities, bans on mass events, and travel restrictions, including cultural live events and the operation of venues. Such measures, according to Mattei and Heinei (2020), negatively impacted the Brazilian workforce, which presented the biggest drop in the population employment rates since the year 2012. The main reason for the drop, in addition to the restrictive measures, is related to the ineffectiveness of established economic policies and the lack of expectation of the population to find a job in the current situation of crisis in the country. There is still, according to a survey carried out by the Banco Central do Brasil, a significant number of companies that have ended their activities, permanently or temporarily, mainly small ones (Banco Central do Brasil, 2021).

The new living conditions in times of pandemic impacted economic activities in general, creating opportunities, but also generating negative effects in several sectors. According to Premebida (2021), the COVID-19 pandemic scenario was favorable for the e-commerce sector, which in 2020 had an increase in sales of 47% when compared to the previous year. The pandemic was the most cited factor among new online shoppers, who were motivated by the convenience of not having to leave their homes and the security of following the quarantine protocols established.

In the sector of products and services related to art, culture and entertainment, it is possible to observe the increase in the consumption of streaming platforms during the period. A comprehensive study conducted by the internet authority in Brazil in 2019 showed that, considering the total number of internet users (71% of the population) as a universe, 74% reported watching videos, programs, series and movies and 72% listened to music online (CGI.BR, 2020). This means that half of the population declared the habit of consuming audiovisual production with the support of technology, considering all segments of society. Estimates for 2021, as indicates a survey carried out by the Kantar Ibope institute (Silva, 2021), show an even higher number, reaching 58% of the total population. Another evidence of this growth is the research data presented in Laycock (2021), which show that, among respondents from 18 countries, 56% said they had access to at least one streaming service, and in Brazil this proportion is even higher, with 64.6% (the second highest in the survey, behind only New Zealand). Brazil is already the second largest Netflix market in the world, with 17.9 million active users of the platform (Silva, 2021).

Considering the closing of the main art and entertainment centers in the country, such as museums, cinemas and theaters, we can suggest that digital entertainment services have gained strength as the main source of leisure and distraction for the population, which is the main interest of the conducted research.

RESULTS

Research: Purpose and Method

The present study was carried out in the first half of 2020 with the purpose of investigating possible changes in the consumption habits of artistic and cultural products in the Brazilian market during the coronavirus pandemic. This is an exploratory study with a quantitative approach, which took advantage of the temporal opportunity to approach informants at a time when they were experiencing the restrictions of lockdown and social isolation. The data collection was made online and the method adopted to obtain the sample was the *virtual snowball*, through which online messages were sent out inviting seeds (initial groups of people related to the researchers, with a large number of connections, not connected with each other) to answer the questionnaire and share with their friends and social networks. This method is widely used in procedures in which the sample is obtained for convenience, but it also serves to access audiences that are not always easily available (Baltar, Brunet, 2012).

To define aspects of the consumption practices of cultural products of interest to the study, a qualitative discussion was initially held with students participating in a discipline in an undergraduate course at a Brazilian university, focusing on the main habits they developed in isolation, especially consumption of artistic and cultural offers and what types of products they considered among the possible options. This discussion helped guide the formatting of the data collection instrument that was organized as follows: in the first block, a scale adapted from the proposed by Fonseca and Rossi (1998) was used, to identify aspects that motivate the involvement of respondents with cultural and artistic products. The dimensions suggested in the original study are: (i) the relevance of the art to the respondent; (ii) the pleasure in consuming art; (iii) the consideration of sacrifices necessary for consumption; (iv) the symbolic value related to the process; and (v) assuredness in choice of alternatives. For each of these constructs, 3 items were used, all of them requiring dichotomous responses, with 7 points.

Statement: Consider that consuming art involves the following activities: watching movies, listening to music, reading books of literature and poetry, seeing dance performances, going to photography shows, going to museums and exhibitions, among other possible activities.

Now use the options below to rate your personal opinion regarding art consumption (use a scale from 1 to 7 to rate your condition, with numbers closer to the words indicating closer proximity). For you, these art consumption activities are...

Table 1. Engagement Items with the Consumption of Artistic and Cultural Products

Construct	Dichotomous item (1 a 7)
Relevance	• Not Essential / Essential • Non-Beneficial / Beneficial • Unnecessary / Necessary
Pleasure	• Not Pleasant / Pleasant • Not Exciting / Exciting • Not Fun / Fun
Consideration of Sacrifices for Consumption	• Annoying / Non-Annoying • Waste of Time / No Waste of Time • Waste of money / Not a waste of money
Symbolic Value	• Not important to what people think of me / Important to what people think of me • They don't communicate status in my relationship groups / They communicate status in my relationship groups • They say who I am / They do not say who I am
Assuredness in the choice	• They cause a lack of confidence when choosing / Do not cause a lack of confidence when choosing • Represent risk when choosing / Do not represent risk when choosing • Make me confused to evaluate options / Don't make me confused to evaluate options

In a second block, the informants declared the type of technological device that was most used in the consumption of products of artistic or cultural nature during the pandemic, to which they could define the intensity from "Never" to "Always", in a 5-point Likert scale. Then, the 13 most common types of offers of artistic and/or cultural nature considered are presented, so that the informant could assign a degree of intensity in their routine consumption of these types of products ("Never" to "Always") BEFORE the decree of social isolation. The same assessment of consumption intensity was carried out, with the same types of products and services, AFTER the enactment of quarantine restrictions.

A statement related to the self-perception of the increase or decrease in the consumption of artistic and cultural products and services after the enactment of quarantine was also requested, which served as a dependent variable of a series of comparisons carried out in terms of sociodemographic profile and attitudinal dimensions related to involvement with the consumption of artistic and cultural products. Finally, each respondent was qualified in terms of gender, age, household income and educational level.

Data collection took place in May and June 2020, with 615 valid responses obtained. The results are described below.

Profile of Respondents and Technical Conditions to Internet Access

Most of the sample is made up of females (62.9%), with an average age of 37.8 years and situated in the upper strata of the Brazilian socioeconomic qualification: 85.9% declared a higher level of education, including post-graduation and 46.3% with monthly household income (including all people who live in the same household) above US$ 1,500.00, which is high by country standards.

Asked about their condition during the quarantine, 84.1% of respondents declared to be carrying out most of their activities at home, while 12.4% declared to carry out activities partly at home, partly outside and only 3.6% declared to develop most of their activities outside the home.

As for their technical conditions for internet access during the pandemic, 79.5% rated the network availability between good and excellent; 62.6% declared that the speed to access the internet was good or excellent and 55.0% evaluated the stability of the network in the same way.

The main means of accessing and consuming artistic products, as stated by respondents, is the smartphone (76.3%) and the least important for the activity is the tablet (10.1%). Figure 1 systematizes these data.

Figure 1. Main means to access products of an artistic / cultural nature (%)

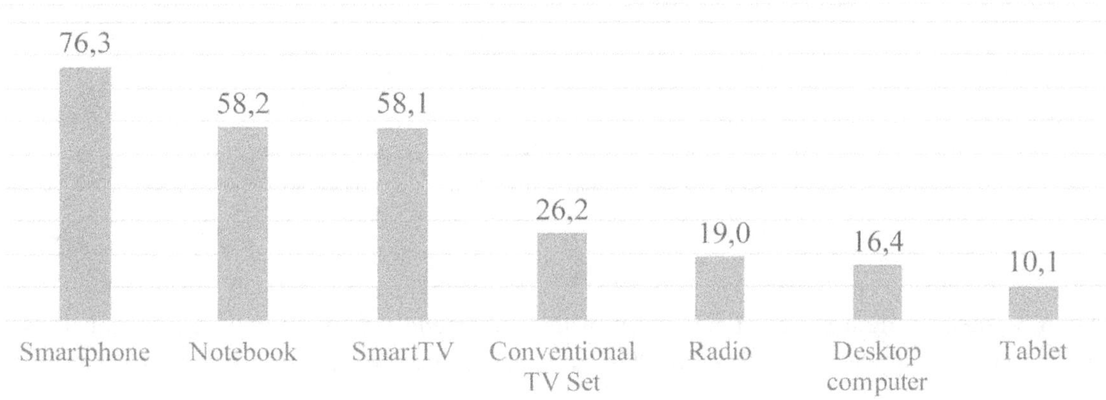

Art Consumption during the Lockdown

Most respondents (53.0%, adding the answers "More" and "Much More") have a self-declared perception that they began to consume more artistic and cultural products during the pandemic.

Table 2. Perception of intensity on consumption of artistic and cultural products during the lockdown

During the pandemic, you started to consume artistic or cultural products...	n	%
Much less	31	5.0
Less	113	18.4
As much	145	23.6
More	236	38.4
Much more	90	14.6
Total	615	100.0

Figure 2 shows the frequencies of added responses "Many Times" and "Always" for activities declared by respondents, as carried out during the lockdown condition. It is possible to see that the activity of watching series and movies via streaming is the most frequent, followed by listening to music on websites and apps. On the other hand, the activities of attending art exhibitions on websites and virtual museums and attending lectures and courses online were the ones that presented the least responses "Many Times" and "Always".

Figure 2. Main activities declared during the pandemic (in %)
(Sum of the answers "Many Times" and "Always")

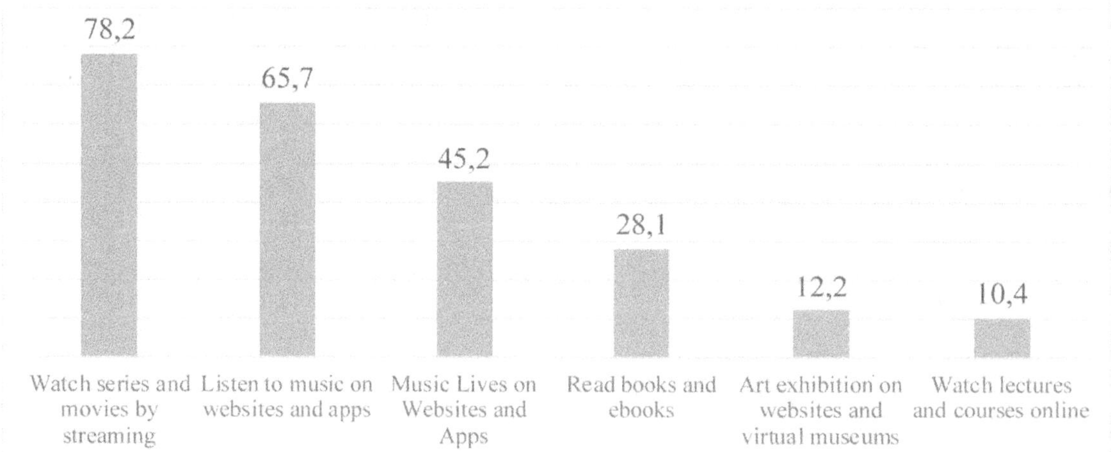

As can be seen in Figure 3, the assessment of the importance of this type of consumption is more linked to entertainment and distraction (96.9% of the added answers attributing "Great Importance" or

"Total Importance" to this motivation), followed by "spend time", with 90.2%. On the other hand, the motivation associated with engagement with social groups is, according to the respondents, the least important for the consumption of artistic and cultural products (only 66.8% of the responses "Great Importance" added to "Total Importance").

Figure 3. Reasons for the importance attributed to the consumption of artistic/cultural products (in %)
(Sum of the answers "Great Importance" plus "Total Importance")

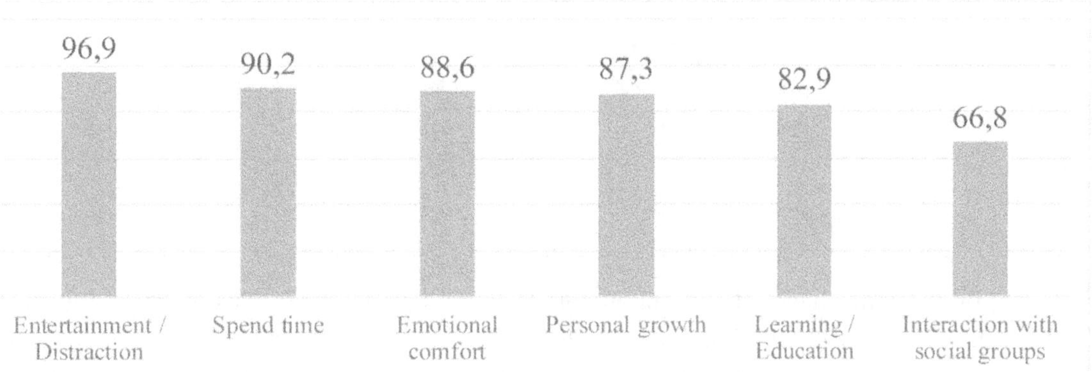

The Figures below present the percentage sum of the frequency of the responses "Many Times" and "Always" for 13 different types of artistic and cultural offers that are normally made available for consumption. Figure 4 shows the frequency of responses related to the period prior to the declaration of social isolation resulting from sanitary measures to contain the coronavirus epidemic in Brazil. It is possible to see that the consumption of music (73.3%), movies (64.6%) and series and TV shows (59.9%) were the most relevant. On the other hand, consumption of circus shows (2.0%), dance shows (8.3%) and artistic performances (10.1%) were the least frequent in the sample surveyed.

Figure 4. Habit of consumption of artistic and cultural goods and offers BEFORE the enactment of social isolation measures (in %)
(Sum of the answers "Many Times" and "Always")

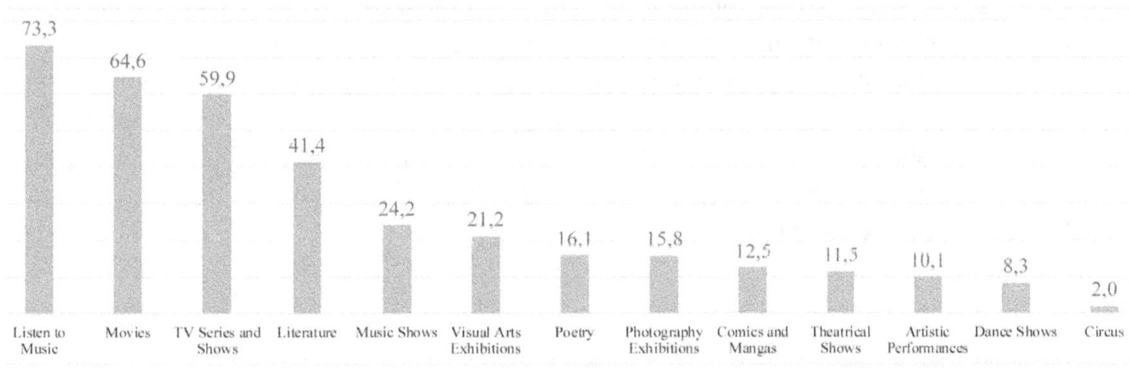

Figure 5. Habit of consumption of artistic and cultural goods and offers AFTER the enactment of social isolation measures (in %)
(Sum of the answers "Many Times" and "Always")

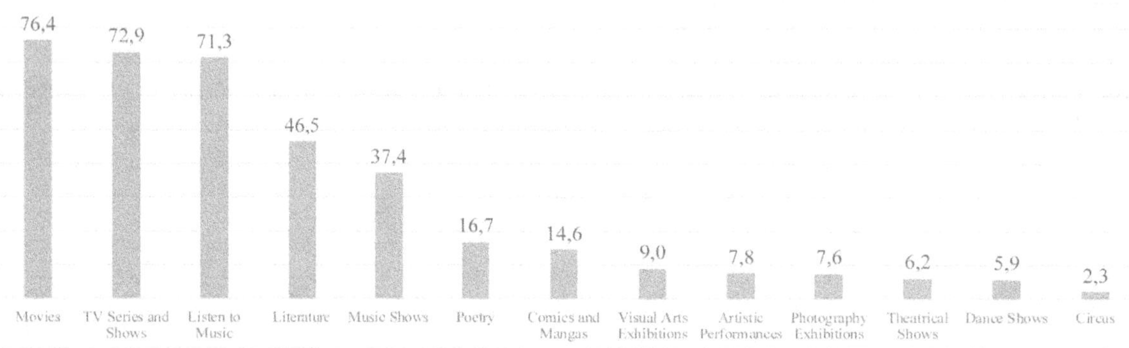

Figure 5, on the other hand, shows statements for the same 13 categories, considering the period AFTER the enactment of social isolation measures. It is possible to notice a sharp growth in the consumption of audiovisual content, with movies (76.4%) and TV series and programs (72.9%) becoming the two types of offer that received the most responses "Many Times" and "Always". Interestingly, the data show a drop in the statements "Many Times" and "Always" for the category "Listening to Music", which was the most mentioned modality previously. It also could be seen that there is an increase in the "Music Shows" categories and "Artistic Performances", and this can be explained by the large number of musical performances and online concerts held during the pandemic, which would change the nature of the experience: instead of "listening" to music, people began to "watch" music, in greater intensity than they did before. The modalities with lower frequencies of answers "Many Times" and "Always" (Circus, with 2.3%; Dance Shows, 5.9%; Theatrical Shows, 6.2%) are experiences that are linked to a tangible venue, despite several attempts to adapt the offer in times of social isolation.

The last column of Table 3, below, systematizes the difference in percentage points of the sum of the frequency of responses "Many Times" and "Always", comparing the two moments, (a) before the decree of social isolation measures and (b) after the lockdown. From this perspective, the artistic/cultural offer that showed the greatest evolution in terms of declared habits was the consumption of music shows, with a jump of +13.2 percentage points, followed by the consumption of TV series and programs (+ 13.0 percentage points) and the consumption of movies (+ 11.8 percentage points).

The necessary counterpoint is related to the activities that had the greatest losses in the process, all of them associated with the on-site experience: the attendance of Visual Arts Exhibitions presented a drop of 12.2 percentage points in the sum of the responses declared "Many Times" and "Always", a decrease that also happened with Photography Exhibitions (down 8.2 percentage points) and Theatrical Shows (down 5.3 percentage points).

Table 3. Differences between consumption before and after lockdown

Type of Artistic Offer		Many Times		Always		Many Times + Always		Percentage Points Differences
		n	%	n	%	n	%	
Music Shows	BEFORE	96	15,6	53	8,6	149	24,2	+13,2
	AFTER	136	22,1	94	15,3	230	37,4	
TV Series and Shows	BEFORE	185	30,1	183	29,8	368	59,9	+13,0
	AFTER	175	28,5	273	44,4	448	72,9	
Movies	BEFORE	199	32,4	198	32,2	397	64,6	+11,8
	AFTER	206	33,5	264	42,9	470	76,4	
Literature	BEFORE	136	22,1	119	19,3	255	41,4	+5,1
	AFTER	132	21,5	154	25	286	46,5	
Comics and Mangas	BEFORE	42	6,8	35	5,7	77	12,5	+2,1
	AFTER	48	7,8	42	6,8	90	14,6	
Poetry	BEFORE	63	10,2	36	5,9	99	16,1	+0,6
	AFTER	64	10,4	39	6,3	103	16,7	
Circus	BEFORE	9	1,5	3	0,5	12	2	+0,3
	AFTER	10	1,6	4	0,7	14	2,3	
Listen to Music	BEFORE	150	24,4	301	48,9	451	73,3	-2,0
	AFTER	130	21,1	309	50,2	439	71,3	
Artistic Performances	BEFORE	42	6,8	20	3,3	62	10,1	-2,3
	AFTER	35	5,7	13	2,1	48	7,8	
Dance Shows	BEFORE	40	6,5	11	1,8	51	8,3	-2,4
	AFTER	25	4,1	11	1,8	36	5,9	
Theatrical Shows	BEFORE	45	7,3	26	4,2	71	11,5	-5,3
	AFTER	26	4,2	12	2	38	6,2	
Photography Exhibitions	BEFORE	64	10,4	33	5,4	97	15,8	-8,2
	AFTER	34	5,5	13	2,1	47	7,6	
Visual Arts Exhibitions	BEFORE	81	13,2	49	8	130	21,2	12,2
	AFTER	38	6,2	17	2,8	55	9,0	

(Difference, in percentage points of the Sum of responses "Many Times" plus "Always")

Degree of Declared Change and Sociodemographic Groups

After analyzing the univariate dimensions of the responses, researchers sought to understand whether there are sociodemographic characteristics associated with the increase or decrease in the consumption of products of an artistic and cultural nature during the pandemic. The nominal variable (a self-declaration) asked the informants to respond: "In my perception, after the lockdown decree, I am consuming art...", with the possibility of a response graded into 5 levels, from 1 = "Much Less" up to 5 = "Much more". In order to better discriminate the possible differences, the categorical answers were regrouped into

3 levels: "Less consumption" (adding answers 1 and 2); the intermediate level "Same Consumption" (answers 3) and the level "Higher consumption" (adding answers 4 and 5).

The data from the crossings, as well as the statistical tests of association (Chi-Square) and the analysis of their significance can be seen in Table 4, presented below.

Table 4. Degree of change in the consumption of artistic and cultural goods x sociodemographic

Profile		Less Consumption		Same Consumption		Higher Consumption		Total		$\chi 2$	PValue	Sig
		n	%	n	%	n	%	n	%			
Gender	Female	96	**66.7**	73	50.3	218	**66.9**	387	**62.9**	16,689	0,002	S***
	Male	46	31.9	71	**49.0**	108	33.1	225	**36.6**			
Age Groups	Up to 20 yo	27	18.8	36	24.8	92	**28.5**	155	**25.3**	26,106	0,004	S***
	21 / 30 yo	23	16.0	18	12.4	65	**20.1**	106	**17.3**			
	31 / 40 yo	22	**15.3**	11	7.6	36	11.1	69	11.3			
	41 / 50 yo	26	18.1	26	17.9	64	19.8	116	19.0			
	51 / 60 yo	31	**21.5**	40	27.6	40	12.4	111	18.1			
	Over 60 yo	15	10.4	14	9.7	26	8.0	55	9.0			
Household Income Range (in R$)	Up to R$ 2.994,00	22	15.3	18	12.4	44	13.5	84	13.7	6,727	0,566	NS
	From R$ 2.995,00 to R$ 5.988,00	33	22.9	29	20.0	84	25.8	146	23.7			
	From R$ 5.989,00 to R$ 8.982,00	29	20.1	25	17.2	46	14.1	100	16.3			
	From R$ 8.983,00 to R$ 11.976,00	20	13.9	21	14.5	55	16.9	96	15.6			
	Over R$ 11.976,00	40	27.8	52	35.9	97	29.8	189	30.7			
Level of Education	Up to Highschool	20	13.9	22	15.2	45	13.8	87	14.1	4,573	0,334	NS
	Up to College	71	49.3	81	55.9	191	58.6	343	55.8			
	Post-Graduates	53	36.8	42	29.0	90	27.6	185	30.1			

Tests indicate statistically significant differences in two categories: related to the Gender of respondents ($\chi 2$=16,689, PValue=0.002) and that related to Age Groups ($\chi 2$=^{2}6.106, PValue=0.004).

Regarding to Gender, the survey data suggest that Women have a complex behavior: while there are respondents who reported an increase in the level of consumption, there are also those who reported lower levels of consumption, given the frequency distribution expected, determined by the percentage attributed to Female Gender in the total sample. Thus, in the "Less Consumption" group, women represent

66.7% and in the "Higher Consumption" group they represent 66.9%, levels higher than the participation of this gender in the total sample (62.9%). Men, on the other hand, have a higher percentage in the composition of the "Same Consumption" group (49.0%), in relation to the frequency distribution of the male gender in the total sample (36.6%). Further investigation is needed to understand these results, but it is possible to assume that the new dynamics of households' chores during the pandemic may have created two types of behaviors and profiles: women with less time (and perhaps interest) in consuming artistic and cultural products and, on the other hand, those who turned to this type of offer to pass the time and pursue well-being.

In the Age Groups, what is observed is a greater proportion of younger people in the group that reported increased consumption of artistic and cultural goods and products, in relation to the distribution of the sample; that is, people under 20 are 28.5% of the group with the higher consumption, while they represent 25.3% of the sample as a whole, and people between 21 and 30 years are 20.1% of the group with the higher consumption, while they constitute 17.3% of the sample taken as a whole. There is, however, important information regarding older segments: the ranges of respondents between 31 and 40 years old and respondents between 51 and 60 years old have a higher participation in the frequency distribution of the "Less Consumption" group, than their participation in the sample. This is another aspect that deserves reflection and investigation, but which may be associated with the fact that older populations are those with greater consumption of events, shows and physical exhibitions before the pandemic, which may have generated the perception of a decrease in the consumption of artistic and cultural products, with no other offer compensating for this loss.

There are no indications found in the data and tests performed that the other sociodemographic categories analyzed present statistically significant differences.

Degree of Declared Change and Attitudinal Groups

The last analytical procedure performed in the study addressed the attitudinal profile of respondents, considering their involvement with the artistic and cultural product. For this purpose, the involvement scale proposed by Fonseca and Rossi (1998) was adopted, whose constructs and items are presented in Table 1, before in this text. Initially, the statistical procedure of Factor Analysis was used to verify the data structure and correspondence to factors predicted in the model. In the processing, the Principal Components Method was used, with Varimax rotation and considered factors/components with eigenvalue greater than 1.0 (Hair et. al. 2005).

As for the adequacy of using the technique, the model was adequate and robust (KMO=0.843 and Bartlett = 0.000). The 15 items were consistently distributed in the 5 predicted constructs, which explain 71.6% of the data variance as shown in Table 4.

Table 5. Total variance explained by the factors

Component	Initial Eigenvalues			Extraction Sums of Squared Loadings			Rotation Sums of Squared Loadings		
	Total	% of Variance	Cumulative %	Total	% of Variance	Cumulative %	Total	% of Variance	Cumulative %
1	5.064	33.757	33.757	5.064	33.757	33.757	2.439	16.257	16.257
2	1.952	13.011	46.768	1.952	13.011	46.768	2.204	14.694	30.951
3	1.636	10.908	57.675	1.636	10.908	57.675	2.045	13.633	44.585
4	1.022	6.812	64.487	1.022	6.812	64.487	2.023	13.488	58.073
5	1.002	6.678	71.165	1.002	6.678	71.165	1.964	13.092	**71.165**

In Table 6 is possible to see the factor loadings properly assigned to the predicted constructs. As a reminder, what is being measured with this procedure is the attitude of respondents to attitudinal factors that are considered in the choice and consumption of artistic and cultural products. These factors were then named according to literature as 1 = Pleasure (involved in the consumption of artistic and cultural products); 2 = Consideration of Sacrifices in Consumption (of artistic and cultural products); 3 = Symbolic Value (related to the consumption of artistic and cultural products); 4 = Assuredness in the Choice (between alternatives for the consumption of artistic and cultural products); and 5 = Relevance (attributed to the consumption of artistic and cultural products).

It is important to note that the first construct, which combines the items of pleasure, emotion and fun, explained the greatest variance in the data, that is, the one with greater dispersion of data in relation to the other items, but greater internal consistency, when considering the component items of the construct.

Table 6. Rotated component matrix

Item	Component				
	1	2	3	4	5
Level of Involvement - Pleasure	**.808**	.191	.071	.106	.261
Level of Involvement - Emotion	**.838**	.155	.143	.107	.210
Level of Involvement - Fun	**.807**	.253	.097	.096	.145
Level of Involvement - Irritation (inverse)	.294	**.696**	.017	.227	.057
Level of Involvement - Waste of Time (inverse)	.178	**.848**	.086	.179	.179
Level of Involvement - Waste of Money (inverse)	.168	**.803**	.077	.140	.301
Level of Involvement - Important to what they think about me	.016	.076	**.850**	-.014	-.038
Level of Involvement - Status	.059	.046	**.853**	.032	.028
Level of Involvement - Tell who I am	.197	.024	**.727**	.040	.203
Level of Involvement - Provoke lack of confidence (inverse)	.084	.137	-.030	**.839**	.034
Level of Involvement - Represent risk on choice (inverse)	.154	.284	.065	**.694**	.018
Level of Involvement - Confuse to evaluate options (inverse)	.029	.060	.027	**.830**	.104
Level of Involvement - Essentiality	.198	.132	.062	.084	**.822**
Level of Involvement - Benefit	.383	.285	.052	-.001	**.556**
Level of Involvement - Necessity	.158	.146	.075	.073	**.815**
Total Variance Explained by Component / Factor	33.757	13.011	10.908	6.812	6.678

After analyzing the use of the technique adequacy, identifying and naming the factors/constructs that would be used in the analyses, groups of respondents were formed, according to the declared importance of each factor found. This procedure was carried out as follows: each respondent was assigned a score associated with each of the 5 factors. This was done considering all responses, and an individual position was then calculated within a normal distribution of mean 0 and standard deviation 1. That is, each respondent was placed on a continuum that went from the individual lowest negative score to the highest value obtained, which indicated their greater or lesser attitudinal agreement/adherence to the ideas expressed by the constructs found.

Considering this, it was possible to form groups in each construct, organizing the cases by score values, which express attitudinal intensity in relation to the analyzed construct. The procedure adopted was to separate, for each construct, the respondents into 3 groups formed by quartiles. Thus, the 109 respondents with the lowest scores formed the quartile considered to have the lowest agreement/adherence to the construct analyzed, the next 217 respondents, who correspond to the second and third quartiles, formed an intermediate group and the 109 respondents with higher scores formed the upper quartile, which expresses greater agreement/adherence to the construct analyzed. Instead of using tertiles directly, this methodological choice seeks to emphasize possible differences between the extreme groups, the first and fourth quartiles.

The next step was to compare the responses to the nominal variable on self-perception (declared) of change in the consumption of artistic and cultural products during the isolation determined by the pandemic, using the 3 groups formed by levels of the answer to the question "In my perception, after the decree social isolation, I'm consuming art...", with the "Less Consumption" group formed by respondents who attributes themselves an answer 1 or 2 ("Much Less" and "Less"); the group "Same Consumption" formed by respondents who gave themselves a score of 3 ("Same"); and "More Consumption" by respondents who declared a score of 4 or 5 ("More" and "Much more") to the question. Comparisons using crosstabs were made between (i) the groups formed by the scores in the 5 involvement constructs, crossing these frequencies with (ii) the groups formed by declared self-perception of change in the level of consumption of artistic and cultural products. The results are summarized in Table 7, presented below.

Table 7. Comparison of groups by frequency distribution (in %)

Constructs		Less Consumption		Same Consumption		More Consumption		Total		$\chi2$	PValue	Sig
		n	%	n	%	n	%	n	%			
Pleasure	Lower Pleasure	27	18.8	41	28.3	85	26.1	153	24.9	4,825	0,306	NS
	Medium Pleasure	82	56.9	69	47.6	158	48.5	309	50.2			
	Higher Pleasure	35	24.3	35	24.1	83	25.5	153	24.9			
Consideration of Sacrifices involved in consumption (inverse)	Higher Sacrifice	32	22.2	45	31.0	76	23.3	153	24.9	4,831	0,305	NS
	Medium Sacrifice	73	50.7	64	44.1	172	52.8	309	50.2			
	Lower Sacrifice	39	27.1	36	24.8	78	23.9	153	24.9			
Symbolic Value	Lower Symbolic Value	32	22.2	34	23.4	87	26.7	153	24.9	2,231	0,693	NS
	Medium Symbolic Value	71	49.3	74	51.0	164	50.3	309	50.2			
	Higher Symbolic Value	41	28.5	37	25.5	75	23.0	153	24.9			
Assuredness on the Choice	Lower Assuredness	32	22.2	56	**38.6**	65	**19.9**	153	**24.9**	19,652	0,001	S***
	Medium Assuredness	73	50.7	60	**41.4**	176	54.0	309	**50.2**			
	Higher Assuredness	39	**27.1**	29	20.0	85	**26.1**	153	**24.9**			
Relevance	Lower Relevance	31	21.5	48	**33.1**	74	22.7	153	**24.9**	14,845	0,005	S***
	Medium Relevance	87	**60.4**	65	44.8	157	48.2	309	**50.2**			
	Higher Relevance	26	18.1	32	22.1	95	**29.1**	153	**24.9**			

Importance Attributed to Factors of Involvement with Consumption of Artistic and Cultural Products (in the rows) versus Declaration of Intensity of Consumption Change during the Pandemic (in the columns)

The data from the association of categorical variables tests ($\chi2$) indicate statistical significance in two constructs: the Assuredness on the Choice (for the consumption of artistic and cultural products) ($\chi2$ = 19.652, PValue = 0.001) and the Relevance (of the consumption of artistic and cultural products) ($\chi2$ = 14,845, PValue = 0.005).

In the first situation, it is observed that those who assigned themselves a lower status in the Assuredness on the Choice (that is, those with a low degree in self-assuredness choosing an artistic or cultural product to consume) are the respondents who participated more than proportionally to the total sample in the composition of the "Same Consumption" group (38.6% versus 24.9% of the frequency of this group in the total sample). While those who attributed to themselves a more positive status regarding Assuredness on the Choice were those who had a complex behavior: they had proportionally greater participation in the "Less Consumption" group and also greater participation in the "More Consumption" group, when one compares the distribution of frequency with the total sample analyzed. As with any study with an exploratory purpose, these findings raise more questions than answers. It is possible to suppose that the state of Assuredness on the Choice, as a criterion for selection and consumption of goods and offers of an artistic and cultural nature, has changed with the conditions of social isolation or, in other words, a new condition was established in which less self-assured people maintained consumption levels and people who were more confident about the risks and complexities of their choices gave different answers: either they decreased the consumption of artistic and cultural goods and products or they increased such levels. This may be related to life outside the pandemic and it is possible to suppose that self-assured people had a more intense life of consumption of art and culture in normal times, which leads to a perception of reduction. At the same time, other people with the same attitudinal profile have adapted themselves more easily to the new scenario and, therefore, started to consume more.

The second difference found was in the group formed by the Relevance attributed to the consumption of artistic and cultural products. The data indicated that people who attributed less Relevance to this type of consumption are those who maintained consumption levels comparable to their status before the pandemic (group participation of 33.1%, versus 24.9% of the sample as a whole), so it is possible to say that art and culture have not gained importance in their daily lives. On the other hand, the group that attributed more relevance to the consumption of artistic and cultural products was the one with a participation (29.1%) higher than the distribution of the total sample (24.9%), which indicates that these people moved to consume, proportionally, more art and culture offers than others.

CONCLUSION

The research presented in this chapter brings on several insights and contributions on the state of consumption of artistic and cultural products during the coronavirus pandemic, specifically under lockdown conditions in Brazil.

The most central finding of the study, based on the answers of more than half of the respondents, is that there was an increase in the consumption of this kind of product during the quarantine decreed by health authorities. The reasons associated with this practice are related to escapism and relaxation: 96.2% of respondents associate the consumption of artistic and cultural products with entertainment and distraction, while 90.2% associate this habit with the need for "time spending". Time becomes different in lockdown, since the routine of isolated people in their homes implies fewer alternatives and possibilities of choice, than on normal days. In this sense, technology facilitates access to content and contributes to a new being-in-the-world mediated by technology. The offer of audiovisual content, movies, series and television programs, music, and even the transmission of events and presentations of an artistic nature (concerts, dance and theater performances) is facilitated by the internet, making producers and consumers meet on the virtual space, the new *locus* for interaction, without the need for physical, tangible and in-person conditions.

The findings indicate a significant growth in the consumption of audiovisual products that can be distributed online (TV series and programs, movies and music), while, as expected, other forms of expression, highly connected with the need for face-to-face experience in a physical environment, had a significant reduction in consumption, especially theatrical performances and photography and visual arts exhibitions.

An interesting finding has to do with music consumption: despite being the most popular modality in the respondents' habits BEFORE the conditions of social isolation, there was a small drop AFTER the lockdown. On the other hand, there was a significant growth in consumption of the modality that involves watching music shows. This means saying that music has not lost its relative importance, it has only changed its form of expression and the human sense used in the experience, from the act of listening to what involves looking (watching).

The data indicate that women and younger people are profiles that reported, proportionally, a greater increase in the consumption of cultural and artistic products. Paradoxically, it is also women who reported a lower proportion of consumption, which suggests a complex behavior, in a "U" shape. A possible explanation, which deserves further investigation, may be the modified domestic routine, with women performing domestic tasks that restrict the time available for the consumption of artistic and cultural products.

Using an attitudinal scale, 5 possible dimensions that express reasons for involvement with artistic and cultural products were analyzed. Differences in the dimensions "Assuredness in Choice" and "Relevance" were statistically significant.

In the first case, "Assuredness in Choice", there are suggestions that people who feel less assured in the process of assessing risk and feel comfortable in choosing options for artistic and cultural offerings, maintained the level of consumption; while people who are more confident in their choices also manifested a "U-shaped" behavior, having proportionally more responses that indicate a lower consumption and, simultaneously, also proportions of responses that indicate a higher consumption. More studies are needed to deepen the understanding of these behaviors, but it is possible to suggest that people who were more assured in their choices were perhaps the ones who most consumed cultural and artistic offerings before the pandemic was decreed, which justifies the perception of decrease; while, on the other hand, another group of people with the same attitudinal profile understands that in the pandemic there were conditions for increased consumption.

In the case of the second construct, "Relevance", the study data indicate that people who attribute greater relevance to the consumption of artistic and cultural products are those who consumed this kind of offer in greater proportions than the research sample.

The survey, by itself, is a picture taken from a particular moment in time. The question that emerges is whether this situation will continue in the future, with the reopening of public spaces and access to in-person events. In any case, the study provides subsidies to confirm the common perception that new technologies that alter the artistic experience are consolidating new ways of accessing content that previously only became available in person, as proposed by several authors (Coman, 2020; Noehrer, 2021; Pennington, Eltham, 2021; Respini, 2018). This transformation process is quite sensitive, as the data confirmed, in some segments, namely among the younger ones and women, and in some modalities, especially those related to audiovisual and music.

From a managerial point of view, the pandemic can be seen as a turning point in which technology has assumed greater relevance and indispensability for the creation and distribution of artistic and cultural products. Research data show that some sociodemographic and attitudinal segments (younger people, women, those who attribute more relevance to art and culture, those with more assuredness in the choice of cultural and artistic offers) increased their consumption and that some types of experiences (music, movies, tv shows) showed higher levels of consumption in the period. More research is needed, but it is possible to assume that, given the conditions of isolation, people who had less frequent habits of online consumption of art and culture were exposed to experiences mediated by technology because they had no other option, and this represents a form of forced learning. The increase in the number of streaming service contracts during the pandemic in Brazil serves as a factual indication of this change. It is therefore necessary to analyze the trade-off that is established: spending limited resources on art and culture online competes to live and in-person artistic and cultural events. Another point to be emphasized is that the urgent need for adaptation, given the circumstances faced, accelerated the movement of cultural institutions and producers towards the opportunities that the internet opens up for the sector. This goes beyond maintaining online communities and promotional and communication efforts, but involves the very nature of the product. Collections and virtual visits, new audiovisual experiences, the understanding of the specific language of the medium, which involves interaction and feedback in real time, have become the result of a learning process that many producers had to adapt to. In the environments mediated by the internet, data collection and analysis becomes a tool with great power to transform the way in which artistic and cultural services and products consumption are evaluated and the relationship with consumers are managed.

In conclusion, it is needed to point out that only a few years after the early events of the pandemic, a large segment of the population evolved from adolescence to adulthood during the conditions of isolation and lockdown determined by the authorities. The extent to which this impacts the value attributed to forms of artistic experience is a topic of great interest for future studies.

REFERENCES

Aquino, E. M., Silveira, I. H., Pescarini, J. M., Aquino, R., Souza-Filho, J. A. D., Rocha, A. D. S., Ferreira, A., Victor, A., Teixeira, C., Machado, D. B., Paixão, E., Alves, F. J. O., Pilecco, F., Menezes, G., Gabrielli, L., Leite, L., Almeida, M. C. C., Ortelan, N., Fernandes, Q. H. R. F., ... Lima, R. T. D. R. S. (2020). Medidas de distanciamento social no controle da pandemia de COVID-19: Potenciais impactos e desafios no Brasil. *Ciencia & Saude Coletiva*, *25*(suppl 1), 2423–2446. doi:10.1590/1413-81232020256.1.10502020 PMID:32520287

Banco Central do Brasil. (2021). Estudos Especiais do Banco Central. Fechamento de empresas durante a pandemia. *Relatório de Inflação*, *99*. Available at: https://www.bcb.gov.br/conteudo/relatorioinflacao/EstudosEspeciais/EE099_Fechamento_de_empresas_na_pandemia.pdf. Accessed in: Dec. 2021

Baltar, F., & Brunet, I. (2012). Social research 2.0: Virtual snowball sampling method using Facebook. *Internet Research*, *22*(1), 57–74. doi:10.1108/10662241211199960

Bianconi, F., Catalucci, S., Filippucci, M., Marsili, R., Moretti, M., Rossi, G., & Speranzini, E. (2017). Comparison between two non-contact techniques for art digitalization. *Journal of Physics: Conference Series*, *882*(1), 012005. doi:10.1088/1742-6596/882/1/012005

CGI.BR. (2019). *Pesquisa TIC Domicílios*. Resumo Executivo. Available at: https://cetic.br/media/docs/publicacoes/2/20201123115919/resumo_executivo_tic_dom_2019.pdf

Coman, I. (2020). Art Consumption During COVID-19 Pandemic: Influence upon the Sentiment of Life Fulfilment. *Business Excellence and Management, 10*(SI1), 112-126.

Dahlgren, A.N, & Wasielewski, A. (2021). Cultures of Digitization: A Historiographic Perspective on Digital Art History. *Visual Resources*, 1-21.

Dowbor, L. (2020). *O capitalismo se desloca: novas arquiteturas sociais*. Available at: https://sesc.digital/conteudo/programacao/42778/o-capitalismo-se-desloca-novas-arquiteturas-sociais

Ebrahimi, A., Ebrahimi, S., & Esfahani, S. A. (2020). How COVID-19 pandemic can lead to promotion of remote medical education and democratization of education? *Journal of Advances in Medical Education & Professionalism, 8*(3), 144. PMID:32802909

Pais, E. (2021). *Sob ataque de Bolsonaro, Cultura defende seu impacto na economia com receita de 170 bilhões de reais*. Available at: https://brasil.elpais.com/cultura/2019-12-27/sob-ataque-de-bolsonaro-cultura-defende-seu-impacto-na-economia-com-receita-de-170-bilhoes-de-reais.html

FGV. (2020). *Relatório sobre os Impactos Econômicos da Covid-19*. Economia Criativa. Available at: https://fgvprojetos.fgv.br/sites/fgvprojetos.fgv.br/files/economiacriativa_formatacaosite.pdf

Firjan. (2014). *Mapeamento da Indústria Criativa no Brasil*. Available at: https://www.firjan.com.br/EconomiaCriativa/downloads/MapeamentoIndustriaCriativa-Firjan2014.pdf

Fonseca, M. J. & Rossi, C A. V. (1998). O estudo do envolvimento com o produto em comportamento do consumidor: fundamentos teóricos e proposição de uma escala para aplicação no Brasil. *Anais do Encontro Anual da Anpad*.

Fossatti, M., & Gemetto, J. (2011). *Arte joven y cultura digital*. Available at: https://www.articaonline.com/wp-content/uploads/2017/08/Arte-joven-y-cultura-digital.pdf

Hair, J. F., Black, W. C., Babin, B. J., Anderson, R. E., & Tatham, R. L. (2009). *Análise multivariada de dados*. Bookman.

Hesmondhalgh. (2002). *The Cultural Industries*. London: Sage.

Howkins, J. (2002). *The creative economy: how people make Money from ideas*. Penguin Global.

Laycock, R. (2021) *Serviços de Streaming mais Populares*. Available at: https://www.finder.com/br/streaming-estatisticas

Markusen, A., Wassall, G., Denatale, D., & Cohen, R. (2008). Defining the Creative Economy: Industry and Occupational Approaches. *Economic Development Quarterly, 22*(1), 24–45. doi:10.1177/0891242407311862

Mattei, L., & Heinen, V. L. (2020). Impacts of the COVID-19 crisis on the Brazilian labor market. *Brazilian Journal of Political Economy, 40*(4), 647–668. doi:10.1590/0101-31572020-3200

Nobre, G. (2020). *Creative Economy and Covid-19, Technology, Automation and the New Economy*. Available at: http://www. researchgate.net/profile/Guilherme_Nobre/publication/340438912_Creative_Economy_and_Covid19_technology_automation_and_the_new_economy/links/5e8a71f4299bf130797ffc1e/Creative-Economy-and-Covid-19-technology-automation-and-the-new-economy.pdf

Lukas, N., Gilmore, A., Jay, C., & Yo, Y. (2021). The impact of COVID-19 on digital data practices in museums and art galleries in the UK and the US. *Humanities & Social. Science Communication*, *8*(1). https://www.researchsquare.com/article/rs-535272/v1

Pennington, A., & Eltham, B. (2021). *Creativity in crisis: Rebooting Australia's arts and entertainment sector after COVID*. Academic Press.

Premebida, E. A. (2021). E-commerce in 2020, a scenario of opportunities amid a pandemic. *Research. Social Development*, *10*(2).

Radermecker, A. S. V. (2021). Art and Culture in the COVID-19 era: For a Consumer-oriented Approach. *SN Business & Economics*, *1*(1), 1–14. doi:10.100743546-020-00003-y PMID:34778811

Respin, E. (2018). No Ghost, Just a Shell. In *Art in the Age of the Internet: 1989 to Today* (pp. 13–40). Yale University Press.

Ryder, B. N. (2020). *Cultural Institutions' Digital Responses To COVID-19 Temporary Closures*. Available at: https://stars.library.ucf.edu/honorstheses/820

Salvador, E., Navarrete, T., & Srakar, A. (Eds.). (2021). *Cultural Industries and the Covid-19 Pandemic: A European Focus*. Routledge. doi:10.4324/9781003128274

Silva, R. (2021). *Um ano depois do início da pandemia, plataformas de streaming contabilizam ganhos*. Available at: https://forbes.com.br/forbes-money/2021/03/um-ano-depois-do-inicio-da-pandemia-plataformas-de-streaming-contabilizam-ganhos/

Sogabe, M. (2016). Arte pós-digital. *Proceedings of International Meeting of Art and Technology*. Available at: https://files.cercomp.ufg.br/weby/up/779/o/milton_sogabe.pdf

UNESCO. (2021). *UNESCO e Banco Mundial lançam marco de ação para recuperação, desenvolvimento e crescimento econômico das cidades criativas*. Available at: https://pt.unesco.org/news/unesco-e-banco-mundial-lancam-marco-acao-recuperacao-desenvolvimento-e-crescimento-economico

Willard, T., & Halder, M. (2003). *The information society and sustainable development*. International Institute for Sustainable Development (IISD), Winnipeg, Canada. http://www. iisd. org/PUBLICATIONS/pub.aspx

KEY TERMS AND DEFINITIONS

Art and Culture Digitization: The process to produce and reproduce artistic and cultural expressions based on technology and digital platforms, that dematerializes the experience, creating new forms to preserve, produce, publish, distribute contents, and engage publics.

Artistic and Cultural Products: Set of goods and services related to arts, cultural expression, heritage conservation and other forms of activities that offer opportunities to intellectual reflection, entertainment, or evasion experiences, which elevate the spiritual state of individuals.

Consumer Behavior: The study of the behavior of individuals, groups and organizations, all activities related to how they search for information, take decisions, use and adopt products and services to satisfy their desires and needs.

Creative Economy: Set of activities based on human creativity and knowledge that obtain economic value from consumers, a range that encompass activities related to business and consumption, activities related to cultural expression, activities related to the media and activities related to technology.

Involvement Scale: Set of items used to measure attitudes towards some specific objects; these items express, numerically, a degree of psychological state of agreement or disagreement with sentences; adherence or rejection of abstract concepts from an individual point of view.

Live Cultural Events: Events that counts on the physical presence of an performer and their audiences in an tangible space or venue; typically exhibitions, concerts, plays and theatrical performances.

Streaming Services: A technological method do deliver cultural, informative and/or of entertainment content in a continuous way, from a particular provider to a subscriber computer, TV, or mobile device via an internet connection.

Section 3

New Trends on Information and Communication Technology

Chapter 8
A Survey on the Deployment of Smart Factories in the Post-COVID-19 Era:
The Role of 5G, Deployment Options, Benefits, and Business Models

Alexandros Psyrris
National and Kapodistrian University of Athens, Greece

Antonios Kargas
https://orcid.org/0000-0001-6157-1761
Department of Business Administration, University of West Attica, Greece

Dimitrios Varoutas
https://orcid.org/0000-0002-9101-6221
National and Kapodistrian University of Athens, Greece

ABSTRACT

Smart Factory and 5th Generation Mobile Communication Systems gained much scientific and business attention during the years before the COVID-19 pandemic, as part of the so-called 4th Industrial Revolution (Industry 4.0). Even though there are second thoughts about whether the pandemic crisis will slow up Industry's 4.0 implementation, there has been an acceleration in the use of intelligent and reliable communications solutions in all business aspects, leading to the need for deepening our understanding about digital transformation and digitalization strategies. The current chapter aims to describe the concept of Smart Factory as a key factor of the 4th Industrial Revolution and to deliver its most important factors for a successful implementation. Moreover, smart factory is interrelated with 5th generation of mobile communication systems (5G), which seems to offer the capabilities needed for the advanced industrial digitalization.

DOI: 10.4018/978-1-7998-9227-4.ch008

INTRODUCTION

Each one of the last 3 centuries brought an industrial revolution, capable to transform the whole economic landscape, in terms of: (a) jobs created and abolished, (b) technologies and processes massively introduced and (c) an overall societal change. In the 21st century, **business environment has entered in new era**, that many researchers and professionals claim to be the Fourth Industrial Revolution, the so-called "**Industry 4.0**". Industry 4.0 aim to deliver "fundamental improvements to the industrial process involved in manufacturing, engineering, material usage and supply chain and life cycle management" (Kagermann et al., 2013) by enabling the communication between people, machines and resources. This will be achieved by integrating physical, machinery and devices with networked sensors and software, creating complex but accurate systems capable to predict, plan and control societal and business outcomes.

The whole idea is based on **embedding networks and computers to physical process**, in order: to support **unique identification**, to **collect, store and analyze data** and finally to **create networks** from physical processes to computation (e.g. structured information) and vice versa (e.g. processes reengineering) (E. A. Lee, 2008). This side of Industry 4.0 is the so-called **Cyber Physical System** (CPS) and it aim to the **fusion of physical and virtual world** (Kagermann, 2014). Another side is the **integration of Internet of Things** (IoT) into various manufacturing and business processes / operations in order to allow "things" such as mobile devices, sensors, RFID and actuators to **interact** and **cooperate** to **reach common goals** (Giusto, Iera, Morabito, & Atzori, 2016).

Industry 4.0's main goal at the time is to achieve the integration between physical, machinery and devices (CPS) with networked sensors and software (IoT), creating complex but accurate systems capable to predict, plan and control **business outcomes** (Industrial Internet Consortium, 2013). By incorporating both business and societal aspects to the Fourth Industrial Revolution's outcomes the boundaries of expected change elevate to business sector that lie out from manufacturing (such as transports and logistics), while in societal level aspects of everyday life (such as cultural and tourism activities) will embed technological elements and change how both services providers and consumers think and act (Kargas & Varoutas, 2020). By accepting so, authors recognize that gradually **Industry 4.0 can and will find apply to any business sector and industry** where internet and embedded systems can serve as a backbone to integrate physical objects, human actors, intelligent machines, production lines and processes in order to develop a new agile, networked and intelligent value chain (Schumacher, Erol, & Sihn, 2016).

Taking into consideration one of the first scenarios (Wahlster, 2013) about how Industry 4.0 will transform business environment, reader can see how multiple users / consumers personal choices are transformed to an optimized process for the supply chain or the packaging. Sensors, actuators and microprocessors can be used to transform objects to smart objects. These objects are not only digital devices, but common, everyday objects augmented with the above-mentioned digital technology. The IoT connects smart objects that have common goals with an online database which tracks and collects data from real world through Cloud Computing technologies. These data can be used in various ways including (indicative): (a) to change smart objects' behavior (new goal to serve), (b) redesign a product / service according to users measured needs / desires in a decentralized procedure that can be dynamically reconfigured when needed (Löffler & Tschiesner, 2013), (c) creating the framework for bespoke design focusing on values and experiences of users instead of typical production optimization.

These features create the vision of products / services with embedded knowledge, capable to rearrange their characteristics, production and distribution (with minimal human intervention) according to their tracked lifecycle and customer use (Hermann, Pentek, & Otto, 2016). Industry 4.0 aspire to keep mass production's best elements (e.g. reliability and quality) and transform its process in order to meet mass customization on demand (Petrelli, 2017) creating unique designs (e.g. product / services' characteristics according to grouped customers' needs) to offer different user experiences.

Even though there were second thoughts about whether COVID-19 pandemic will slow up Industry's 4.0 implementation, there has been an acceleration in the use of intelligent and reliable communications solutions in all business aspects, leading to the need for deepening our understanding about digital transformation and digitalization strategies. Industries in many countries are already moving to the digitalization of the production lines to full automatize their functions with the support of operation technologies (OT) and information and communication technologies (ICT).

Current Chapter aim to describe the concept of **Smart Factory**, as a key factor of the 4th industrial revolution and to deliver its most important factors for a successful implementation. Moreover, smart factory is interrelated with **5th generation of mobile communication systems (5G)**, which seems to offer the capabilities needed for the advanced industrial digitalization. The Chapter aim to present the 5G related smart factory use cases and the benefits for the Mobile Network Operators (MNO) and the manufacturers from the proposed digital transformation / digitalization of the traditional factory to a smart factory. Finally, a comprehensive analysis of the options related with private networks with spectrum usage, network slicing and management of SLA are examined.

CHALLENGES AND OBJECTIVES OF INDUSTRY 4.0

Industry 4.0 created new challenges to researchers, research institutes and industries. In contrast to all previous Industrial Revolutions, Industry 4.0 is an ongoing process instead of an ex-post observed phenomenon (Drath & Horch, 2014). Facing an a-priori phenomenon, researchers, companies and governments can take part in shaping the future by developing the scenarios, getting mature to face changes and creating the required policies respectively (Hermann et al., 2016). Even though "change" hides dangers, participating in the change process can reduce risks or even offer benefits and competitive advantages.

Moreover, this is point is crucial especially for industries in smaller countries, where gaining a competitive advantage in European or Global level is much more difficult (Kargas, Kiriakidis, & Zacharakis, 2020; Laitsou, Kargas, & Varoutas, 2020). Even in manufacturing industry of heavily industrialized countries, it is accepted that Industry 4.0 can bring increased complexity in both macro and micro level (Schuh, Potente, Varandani, & Schmitz, 2014), while smaller companies are not aware of the financial effort needed to implement the required hardware and applications taking into account that the overall impact on their business models seem uncertain (Schumacher et al., 2016). The problems are not only financial / profit related but mainly related with how to create value from the core idea. Companies find it difficult to relate Industry 4.0 with their specific domain and with their business strategy (Erol, Schuhmacher, & Sihn, 2016), which leads to failures in identifying implementation programmes, fields of action and developmental projects.

These challenges are even greater when Industry 4.0 is to be implemented in SME's business environment, where resource capabilities, in IT Systems and infrastructures, are less than what basic requirements imply (Schröder, 2016). Even under the German business environment and only for the manufacturing sector (not the whole economy) roughly 5% merely adopt technologies related with Industry 4.0 and just on third of them (around 1,6% in the whole economy) are developing strategies for a full adoption (Pereshybkina, Conde, Kalyesubula, & Kirner, 2017). Creating scenarios is revealed as crucial for enlarge adoption and deepen its extent, taking into consideration that lack of general standards and data security norms make it difficult, especially for SME's, to take part in value chain networks and innovational joint collaborations (Pereshybkina et al., 2017).

SMART FACTORY AS AN INDUSTRY'S 4.0 KEY FACTOR

According to Lee (J. Lee, 2015) we can define smart factory as "*the integration of all recent IoT technological advances in computer networks, data integration, and analytics*" aiming to bring transparency to all manufacturing factories. The smart factory is based on advanced technology, virtual production systems by digital platform connected with IoT, uses human-machine collaboration, supports minimal incremental cost for new products and enables new business models. Some of the smart factory's capabilities are:

- Machine alarm aggregation, prioritization and analysis.
- Improvements in overall equipment effectiveness (OEE).
- Human-machine interfaces (HMI) for real-time monitoring of production resources.
- Sensor based manufacturing and reporting of key performance indicators (KPIs).
- Shorter time to market for new products.
- End-to-end supply chain synchronization.
- In-process quality control based on real time data analysis.

To reach smart factory's capabilities, it is required to transform existing physical facilities / equipment, as well as firm's existing intellectual capital, in a procedure called digital transformation. The digital transformation of a factory consists of the use of devices and equipment capable of transmitting and receiving data for controlling, monitoring and maintenance purposes consequently moving to advanced functionalities for production lines (Figure 1). There are several stages of digital transformation of a factory into a smart factory (Pricewaterhouse Coopers, 2016), starting from the adoption of isolated digital equipment, and then implementing a vertical integration by digital production and services. The next proposed stages are the transformation with a horizontal collaboration by integration of customer, supply chain and external partners.

An essential technological factor for the digital transformation of a factory is the **Internet of Things (IoT)** which is defined by ITU-T Y.4000 as "*a global infrastructure for the information society, enabling advanced services by interconnecting (physical and virtual) Things based on existing and evolving interoperable information and communication technologies*". In such a procedure, "**security**" seems to play a crucial role. The use of authentication credentials issued by either the manufacturing company or the device manufacturer is a reliable solution, while different types of credentials can be used (ETSI, 2018b). TCP/IP technologies (Transmission Control Protocol / Internet Protocol) like OPC Unified Architecture (OPC UA) are usually deployed throughout the entire factory and are therefore an important driver for the selection of the authentication mechanisms to be used. An approach is presented in (Giaretta, Dragoni, & Massacci, 2019) where the security-by-contract paradigm is combined with fog computing to secure IoT devices.

Another important factor for the implementation of a smart factory is the **communication network**. An example is the communication initiated by the manufactured part called Manufactured Product as a Smart Client (MPSC). This MPSC is often moved by an Automated Guided Vehicle (AGV) and there are special requirements for the communication between employees, material, machines, manufacturing execution systems (MES) and MPSC (3GPP, 2020).

Figure 1. Digital factory communication network (Source: ETSI TR22804)

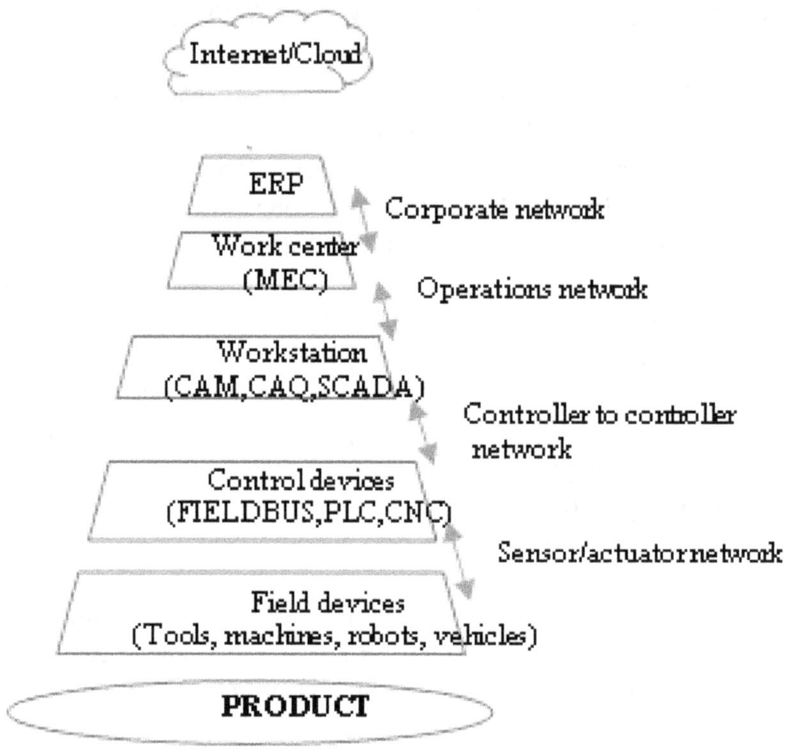

Communication networks play a significant role to both smart factory and to Industry 4.0 as a while. The Industry 4.0 aims to transform the physical production systems to cyber physical ones that can be operated beyond the local factory premises with a variety of applications based on communication networks which shall be capable to provide:

- Critical communication applications such as real-time optimization based on instantly received information from monitoring or interaction between different operators of machines, remote control of robotic operations and collaborative robots in closed-loop control systems. The use case is characterized by communication latency that may go below 1 ms.
- Non-time critical communications concerning applications such as localization of assets and goods, quality control and sensor data collection. Remote control applications based on augmented reality (AR) and virtual reality (VR) to provide support in production and maintenance.
- Seamless communications across multiple mediums such as wired and fixed networks, multiple vendors, multiple technologies, different production sites and other parties.
- A fast and reliable reconfiguration of Quality of Services (QoS) is necessary to enable fast network adaptation to current specific delay requirements.

The wireless connectivity can provide the flexibility, mobility and versatility required for the smart factory. According to (ETSI, 2011) the wireless communication has the following benefits for the industrial manufacturing process:

1) Increased productivity by:
    a. reduced downtime of production lines.
    b. improved product quality.
    c. faster installation and commissioning of production lines and higher flexibility due to easier reconfiguration of manufacturing systems.
    d. more efficient manufacturing process due to data analytics.
2) Lower energy consumption due to energy efficient wireless communications.
3) New possibilities for manufacturing automation such as mobility.
4) Improvement in safety at work.
5) Lower installation cost compared to wires especially in large areas with difficult access, or in high risk environment.

Even though there exist the above-mentioned benefits, the wired technologies dominate industry automation, including dedicated Industrial Ethernet technologies (e.g. Sercos, PROFINET, EtherCAT) and fieldbuses (e.g. PROFIBUS, CC-Link, CAN). In 2017, while wireless technologies such as Bluetooth and WLAN make up only of 4% of the market. These technologies cannot provide the necessary reliability and low latency needed for the most stringent Industry 4.0 applications. On the other hand, 5G can achieve simultaneous ultra-low latency of less than 1 ms and 99.999% reliability, making it the only mobile technology suitable for stringent Industry 4.0 applications according to (Nokia, 2017).

Different to wired technologies, the wireless communication devices may interfere with others on the same premises or environment, disturbing each other, and this fact is leading to the recognition that coexistence management is needed (IEC, 2017). Even in the case a critical wireless link of an industrial application would be interrupted or not respond instantaneously, safety measures beyond communication take effect immediately, according to EN/IEC[1] 61508 and EN/IEC 61784-3-series.

Examples of wireless networks for short range are Bluetooth low energy, IEEE 802.11ah, IEEE 802.15.4, ZigBee, Z-Wave etc. which do not have very high requirements for low latency communications. Examples of wireless networks for wide range (LPWA) are Sigfox, Weightless, Ingenu, LoRaWAN, etc. (Radio Spectrum Policy Group, 2016). Industrial wireless communication indicated in (ETSI, 2011) exist for frequencies such as 169 MHz, 433 MHz, 863-870 MHz, 1,880 MHz to 1,900 MHz (DECT) also 2,400 to 2,4835 GHz (ISM-band), 5,15-5,35 GHz and 5,47-5,725 GHz (WLAN).

In a factory, examples of networks are IEC 62591-2 (WirelessHART®3), IEC 62601 (WIA-PA) and IEC 62734 (ISA100.11a) that use IEEE 802.15.4 for the process automation applications. There are also wireless networks specified in IEC 61784-1 and IEC 61784-2 that use IEEE 802.11 and IEEE 802.15.1 for factory automation applications. The 3GPP has introduced in Rel.13 the LTE Cat-M1 (eMTC) supporting up to 350kbps data rates, voice, roaming suitable for real-time fixed or mobile applications and Cat-NB1 (NB-IoT) supporting up to 65kbps data rates for static sensor applications. Finally, 5G is a significant technological and managerial enabler for smart factory with more advanced capabilities, compared to other communication wireless technologies solutions.

Another enabler of a smart factory is the **digital manufacturing platform** which combines technical and management systems and analyses real time KPIs from the factory floor and the supply chain network enabling the operator to task scheduling and tracking leading to increased process reliability and Overall Equipment Effectiveness (OEE). The main architectures are (World Economic Forum, 2019):

- Industrial Internet Reference Architecture (IIRA), which is built on top of the IoT Analysis Framework (IIAF).
- Reference Architectural Model Industry 4.0 (RAMI4.0) which consists of three dimensions: hierarchy levels, life cycle and value (Strufe et al., 2019).
- oneM2M[2] architecture enables interoperability across IoT applications regardless of the underlying technology used.

Also, the new cloud based models (Platform-as-a-Service, Infrastructure-as-a-Service, Software-as-a-Service, etc.) are significant enablers for the smart factory ecosystem. Some of the advantages for using a cloud infrastructure (public or hybrid) are the processing of data from multiple factory premises and the need for special computing capabilities and algorithms not available on-premises resources.

Additionally, the Artificial Intelligence (AI) mechanisms are not only used in use cases equipment but also used in 5G network for optimization, enhanced customer experience, network management by controlling network slicing and solving complex data problems. The use case of equipment with computer vision is evaluated in paper (Villasante Marcos, 2022) as an URLLC service with the combination of 5G edge computing and AI resulting to lower end-to-end (E2E) latency.

5G AS KEY ENABLER OF SMART FACTORY

The role and the importance of 5G networks seems to be constantly growing, related with overall technological development, as well as related with new forms of economic and social life, such as smart and sustainable cities (Psyrris, Kargas, & Varoutas, 2020). According to its performance requirements 5G can offer lower cost, lower energy consumption, massive connectivity and a high level of security. Moreover, 5G is characterized for its capability to transport very high data volumes with advanced management and its low latency applications. The 5G with the Software Defined Networks (SDN) flexible control allows prioritization and proactive resource reservation ensuring a specific level of Quality of Services leading to advanced Service Level Agreements (SLA) support.
In the following sub-sections, some main characteristics and challenges for 5G in industry are presented:

5G Integration with Industrial Ethernet

A challenge for 5G is the integration with industrial Ethernet especially in brownfield deployments, while the concept of transparent integration may be beneficial (Neumann, Wisniewski, Ganesan, Rost, & Jasperneite, 2018). Due to the adaptive system architecture of 5G, it is possible to transparently integrate industrial networks with the 5G mobile networks e.g. the Time Sensitive Network (TSN-IEEE 802.1Qcc) Txl maps the 5G Quality of Services Class Indicator (QCI). The standardized 5QI to Quality of Services characteristics mapping are presented in (ETSI, 2021) including the process automation. Alongside with 5G's IP capability, it should be possible to either use:

- Standardized IP based protocols such as OPC Unified Architecture, ModbusTCP, HARTip.

- Pack non-IP-based protocols into IP-frames in a proprietary way. This can be inside standardized protocols such as http or proprietary IP-based.
- Proprietary IP-based protocols.

Network Slicing

Another characteristic of 5G is the provision of end-to-end slice capabilities, virtualized edge and platform. An IoT system can be considered as a 5G network slice where sensors communicate wirelessly via e.g. Bluetooth, ZigBee, LoRa technologies with an IoT Gateway, which is capable of handling, storing and transferring data through 5G facilities. The IoT platform then enables the communications between IoT devices and applications in a service-oriented base.

In the cloud environment, an IoT Broker is in charge of interacting with external applications while optimally delivering different data information via resource policies. In addition, the Broker influences IoT traffic shape by application of service aware Quality of Services at the application level. The ability to optimize sliced network capacity enables resource efficiency in the network.

Security

The 5G networks are expected to support heterogeneous connected devices and networks. In particular the 5G-IoT network security will be much more complicated. Integrators and providerS of 5G-IoT services must comply with regulations such as the General Data Protection Regulation (GDPR) in Europe. The HORIZON 2020 project SecureIoT (SECUREIoT, 2021) developed an architecture which can enable the offering of security services (e.g., risk assessments, compliance auditing reports) based on a managed, cloud based and utility-based model i.e. as SECaaS (Security as a Service).

Also, the (Haider, Baig, & Imran, 2020) presents AI and ML mechanisms for 5G security issues such as identity, authentication, privacy and E2E protection. The proposed architecture integrates AI and Machine Learning (ML) to detect threats for classification and testing of security protocols against detected threats/attacks in 5G and future networks.

Standardisation And Pilot Projects

3rd Generation Partnership Project, known as 3GPP, aim to unite telecommunication's standards coming from seven (7) development organizations. 3GPP is in the process of studying mechanisms to allow Narrowband Internet of Things (NB-IoT) and LTE-M[3] to connect to the 5G core network and to coexist with a New Radio (NR) carrier independently from an LTE one. This will allow the 5G systems of the future to support LTE, NR, NB-IoT and LTE-M using the same core network. 5G adds support for Time-Sensitive Networking (TSN) Ethernet adaptation, TSN time synchronization with generic Precision Time Protocol (gPTP) and Quality of Services.

The New Radio Unlicensed (NR-U) will be able to operate in existing unlicensed bands or in greenfield unlicensed or shared bands. Rel. 16 will bring the first set of vertical features such as ultra-reliable low latency with expected devices in 2022-2023 timeframe. The Rel.16 introduces 5G NR positioning and defines the standards for private 5G networks and network slicing, a feature that allows the creation of guaranteed performance profiles to match specific applications' requirements. The full 5G vertical feature set and finalization of Rel.16 items will come with Rel.17 targeted for standardization in 2022 with devices 1-1.5 years later. The additional elements are 5G massive IoT, TSN and other vertical features.

ETSI[4] has developed the "Smart Anything REFerence ontology" (SAREF) which enables better integration of semantic data from various vertical domains (smart city, smart agricultural, smart manufacturing, automotive, eHealth/ageing-well and wearables) in the IoT use of various network and communications technologies. The ETSI TS 103 410-5 was developed to solve the lack of interoperability between various types of production equipment that manufacture items in a factory.

In the area of 5G and manufacturing there are pilot projects in European Union such as the TANGO project aiming to connect multiple factory premises at different geographical locations to a common company network. Factory premises comprise several machines and additional user-equipment like AR/VR glasses. These premises must be interconnected and usually have access to the Internet through the Company IT network (5Gtango, 2021). Another project is the VINNI (5G-VINNI, 2021) aiming to build a network infrastructure for verticals with network slicing supporting also traffic isolation and multi-tenancy.

USE CASES AND PERFORMANCE REQUIREMENTS

The digital transformation of a factory consists of the following applications as described in (3GPP, 2020):

- Factory or discrete automation refers to the automated control (control-to-control, motion control), monitoring and optimization of processes and workflows within a factory e.g. an automotive manufacturing factory. Involves a large number of mobile production assets, for which massive high-speed wireless communication and localization services are required (mobile robots, massive wireless sensor networks).
- Process automation (PA) refers to the control of production and handling of substances such as chemicals, food & beverage, etc. The use cases are mobile robots, massive wireless sensor networks, closed-loop process control, process monitoring, plant management.
- Production IT and Human-machine interfaces (HMIs) such as panels in production line, laptops, tablet PCs, smartphones. Production IT based applications, such as manufacturing execution systems (MES) and enterprise resource planning (ERP) systems, augmented and virtual reality (AR/VR) applications.
- Logistics and warehousing use cases such as control-to-control, mobile robots.
- Monitoring and maintenance refers to massive wireless sensor networks, remote access and maintenance.

In the following Table 1 the performance characteristics of indicative use cases of the smart factory applications are presented:

Table 1. Performance characteristics

KPI \ USE CASE	Motion control	Control-to-control comm.	Mobile control panels	Mobile robots	Massive wireless sensor networks
Communication service availability	99,9999% to 99,999999%	99,9999% to 99,999999%	99,9999% to 99,999999%	> 99,9999%	> 99,9999%
End-to-end latency: target value	< transfer interval	< transfer interval	< 30 ms	< transfer interval	≤ 10 ms
End-to-end latency: jitter			< 50% of end-to-end latency	< 50% of transfer interval	
Service bit rate: user-experienced data rate			> 5Mbit/s		≤ 100 Mbit/s
Message size [byte]	50	1 k		40 to 250	
Transfer interval: target value	0,5 ms	≤ 4 ms		1 ms	
Survival time	0,5 ms			1 ms	
UE speed	≤ 20 m/s			≤ 14 m/s	
number of UEs	≤ 20	5 to 10		≤ 100	connection density up to 1/m2

A **motion control system** is responsible for controlling moving and/or rotating parts of machines in a defined manner, e.g. in printing machines, machine tools or packaging machines.

Control-to-control (C2C) communication, is the communication between different industrial controllers (e.g., programmable logic controllers or motion controllers).

Control panels are devices for the interaction between people and production machinery as well as for the interaction with moving devices. These panels are used for configuring, monitoring, debugging, controlling and maintaining machines, robots, cranes or complete production lines. Also the control panels can be equipped with an emergency stop button and an enabling device, which an operator can use in case of a safety event in order to avoid damage to workers or machinery.

A mobile robot is a programmable machine able to execute multiple operations, following programmed paths to fulfil a large variety of tasks. A mobile robot can perform activities like assembly of parts, assistance in workers and transportation of materials and products and can move around a space.

Wireless sensor networks (WSN) are monitoring the environment, the processes and the corresponding parameters in an industrial environment. This environment is typically monitored using various types of sensors such as microphones, CO2 sensors, pressure sensors, humidity sensors, and thermometers.

The monitored data is used to detect anomalies in the data, i.e., by leveraging ML algorithms. These algorithms usually require a training phase before a trained ML algorithm can later work on a subset of the available measured data.

The 5G system in the smart factory should be able to support continuous monitoring of the current network state in real-time, to take quick and automated actions in case of problems and to do efficient root-cause analyses in order to avoid any undesired interruption of the connectivity and consequently to the production processes which may incur huge financial damage. In case a third-party network operator is involved in various network domains i.e. access, edge, core, cloud, then an accurate Service Level Agreements (SLA) monitoring is mandatory. There are 5G capabilities which can act as a contributing factor to the successful implementation of smart factory such as:

- Real-time video for monitoring and guidance.
- Massive connectivity for non-time-critical sensing.
- Massive connectivity for time-critical sensing and feedback.

ARCHITECTURE OPTIONS OF PRIVATE NETWORKS

The deployment of 5G network in factory premises uses available spectrum resources which can offer a great number of deployment options. The spectrum sharing is a beneficiary solution as the spectrum is a scarce asset and demand is growing. The network deployment shall be suitable to the required use case or scenario as some applications involve high data transmission with the use of wearables, for instance 3D video or AR content while other applications involve low data transmitted by the different sensors. The mobile network operator (MNO) through Cognitive Radio (CR) and SDN technologies can reserve spectrum and network slices for IoT traffic giving the manufacturing company the opportunity to build and manage its own network (Figure 2).

Figure 2. Example of industrial 5G network

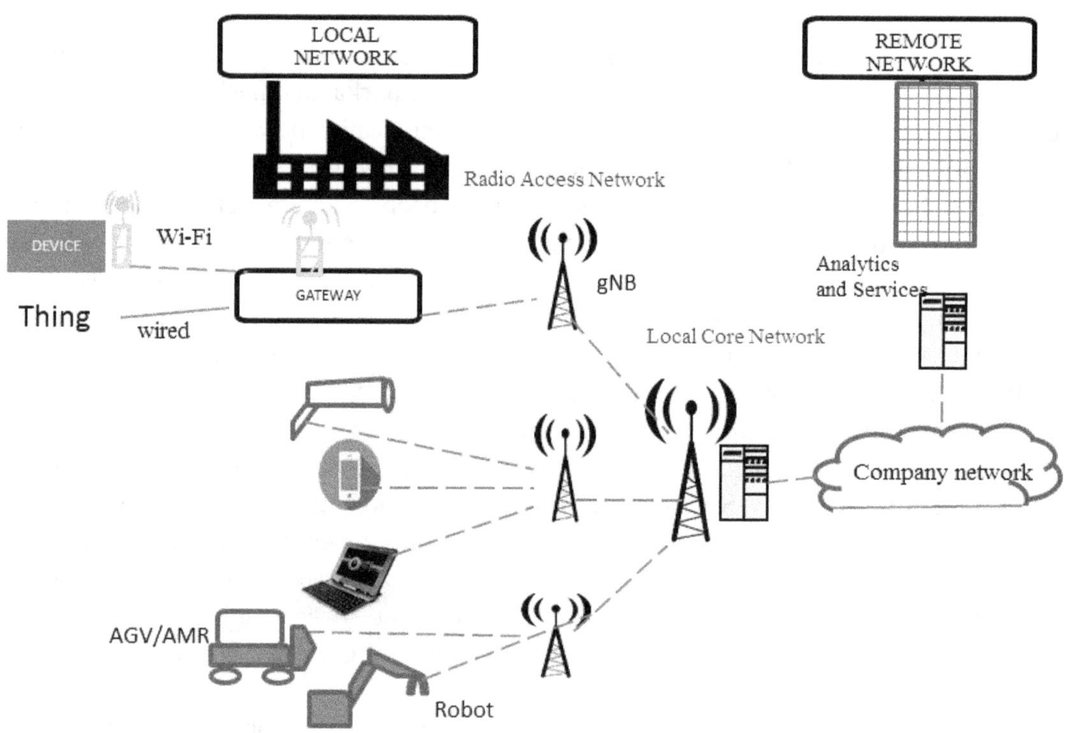

Many manufacturing companies require management, network security, liability, and increased availability which can be offered by 5G private network within the factory. In some use cases seamless interoperability and seamless handovers between 5G public land mobile networks (PLMNs) and private 5G systems is required. In (3GPP, 2020) a network option is identified as a 3GPP network that is not for public use and for which service continuity and roaming with a PLMN is possible. Also, another network option is identified as an isolated 3GPP network that does not interact with a PLMN. Intersystem mobility supported subject to an agreement between the MNOs and service providers, operator policies and the regional or national regulatory requirements. Also, the study in (Prakash, 2019) presents two options for private network: an integrated private network by sharing of Radio Access Network (RAN) or control plane or user plane with 5G network of MNO or independent private network with private network domains.

Private networks are especially needed for supporting URLLC (Ultra-reliable low-latency communication) and may be limited to authorized users, isolated from networks or network resources used by other cellular users. Deployed for use cases with high requirements on the communications system regarding communication service availability with specific requirements for determinism, reliability, redundancy, cyber security and functional safety.

Another scenario is where the manufacturing equipment is limited to connecting on the private network but the employee UEs (User Equipment) are capable of being used both on the private network for communicating with other devices on that network and on the PLMN for communicating to other UEs outside of the private network.

In (Siriwardhana et al., 2019) and (Siriwardhana, Porambage, Ylianttila, & Liyanage, 2020) the advantages in performance are presented for low latency use cases for a private network by deploying core network functions locally in factory premises compared to a MNO with a remote core network. The latency measurements are based on different architecture options for the use cases of AR, massive wireless sensor networks and mobile robots.

In (Rostami, 2019) a qualitative evaluation of deployment models (local, remote) and operation models (private, shared-isolated, shared-integrated) is performed with specific qualitative criteria (performance, security, simplicity, efficiency). As there are many combinations of deployment and operation models the selection is based on the use case and the business model selected.

Another deployment option based on NS is presented in (Valtanen, Backman, & Yrjola, 2019) with blockchain (BC). The manufacturing equipment of a production line can lease independently the network slice required for operations on-demand, approve Service Level Agreements (SLA) and pay for the service according to actual usage. BC smart contract orders slice orchestration according to agreed SLA from a 5G network slice broker. Time stamping of the utilized network slice and dynamic billing according to actual usage is handled by BC.

Some Options for 5G private networks for industrial premises in terms of wireless access are:

Unlicensed Spectrum

For the unlicensed spectrum there are the options of asynchronous and synchronized sharing. The NR-U (New Radio Unlicensed) capability in 3GPP Rel.16 with asynchronous sharing can be used for private 5G networks that do not require eURLLC. The disadvantages are the unpredictable QoS and random access.

The unlicensed spectrum with synchronized sharing can provide higher network capacity, data speeds, predictable QoS and 99.9999% reliability with Coordinated Multipoint (CoMP) spatial diversity. With synchronized sharing, adjacent deployments are possible for simultaneous use of the same spectrum. The synchronized sharing supports IoT in unlicensed spectrum in the 5 GHz band currently used by existing technologies such as Wi-Fi and LTE-based Licensed Assisted Access (LAA). The 6 GHz band is an unlicensed band, in the USA extends between 5,925 – 7,125 GHz with allocation of a portion where time synchronized operation has priority while, in Europe, it extends between 5,925 – 6,425 GHz.

Licensed Spectrum

The Licensed Shared Access (LSA) provided by exclusive licensed and not license exempt spectrum aims to ensure a certain level of guarantee regarding radio spectrum access and protection against harmful interference for both the incumbent and LSA licensees, thus allowing them to provide a predictable QoS (Figure 3). ETSI has set up the specifications in (ETSI, 2015) for the access the spectrum in the 2,3 GHz - 2,4 GHz band (Table 2).

Figure 3. LSA with infrastructure sharing

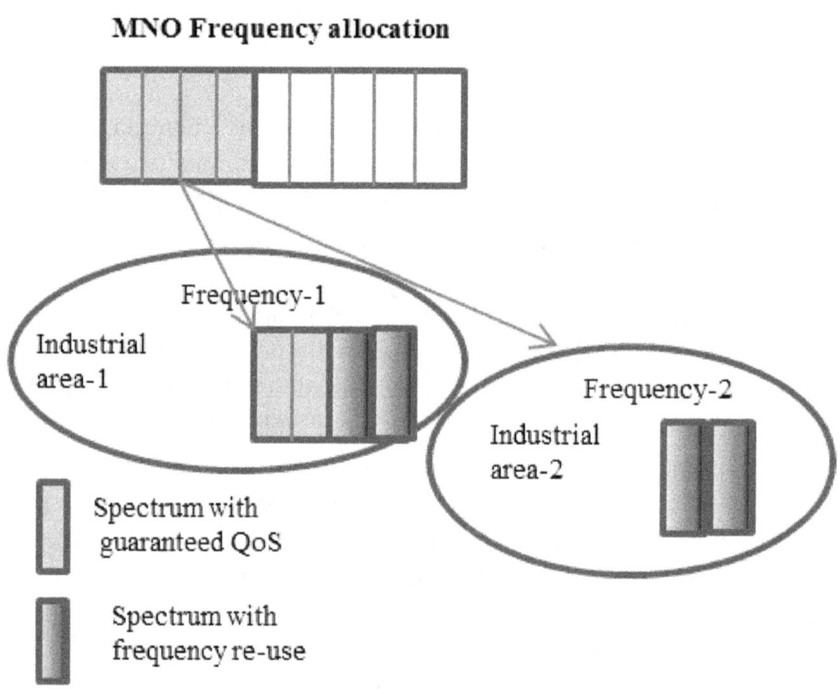

The sharing schemes enable local industrial 5G networks by allowing:

- Mobile network operators to offer dedicated local area services in their licensed frequencies
- Mobile network operators to sublease part of their spectrum locally to local area service providers
- Spectrum to be licensed to local area service providers

The benefits are the large coverage and avoidance of the risk of interference and consequently the production downtime.

Table 2. Local industrial 5G network (ETSI, 2018a)

Domain	Public network	Private network by subleasing	Private network by local licensing
Spectrum	Managed by MNO	Subleased from MNO to the vertical service provider	Allocated by Spectrum Resource Repository to the vertical service provider
Network infrastructure	MNO infrastructure (e.g. Network Slicing) Private attached to public MNO (Network Densification)	Private	Private
Radio Access Technology	Used by MNO	Any, following harmonised standards	Any, following harmonised standards
Network management	National, MNO-supported	Local, stand-alone	Local, stand-alone

LAA (Licensed Assisted Access) uses licensed spectrum for control-related transmissions while sending data over both licensed and license-exempt carriers. Non-critical IoT traffic could be transmitted via the license-exempt band (e.g Wi-Fi) while being controlled from the licensed band (5G NR).

Dedicated shared spectrum for 5G private networks, are considering in countries such as: U.K., Sweden, Finland, Netherlands, France, Australia, Hong Kong, and Japan. In US the Citizen Broadband Radio Service (CBRS) with Spectrum Access System (SAS) has been introduced for relatively low powered network technologies in the band 3,550 GHz – 3,700.

In Germany the Regulator Authority has set fees for 3,7 – 3,8 GHz spectrum for local use (Bundesnetzagentur, 2019). Each assignment fee is calculated using the following formula:

$$Fee = 1000 + B * t * 5 (6a1 + a2)$$

The fee comprises a base amount of €1,000, the assigned bandwidth (B) from 10 MHz to 100 MHz, the assignment term t, in years or fractions of a year based on each month commenced and the surface area covered by the assignment in square kilometers (a1 for land for settlements and transport infrastructure, a2 for other types of land).

Also, the mmWave[5] (24GHz to 100GHz) is promising due to frequency availability in licensed and unlicensed bands with massive multiple-input-multiple-output (massive MIMO) antennas that can overcome path losses and Non-Line of Sight (NLOS) conditions.

CONCLUSION

The benefits arising from the digital transformation of an industry to a smart factory are significant in terms of productivity, cost and time saving. The 5G in specific use cases such as mobile robots, real-time monitoring, AR/VR is a significant enabler for the smart factory combined with its operational and managerial capabilities i.e network slicing, advance data analytics, security and QoS.

The 5G can enable a manufacturing company to transform into a digital integrator and can provide enhanced capabilities to its production lines, company's functional processes involving customers, suppliers and other stakeholders to products and services. There are great expectations regarding manufacturing companies and the MNOs from the digital transformation accompanied with the adoption of 5G capabilities.

Moreover, there are many challenges that have to be answered before the successful deployment of 5G communication systems in factory premises regarding the radiofrequencies planning, the interoperability and the integration with the legacy industrial systems. Especially the deployment of a private network with or without a MNO is under investigation since there are many deployment options and spectrum issues needed to be specified. Also, SLA mechanisms need to be established among the industrial 5G ecosystem players. It is very challenging to investigate the different deployment options of 5G by a manufacturing company in techno-economic terms with benefits monetization.

LIST OF ABBREVIATIONS

Augmented reality	AR
Automated Guided Vehicle	AGV
Citizen Broadband Radio Service	CBRS
Cognitive Radio	CR
Coordinated Multipoint	CoMP
Cyber Physical System	CPS
Enhanced Ultra Reliable Low Latency Communication	eURLLC
Enterprise resource planning	ERP
European Telecommunications Standards Institute	ETSI
generic Precision Time Protocol	gPTP
Human-machine interfaces	HMI
Industrial Internet Reference Architecture	IIRA
Information and communication technologies	ICT
IoT Analysis Framework	IIAF
Internet of Things	IoT
Key performance indicators	KPIs
Licensed Assisted Access	LAA
Low Power Wide Area	LPWA
Long Term Evolution	LTE
Long Term Evolution-Machines	LTE-M
Licensed Shared Access	LSA
Manufacturing execution systems	MES
Manufactured Product as a Smart Client	MPSC
Multiple-input-multiple-output	MIMO
Mobile Network Operators	MNO
Narrowband Internet of Things	NB-IoT
New Radio Unlicensed	NR-U
Non Line of Sight	NLOS
Network Slice	NS
Operation technologies	OT
Overall equipment effectiveness	OEE
Open Platform Communications	OPC
OPC Unified Architecture	OPC UA
Process automation	PA
Public land mobile networks	PLMNs
Quality of Services	QoS
Quality of Services Class Indicator	QCI
Radio Access Network	RAN
Reference Architectural Model Industry 4.0	RAMI4.0
Service Level Agreements	SLA
Smart Anything REFerence ontology	SAREF
Spectrum Access System	SAS

Continued on following page

List of Abbreviations Continued

Software Defined Networks	SDN
Small, Medium Enterprises	SME
Time-Sensitive Networking	TSN
Transmission Control Protocol / Internet Protocol	TCP/IP
User Equipment	UE
Ultra-reliable low-latency communication	URLLC
Virtual reality	VR
3rd Generation Partnership Project	3GPP
5th generation of mobile communication systems	5G

REFERENCES

Bundesnetzagentur. (2019). *5G spectrum fees for local usages*. Retrieved July 1, 2021, from https://www.bundesnetzagentur.de/SharedDocs/Pressemitteilungen/EN/2019/20191031_LokalesBreitband.html

Drath, R., & Horch, A. (2014). Industrie 4.0: Hit or Hype? *IEEE Industrial Electronics Magazine*, *8*(2), 56–58. https://doi.org/10.1109/MIE.2014.2312079

Erol, S., Schuhmacher, A., & Sihn, W. (2016). Resource Efficiency for Global Competitiveness. In *International Conference on Competitive Manufacturing (COMA)* (pp. 495–500). Retrieved from http://publica.fraunhofer.de/documents/N-382579.html

ETSI. (2011). *TR 102 889-2 - V1.1.1 - Electromagnetic compatibility and Radio spectrum Matters (ERM); System Reference Document; Short Range Devices (SRD); Part 2: Technical characteristics for SRD equipment for wireless industrial applications using technologies different from Ultra-Wide Band (UWB)*. Sophia Antipolis Cedex. Retrieved from https://www.etsi.org/deliver/etsi_tr/102800_102899/10288902/01.01.01_60/tr_10288902v010101p.pdf

ETSI. (2015). *TS 103 235 - V1.1.1 - Reconfigurable Radio Systems (RRS); System architecture and high level procedures for operation of Licensed Shared Access (LSA) in the 2 300 MHz - 2 400 MHz band*. Sophia Antipolis Cedex.

ETSI. (2018a). *Reconfigurable Radio Systems (RRS); Feasibility study on temporary spectrum access for local high-quality wireless networks*. Sophia Antipolis Cedex.

ETSI. (2018b). *TR 103 515 - V1.1.1 - Digital Enhanced Cordless Telecommunications (DECT); Study on URLLC use cases of vertical industries for DECT evolution and DECT-2020*. Sophia Antipolis Cedex. Retrieved from https://www.etsi.org/deliver/etsi_tr/103500_103599/103515/01.01.01_60/tr_103515v010101p.pdf

ETSI. (2021). *TS 123 501 - V15.12.0 - 5G; System architecture for the 5G System (5GS) (3GPP TS 23.501 version 15.12.0 Release 15)*. Sophia Antipolis Cedex. Retrieved from https://www.etsi.org/deliver/etsi_ts/123500_123599/123501/15.12.00_60/ts_123501v151200p.pdf

Giaretta, A., Dragoni, N., & Massacci, F. (2019). IoT security configurability with security-by-contract. *Sensors (Basel)*, *19*(19), 4121. https://doi.org/10.3390/s19194121

Giusto, D., Iera, A., Morabito, G., & Atzori, L. (2016). Internet of Things (IoT) – A Technological Analysis and Survey on Vision, Concepts, Challenges, Innovation Directions, Technologies, and Applications. *American Journal of Electrical and Electronic Engineering*, *4*(1), 23–32. http://www.sciepub.com/reference/146416

GPP. (2020, June). *TR 22.804 (2Q20/197 p.) – on Automation in Vertical Domains*. Retrieved July 1, 2021, from https://www.tech-invite.com/3m22/tinv-3gpp-22-804.html

Gtango. (2021). *5GTANGO*. Retrieved July 1, 2021, from https://www.5gtango.eu/

Haider, N., Baig, M. Z., & Imran, M. (2020). Artificial Intelligence and Machine Learning in 5G Network Security: Opportunities, advantages, and future research trends. *Computer Science*.

Hermann, M., Pentek, T., & Otto, B. (2016). Design Principles for Industrie 4.0 Scenarios. In *2016 49th Hawaii International Conference on System Sciences (HICSS)* (pp. 3928–3937). IEEE. doi:10.1109/HICSS.2016.488

IEC. (2017). *IEC 62657-2:2017 Industrial communication networks - Wireless communication networks - Part 2: Coexistence management*. Retrieved from https://cdn.standards.iteh.ai/samples/22382/3f887e55ed074e2ba81dd356a18b176f/IEC-62657-2-2017.pdf

Industrial Internet Consortium. (2013). *Fact Sheet*. Retrieved March 2, 2019, from https://www.iiconsortium.org/docs/IIC_FACT_SHEET.pdf

Kagermann, H. (2014). Chancen von Industrie 4.0 nutzen. In *Industrie 4.0 in Produktion, Automatisierung und Logistik* (pp. 603–614). Wiesbaden: Springer Fachmedien Wiesbaden. doi:10.1007/978-3-658-04682-8_31

Kagermann, H., Wahlster, W., Helbig, J., Hellinger, A., Stumpf, M. A. V., & Treugut, L. … Findeklee, U. (2013). *Recommendations for implementing the strategic initiative Industrie 4.0: Final report of the Industrie 4.0*. Retrieved from http://alvarestech.com/temp/tcn/CyberPhysicalSystems-Industrial4-0.pdf

Kargas, A., Kiriakidis, M., & Zacharakis, E. (2020). Europe's Economic Crisis: Re - Clustering European Economies. *European Journal of Social Science Education and Research*, *7*(1), 41. https://doi.org/10.26417/ejser.v7i1.p41-50

Kargas, A., & Varoutas, D. (2020). Industry 4.0 in Cultural Industry. A Review on Digital Visualization for VR and AR Applications. In C. M. Bolognesi & S. Cettina (Eds.), Impact of Industry 4.0 on Architecture and Cultural Heritage (pp. 1–19). IGI Global. https://doi.org/10.4018/978-1-7998-1234-0.CH001.

Laitsou, E., Kargas, A., & Varoutas, D. (2020). Digital Competitiveness in the European Union Era: The Greek Case. *Economies, 8*(4), 85. doi:10.3390/economies8040085

Lee, E. A. (2008). Cyber Physical Systems: Design Challenges. In *2008 11th IEEE International Symposium on Object and Component-Oriented Real-Time Distributed Computing (ISORC)* (pp. 363–369). IEEE. doi:10.1109/ISORC.2008.25

Lee, J. (2015). Smart Factory Systems. *Informatik-Spektrum, 38*(3), 230–235. doi:10.1007/S00287-015-0891-Z

Löffler, M., & Tschiesner, A. (2013). *The Internet of Things and the Future of Manufacturing*. Retrieved from https://www.ocf.co.uk/uploads/manufacturing_whitepaper.pdf

Neumann, A., Wisniewski, L., Ganesan, R. S., Rost, P., & Jasperneite, J. (2018). Towards integration of Industrial Ethernet with 5G mobile networks. In *14th IEEE International Workshop on Factory Communication Systems - Proceedings, WFCS* (pp. 1–4). Institute of Electrical and Electronics Engineers Inc. doi:10.1109/WFCS.2018.8402373

Nokia. (2017, April 18). *Nokia studies outline business return-on-investment from 5G services*. Retrieved July 22, 2021, from https://www.nokia.com/about-us/news/releases/2017/04/18/nokia-studies-outline-business-return-on-investment-from-5g-services/

Pereshybkina, A., Conde, M. E. C., Kalyesubula, T., & Kirner, E. (2017). *Industry 4.0 Scenario Planning. How will the industry 4.0 transformations affect SMEs in Germany by 2030?* Retrieved from https://opus.hs-furtwangen.de/frontdoor/deliver/index/docId/2467/file/Project+A_Scenario+Industry+4.0+and+SMEs_EK2.pdf

Petrelli, D. (2017). Industry 4.0: Is It Time for Interaction Design Craftsmanship? *The Design Journal, 20*, 2735–2745. doi:10.1080/14606925.2017.1352785

Prakash, R. (2019, May 30). *Transforming enterprise and industry with 5G private networks*. Retrieved July 22, 2021, from https://www.qualcomm.com/media/documents/files/the-role-of-5g-in-private-networks-for-industrial-iot.pdf

Pricewaterhouse Coopers. (2016). *Industry 4.0: Building the digital enterprise*. Retrieved from https://www.pwc.com/gx/en/industries/industries-4.0/landing-page/industry-4.0-building-your-digital-enterprise-april-2016.pdf

Psyrris, A., Kargas, A., & Varoutas, D. (2020). 5G networks' implementation and development of smart sustainable cities evidence and key issues. *13th CMI Conference on Cybersecurity and Privacy - Digital Transformation - Potentials and Challenges, CMI 2020*. doi:10.1109/CMI51275.2020.9322717

Radio Spectrum Policy Group. (2016). *A Spectrum Roadmap for IoT. Opinion on the Spectrum Aspects of the Internet-of-things (IoT) including M2M FINAL 2 A Spectrum Roadmap for IoT Opinion on the Spectrum Aspects of the Internet-of-things (IoT) including M2M Background and scope of work*. Retrieved from https://circabc.europa.eu/sd/a/a0faa1a5-ca41-42c3-83d5-561b197419b0/RSPG17-006-Final_IoT_Opinion.pdf

Rostami, A. (2019). Private 5G networks for vertical industries: Deployment and operation models. In *IEEE 5G World Forum, 5GWF 2019 - Conference Proceedings* (pp. 433–439). Institute of Electrical and Electronics Engineers Inc. doi:10.1109/5GWF.2019.8911687

Schröder, C. (2016). *The Challenges of Industry 4.0 for Small and Medium-sized Enterprises*. Bonn. Retrieved from www.fes-2017plus.de

Schuh, G., Potente, T., Varandani, R., & Schmitz, T. (2014). Global Footprint Design based on genetic algorithms – An "Industry 4.0" perspective. *CIRP Annals, 63*(1), 433–436. https://doi.org/10.1016/J.CIRP.2014.03.121

Schumacher, A., Erol, S., & Sihn, W. (2016). A Maturity Model for Assessing Industry 4.0 Readiness and Maturity of Manufacturing Enterprises. *Procedia CIRP*, *52*, 161–166. https://doi.org/10.1016/J.PROCIR.2016.07.040

SECUREIoT. (2021). *SECUREIoT Project*. Retrieved October 8, 2021, from https://secureiot.eu/

Siriwardhana, Y., Porambage, P., Liyanage, M., Walia, J. S., Matinmikko-Blue, M., & Ylianttila, M. (2019). Micro-Operator driven Local 5G Network Architecture for Industrial Internet. In *IEEE Wireless Communications and Networking Conference, WCNC* (Vol. 2019-April, pp. 1–8). Institute of Electrical and Electronics Engineers Inc. doi:10.1109/WCNC.2019.8885900

Siriwardhana, Y., Porambage, P., Ylianttila, M., & Liyanage, M. (2020). Performance Analysis of Local 5G Operator Architectures for Industrial Internet. *IEEE Internet of Things Journal, 7*(12), 11559–11575. doi:10.1109/JIOT.2020.3024875

Strufe, M., Gundall, M., Schotten, H. D., Markwart, C., Ganesan, R. S., & Aleksy, M. (2019). Design of a 5G Ready and Reliable Architecture for the Smart Factory of the Future. *Computer Science*.

Valtanen, K., Backman, J., & Yrjola, S. (2019). Blockchain-Powered Value Creation in the 5G and Smart Grid Use Cases. *IEEE Access: Practical Innovations, Open Solutions*, *7*, 25690–25707. https://doi.org/10.1109/ACCESS.2019.2900514

Villasante Marcos, C. (2022). Artificial Intelligence Edge Applications in 5G Networks. In Proceedings of Sixth International Congress on Information and Communication Technology (pp. 269–279). Springer. https://doi.org/10.1007/978-981-16-2380-6_24.

VINNI. (2021). *5G-VINNI – 5G Verticals Innovation Infrastructure*. Retrieved July 1, 2021, from https://www.5g-vinni.eu/

Wahlster, W. (2013). Industry 4.0: The Semantic Product Memory as a Basis for Cyber-Physical Production Systems. In *Recent Trends in Artificial Intelligence and Cognitive Science*. Zuruch: SGAICO Forum.

World Economic Forum. (2019). *Fourth Industrial Revolution: Beacons of Technology and Innovation in Manufacturing*. Retrieved from https://www3.weforum.org/docs/WEF_4IR_Beacons_of_Technology_and_Innovation_in_Manufacturing_report_2019.pdf

KEY TERMS AND DEFINITIONS

5th Generation of Mobile Communication Systems (5G): 5G is the fifth-generation technology standard for broadband cellular networks, which cellular phone companies began deploying worldwide in 2019.

Cyber Physical System (CPS): A whole process enabling the communication between people, machines and resources. The whole idea is based on embedding networks and computers to physical process, in order: (a) to support unique identification, (b) to collect, store and analyze data and finally (c) to create networks from physical processes to computation (e.g., structured information) and vice versa (e.g., processes reengineering).

Digital Transformation: The integration of digital technology into all areas of a business resulting in fundamental changes to how businesses operate and how they deliver value to customers.

Industry 4.0: A "marriage" between the physical world / sciences with digital technologies. Digital technologies offer new ways of interconnection with "physical", effective data collection and wise systems capable to interpret the gathered data for a more holistic, informed decision making (action back to physical world).

Internet of Things (IoT): It is the integration of Internet into various "manufacturing – business – everyday" processes / operations in order to allow "things" such as mobile devices, sensors, RFID and actuators to (a) interact and (b) cooperate in order to (c) reach common goals.

ENDNOTES

1 European Standards

2 global partnership project founded in 2012 and constituted by 8 of the world's leading ICT standards development organizations, notably: ARIB (Japan), ATIS (United States), CCSA (China), ETSI (Europe), TIA (USA), TSDSI (India), TTA (Korea) and TTC (Japan)

3 simplified industry term for the LTE-MTC low power wide area (LPWA) technology standard published by 3GPP in the Release 13 specification

4 European Telecommunications Standards Institute

5 Millimeter wave spectrum

Chapter 9
ICT Process Optimization Framework:
A Systematic Literature Review

Joaquina Marchão
https://orcid.org/0000-0002-9174-9871
Universidade do Algarve, Portugal

Leonilde Reis
https://orcid.org/0000-0002-4398-8384
Instituto Politécnico de Setúbal, Portugal

Paula Ventura Martins
https://orcid.org/0000-0002-3199-4517
University of Algarve, Portugal

ABSTRACT

Organizations need to provide more efficient services with increasingly optimized costs. Organizations may have an area of management control with transversal responsibilities in information and communication technology (ICT) support function, operating information technology front office, monitoring information technology (IT) service catalog and performance, reporting the service level agreements with stakeholders, controlling software and equipment installed or under maintenance, department budget control, management of suppliers' contracts, and financial analysis. The chapter presents a systematic literature review related to relationship management, optimization, and alignment of business processes between ICT areas and other organizational business units in a multidisciplinary way. The proposed framework pretends to contribute to creating strategies and indicators that allow optimized risk management, resources management, cost control, and streamlining of the defined processes in a continual improvement cycle.

DOI: 10.4018/978-1-7998-9227-4.ch009

INTRODUCTION

Currently, organizations must have defined communication strategies between employees and stakeholders that are swift and assertive. However, in large number of organizations, there is informal information that runs the risk of being lost when an employee is promoted or left. Thus, it is urgent to optimize the processes using ICT to include parameters and metrics that enhance digitalization towards the digital transformation of processes.

Digitalization can be considered a transforming factor in a globalized business context. The introduction of novel digital technologies into the market has been driving organizations to digitally transform their businesses (Feroz et al., 2021). In the management of Information and Communication Technologies (ICT) services and support of business, has more complexity, and new challenges appear. An increase of complexity is resulting, among other factors, from the diversity of ICTs and components used: in hardware, software, and communications (Veronica & Debora Suryawan, 2018).

Digitization affects not only businesses but also the entire society. Each industry should adapt to the changes brought by Digital Era (Osman & Ghiran, 2019). Digitalization can drive the sustainable transformation of society and industry. Many of the opportunities are, however, closely linked with risks. The dynamics and uncertainties of digitalization are complex, and to make it a sustainable success, all actors involved should be engaged in a co-design process to develop a governance structure that is in line with sustainability (Renn et al., 2021).

Digital transformation dominates the practical and scientific discourse. Still, many companies do not have a clear plan on how to approach it. Small- and medium-sized enterprises, in particular, struggle to initiate their digital journey as they lack resources and expertise (Fischer et al., 2020). Digital transformation is not a single step undertaken for upgrading specific functions of organizations but is more of a process that brings fundamental changes in organizations and results in creating additional opportunities for improvement (Feroz et al., 2021).

To accelerate the business, it is expected IT Development bring as much change as possible. IT Operations tend to come with an outlook where change is the enemy. The business folks depend on them to keep the lights on and deliver the services that make the business money today. Between IT development and IT operations, are issues caused by a miscellaneous of conflicting motivations among people, processes, and technology/tooling. Hence there is a pressing need for strengthening the harmonization of Development and Operations functions of an IT organization (Shinn & Lunz, 2015).

It is considered that the management and governance of ICT have today high importance to organizations, involving multidisciplinary knowledge. Themes of operational efficiency, cost optimization, and stakeholder satisfaction, are relevant topics in any organization strategy, directly influencing the financial return. ICT is now inseparable from the organizations' business, so, it is important for the ICT department to align IT management and governance with the organization's management and governance.

COVID-19 pandemic has forced many organizations to undergo significant transformation, rethinking key elements of their business processes and use of technology to maintain operations whilst adhering to a changing landscape of guidelines and new procedures (Dwivedi et al., 2020).

A fundamental aspect that influences the competitiveness of an organization is how it responds, learns, and adapts to market challenges, opportunities, and threats. Managing these requirements requires the ability to constantly analyze and redefine the processes involved, control their execution, and assess performance, in a continuous periodic cycle.

Business Process Modelling (BPM) is a way to support business processes using several techniques, methods, models, and systems to design, control, and analyses business processes, where many resources are used: humans, technologies, organizations, applications (Alotaibi & Liu, 2013).

BPM promotes a baseline for communication. BPM can not only enable the realization of optimization but also foster process innovation and creativity. BPM provides an overview of organizational resources and competencies and assigns them to tasks and activities within the company's value creation processes. BPM was primarily used to reduce costs and to increase customer orientation, transparency, and product and service quality. However, as digital transformation demands the realization of socio-technical assets, and BPM yields adaptations to their social, technological, and operational setup, each company developed an individual strategy to manage the underlying change processes successfully (Fischer et al., 2020).

Human tasks (or activities) within processes represent crucial elements that strongly affect the results, in terms of the performance of the processes (Ciasullo et al., 2018).

The chapter's objectives are to present a systematic literature review (SLR) in BPM domain and in ICT management, focusing on human relationship, interdepartmental alignment processes, and related features. It is intended to obtain guidelines for the development of a multidisciplinary framework within the scope of the alignment of processes, enhancing the digital transformation through the aggregation of informal and relevant knowledge for adequate decision-making.

The applied methodology is a systematic literature review related to BPM domain and concepts of relationship management and alignment processes in organizations.

The structure of this paper has eight sections. The first section is the Introduction to the research theme. The second section presents the Background. The Research Methodology is in the third section. The fourth section presents the Results. In the fifth is presented the Framework, the sixth has the Recommendations, the seventh presents Future research directions and in the last one, is the Conclusion.

BACKGROUND

In this Digital Age, organizations increasingly face the need to increase the level of usability of digital technologies to leverage their business. The support of ICT professionals in this transition has been crucial. The support was based not only on helping to work with new technologies, but also contributed to changing the organizational culture, boosting the use of collaboration tools, promoting the transformation of organizational processes related to distance work.

With the turbulent external business environment, the complexity of internal relations of the organization, and the emergence of IT roles, the alignment between business and IT alignment has become increasingly difficult. The unsuccessful realization of the alignment will lead to the waste of organizational resources, the reduction of return on investment, and loss of competitive advantage (Menglong et al., 2020).

The organizational culture can facilitate that employee's owns process organizational relevant information that is not systematized and, therefore, be informal and not recorded. It is intended that the multidisciplinary framework can contribute identify e prevent these situations, thru alignment processes between departments. When employees leave or are promoted, the unrecorded information may be lost and cause an impact on the process, e.g. delays on workflow or tasks executed in an inadequate way.

Processes associated with digital transformation began to be implemented in companies after 2012. The cross-functional nature of digital transformation and new cloud service models, prompted a complete rethink of corporate IS architectures, providing agility in response to the needs of business, but also to take advantage of hybrid solutions offering a boost to corporate performance (Cigref, 2018). Strong impulse to digitize processes and operations in companies and enterprises have resulted in the creation and automatic recording of an increasingly large amount of process data in information systems (Pegoraro et al., 2021).

Digitization can drive the sustainable transformation of society and industry, and opportunities are often closely linked to risks. The risk-benefit perspective can help in reviewing and categorizing the main impacts and trade-offs related to the ecological, economic, and social dimensions of sustainability. The dynamics and uncertainties of digitization are complex – to make digitization a sustainable success, all actors involved must be committed to the process of developing a governance structure aligned with sustainability (Renn et al., 2021).

The objectives of improving stakeholder satisfaction and optimizing costs in the ICT service support front-end area led to the search for best international ICT management practices. The selected best practices were the Information Technology Infrastructure Library (ITIL) and Information Technology and Related Control Objectives (COBIT) references, in the perspective of managing ICT processes and services, seeking to optimize costs and satisfaction of the stakeholders involved. It is intended to analyze and contribute to the resolution of some problems faced by organizations, using models/frameworks, a powerful way to address the complexity of organizations (Roquete, 2018).

Figure 3 is an example of IT operational areas and related processes, with three main ICT areas: Infrastructures, Applications Systems, and Support, and four/five processes related to operations. ICT Infrastructures Management area has, among others, the responsibility of specialized support team of second intervention level. This team has high expertise and is responsible for: maintenance and technological evolution of ICT communications' infrastructure - voice and data networks, monitoring and administration of servers that support corporate systems, implementation and management mechanisms to control infrastructures' security - logical and physical, including data centers and maintenance of ICT recovery plan in case of disaster.

Application and Systems Management area is responsible for corrective maintenance and evolution of systems or new solutions development that respond to business or regulatory needs, managing changes' impact in the existing systems architecture and related interfaces.

The responsibilities of the ICT Support Management area focus on the Helpdesk function, frontend team, basic resolution support the first intervention level in data network access, roll-out and assistance on workstations, and support on peripherals, software configurations, installations, and standard upgrades.

The main processes analyzed were Incident Management and Request Management (both processes related to the service catalog, used by the same teams, can be joined in one workflow). Incident Management is the main process for IT frontend support, used in direct contact with stakeholders, asking for assistance, or asking for a new service. Through this process, the stakeholders interact with the technical team and form their opinion on the IT services performance in general (Persse, 2012). Through the problem management process, an expert team with different skills analyzes and solves complex incidents. The problem management process interacts with incident management, when the frontend team cannot resolve an incident based on existing procedures or known errors, the issue is transferred to an expert team. The maturity of the teams and their knowledge of IT architecture implemented are important factors for the success of the operationalization of this process.

Change management is related to both areas: Infrastructure and Application Systems. Change management ensures documentation and control of changes in software development and systems implemented in the production environment and other ICT configuration items such as network infrastructure and hardware assets that support the systems. Service asset and configuration management have service assets that support the production environment, under configuration control. Multiple data are structured in a database of configuration items, and the information is used to support other processes (Marchão et al., 2021). Most aspects of work in an organization are based on predefined business processes (Prasetyo et al., 2021). Activities in one business process are connected through flow structures, and actions or decisions in service can trigger changes or additional actions in other services (Nasiriasayesh & Yari, 2019).

Business Process Management (BPM) has proven great value for process control and process optimization. Organizations face the need to both optimize existing processes and to innovate and disrupt them. Studies have recently moved beyond the paradigm of aligning IT with business strategies towards the concept of IT being the strategy (Helbin & Van Looy, 2019). Business process management provides tools, methods to design, optimize, and maintain business processes. Typically, BPM requires five steps: process identification, process discovery, process analysis, process redesign, process implementation, process monitoring, and controlling. Business environment' complexity often causes organizations to produce several inconsistent views on the same business process, leading to fragmentation and inefficiencies (Belchior et al., 2020). The implementation of BPM is a complex process and requires many technical and non-technical aspects (Handayani & ER, 2019).

Business processes represent one of the main assets of organizations as they have a direct impact on the attractiveness of products and services, including customer experiences and even revenue. Processes orchestrate corporate resources to fulfill orders and are a key factor in determining cost of service and operational efficiency. They determine tasks, roles and responsibilities and therefore shape the future work of each employee and machine throughout a business process. the processes they are pillars within organizations. Consequently, any process failure can impact corporate life and the entire ecosystem of processes. Processes determine the potential and speed of an organization to adapt to new circumstances and comply with rapid growth in the number of legislative requirements. Despite of that, unlike other corporate assets such as products, services, workforce, brand, physical or monetary assets, the significance of business processes had not been appreciated for a long period. The growing demands for globalization, integration, standardization, innovation, agility, and operational efficiency, coupled with the opportunities raised by digital technologies, have finally increased the appetite for reflecting on and ultimately improving existing as well as designing entire new business processes (Dumas et al., 2018b)

Business Process Management is dynamically changing in the era of IT and Digital Innovations and business process modeling and design remain highlighted areas (Ahmad, 2019). Fast-changing business environments and the costly process of in-house development of BPM Systems drives the businesses to outsource their business processes, migrating to the Cloud (Nasiriasayesh & Yari, 2019).

A common problem among BPM practitioners is how to relate perceived BPM success to actual success. BPM success should link to business success, i.e., to the ability to meet or exceed the business performance objectives that are part of the corporate strategy. Common reasons for the failure of BPM programs include: A sole focus on BPM methods and tools, not on business goals; the belief that BPM is the single source of truth; BPM projects that are managed as isolated silos and an overall inability to the change. However, introducing transversal aspects of BPM, such as governance and strategic alignment, these fail reasons can be avoided (Dumas et al., 2018a).

COVID-19 has forced the manufacturing organizations to pause the production system for a longer time and search for sustainable solutions to ensure smooth supply and operations from both the businesses and the customers' perspectives. Some impact reported are related to organizational workforce management, for better sustainability; adoption of virtual training programs, focusing on training and coaching so that the team becomes resilient; knowledge sharing, create a digital workplace for the future and adoption of social media, which can be crucial for businesses to evaluate the behavior and consumption trends of customers; supply chain and logistics domain, an opportunity for managers to transform supply chain networks to Digital Supply Networks (DSNs). Apart from minimizing cost, inventories, and increased asset utilization, the DSNs helps to develop end-to-end visibility, collaboration, responsiveness, agility, and resilient supply chain and logistics (Kumar et al., 2020).

With COVID-19, organizations suddenly had to navigate thru the uncertainty and unknown, and thus find new solutions to the challenges that arose in many areas of their operations. This pandemic has created a particularly challenging environment for human resource management trying to help workforce adapt to and cope with radical changes occurring in the work and social environment. In case of employees who formerly spent all or most of their time working inside their organization's physical boundaries, quickly had to adjust to remote work environments. Due to closure of non-essential businesses, even those who might be well adjusted to remote working conditions were faced with the challenges of an inability to seek alternative workspaces (e.g., cafés, libraries) outside of the home itself. This has likely further limited the segmentation between work and private life, leading to greater difficulties in "unplugging" from work demands. Organizations continue to adapt their human resources practices transitioning to virtual forms of work in distance (Carnevale & Hatak, 2020).

Pos covid19 era has accelerated the increased number of remote workers. The emergence of computer-mediated groups has propelled the use, deployment, and growth of virtual teams in the past decade. A recent survey of 1,372 business respondents from 80 countries found that 85% of the respondents worked on virtual teams. The increasingly important role of virtual teams in organizations has spurred a parallel growth in research examining various aspects and challenges of these teams. Communication challenges in virtual settings may lead to misinterpretation in tasks and project requirements, duplication of effort, and hindrances in accomplishing project goals (Alaiad et al., 2019).

Digitization has increased and the fulfillment of business requirements in a virtual setting has led to massive cyber-attacks that have stolen assets, with loss of reputation, lost business, financial losses, stock market impact and intellectual property theft. Digital transformation has not only accelerated business, it has also become a huge market for cybercriminals. The Covid19 pandemic required a remote workforce that involved bringing your own device (BYOD) and organizations moving to the cloud opened huge doors, exponentially expanding the attack surface. On the other hand, mixing corporate and social media tools without adequate safeguards has raised concerns about data leakage, leading to regulatory issues. Safety efficiency is achieved through the development of a safety-conscious workforce, balancing the relationships between people, processes and technology (Vadlamudi & De, 2021).

COVID-19 has changed the way companies and employees work, requiring a constant reinvention of how they operate and causing actions never seen before, generating deep changes in the workplace. The idea of the workplace is different from what was expected before COVID-19, where reinvention of work, technology and safety are key points in its transformation process. COVID-19 exposed many weaknesses and issues that have been present in business for a long time, especially how to carry out daily activities from physical to virtual interactions perspective. Temptation to return to pre-pandemic approaches should be avoided, preventing previous mistakes. It is necessary to build new processes for a digital world, educating and preparing the organization so that there are no differences between the processes related to face-to-face and remote work (de Lucas Ancillo et al., 2021).

RESEARCH METHODOLOGY

The approach is a systematic literature review to find the relevant prior work to support the framework under construction. The first step began with planning the research after identifying the problems. Then formulating research questions, define parameters and criteria, refine keywords, generate research, applying Boolean operators. The following steps are revision of research questions and change them if needed, separate concepts to search, conduct research using online sources and obtain studies, evaluate, record, in a loop process until the achievement of the desired results. The last phase is organizing studies, analyze them with a critical perspective focusing on answering research questions, finding gaps, group concepts and write the Systematic Literature Review report.

Preliminary Research

For understanding the relevance and actuality of the subject under study, specifically applicable in the management of ICT operations, using ITIL and COBIT framework, before this work it was performed an analysis of existing literature (Marchão et al., 2020). The definition of the research process scope was based on the literature found in conference abstracts (IEE Explore), conference abstracts and research articles (ScienceDirect), from 2010-2020. Based on two sources, it was used in the search Boolean operators and keywords. The search was restricted to abstract field. The keywords or group of keywords used to find the literature were: "Implement"; "Case"; "Process"; "Framework"; "Approach"; "Model"; "ITIL"; COBIT; Operation. During the first execution, some similar expressions were detected, it was decided to use all.

The complete string was: ((((((((“Abstract”:Implement) OR “Abstract”:Case) OR “Abstract”:Process) OR “Abstract”:Framework) OR “Abstract”:Approach) OR “Abstract”:Model) AND “Abstract”:ITIL) AND “Abstract”:COBIT) AND “Abstract”:Operation) AND “Abstract”:medium-size). The analysis shows the subject of management of ICT operations, using ITIL and COBIT framework has a multidisciplinary character.

As a result of the quantity and quality of the information obtained, it was decided to continue the research on online sources, literature related to the theme but focusing on business processes, relationship, and interdepartmental alignment frameworks studies. The conception of the multidisciplinary framework implies the analysis of existing gaps in the literature and in international references. Thus, a systematic literature review was carried out in the domain of BPM to validate the research questions (Q1, Q2 and Q3), to assess the existing studies and analyze the gaps that will enhance the creation of the framework.

Research Scope

The definition of the research process scope is based on the literature found in three online sources:

1. . IEE Explore Digital Library
2. . Science Direct Library
3. . Emerald Library.

Based on these sources, several keywords were used in the search with Boolean operators. Filters, exclusion, and inclusion criteria was applied. Keywords used were: “Business Process Management”; “BPM”; “Framework”; “Relationship management”; “Alignment”.

The formulations of the research objectives are:

- Q1: Are there a business processes management framework related to relationship?
- Q2: Those frameworks focus on interdepartmental alignment?
- Q3: What features are essential to interdepartmental alignment?

Final string defined was: ((“Abstract”:Business Process Management”) OR (“Abstract”:BPM) AND (“Abstract”:Framework) AND (“Abstract”:Relationship management) AND (“Abstract”:Alignment)

Table 1 presents the results based on the defined criteria.

Table 1. Primary results of the research based on the defined criteria (Studies Found)

Search Terms - Scientific Database	IEE Explore	ScienceDirect	Emerald
Business process management or “BPM”	3273	3368	637
“Business process management” or “BPM” and “Framework” and “Relationship” and “Alignment”	1336	233	256
“Business process management” or “BPM” and “Framework” and “Relationship Management” and “Alignment”	1336	63	58

Table 2 presents the result after applying incremental exclusion criterion to find candidates studies to analyze and select. To reduce the number of studies it was applied period 2018-2021. Removed studies that were not a final version.

Table 2. Results after applying exclusion criteria (Candidate Studies)

Incremental Exclusion Criteria	IEE Explore	ScienceDirect	Emerald
Abstract Field	857	38	1
Only conferences/research articles	800	33	0
2018-2021	240	11	0
Related to a Department	36	11	0

Table 3 shows the studies considered relevant to the development of the framework. Selected those that could answer the research questions. Removed duplicates studies. Reject studies not related with ICT management area.

Table 3. Final results

Source	Studies Found	Candidate	Selected
IEE Explore	3.273	36	11
ScienceDirect	3.368	11	8
Emerald	637	0	0
Total	7.278	47	19

After analyzing the 47 candidate studies, it was selected 19 that should answer to the research questions.

RESULTS

The selected studies (19) are listed in Appendix A and in Table 4. The studies were analyzed and selected the ones that could answer, at least, to one of the research questions (Q1; Q2; Q3), and consequently contribute to the development and improvement of the framework.

In the analysis of selected studies, was also carried out a comparison between the studies, searching for common or contradictory aspects. It was possible to group them into 3 different capabilities of the Business Process: Process Management, Process Optimization and Process Modeling; and 9 areas of knowledge: Tools, Risk analysis, Decision-making, Process perspective, Quality, Collaboration, Big Data, Mining and Blockchain.

Following graphics show the analysis grouped by Business Process capabilities and focus area found.

Figure 1 presents the studies selected organized according to the Business Process capability area considered in each article.

Figure 2 shows the studies selected and organized according to the focus area considered in each article.

The Systematic Literature Review selected studies with different themes of knowledge/focus area and different Business Process capability area. This diversity is enriching and shall be considered in the construction of the framework.

Table 4. Systematic literature review analysis

Title	Author	Publication Forum	BP Capabilities	Focus area
Business Process Management (BPM) in Operational BINUS Online Learning	Desak, G.; Saputra, W.; Titan; Mariani, V.	International Conference on Information Management and Technology	Process Modeling	Tools
A Conceptual Model for Information Security Risk Considering Business Process Perspective	Hariyanti, E.; Djunaidy, A.; Siahaan, D.	4th International Conference on Science and Technology	Process Modeling	Risk analysis
A Literature Review on Business Continuity Based on ISO 22301, Six Sigma and Customer Satisfaction Evaluation	Hersyah, M.; Derisma	International Conference on Information Technology Systems and Innovation	Process Management	Risk analysis
Business Process Management System Implementation Model for Improving Employee Performance	Juwitasary, H.; Christian, L.; Putra, E.; Fifilia; Sardjono, W.	International Conference on Information Management and Technology	Process Optimization	Tools
Business process outsourcing enhanced by fuzzy linguistic consensus model	Ciasullo, M.; Fenza, G.; Herrera-Viedma, E.; et al.	Applied Soft Computing	Process Management	Decision-making
Factors Affecting Business Process Management in the Bulgarian Enterprises to Achieve Sustainable Development	Mihova, T.; Nikolova-Alexieva, V.; Angelova, M.	International Conference on High Technology for Sustainable Development	Process Optimization	Process perspective
Modeling flexibility on internal quality assurance system business process	Yulherniwati; Jama, J.; Ganefri; Ikhsan, A.	International Seminar on Research of Information Technology and Intelligent Systems	Process Management	Quality
Research and Implementation of Financial Approval System Based on jBPM Engine	Jiang, H.	IEEE 3rd Advanced Information Technology, Electronic and Automation Control Conference	Process Optimization	Tools
Tactical Business-Process-Decision Support based on KPIs Monitoring and Validation	Pérez-Álvarez, J.; Maté, A.; Trujillo, J.; et al	Computers in Industry	Process Modeling	Decision-making
A Conceptual Model for the Use of Social Software in Business Process Management and Knowledge Management	Ramadhani, F.; Mahendrawathi ER	Procedia Computer Science	Process Modeling	Collaboration
An open-minded strategy towards eco-innovation: A key to sustainable growth in a global enterprise	Cegarra-Navarro, J.; Papa, A.; Fiano, F.; et al.	Technological Forecasting and Social Change	Process Management	Process perspective
Business Process Mapping: A Case Study	Al-Fedaghi, S.; Mohamad, Y.	IEEE/ACS 16th International Conference on Computer Systems and Applications	Process Optimization	Process perspective
Factors influencing effective use of big data: A research framework	Surbakti, F.; Wang, W.; Sadiq, S.; et al.	Information & Management	Process Management	Big Data
Influence of Digital Technology on Roadmap Development for Digital Business Transformation	Strutynska, I.; Kozbur, G.; Dmytrotsa, L.; Sorokivska, O.; Melnyk, L.	9th International Conference on Advanced Computer Information Technologies	Process Management	Mining

Continued on following page

Table 4. Continued

Title	Author	Publication Forum	BP Capabilities	Focus area
Towards a maturity model for big data analytics in airline network planning	Hausladen, I.; Schosser, M.	Journal of Air Transport Management	Process Management	Big Data
Firm-level capabilities towards big data value creation	Brinch, M.; Gunasekaran, A.; Wamba, S.	Journal of Business Research	Process Management	Big Data
Towards an integrated methodology for the development of blockchain-based solutions supporting cross-organizational processes	Sousa, V.; Corentin, B.	13th International Conference on Research Challenges in Information Science	Process Management	Blockchain
Enterprise modelling: Research review and outlook	Vernadat, F.	Computers in Industry	Process Modeling	Process perspective
Increasing process maturity through a Business Process Management System: Case study at a financial institution	Cabrita, M.; Antunes, C.; Costa, J.	16th Iberian Conference on Information Systems and Technologies	Process Management	Tools

Figure 1. Selected studies organized by business process capability area

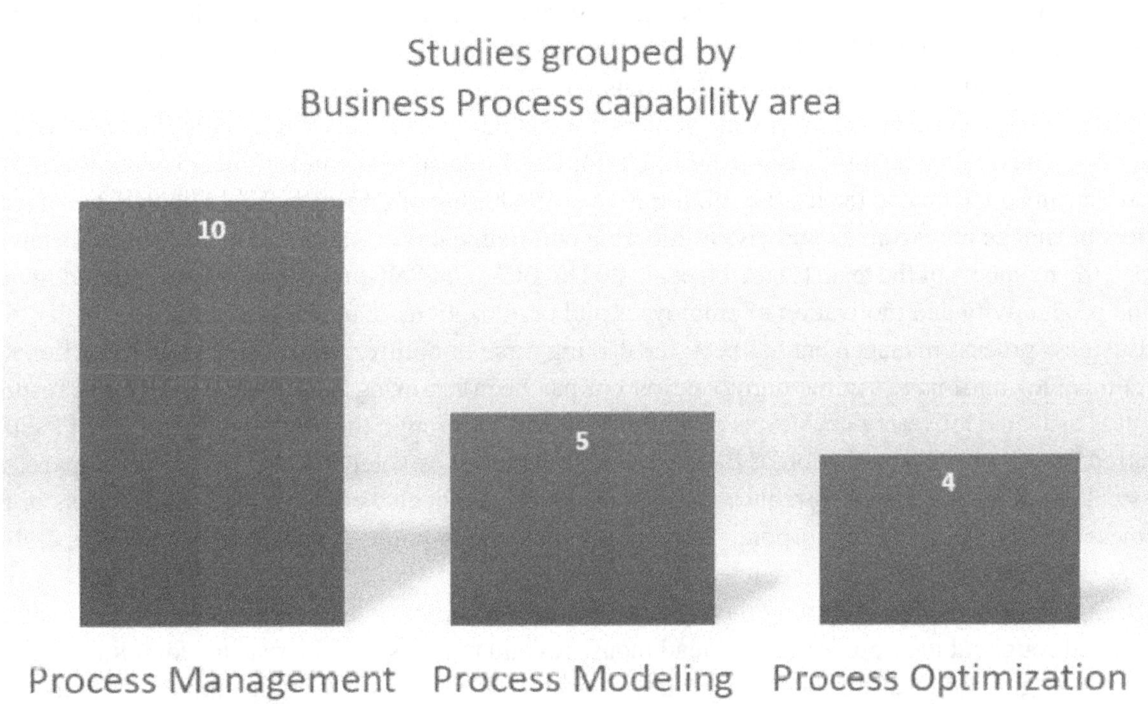

Figure 2. Selected studies organized by focus area

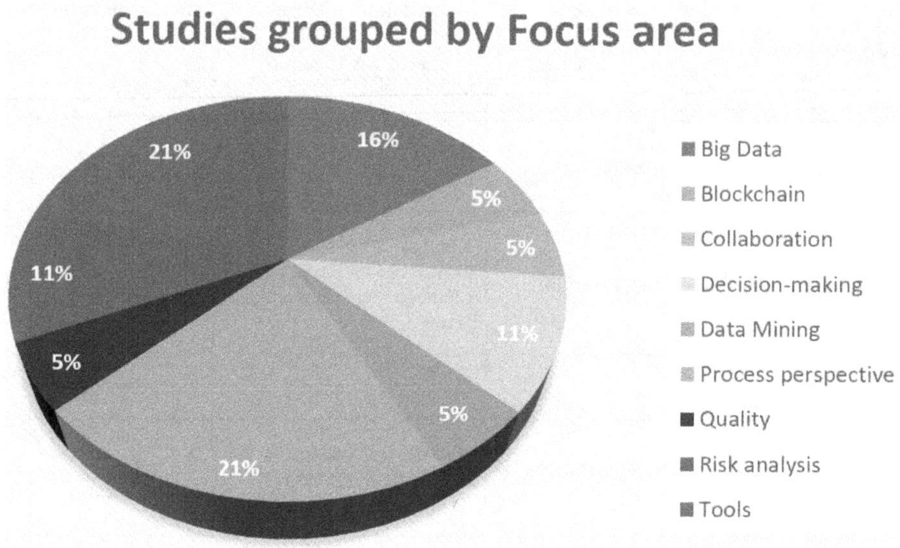

Related Work

Literature found in research presented BPM frameworks in different dimensions, with focus on system implementation (Alotaibi & Liu, 2013); Artifact-centric automation approach to business process modeling (Kunchala et al., 2020); Business process outsourcing as a strategical option to obtain improvement of performance in business process management context and it consists in externalizing whole or part of a process of a value chain (Ciasullo et al., 2018); BPM related to organizational change, it is stated that trust can be repaired at the team level, improving the sharing of information and knowledge of team leaders in change management and also reinforcing communication, collaboration and ethical behavior among the members of the team (Ogbeibu et al., 2021). BPM and Self-management concept, and impact on the productivity and motivation of employees and organizations (Gutierrez et al., 2019).

Business process management has been the driving force of optimization and operational efficiency for companies until now, but the digitalization era has been requiring businesses' agility and responsiveness as well. Delivering new levels of automation agility through the digitalization of BPM itself is required. However, the automation of BPM cannot be achieved by solely focusing on process space and classical planning techniques. It requires a holistic approach that also captures the social aspects of the business environment, such as corporate strategies, organization policies, negotiations, and cooperation (Kir & Erdogan, 2021).

Digital transformation is driving the emerge of a new breed of organizations able to scale quickly, innovate throughout their processes, and lead industries and markets. The increasing adoption of cognitive technologies, like artificial intelligence, advanced analytics, high-performing computing, and cyber-physical systems, allow organizations to create new value based on increased reactivity and resilience, situational awareness, agility, and operational excellence. Although the idea of cognitive enterprise is rapidly emerging, a theoretical framing of the concept is still not present in literature (Elia & Margherita, 2021).

Based on the analysis of international best practices ITIL and COBIT it is intended to contribute to the alignment of IT goals with business goals, a departmental and organizational view. The framework will present the mechanisms to solve some GAPs found in ITIL and COBIT, in particular: describing some process maps, how to assess them and how to align some business processes. Using ITIL to organize work and manage IT services will improve operational efficiency. Using COBIT from its top-down perspective, the alignment of business goals to IT goals can be achieved and controlled evidencing in that way IT value to the business, thus enabling a multidisciplinary and integrative strategic vision (Marchão et al., 2021).

FRAMEWORK

The framework in the business process domain has a particular interest given the current problem of gaps in the management domain. The information could be dispersed, not registered, and not available, and the lack of this informal knowledge can delay tasks, timely and inadequate decision-making. Thus, a multidisciplinary and aggregating framework is under construction, to encourage the inclusion of relevant informal information in workflow the underlying organizational processes.

Figure 3 is an example of IT processes, with intradepartmental relationships with information flow, such as infrastructures management, application systems management, and support management.

Infrastructure and application systems areas share processes like service asset and configuration management and change management. Both interact with support management through the incident and request management process. Problem management is a distinct process, which aims to solve complex situations. The concept of this process is to activate and manage the problem as a project, bringing together the technical teams with the appropriate skills and expertise to find a satisfactory answer or resolution.

The bidirectional flow presented in Figure 3 is based on the necessary and constant feedback to optimize and adjust the processes, in a continual improvement cycle.

Figure 3. IT operational areas and related processes
(Marchão et al., 2021)

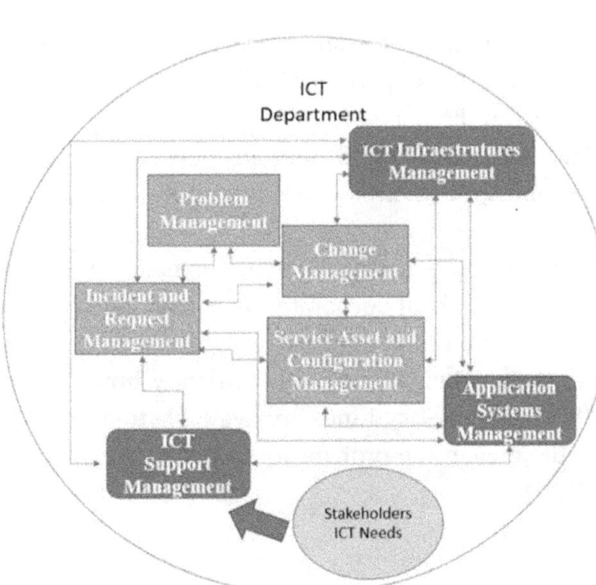

ITIL has the best practices guidance for IT Service Management (ITSM) and has been well accepted by organizations world-wide. ITILv3 presents five stages in the service lifecycle management: Service Strategy, Service Design, Service Transition, Service Operation and Continual Service Improvement (OCG, 2007). ITIL bundle established best practices to support the task of IT service operation (Kubiak & Rass, 2018), but briefly explains and guides the main tasks of IT operations (Mahalle et al., 2018).

Control Objectives for Information and Related Technology (COBIT) is an IT governance framework, shows a clear distinction between IT management and IT governance. COBIT19 refers the possibility to define factors and components that should be considered by organizations to build and maintain a governance system: processes, organizational structures, politics, procedures, information flows, culture, ethic and behavior, skills, services, applications and infrastructure of an organization, not only in the ICT domain. This framework treats information and related technologies as assets, which must be managed (ISACA, 2019).

Comparing ITIL and COBIT, the gaps considered are presented in Table 5.

Table 5. Identifying gaps between ITIL and COBIT

Analysis	ITILv3	COBIT5.0
Gaps	Does not contain detailed process maps.	Does not guide how to assess processes.
	Does not define measures for process improvement.	Does not provide a "road map" for continuous improvement.
	Difficult implementation.	Difficult implementation.
	Does not provide working instructions.	
	Does not align IT processes and business objectives.	

(Marchão et al., 2021)

Based on several studies and research it is considered that COBIT and ITIL frameworks are relevant references to support the design of an approach for service operation management in a medium-sized organization, to improve operational efficiency, cost optimization, and stakeholder satisfaction (Marchão et al., 2021).

It is considered that the framework under construction should include other aspects, namely interaction in a more assertive manner with the department's Financial Management area, whose foundation is based on COBIT guidelines from the perspective of governance and ICT management. A problem that the organization often face is the difficulty of measuring the effectiveness of IT investment, aligning with a business objective, and show them a benefit map into the part of the organization affected (Saputra et al., 2019).

The resources for investment planning and ICT budget management must, regardless of the size of the organization, comply with the criteria of corporate finance and the constant observation of the cost/benefit ratio, in which the benefit should be evidence, when possible, as a service level commitment to stakeholders, internal or external. Budget control is critically important to ensure that there are no unexpected deviations and that the necessary funds are available to carry out the planned projects. The better the budgetary control, the greater the probability of achieving the objectives and the greater the credibility (Silva & Torres, 2010).

The Figure 4 presents an interdepartmental relationship between some departments of an organization, such as ICT, corporate Procurement, corporate Finance, legal and commercial department.

Figure 4. Interdepartmental relationship: information workflows

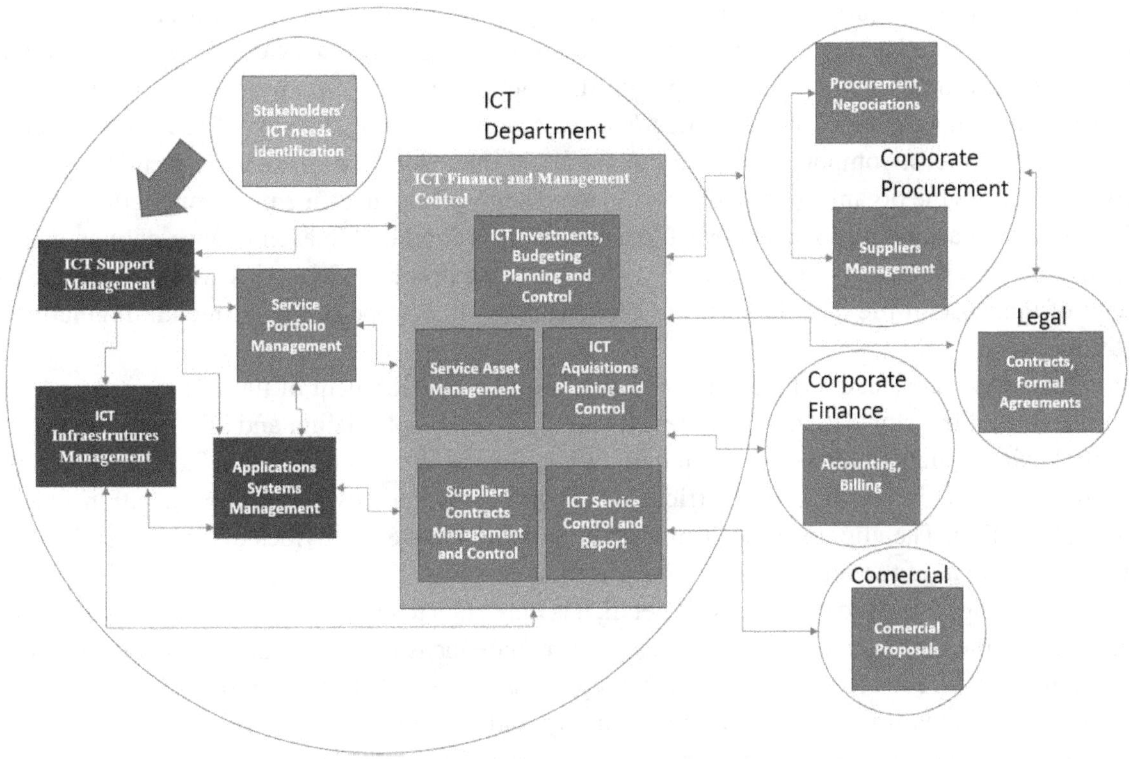

In the context of the process of interdepartmental information management and the domain of gaps underlying informal information in organizations, Figure 4 shows an example of functional interdepartmental relationships between the ICT department and other departments of a medium-sized organization, related to information flow. In addition to the formal communication and team's relationship, an invisible informal communication network is maintained in the organizations. It is essential to facilitate the efficiency of the processes and organizations' strategic and operational objectives but must be supervised to avoid loses information not registered.

The processes managed in the ICT financial and management control area, are related to all processes and/or activities that are related to financial studies, investments or budgeting control, schema is presented in Figure 4. This area controls the acquisitions and manages budget costs, especially contracts related to software licensing, equipment maintenance, telecommunications, or specialized technical support. This area has an inevitable relationship with the corporate finance area, from which the guidelines for budget and financial resources available came, to pursuit the maintenance of ICT daily operation and to innovate, in a balance between exploration and exploitation (Helbin & Van Looy, 2019).

The ICT financial and management control area is related to several corporate areas, with different functions, e.g. supervising financial and budgeting aspects or clarifying some ICT concepts requested.

Corporate Purchasing Area and Legal Area are two of them. The Purchasing area processes material acquisitions or services, in supplier market. They look for products or services in different companies in the market and negotiate commercial proposals for the best prices. The process goes through the internal legal area and aims to ensure compliance with internal policies and regulations and legal requirements applicable in external contracts before a formal commitment from the organization.

The organization can provide internal services, only to the organization, or to different clients to obtain financial returns. The services are supported by the catalog of ICT services. If working to outsider clients, ICT department has a relationship with the commercial area in a partnership model, and this area establishes an agreement with the client/stakeholder. Controlling the cost of each service, considering the different cost components that comprise it and the respective financial return on the services it provides, allows the organization to define the most appropriate investment and marketing strategies.

The asset management process allows the control of items related to each service delivered, during its lifecycle. Plan scheduled technical interventions or / and replace the assets when obsolescence at the end of their useful life, should ensuring compliance with European environmental regulations for electronic waste.

It is intended that selected studies can contribute to the development of the framework under construction. Digital transformation applied to existing processes, optimizing, and aligning them between different business units, interconnected in daily work. One of the focuses can be the team relationship and individual behavior, leading to the efficiency of transformed processes, cost optimization and stakeholder satisfaction. The alignment of IT processes with the business provides evidence of added value for the achievement of the organizations' objectives.

Before starting to analyze any process in detail, it is important to identify which are the target processes to analyze and then define clearly the process performance measures (also called process performance metrics) that will be used to determine whether a process is in good shape or in bad shape. Typical process performance measures relate to cost, time, quality, and flexibility. The identification of performance measures (and associated performance objectives) is crucial in any BPM initiative. This identification is generally seen as part of the process identification phase, although in some cases it may be postponed until later phases. Next phase for the team is to understand the business process in detail (*as-is* process models), is process discovery phase and reflect the understanding that people in the organization have about how work is done. It is common practice to use diagrams to model business processes, diagrams allow us to comprehend the process more easily and they may still be complemented with textual descriptions. There are many languages for modeling business processes, one of the oldest are *flowcharts.* Other are Unified Modeling Language (UML), Event-driven Process Chains (EPCs), data-flow diagrams and Integrated DEFinition for Process Description Capture Method (IDEF3). There is a widely used standard for process modeling, namely the Business Process Model and Notation (BPMN). It was released as a standard by the Object Management Group (OMG). The identification and assessment of issues and opportunities for process improvement is called the process analysis phase. Once issues in a process have been analyzed and possibly quantified, the next phase is to identify and analyze potential remedies for these issues. It is important to keep in mind that a change in a process to address one issue may potentially cause other issues. Changing a process is not easy, people often inclined to resist changes. The *to-be* process design is the main output of the process redesign phase. Once redesigned, the necessary changes in the ways of working and the IT systems of the organization should be implemented so that the *to-be* process can eventually be put into execution. This phase is called process implementation. Process implementation involves two complementary aspects: organizational change management and process automation. Organizational change management refers to the set of activities required to change the way of working of all participants involved in the process, Process automation, on the other hand, involves the configuration or implementation of an IT system (or the re-configuration of an existing IT system) to support the to-be process. Over time, adjustments may be required in the implemented business process when it does not meet expectations any longer. To find out that, data must be collected, and process monitored, to identify needed adjustments. These activities are related to the process monitoring phase. Lack of continuous monitoring and improvement of a process leads to degradation, This is why the BPM lifecycle should be seen as circular: the output of the monitoring phase feeds back into the discovery, analysis, and redesign phases (Dumas et al., 2018b).

(Stravinskiene & Serafinas, 2020) reported four dimensions of BPM: process awareness, process ownership, process measurement, and process improvement. Process awareness is defined as the most important criterion of process management, i.e., business processes should be identified, named, and documented. This is shown in a comprehensive process map that visualizes the processes of the organization and their interrelationships. It should be supplemented by a set of documents describing individual processes and distinguishing activities, roles, resources, rules, and results. However, to meet the criteria of understanding the processes, having documents alone is not enough. Managers and employees should comprehend these processes; employees should have a deep understanding of the processes they are involved in from the beginning to the end. This most important criterion is about how employees and managers perceive the organization, i.e., how it is structured, how it works. Moreover, in case processes are immeasurable, it is impossible to define the value they create.

RECOMMENDATIONS

Currently, companies support their activities in IS / ICT, and it is intended to optimize this relationship by fulfilling the goals of digital transformation. ICT management is a highly complex activity in the context of most organizations.

Taking into account the relevance of ICT in the context of the organization, ICT Governance is today an inseparable vertex of Corporate Governance, and the constant alignment with the needs of stakeholders should be the basis for creating value for the organization's ICT area., proposing solutions to leverage the business or create new opportunities. It is intended that the framework will allow to identify and reduce gaps between established practices and those suggested by international references, proposing process optimization or integration. The added value of the approach in an organizational context is to allow an integrative and multidisciplinary view, improving the aspects of cost optimization, communication, and stakeholder satisfaction.

FUTURE RESEARCH DIRECTIONS

As perspectives for future work, it is recommended that the contribution of the systematic literature review can support and improve the development of a framework to solve the problem in the organizational context, thus allowing the detection of gaps in the alignment of ICT processes. It is also considered an advantage that the framework can integrate cross-cutting business processes relevant to other departments, which are related to the flow of information to and from the ICT processes.

The approach to be created should be validated through a focus group, to assess its viability and contribute to the improvement of the service provided to the various stakeholders involved, valuing professionalism and work quality.

CONCLUSION

Digital transformation can be built as the engine of change to enhance the use of ICT in an organizational context, to optimize processes and include informal knowledge. Thus, it is considered that the workflows underlying the processes must be re-analyzed so that the decision-making can be supported by the information contained in the business support IS.

Currently, organizations in their business relationships rely heavily on ICT to involve more and more stakeholders to provide better services given the need for fast and quality service markets. It is considered that digital transformation can contribute towards optimizing processes, creating added value.

Digital transformation is not just about technology, it is also about organizational processes, the way of doing work, and human relationships. Digital technology is changing the world, transforming business models, and forcing management methods to change. Organizations are increasingly based on trust, sharing, and collaboration between individuals (Cigref, 2018).

The focus on human resources should be on a vision of the future, the challenges constitute a "new reality", it offers new opportunities for which academics and professionals in the organization will need to remain attentive. The long-term implications of COVID-19 are currently unknown, and its impact on organizational life is believed to continue (Carnevale & Hatak, 2020).

It is intended to identify existing problems in the function of supporting ICT operations and informal information relevant to the processes that is not registered. Also analyze best practices, related areas and relevant cross-cutting processes. The elaboration of a Framework has a particular interest centered on continuous improvement based on the function of supporting the ICT services provided and related areas.

The Information Technology Infrastructure Library (ITIL), universally known, presents the best practices for the management of IT services to be implemented in an organizational context. The ITIL service management lifecycle has Strategy, Design and Conception, Transition, Operations, and Continuous Improvement areas.

The ITIL v3 is compliant with international standard ISO 20000, oriented to IT services management, allows organizations that provide IT services to demonstrate compliance with requirements organized by processes, being these requirements generic and intended to be applicable to all types of organizations, regardless of the sector, size, and nature of the provided service.

The Control Objectives for Information and related Technology (COBIT) is a standard that considers the culture of excellence an important and differentiating pillar of any organization. The COBIT methodology, principles, tools, and models are globally accepted by many organizations. The implementation is based on a set of governance indicators associated with IT service operations.

SLR allowed the study of several authors and references in the field of the subject, supporting the creation of the ICT Process Optimization Framework, based on research questions. The need to develop the Framework arises from the finding of a set of gaps in organizational practice.

The COVID-19 pandemic forced many organizations to make considerable changes to their normal business processes. Human beings will continue to adapt, innovate, create new technologies and integrate them to make tasks that were once time-consuming and difficult to do, easier and faster to complete.

Thinking outside the box and innovating for different ways of doing things will create new opportunities to improve lives by carefully integrating man and technology, working together sustainably.

REFERENCES

Ahmad, T. (2019). The Impact of New IT Adoption on Business Process Management. *Proceedings - International Conference on Research Challenges in Information Science*. 10.1109/RCIS.2019.8877085

Alaiad, A., Alnsour, Y., & Alsharo, M. (2019). Virtual teams: Thematic taxonomy, constructs model, and future research directions. IEEE Transactions on Professional Communication, 62(3), 211–238. doi:10.1109/TPC.2019.2929370

Alotaibi, Y., & Liu, F. (2013). Business process modelling towards derive and implement IT goals. *Proceedings of the 2013 IEEE 8th Conference on Industrial Electronics and Applications, ICIEA 2013*. 10.1109/ICIEA.2013.6566649

Belchior, R., Guerreiro, S., Vasconcelos, A., & Correia, M. (2020). *A survey on business process view integration*. ArXiv.

Carnevale, J. B., & Hatak, I. (2020). Employee adjustment and well-being in the era of COVID-19: Implications for human resource management. *Journal of Business Research, 116*, 183–187. doi:10.1016/j.jbusres.2020.05.037 PMID:32501303

Ciasullo, M. V., Fenza, G., Loia, V., Orciuoli, F., Troisi, O., & Herrera-Viedma, E. (2018). Business process outsourcing enhanced by fuzzy linguistic consensus model. *Applied Soft Computing, 64*, 436–444. doi:10.1016/j.asoc.2017.12.020

Cigref. (2018). *Cigref Nomenclature Information Systems job profiles Framework*. https://www.cigref.fr/cigref-nomenclature-information-systems-job-profiles-framewok-update-2018

de Lucas Ancillo, A., del Val Núñez, M. T., & Gavrila, S. G. (2021). Workplace change within the COVID-19 context: A grounded theory approach. *Economic Research-Ekonomska Istraživanja, 34*(1), 2297–2316. doi:10.1080/1331677X.2020.1862689

Dumas, M., La Rosa, M., Mendling, J., & Reijers, H. A. (2018a). BPM as an Enterprise Capability. Fundamentals of Business Process Management. doi:10.1007/978-3-662-56509-4_12

Dumas, M., La Rosa, M., Mendling, J., & Reijers, H. A. (2018b). *Fundamentals of Business Process Management*. Springer Berlin Heidelberg. doi:10.1007/978-3-662-56509-4

Dwivedi, Y. K., Hughes, D. L., Coombs, C., Constantiou, I., Duan, Y., Edwards, J. S., Gupta, B., Lal, B., Misra, S., Prashant, P., Raman, R., Rana, N. P., Sharma, S. K., & Upadhyay, N. (2020). Impact of COVID-19 pandemic on information management research and practice: Transforming education, work and life. *International Journal of Information Management, 55*, 102211. doi:10.1016/j.ijinfomgt.2020.102211

Elia, G., & Margherita, A. (2021). A conceptual framework for the cognitive enterprise: Pillars, maturity, value drivers. *Technology Analysis and Strategic Management*, 1–13. doi:10.1080/09537325.2021.1901874

Feroz, A. K., Zo, H., & Chiravuri, A. (2021). Digital transformation and environmental sustainability: A review and research agenda. *Sustainability (Switzerland), 13*(3), 1–20. doi:10.3390u13031530

Fischer, M., Imgrund, F., Janiesch, C., & Winkelmann, A. (2020). Strategy archetypes for digital transformation: Defining meta objectives using business process management. *Information & Management, 57*(5), 103262. doi:10.1016/j.im.2019.103262

Gutierrez, G., Garzas, J., De Lena, M. T. G., & Moguerza, J. M. (2019). Self-Managing: An Empirical Study of the Practice in Agile Teams. *IEEE Software, 36*(1), 23–27. Advance online publication. doi:10.1109/MS.2018.2874324

Handayani, S. F., & Er, M. (2019). Antecedent and Business Process Management Non-Technical Capabilities in Social Media Implementation for Micro, Small and Medium Enterprises: A Conceptual Model. *Procedia Computer Science, 161*, 1114–1121. doi:10.1016/j.procs.2019.11.223

Helbin, T., & Van Looy, A. (2019). Business Process Ambidexterity and its impact on Business-IT alignment. A Systematic Literature Review. *2019 13th International Conference on Research Challenges in Information Science (RCIS)*, 1–12. 10.1109/RCIS.2019.8877073

Kir, H., & Erdogan, N. (2021). A knowledge-intensive adaptive business process management framework. *Information Systems, 95*, 101639. doi:10.1016/j.is.2020.101639

Kubiak, P., & Rass, S. (2018). An Overview of Data-Driven Techniques for IT-Service-Management. *IEEE Access: Practical Innovations, Open Solutions, 6*, 63664–63688. doi:10.1109/ACCESS.2018.2875975

Kumar, A., Luthra, S., Mangla, S. K., & Kazançoğlu, Y. (2020). COVID-19 impact on sustainable production and operations management. *Sustainable Operations and Computers, 1*, 1–7. doi:10.1016/j.susoc.2020.06.001

Kunchala, J., Yu, J., Yongchareon, S., & Liu, C. (2020). An approach to merge collaborating processes of an inter-organizational business process for artifact lifecycle synthesis. *Computing, 102*(4), 951–976. doi:10.100700607-019-00770-z

Mahalle, A., Yong, J., & Tao, X. (2018). ITIL Processes to Control Operational Risk in Cloud Architecture Infrastructure for Banking and Financial Services Industry. *2018 5th International Conference on Behavioral, Economic, and Socio-Cultural Computing (BESC)*, 197–200. 10.1109/BESC.2018.8697294

Marchão, J., Reis, L., & Martins, P. V. (2021). A Framework to Align Business Processes: Identification of the Main Features. *Advances in Science. Technology and Engineering Systems Journal, 6*(2), 746–753. doi:10.25046/aj060286

Marchão, J., Reis, L., & Ventura, P. (2020). Operation management using ITIL and COBIT framework. *Conference Proceedings (Part of ITEMA Conference Collection)*, 201–207. 10.31410/ITEMA.2020.201

Menglong, L., Shuanghui, Y., Mengmeng, Z., Tao, C., Honghui, C., & Xiaoxue, Z. (2020). A coevolutionary framework of business-IT alignment via the lens of enterprise architecture. *Journal of Systems Engineering and Electronics, 31*(5), 983–995. doi:10.23919/JSEE.2020.000073

Nasiriasayesh, H., & Yari, A. (2019). A Model for Policy-Aware Execution of Business Process in Federated Clouds. *9th International Symposium on Telecommunication: With Emphasis on Information and Communication Technology, IST 2018*, 700–704. 10.1109/ISTEL.2018.8661051

OCG. (2007). *The official Introdution to ITIL Service Lifecycle*. Stationery Office.

Ogbeibu, S., Chiappetta Jabbour, C. J., Burgess, J., Gaskin, J., & Renwick, D. W. S. (2021). Green talent management and turnover intention: The roles of leader STARA competence and digital task interdependence. *Journal of Intellectual Capital*. Advance online publication. doi:10.1108/JIC-01-2021-0016

Osman, C.-C. C., & Ghiran, A.-M. M. (2019). When Industry 4.0 meets Process Mining. *Procedia Computer Science*, *159*, 2130–2136. doi:10.1016/j.procs.2019.09.386

Pegoraro, M., Uysal, M. S., & van der Aalst, W. M. P. (2021). Conformance checking over uncertain event data. *Information Systems*, *102*, 101810. doi:10.1016/j.is.2021.101810

Persse, J. (2012). The ITIL Process Manual - Key Processes and their Application. *The ITIL Process Manual*, 55.

Prasetyo, H. N., Sarno, R., Budiraharjo, R., & Sungkono, K. R. (2021). The Effect of Duration Heteroscedasticity to the Bottleneck in Business Process Discovered by Inductive Miner Algorithm. *Proceedings - 2021 IEEE Asia Pacific Conference on Wireless and Mobile, APWiMob 2021*, 52–58. 10.1109/APWiMob51111.2021.9435199

Renn, O., Beier, G., & Schweizer, P. J. (2021). The opportunities and risks of digitalisation for sustain able development: A systemic perspective. *Gaia (Heidelberg)*, *30*(1), 23–28. doi:10.14512/gaia.30.1.6

Roquete, M. M. F. (2018). *Modelo de maturidade para apoio à implementação de uma filosofia de gestão orientada a processos numa organização*. Academic Press.

Saputra, D. A., Nugroho, W. S., & Ranti, B. (2019). Benefits Analysis of IT Investment in Business Support System (BSS) Projects Using Ranti's Generic IS/IT Business Values: Case Studies of the Indonesian Telecommunication Company. *2019 International Conference on Advanced Computer Science and Information Systems (ICACSIS)*, 331–336. 10.1109/ICACSIS47736.2019.8979945

Shinn, S. A., & Lunz, V. A. (2015). Managing Cost, schedule, and technical performance through a sustained change framework. *IEEE Aerospace Conference Proceedings*. 10.1109/AERO.2015.7119116

Silva, P., & Torres, C. (2010). *Gestão e Liderança* (F. C. A. Editora, Ed.). Lidel Edições.

Stravinskiene, I., & Serafinas, D. (2020). The Link between Business Process Management and Quality Management. *Journal of Risk and Financial Management*, *13*(10), 225. doi:10.3390/jrfm13100225

Vadlamudi, S., & De, S. (2021). A Novel Approach in Cyber Security for securing the Workplace of the Future in large Industry Setups. *2021 International Conference on Intelligent Technologies (CONIT)*, 1–6. 10.1109/CONIT51480.2021.9498468

Veronica & Debora. (2018). Information technology service performance management using COBIT and an ITIL framework: A systematic literature review. *Proceedings of 2017 International Conference on Information Management and Technology, ICIMTech 2017*. doi:10.1109/ICIMTech.2017.8273528

KEY TERMS AND DEFINITIONS

COBIT: Framework for the governance and management of information and technology, aimed at the whole enterprise, not limited to the IT department of an organization but certainly includes it.

Information and Communication Technologies: A technological resource set used to process information and ensure communication. When used in an integrated way it enhances information transmission and communication processes.

Information Systems: Is the organized set of components such as people, processes of collection and transmission of data and material resources, automated or manual. The interaction of components enhances the processing and dissemination of information.

International Standards: A set of technical standards that establish a quality management model for organizations in general, whatever their type or size, covering various areas within organizations.

ITIL: Framework the most widely accepted IT service management system in the world. ITIL is a set of practices used by organizations to manage IT services.

APPENDIX

Included Studies

This appendix contains the included selected studies, as well as their author, year of publication, title, and publication forum.

Table 6.

#	Year	Author	Title	Publication Forum
1	2018	Desak, G.; Saputra, W.; Titan; Mariani, V.	Business Process Management (BPM) in Operational BINUS Online Learning	International Conference on Information Management and Technology (ICIMTech)
2	2018	Hariyanti, E.; Djunaidy, A.; Siahaan, D.	A Conceptual Model for Information Security Risk Considering Business Process Perspective	4th International Conference on Science and Technology (ICST)
3	2018	Hersyah, M.; Derisma	A Literature Review on Business Continuity Based on ISO 22301, Six Sigma and Customer Satisfaction Evaluation	International Conference on Information Technology Systems and Innovation (ICITSI)
4	2018	Juwitasary, H.; Christian, L.; Putra, E.; Fifilia; Sardjono, W.	Business Process Management System Implementation Model for Improving Employee Performance	International Conference on Information Management and Technology (ICIMTech)
5	2018	Ciasullo, M.; Fenza, G.; Herrera-Viedma, E.; et al.	Business process outsourcing enhanced by fuzzy linguistic consensus model	Applied Soft Computing, 27 December 2017, Volume 64 (Cover date: March 2018) Pages 436-444
6	2018	Mihova, T.; Nikolova-Alexieva, V.; Angelova, M.	Factors Affecting Business Process Management in the Bulgarian Enterprises to Achieve Sustainable Development	International Conference on High Technology for Sustainable Development (HiTech)
7	2018	Yulherniwati; Jama, J.; Ganefri; Ikhsan, A.	Modeling flexibility on internal quality assurance system business process	International Seminar on Research of Information Technology and Intelligent Systems (ISRITI)
8	2018	Jiang, H.	Research and Implementation of Financial Approval System Based on jBPM Engine	IEEE 3rd Advanced Information Technology, Electronic and Automation Control Conference (IAEAC)
9	2018	Pérez-Álvarez, J.; Maté, A.; Trujillo, J.; et al	Tactical Business-Process-Decision Support based on KPIs Monitoring and Validation	Computers in Industry,18 August 2018, Volume 102 (Cover date: November 2018) Pages 23-39
10	2019	Ramadhani, F.; Mahendrawathi ER	A Conceptual Model for the Use of Social Software in Business Process Management and Knowledge Management	Procedia Computer Science,2019, Volume 161Pages 1131-1138
11	2019	Cegarra-Navarro, J.; Papa, A.; Fiano, F.; et al.	An open-minded strategy towards eco-innovation: A key to sustainable growth in a global enterprise	Technological Forecasting and Social Change,4 September 2019, Volume 148 (Cover date: November 2019) Article 119727
12	2019	Al-Fedaghi, S.; Mohamad, Y.	Business Process Mapping: A Case Study	IEEE/ACS 16th International Conference on Computer Systems and Applications (AICCSA)
13	2019	Surbakti, F.; Wang, W.; Sadiq, S.; et al.	Factors influencing effective use of big data: A research framework	Information & Management,19 February 2019, Volume 57, Issue 1 (Cover date: January 2020) Article 103146
14	2019	Strutynska, I.; Kozbur, G.; Dmytrotsa, L.; Sorokivska, O.; Melnyk, L.	Influence of Digital Technology on Roadmap Development for Digital Business Transformation	9th International Conference on Advanced Computer Information Technologies (ACIT)
15	2019	Hausladen, I.; Schosser, M.	Towards a maturity model for big data analytics in airline network planning	Journal of Air Transport Management,24 October 2019, Volume 82 (Cover date: January 2020) Article 101721
16	2019	Sousa, V.; Corentin, B.	Towards an integrated methodology for the development of blockchain-based solutions supporting cross-organizational processes	13th International Conference on Research Challenges in Information Science (RCIS)
17	2020	Vernadat, F.	Enterprise modelling: Research review and outlook	Computers in Industry,29 June 2020, Volume 122 (Cover date: November 2020) Article 103265
18	2020	Brinch, M.; Gunasekaran, A.; Wamba, S.	Firm-level capabilities towards big data value creation	Journal of Business Research,10 August 2020, Volume 131 (Cover date: July 2021) Pages 539-548
19	2021	Cabrita, M.; Antunes, C.; Costa, J.	Increasing process maturity through a Business Process Management System: Case study at a financial institution	16th Iberian Conference on Information Systems and Technologies (CISTI)

Chapter 10
Digitalization and Drivers of Innovative Behavior for a Smart Economy in the Post-COVID-19 Era:
Technology Student Course Design Characteristics

James Kiarie Ngugi
University of South Africa, South Africa

Leila Goosen
https://orcid.org/0000-0003-4948-2699
University of South Africa, South Africa

ABSTRACT

To summarize the content and provide readers with an overview, the purpose of this chapter is stated as investigating digitalization and the drivers of individual innovative behavior (IIB) for a smart economy in the post-COVID-19 era in terms of the effects of information and communication technology (ICT) students' course design characteristics (CDCs) in developing their IIB. Modelling of the mediating effects of knowledge sharing behavior (KSB) and self-regulated learning (SRL) on ICT students' individual and contextual antecedents is also considered.

INTRODUCTION

This section will describe the general perspective of the chapter and end by specifically stating the objective.

DOI: 10.4018/978-1-7998-9227-4.ch010

The COVID-19 pandemic had accelerated emerging trends towards criteria and guidelines for the selection and implementation of internet-based **digitalization** and automation strategies underlying digital transformation (Goosen, 2004; Kalina, 2021). In this way, there has been an exponential increase in the demand for intelligent and reliable communication and collaboration **solutions**. Although the pandemic brings huge **challenges** for all economic agents, Garg and Garg (2021) indicated that the 'smart' capabilities brought by the Internet of Things are leading towards revolutionary applications, which have huge potential to improve efficiency multifold. Resilience and the capacity to adapt to new risks and **challenges** will be fundamental elements in society. Across all industries, recovery demands the incorporation "of the striking features of new business models", new marketing channels and new markets that may be reached using Information and Communication Technologies (ICTs), but also for innovative proposals and flexibility to capture value in a digital world, as well as to start, expand and/or improve businesses (Sufi & Ahmed, 2021). It is agreed that digital technologies played a crucial role during the pandemic to keep society functioning, with new vocabulary coming into daily life, such as groups of Information Technology (IT) students, who are working and learning in their 'remote' class (Mentz & Goosen, 2007), etc. In this context, it is fundamental that **digitalization** brings opportunities for a transition to a smarter economy based on innovation and entrepreneurship, using the potential of ICTs for a sustainable recovery towards the post-COVID-19 era (Ngugi & Goosen, 2021c).

Target Audience

Like the book, this chapter is mainly intended to support an academic audience (academics, university teachers, researchers and post-graduate students – at both Master and Doctorate levels). In addition, this chapter could be of benefit to public and private institutions, and even private and public organizations, as well as developers, business managers, and professionals with regard to this and related sectors of innovation or ICTs.

Recommended Topics

Since this is an edited publication, the authors of this chapter are seeking to publish a chapter covering the broad areas of innovation and ICTs, in line with the **recommended topics** for the book. Based on the list of proposed topics provided, which is necessarily generalist and indicative, the authors aim to cover the widest range possible, while still maintaining a balance of topics that remain within the authors' remit of innovative, engaging and **emergent** approaches. Topics addressed in this chapter include:

- ICT pandemic times adoption
- ICT student **solutions**
- Case study application
- Social aspects of Information Systems (IS) education
- Social demand and innovative proposals
- e-Learning and education in the post COVID-19 era

Objective

According to Ngugi and Goosen (2021a), there is extensive literature that addresses the main topics of, and/or had identified factors promoting, **digitalization**, ICTs and Individual Innovative Behavior (IIB) in an organizational context in post-pandemic times. Against this background, the requirements for a successful recovery includes overcoming huge **challenges**, highlighting the relevance of a multi-disciplinary approach that mixes and complements these topics.

However, the effects of Course Design Characteristics (CDCs), Self-Regulated Learning (SRL) and Knowledge Sharing Behavior (KSB) in facilitating the development of individual innovative behavior among information and communication technology students at university level is not understood well (Ngugi & Goosen, 2017).

The question of how the construct of course design characteristics leads to knowledge sharing behavior among undergraduate ICT students is also not fully understood. If the proposed CDCs construct is indeed a significant antecedent of knowledge sharing behavior, then the construct can be added to the salient contextual **drivers** of IIB, along with ICT *students' perceptions* of self-regulated learning. By leveraging the antecedents of knowledge sharing behavior, SRL and CDCs at the level of an individual, ICT students should be well-placed to compete in a world that is complex and competitive - according to Gravemeijer, Stephan, Julie, Lin and Ohtani (2017), it is also, under the influence of automatization, **digitalization**, globalization and informatization, changing rapidly and leading to societal innovativeness.

Similar to that of the chapter by Ngugi and Goosen (2021c), the **purpose** of the study being reported on in this chapter was to present a description of research in an organizational context in order to optimize the practices established in the most diverse domains of knowledge, attending to the relation between **digitalization** and sustainability in a post-pandemic era. This was accomplished by developing a structural equation model of the drivers of individual innovative behavior for ICT students against a background of research regarding **digitalization** for a smart economy.

Emphasizing the importance of digitization as an organizational support, and crafting and executing strategies in the quest for a competitive advantage (Thompson, Strickland, & Gamble, 2014), can in times of recovery enhance the nature of the impact of changes on stakeholders. This chapter aims to present an African and multi-disciplinary approach that could contribute to an improved understanding of the relationship and mutual influence of ICTs and innovation across scientific areas. It is important that research is emphasized, which disseminates studies in various contexts from a perspective of innovation and ICTs. The **objective** of this chapter is therefore to answer the following research question:

- What implications do digitalization and the drivers of individual innovative behavior have for the smart economy in the post-COVID-19 era in terms of the effects of information and communication technology students' course design characteristics in developing their IIB?

BACKGROUND

This section of the chapter and the next will provide broad *definitions* and discussions on the topics of **digitalization** and the **drivers** of individual innovative behavior for the smart economy in the post-COVID-19 era in terms of the effects of information and communication technology students' course design characteristics. These will also incorporate the views of others (in the form of a *literature review*) into the discussion to support, refute, or demonstrate the authors' position on the topic.

Digitalization

The authors of this chapter (Ngugi & Goosen, 2021c, p. 111) pointed out that **digitalization** is more than just one of the **emerging trends** and ICTs were "common and influential to the wellbeing of millions of people virtually everywhere."

The paper by Gravemeijer, et al. (2017) attempted engaging in fields related to discussing what mathematics was needed for students towards engaging in society, especially with increasing technologies and **digitalization**.

Insufficient digital infrastructure in India may create a digital divide amongst people (Srinivasa Varadhan, 2021). Because of such **digitalization**, however, sales of electronic equipment had soared.

In the context of the chapter by Reis, et al. (2021, p. 244), new digital business models gained popularity in pandemic "times, with the importance of **digitalization**" acting as a transversal factor across all of society.

"The process of converting analogue data into digital data is one of the most fundamental concepts behind the operations of a computer system." It had, however, "been observed that many students" at tertiary education had "little to no knowledge of this fundamental concept". Evans, Fuse, Munekata and Ono (2017, p. 42) therefore investigated the deployment of an interactive JavaScript application to aid in understanding the **digitalization** of sound.

E-Learning and Education in The Post COVID-19 Era

In their **education** conference papers, Goosen and Ngugi (2018) urged their audience to rethink teaching and learning in the 21st century in terms of course design characteristics towards individual innovative behavior for ICT students (Goosen & Ngugi, 2019b).

As both learners at Basic Education (school) and students at Higher Education and Training (HET/university) levels have indicated that they want access to **e-learning** (Goosen, 2016), technology-supported teaching and research methods for educators are needed (Goosen, 2019).

In a history of e-learning, Nicholson (2007, p. 1) expressed the view that in many contemporary sectors, **e-learning** was "often regarded as a 'new' form of learning that uses the affordances of the Internet", computers and education "to deliver customized, often interactive, learning materials and programs to diverse local and distant communities of practice."

In a case study of a private university in Malaysia using Facebook and against the background of e-management and **e-learning**, Sim, Dewika and Devandran (2014, p. 354) indicated that there was "no definite *definition* of mobile learning. Learning on the move can be" a generalization for improving students' engagement through social media, "focusing on devices that are small and portable, for example, handheld computers and smart phones".

While Pereira, Dias, Carvalho and Noronha (2021) investigated *students' perceptions* about **e-learning** within the context of the COVID-19 pandemic in a study in Brazil and Portugal, Van Heerden and Goosen (2021) reported on *students' perceptions* of e-assessment in the context of **COVID**-19 in a case study application at the University of South Africa (UNISA). Earlier, the latter authors (Van Heerden &

Goosen, 2012) had reported on using vodcasts to teach programming in an Open and Distance **Learning** (ODL) environment.

In a case study of the Indian restaurant industry, Sufi and Ahmed (2021) explored how the **COVID-19** crisis could be survived by using new business models, whereas Kalina (2021) presented managerial decision support in the post-COVID-19 era towards information-based management.

Also towards **the post-COVID-19 era**, Ngugi and Goosen (2021b) reported on innovation, entrepreneurship and sustainability for ICT students and Bolton, Goosen and Kritzinger (2021) offered insights on an empirical study into the impact on innovation and productivity in terms of the digital transformation of an automotive enterprise.

Course Design Characteristics

The need to develop a comprehensive measure for course design characteristics was addressed, due to the following three (3) reasons:

Firstly, despite the availability of employee-related measures on the range of jobs, there are limited measures available that are specific to university-level students undertaking an undergraduate program. Such a measure may help to address some policy decisions in the redesign of courses in university education.

Secondly, although there are distinct relationships between work design dimensions and course design dimensions, there has been no attempt to extend work design to the field of course design. By extending the focus of work design to the educational context of course design, the study could form the basis in terms of **further research directions** and the generation of theoretical models.

Thirdly, the question of how the new construct of CDCs affects knowledge sharing behavior among undergraduate ICT students is still not fully understood, especially in a developing country like Kenya. If the proposed CDCs are indeed a significant antecedent of knowledge sharing behavior, then the construct can be added to the salient contextual **drivers** of IIB, along with the SRL of ICT students. By leveraging the antecedents of knowledge sharing behavior and IIB in ICT education, it should be possible to trigger individual innovative behavior in students.

Dimensions of Course Design Characteristics

Based on the work of Morgeson and Humphrey (2006), the adapted latent construct of CDCs has two main dimensions: course task characteristics and course knowledge characteristics.

Course task characteristics

Exploring the relationship between job design and knowledge productivity in a conceptual framework in the context of Malaysian administrative and diplomatic officers, a *journal article against the background of organizational knowledge* by Masrek, Yusof, Noordin and Johare (2013) indicated that course task characteristics involve a measure of the extent of task autonomy, task feedback, task identity, task significance and task variety, where the task in this case relates to a course. Course task characteristics therefore refer to *students' perceptions* of the range of task demands, as well as the type of tasks associated with a course of study in university education. Both Pereira, et al. (2021) and Van Heerden and Goosen (2021) also considered *students' perceptions*.

The five (5) sub-constructs of course task characteristics as quoted in the previous paragraph utilized the definitions provided in Ngugi and Goosen (2018), as well as Goosen and Ngugi (2018), where the former were modelling course-design characteristics, self-regulated learning and the mediating effect of knowledge-sharing behavior as **drivers** of individual innovative behavior.

Consequences of Course Design Characteristics

Previous studies, such as the journal article by Luthans, Norman, Avolio and Avey (2008) in the context of organizational behavior on the mediating role of *psychological capital* in a supportive organizational climate in terms of employee performance relationships, have shown that *job design* characteristics, such as task identity, job feedback, autonomy, skill variety and task significance are associated directly with KSB and directly with IIB (Dorenbosch, Van Engen, & Verhagen, 2005; Thompson & Heron, 2006; De Jong & Den Hartog, 2010; Hartjes, 2010).

In a journal article on business research, Rego, Sousa, Marques and Cunha (2012) considered authentic leadership promoting employees' *psychological capital* and creativity. Also with regard to creativity and on-the-job innovation management, the importance and impact of job design and *human resource management* through production ownership among employees and in organizations have also been established in previous research (Dorenbosch, et al., 2005).

Another *human resource management* journal article by Thompson and Heron (2006) looked at relational quality and innovative performance in Research and Development (R&D) based science and technology firms, while an academy of management **learning** and **education** journal article in a two-wave study investigated stimulating informal **learning** activities through perceptions of performance appraisal quality and *human resource management* system strength (Bednall, Sanders, & Runhaar, 2014).

Consequently, the study reported on in this chapter broke into new ground by extending the Job Characteristics Model (JCM) to the field of ICT education, by introducing the new construct of CDCs. Morgeson and Humphrey (2006, p. 1322) extended the JCM to include work design, which "acknowledges both the job and the link between jobs and the broader environment". The latter authors' Work Design Questionnaire (WDQ) distinguished four (4) key dimensions of work: contextual, knowledge, task, and social characteristics. The task and knowledge characteristics dimensions of work are more relevant to the construct of course design characteristics and were adapted and modified in developing the course design characteristics scale.

Accordingly, the study proposed the following two hypotheses:

Hypothesis 3: Course design characteristics are positively related to ICT students' KSB; and

Hypothesis 4: Course design characteristics are positively related to ICT students' individual innovative behavior.

The hypothesized model suggested that KSB mediates the relationship between CDCs and IIB and between SRL and IIB. The hypothesized model also advocated the existence of a direct relationship between CDCs and IIB, as well as between SRL and IIB. The hypothesized relationships were tested with the aid of structural equation modeling techniques, as explained in a following subsection.

MAIN FOCUS OF THE CHAPTER

Issues, Problems, and Challenges

This section of the chapter will present the authors' perspective on the **issues**, **problems**, **challenges**, etc., as these relate to the main theme of the book on digitalization as a driver for the smart economy in the post-COVID-19 era, and arguments supporting the authors' position. It will also compare and contrast with what has been, or is currently being, done as it relates to the specific topic of the chapter on digitalization and the **drivers** of individual innovative behavior for the smart economy in the post-COVID-19 era, in terms of the effects of information and communication technology students' course design characteristics.

"In technical and vocational education and training systems, **vulnerabilities** *such as low levels of* **digitalization** *and long-standing structural* **weaknesses***, have been highlighted" by the pandemic (Pereira, et al., 2021, p. 286).*

According to Srinivasa Varadhan (2021, p. 377), in India, the passage to an undoubtedly promising future of online education "is packed with many **obstacles**."

In a British journal article on educational technology, Njenga and Fourie (2010, p. 199) expressed the opinion that proponents "have marketed e-learning by focusing on its adoption as the right thing to do while disregarding, among other things, the **concerns** of the potential users" and the **adverse** effects that the myths about e-learning in higher education could have.

The World Bank (2011) development report of that year considered **conflict** and security.

The smart economy

The Internet of Things (IoT) has "witnessed rapid growth in the last decade and is considered to be a promising field that plays an all-important role in every aspect of modern-day life." However, this growth of the IoT was seriously **hindered** by several factors. Abrar, Pottoo, Masoodi and Bamhdi (2021, p. 37) therefore reported on **challenges** and open **issues** related to the IoT and its integration with cloud computing – according to Goosen and Ngugi (2019a), such innovation for computing students matters, of course!

"Today, everything is progressing to '**Smart**' to enhance the environment via technological progress including" the IoT, big data, Artificial Intelligence (AI), ICTs, "and so on. But, in this whole process, the sustainability of being '**smart**' is implemented" through cloud-based technologies towards a cloud-based **smart** society (Tomar, Singh, Bhati, & Tomar, 2021, p. 113).

Using **smart** *sensors* for capture, the "cloud-based **smart** city is a way to provide resources and data on demand. Two technologies used to build cloud-based **smart**" cities, the IoT and cloud computing were explored in the chapter by Malik and Tarar (2021, p. 133).

An Internet of Things-enabled **smart** entry system for telecom sites "is leading towards revolutionary applications with huge potential to" improve efficiency multifold (Garg & Garg, 2021, p. 155). The IoT, through the use of *sensors* had "opened a huge window for applications in almost every area of life".

The Internet of Things "is a network of people and stuff at any moment, anytime, for anyone, with any network or service." The "IoT is therefore a major complex worldwide network backbone for online service providers", with the **smart** grid using the Internet of Things (Kaswan, Dhatterwal, & Gaur, 2021, p. 251).

"The worst natural catastrophes occurring in well-settled intelligent cities are earthquakes. A framework of earthquake warning minimizes destruction and protects countless lives" (Kaswan, Dhatterwal, & Kumar, 2021, p. 272). A blockchain of Internet of Things-based earthquake alarm system in **smart** cities is built on the IoT towards identifying the earthquake in time.

Finally, Ngugi and Goosen (2019) were modelling motivation, *metacognition* and affective aspects of learning towards **smart** innovation for information systems and ICT students, Seraphin, Philippoff, Kaupp and Vallin (2012) looked at *metacognition* as a means to increase the effectiveness of inquiry-based science education internationally.

Against the background of transactions on the smart grid, the paper by Wang, Wang, Wen, Guo and Wang (2021, p. 3185) was dedicated to solving the push-based distributed "economic dispatch problem in smart grids" over time-varying unbalanced directed graphs, which was aimed "at minimizing the total generation cost while satisfying the power supply-demand balance and generation capacity constraints. A distributed algorithm" was proposed to solve this.

Course knowledge characteristics

Course knowledge characteristics refer to the perception of students about the cognitive range of knowledge demands, as well as the nature of knowledge demands associated with a course of study in university education. The study adapted the *job design* construct from Morgeson and Humphrey (2006) to explore the extent of course variety, information processing, course complexity, **problem** solving, and specialization.

According to Oldham (2012), the *design of jobs* can act as a strategy for enhancing the positive outcomes of individuals at work in the context of positive *organizational* scholarship.
The sub-constructs of course knowledge characteristics are discussed in the following:

1. **Course Variety** is **defined** as the measure of the extent to which a course **challenges** and engages the student to engage in varied and complementary skills, in order to accomplish ICT course work.
2. **Course Information Processing** is **defined** as the degree or measure that a course demands differentiated processing of information. It is hypothesized that courses that require higher measures of processing would more likely impact positively on students' individual innovative behavior.
3. **Course Complexity** denotes *students' perceptions* about the complexity of technological tasks and the level of cognitive demands and **challenges** associated with a course.
4. **Problem Solving** is **defined** as the measure of the extent to which a course leads to the creation of novel **solutions**, as well as analyzing and unravelling non-routine situations through active cognitive processing.
5. **Specialization** is **defined** as the degree to which a course provides opportunities for the performance of specific tasks or the accumulation of specialized knowledge and/or skills in a particular field.

Godfrey (1983, p. 71) explored how to structure freedom in an alternative approach to post-graduate course design management education and development. The latter author posited that the structure of an 'alternative' management course needed to be as open as its curriculum, have clear aims and explicit resources. Further, for the course to match its purpose, it had "to evolve, to be as much the creation of its students as of its staff, who are equally committed to its development and who" were "prepared to learn from the experience". For the course design to be viewed as a creation of the students and staff, it requires the right mix and support, and if not done well, it could easily be a potential **challenge** to course design.

Against the background of management learning and education, the dominance of theory-based approaches towards strategy teaching had "not displaced the need for" a core strategy *course* in how to develop strategic management competency by reconsidering the learning goals and *knowledge* requirements towards cultivating broader management skills. Limited attention had, however, been given to explicating why Grant and Baden-Fuller (2018, p. 1) needed to teach these skills.

Research Context

With regard to development **drivers** in Africa and the role of innovation, Hanson and Léautier (2011) posited that for Africa to uncover innovations for development, a critical mass of creative and skilled youth must be produced in an inclusive and open space where they can experiment and tinker with various ideas.

The **context** described for ICT students was employed in delineating the sample population. The nomenclature of the undergraduate program provided for a four (4) year duration, which includes project-based assessment influencing the pass rates of these ICT modules at the applicable institutions (Goosen & Van Heerden, 2013).

According to Bertuglia, Lombardo, and Nijkamp (2012), most empirical studies on individual innovative behavior have paid attention to a manufacturing sector setting, while at the individual level, most studies on innovative behavior have used a sample of *employees*, and not the university sector. Examples of the former include:

- McKinley, Latham, and Braun (2014), who conducted a management review of *organizational* decline and innovation in the context of turnarounds and downward spirals;
- Li and Hsu (2017), who investigated customer participation in services and its effect on *employee* innovative behavior, while their earlier journal article (Li & Hsu, 2016) provided a review of *employee* innovative behavior in services; and
- An international journal article on contemporary hospitality management by Lee (2016), which looked at a sense of calling and the career satisfaction of hotel frontline employees against the background of mediation through knowledge sharing behavior with *organizational* members.

Although Ramayah, Yeap and Ignatius (2014) an evaluation review assessing knowledge sharing among academics in terms of a validation of the Knowledge Sharing Behavior Scale (KSBS), these imply that studies on individual innovative behavior in the context of an university **education** setting are not fully explored.

Further, previous studies, such as those reported on in the book edited by Goelm and Singhal (2016), on *product innovation* through knowledge management and social media strategies, have given prominence to *product innovation*, with less emphasis on the generation of ideas, and the identification of new and innovative procedures.

There are therefore five (5) main reasons that guided the choice of ICT education, and more specifically, students undertaking undergraduate ICT-related programs for this research:

Firstly, in comparison to other undergraduate programs, the field of ICT-related studies is a relatively new area; hence, it is bound to be dynamic in content and scope.

Secondly, the unit of analysis in this study are ICT students, who had undertaken ICT-related project work as part of their course requirement. The expectation for innovation is higher in such a context, unlike in other program areas that are not ICT-based.

Thirdly, the population of this particular area of ICT-related studies makes it easy to obtain a sample, due to the high student enrolment. Fourthly, the teaching of ICT-related studies is highly standardized across universities, based on the accreditation of the programs by the university regulator (Commission for University Education (CUE), 2016). Finally, convenience reasons informed the use of the sample: mainly the easy access that the researcher had within a framework for partnerships promoting the continued support of university lecturers and, in effect, university students (Vorster & Goosen, 2017). Thus, the research setting qualified to form a basis for developing the Structural Equation Model (SEM) and the eventual testing of the attendant hypotheses.

The Structural Equation Model Process

Bollen (1989) provided a new incremental fit index for general **structural equation models** to be used with sociological methods and research, while Bollen and Lennox (1991) explored conventional wisdom on measurement from a **structural equation** perspective.
The SEM analysis followed a five-step logical sequence as indicated in the following:

Model specification

The first initial stage of SEM analysis involved model specification, which is defined as finding relevant theory and previous research towards formulating a theoretical regression model (Schumacker & Lomax, 2010). Hence, before the researcher starts collecting or analyzing data, the particular model needs to be designed using existing information. Specification occurred "when the true population model" was deemed to be "consistent with the implied theoretical model", which was being tested (Schumacker & Lomax, 2010, p. 55).

Model identification

The second stage in SEM is related to model identification, whereby parameters in the specified model are identified. In this stage, the researcher makes a decision on "whether a set of unique parameter estimates can be computed for the regression equation" (Schumacker & Lomax, 2010, p. 131). Simply stated, an identified model occurs when all the parameters are identified, implying that these take on a single value for the model, as well as the observed data (Hoyle, 2012). Further, the "number of distinct values in the sample variance–covariance matrix equals the number of parameters to be estimated; thus, multiple regression models are always considered just-identified" (Schumacker & Lomax, 2010, p. 131).

Model estimation

The third stage of model estimation leads to "estimating the parameters in the regression model" (Schumacker & Lomax, 2010, p. 131). The model estimation process examines the "decomposition of the correlation (or variance–covariance) matrix, parameter estimation in general, and parameter estimation for the confirmatory factor model example" (Schumacker & Lomax, 2010, p. 169). In the study reported on in this chapter, Maximum Likelihood Estimation (MLE) was employed, as it "finds estimates of model parameters that are most likely to give rise to the pattern of observations in the sample data" (Pampel, 2000, p. 40).

Model testing

The fourth stage of model testing, as the name suggests, involved testing how well the data fit the model, through an analysis of the parameter estimates. Simply stated, model testing seeks to explore how well the data support the theoretical model. Model testing examines "model-fit indices for the fit of the entire model and examine the specific tests for statistical significance of individual parameters in the model" (Schumacker & Lomax, 2010, p. 217).

Model Modification or Specification

After model testing, the next stage involves either model modification/specification, or the stage of model interpretation and reporting. Often, model modification occurs "if the fit of an implied theoretical model is not acceptable, which is sometimes the case with an initial model" (Schumacker & Lomax, 2010, p. 218). This stage might also entail a reviewing of the identification, and further estimation and evaluation of fit (Hoyle, 2012).

SOLUTIONS AND RECOMMENDATIONS

This section of the chapter will discuss **solutions** and **recommendations** in dealing with the issues or problems presented in the preceding section.

Solutions

According to Verma and Kharb (2021, p. 236), the integration and implementation of smart farming by using Internet of Things technologies not only provides **solutions** for optimal monitoring, but could also "empower farmers to upgrade profitability going from the amount of manure to be used to the quantity of water for irrigating their fields and also help them to decrease waste."

Indirect Effects of Course Design Characteristics on IIB Mediated by KSB

Radaelli, Lettieri, Mura and Spiller (2014) conducted a micro-level investigation of direct and *indirect effects* in the context of knowledge sharing and innovative work behavior in healthcare, as well as creativity and innovation management.

All tests for *indirect effects* involved the use of bootstrap estimation with 2000 samples (Shrout & Bolger, 2002). The paths linking CDCs and IIB with knowledge sharing behavior acting as the mediator, were examined. The results of the test or direct and *indirect effects* was as presented in Figure 1.

Figure 1. Indirect effect of course design characteristics on individual innovative behavior through knowledge sharing behavior
Source: Ngugi research results

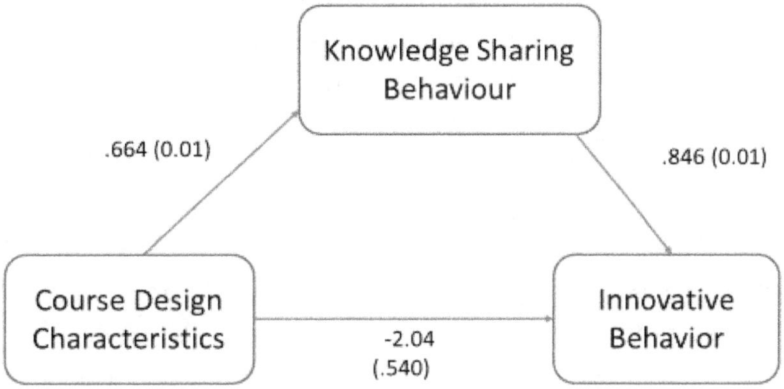

The findings suggested that the indirect effect via knowledge sharing behavior was significant ($b = .846$, $p<0.01$). Further, zero fell outside the Confidence Interval (CI) of the hypothesized indirect effect (95% CI: lower limit =.284, upper limit =.761), which was a necessary condition to support the significance of the path. Thus, there was empirical evidence to support hypothesis 7 as stated in Ngugi and Goosen (2018).

Indirect Effects of SRL on Individual Innovative Behavior Mediated by KSB

The test for the indirect effect of self-regulated learning on individual innovative behavior involved the use of bootstrap estimation with 2000 samples (Shrout & Bolger, 2002). The paths linking SRL and IIB, with knowledge sharing behavior acting as the mediator, were examined. The results of the test of indirect and direct effect was as presented in Figure 2.

The findings provided evidence that there exists an indirect significant relationship ($b = .923$, $p<0.01$) between SRL and IIB that was fully mediated by KSB, thus lending support to Hypothesis 6. The effect of self -regulated learning on individual innovative behavior was mediated by knowledge sharing behavior, thus fully supporting **Hypothesis 6**, which stated that:

Figure 2. Indirect effect of self-regulated learning on individual innovative behavior through knowledge sharing behavior
Source: Ngugi research results

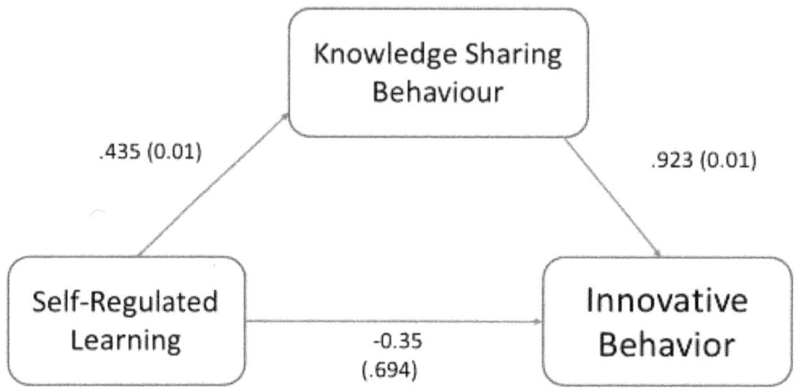

Hypothesis 6: Knowledge sharing behavior mediates the relationship between the interaction of SRL and IIB among information and communication technology students.

Secondly, the indirect relationship between CDCs and IIB was significant and fully mediated by KSB. The interaction of CDCs on IIB performance was fully mediated by KSB ($p < .01$). Hence, there is full support for **Hypothesis 7**, which stated that knowledge sharing behavior mediates the effects of the interaction between CDCs and IIB.

There is evidence of mediation between CDCs and SRL and the endogenous variable of IIB, as well as between SRL and IIB, mediated by KSB, as the two-tailed significance (bias corrected) values are all less than 0.05 ($p<0.05$). Further, SEM bootstrap analysis of the two relevant paths from the exogenous variables of SRL and CDCs to IIB both demonstrated significant effects. Hence, the test of the hypothesis was as summarized in Table 1.

Recommendations

In terms of choosing 'best' practices (Goosen, Mentz, & Nieuwoudt, 2007) in *exploratory factor analysis*, Costello and Osborne (2005) made four **recommendations** for getting the most from an analysis with regard to practical assessment, research and evaluation. In a review of *structural equation modelling* in practice, Anderson and Gerbing (1988) **recommended** a two-step approach.

Shrout and Bolger (2002) **recommended** the use of *bootstrap methods* for small to moderate samples in assessing mediation, describing the benefits of these and showing how these could make a difference in interpreting mediation studies. In their journal article in the context of applied *psychology*, Podsakoff, MacKenzie, Lee and Podsakoff (2003) provided a critical review of the literature and **recommended** remedies for *common method biases* in behavioral research. Against the background of the related context of personality and social *psychology*, the journal article by Baron and Kenny (1986) reflected on the moderator-mediator variable distinction in social psychological research in terms of conceptual, strategic, and statistical considerations.

Table 1. Summary of results on hypothesis testing

Hypothesis	Hypothesis Statement	Result	Confirmed /Rejected
Hypothesis 1	Self-regulated learning is positively related to knowledge sharing behavior.	+	Confirmed
Hypothesis 2	Self-regulated learning is positively related to individual innovative behavior.	+	Confirmed
Hypothesis 3	Course design characteristics are positively related to knowledge sharing behavior.	+	Confirmed
Hypothesis 4	Course design characteristics are positively related to individual innovative behavior.	+	Confirmed
Hypothesis 5	Knowledge sharing behavior is positively related to individual innovative behavior.	+	Confirmed
Hypothesis 6	Knowledge sharing behavior mediates the relationship between the interaction of self-regulated learning and individual innovative behavior.	+ Full mediation	Confirmed
Hypothesis 7	Knowledge sharing behavior mediates the relationship between the interaction of course design characteristics and individual innovative behavior	+ Full mediation	Confirmed

FUTURE RESEARCH DIRECTIONS

This section of the chapter will discuss **future** and **emerging trends** and provide insight about the future of the theme of the book on digitalization as a driver for the smart economy in the post-COVID-19 era, from the perspective of the chapter focus. The viability of a paradigm, model, implementation issues of proposed programs, etc., may also be included in this section. Further **future research directions** within the domain of the topic of the chapter, on **digitalization** and the **drivers** of individual innovative behavior for the smart economy in the post-COVID-19 era, in terms of the effects of information and communication technology students' course design characteristics, will finally be suggested.

According to Ngugi and Goosen (2021b), **digitalization** is more than just one of many **emerging trends**. Kalina (2021, p. 225) indicated that the COVID-19 pandemic accelerated **emerging trends** towards **digitalization** and automation, which allowed for the acquisition of massive datasets, which were "useful for managerial decision making."

Goosen and Van Heerden (2017) recommended taking the learning of programming, which often forms part of IT students' curriculum, beyond the horizon with educational technologies. In their journal article on British educational technologies, "Za, Spagnoletti and North-Samardzic (2014) … looked at the generative role of digital tools in informal organizational learning practices" as **emerging trends** in terms of such processes (Ngugi & Goosen, 2021a, p. 649).

Whereas South Africa leads the continent in terms of innovation investment and output, with, for example, the Ubuntu Operating System (OS), which has found wide application (Hill, Helmke, & Burger, 2009), other countries are also showing **emerging trends** with regard to examples of innovation.

While Gravemeijer, et al. (2017) asked what Mathematics education may prepare students for the society of the **future**, Srinivasa Varadhan (2021, p. 377) indicated that in India, there was "undoubtedly a promising **future** for online education".

In the proceedings of the IEEE, Tresp, et al. (2016, p. 2180) provided an overview of recent **emerging trends** in a survey on going digital, "**digitalization** and large-scale data analytics in healthcare. It" was expected that these **emerging trends** were "instrumental in the dramatic changes" in the way healthcare would be organized in the **future**.

CONCLUSION

This section of the chapter will provide a discussion of the overall coverage of the chapter and concluding remarks.

The World Bank (2011) assessment of Africa came to the **conclusion** that many countries still lack skills and competence in science and technology, which underpin rapid innovation and the development of technologies critical to transforming economies and societies. This makes the need even more explicit for the stimulation of innovation in Africa, as a panacea for societal *development*. This was echoed by an African journal article on science, technology, innovation and *development*, which looked at workplace innovation influence on occupational safety and health (Jilcha, Kitaw, & Beshah, 2016). Goosen (2018) also expressed the opinion that students' access to an Information and Communication Technologies for *Development* (ICT4D) Massive Open Online Course (MOOC) could make a meaningful contribution.

In the context of the so-called 'brain drain', the reporting of results and data analysis, however, needs to be conducted in an ethical way (Jauhar, Ghani, & Islam, 2016), while protecting research confidentiality in terms of what happens when the law and ethics collide (Palys & Lowman, 2014).

Adding even more detail, like the journal article by Ngugi and Goosen (2021c), this chapter has discussed how **digitalization** and other **drivers** of innovative individual behavior, including self-regulated learning and knowledge sharing behavior, can be harnessed for a **smart** economy in **the post-COVID-19 era** by paying careful attention to Computer Science (CS) and Information Technology students' course design characteristics.

REFERENCES

Abrar, I., Pottoo, S. N., Masoodi, F. S., & Bamhdi, A. (2021). On IoT and Its Integration With Cloud Computing: Challenges and Open Issues. In P. Tomar (Ed.), Integration and Implementation of the Internet of Things Through Cloud Computing (pp. 37-64). IGI Global. doi:http://doi:10.4018/978-1-7998-6981-8.ch003

Anderson, J. C., & Gerbing, D. W. (1988). Structural equation modelling in practice: A review and recommended two-step approach. *Psychological Bulletin*, *103*(3), 411–423. doi:10.1037/0033-2909.103.3.411

Baron, R. M., & Kenny, D. A. (1986). The moderator-mediator variable distinction in social psychological research: Conceptual, strategic, and statistical considerations. *Journal of Personality and Social Psychology*, *51*(6), 1173–1182. doi:10.1037/0022-3514.51.6.1173 PMID:3806354

Bednall, T. C., Sanders, K., & Runhaar, P. (2014). Stimulating informal learning activities through perceptions of performance appraisal quality and human resource management system strength: A two-wave study. *Academy of Management Learning & Education*, *13*(1), 45–61. doi:10.5465/amle.2012.0162

Bertuglia, C. S., Lombardo, S., & Nijkamp, P. (Eds.). (2012). *Innovative behaviour in space and time*. Springer Science & Business Media.

Bollen, K., & Lennox, R. (1991). Conventional wisdom on measurement: A structural equation perspective. *Psychological Bulletin*, *110*(2), 305–314. doi:10.1037/0033-2909.110.2.305

Bollen, K. A. (1989). A new incremental fit index for general structural equation models. *Sociological Methods & Research*, *17*(3), 303–316. doi:10.1177/0049124189017003004

Bolton, A., Goosen, L., & Kritzinger, E. (2021). An Empirical Study into the Impact on Innovation and Productivity Towards the Post-COVID-19 Era: Digital Transformation of an Automotive Enterprise. In L. C. Carvalho, L. Reis, & C. Silveira (Eds.), *Handbook of Research on Entrepreneurship, Innovation, Sustainability, and ICTs in the Post-COVID-19 Era* (pp. 133–159). IGI Global. doi:10.4018/978-1-7998-6776-0.ch007

Commission for University Education (CUE). (2016). *Statistics on University Education in Kenya*. CUE.

Costello, A. B., & Osborne, J. W. (2005). Best practices in exploratory factor analysis: Four recommendations for getting the most from your analysis. *Practical Assessment, Research & Evaluation*, *10*(7), 1–9.

De Jong, J. P., & Den Hartog, D. N. (2010). Measuring innovative work behaviour. *Creativity and Innovation Management*, *19*(1), 23–36. doi:10.1111/j.1467-8691.2010.00547.x

Dorenbosch, L., Van Engen, M., & Verhagen, M. (2005). On-the-job innovation: The impact of job design and human resource management through production ownership. *Creativity and Innovation Management*, *14*(2), 129–141. doi:10.1111/j.1476-8691.2005.00333.x

Evans, B. L., Fuse, I., Munekata, N., & Ono, T. (2017). Deployment of an Interactive JavaScript Application to Aid in Understanding the Digitalization of Sound. *Journal of Information Systems Education*, *15*(1), 42–47. doi:10.12937/ejsise.15.42

Garg, R., & Garg, H. (2021). Internet of Things-Enabled Smart Entry System for Telecom Sites. In P. Tomar (Ed.), Integration and Implementation of the Internet of Things Through Cloud Computing (pp. 155-177). IGI Global. doi:10.4018/978-1-7998-6981-8.ch008

Godfrey, E. (1983). Structuring Freedom: An Alternative Approach to Post-Graduate Course Design. *Management Education and Development*, *14*(1), 68–81. doi:10.1177/135050768301400110

Goelm, A., & Singhal, P. (Eds.). (2016). *Product Innovation Through Knowledge Management and Social Media Strategies*. IGI Global. doi:10.4018/978-1-4666-9607-5

Goosen, L. (2004). *Criteria and Guidelines for the Selection and Implementation of a First Programming Language in High Schools*. Potchefstroom Campus: North West University. Retrieved from http://hdl.handle.net/10394/226

Goosen, L. (2016, February 18). *We don't need no education"? Yes, they DO want e-learning in Basic and Higher Education!* Retrieved from https://uir.unisa.ac.za/handle/10500/20999

Goosen, L. (2018). Students' Access to an ICT4D MOOC. In S. Kabanda, H. Suleman, & S. Jamieson (Ed.), *Proceedings of the 47th Annual Conference of the Southern African Computer Lectures' Association (SACLA 2018)* (pp. 183 - 201). University of Cape Town.

Goosen, L. (2019). Technology-Supported Teaching and Research Methods for Educators: Case Study of a Massive Open Online Course. In L. Makewa, B. Ngussa, & J. Kuboja (Eds.), *Technology-Supported Teaching and Research Methods for Educators* (pp. 128–148). IGI Global., doi:10.4018/978-1-5225-5915-3.ch007

Goosen, L., Mentz, E., & Nieuwoudt, H. (2007). Choosing the "Best" Programming Language?! In E. Cohen (Ed.), *Proceedings of the 2007 Computer Science and IT Education Conference* (pp. 269-282). Santa Rosa: Informing Science Press.

Goosen, L., & Ngugi, J. K. (2018). Rethinking Teaching and Learning in the 21st Century: Course Design Characteristics towards Innovative Behaviour. In M. M. Dichaba, & M. A. Sotayo (Ed.), *Proceedings of the South Africa International Conference on Education* (pp. 376 - 394). African Academic Research Forum.

Goosen, L., & Ngugi, J. K. (2019a). Innovation for Computing Students Matter, of Course! In B. L. Tait & J. H. Kroeze (Eds.), *Proceedings of 48th Annual Conference of the Southern African Computer Lecturers' Association (SACLA 2019)* (pp. 19–36). University of South Africa. Retrieved from http://osprey.unisa.ac.za/sacla2019/SACLA2019%20Proceedings.pdf#page=31

Goosen, L., & Ngugi, J. K. (2019b). Towards Innovative Behaviour For Technology Students. In *Proceedings of the 10th Institute of Science and Technology Education (ISTE) International Conference on Mathematics, Science and Technology Education* (pp. 333 - 342). UNISA. Retrieved from https://uir.unisa.ac.za/handle/10500/26055

Goosen, L., & Van Heerden, D. (2013). Project-Based Assessment Influencing Pass Rates of an ICT Module at an ODL Institution. In E. Ivala (Ed.), *Proceedings of the 8th International Conference on e-Learning*. Cape Town: Academic Conferences and Publishing.

Goosen, L., & Van Heerden, D. (2017). Beyond the Horizon of Learning Programming with Educational Technologies. In U. I. Ogbonnaya, & S. Simelane-Mnisi (Ed.), *Proceedings of the South Africa International Conference on Educational Technologies* (pp. 78 - 90). Pretoria: African Academic Research Forum.

Grant, R. M., & Baden-Fuller, C. O. (2018). *How to Develop Strategic Management Competency: Reconsidering the Learning Goals and Knowledge Requirements of the Core Strategy Course.* Academy of Management Learning and Education. doi:10.5465/amle.2017.0126

Gravemeijer, K., Stephan, M., Julie, C., Lin, F.-L., & Ohtani, M. (2017). What Mathematics Education May Prepare Students for the Society of the Future? *International Journal of Science and Mathematics Education, 15*(S1, Suppl 1), S105–S123. doi:10.100710763-017-9814-6

Hanson, K. T., & Léautier, F. A. (2011). *Development drivers in Africa: Role of innovation.* ACBF Occasional Paper, 14. Retrieved February 20, 2015, from http://elibrary.acbfpact.org/collect

Hartjes, B. J. (2010). *Aligning employee competences with organizational innovation strategy: A case study at B.V. Twentsche Kabelfabriek* (Unpublished Master's Thesis). Enschede, The Netherlands: University of Twente. Retrieved March 14, 2015, from http://essay.utwente.nl/59930/1/MA_thesis_B_Hartjes.pdf

Hill, B. M., Helmke, M., & Burger, C. (2009). *The official Ubuntu book*. Pearson Education.

Hoyle, R. H. (Ed.). (2012). *Handbook of structural equation modeling*. Guilford Press.

Jauhar, J. B., Ghani, A. B., & Islam, R. (2016). Results and data analysis. In *Brain Drain* (pp. 127–158). Springer.

Jilcha, K., Kitaw, D., & Beshah, B. (2016). Workplace innovation influence on occupational safety and health. *African Journal of Science, Technology, Innovation and Development*, *8*(1), 33–42. doi:10.1080/20421338.2015.1128044

Kalina, J. (2021). Managerial Decision Support in the Post-COVID-19 Era: Towards Information-Based Management. In L. C. Carvalho, L. Reis, & C. Silveira (Eds.), *Handbook of Research on Entrepreneurship, Innovation, Sustainability, and ICTs in the Post-COVID-19 Era* (pp. 225–241). IGI Global. doi:10.4018/978-1-7998-6776-0.ch011

Kaswan, K. S., Dhatterwal, J. S., & Gaur, N. K. (2021). Smart Grid Using Internet of Things. In P. Tomar (Ed.), Integration and Implementation of the Internet of Things Through Cloud Computing (pp. 251-271). IGI Global. doi:10.4018/978-1-7998-6981-8.ch013

Kaswan, K. S., Dhatterwal, J. S., & Kumar, K. (2021). Blockchain of Internet of Things-Based Earthquake Alarming System in Smart Cities. In P. Tomar (Ed.), Integration and Implementation of the Internet of Things Through Cloud Computing (pp. 272-287). IGI Global. doi:10.4018/978-1-7998-6981-8.ch014

Lee, K. J. (2016). Sense of calling and career satisfaction of hotel frontline employees: Mediation through knowledge sharing behaviour with organizational members. *International Journal of Contemporary Hospitality Management*, *28*(2), 346–365. doi:10.1108/IJCHM-01-2014-0026

Li, M., & Hsu, C. (2017). Customer participation in services and its effect on employee innovative behavior. *Journal of Hospitality Marketing & Management*, *26*(2), 164–185. doi:10.1080/19368623.2016.1215946

Li, M., & Hsu, C. H. (2016). A review of employee innovative behavior in services. *International Journal of Contemporary Hospitality Management*, *28*(12), 2820–2841. doi:10.1108/IJCHM-04-2015-0214

Luthans, F., Norman, S. M., Avolio, B. J., & Avey, J. B. (2008). The mediating role of psychological capital in the supportive organizational climate—Employee performance relationship. *Journal of Organizational Behavior*, *29*(2), 219–238. doi:10.1002/job.507

Malik, I., & Tarar, S. (2021). Cloud-Based Smart City Using Internet of Things. In P. Tomar (Ed.), Integration and Implementation of the Internet of Things Through Cloud Computing (pp. 133-154). IGI Global. doi:10.4018/978-1-7998-6981-8.ch007

Masrek, M. N., Yusof, N. I., Noordin, S. A., & Johare, R. (2013). Exploring the relationship between job design and knowledge productivity: A conceptual framework in the context of Malaysian administrative and diplomatic officers. *Journal of Organizational Knowledge*, 1-8. doi:10.5171/2013.128970

McKinley, W., Latham, S., & Braun, M. (2014). Organizational decline and innovation: Turnarounds and downward spirals. *Academy of Management Review*, *39*(1), 88–110. doi:10.5465/amr.2011.0356

Mentz, E., & Goosen, L. (2007). Are groups working in the Information Technology class? *South African Journal of Education*, *27*(2), 329–343.

Morgeson, F., & Humphrey, S. (2006). The Work Design Questionnaire (WDQ): Developing and validating a comprehensive measure for assessing job design and the nature of work. *The Journal of Applied Psychology*, *91*(6), 1321–1339. doi:10.1037/0021-9010.91.6.1321 PMID:17100487

Ngugi, J., & Goosen, L. (2017). The Effects of Course Design Characteristics, Self-Regulated Learning and Knowledge Sharing in Facilitating the Development of Innovative Behaviour among Technology Students at Universities. In *Proceedings of the Institute of Science and Technology Education (ISTE) Conference on Mathematics, Science and Technology Education* (pp. 80-86). UNISA Press.

Ngugi, J., & Goosen, L. (2018). Modelling Course-Design Characteristics, Self-Regulated Learning and the Mediating Effect of Knowledge-Sharing Behavior as Drivers of Individual Innovative Behavior. *Eurasia Journal of Mathematics, Science and Technology Education*, *14*(8). Advance online publication. doi:10.29333/ejmste/92087

Ngugi, J., & Goosen, L. (2019, October 25). Towards Smart Innovation for Information Systems and Technology Students: Modelling Motivation, Metacognition and Affective Aspects of Learning. Smart Innovation, Systems and Technologies, 111, 90-99. doi:10.1007/978-3-030-03577-8_11

Ngugi, J. K., & Goosen, L. (2021a). Knowledge Sharing Mediating Information Technology Student Innovation. In M. Khosrow-Pour (Ed.), *Handbook of Research on Modern Educational Technologies, Applications, and Management* (Vol. 2, pp. 645–663). IGI Global. doi:10.4018/978-1-7998-3476-2.ch040

Ngugi, J. K., & Goosen, L. (2021b). Innovation, Entrepreneurship, and Sustainability for ICT Students Towards the Post-COVID-19 Era. In L. C. Carvalho, L. Reis, & C. Silveira (Eds.), *Handbook of Research on Entrepreneurship, Innovation, Sustainability, and ICTs in the Post-COVID-19 Era* (pp. 110–131). IGI Global. doi:10.4018/978-1-7998-6776-0.ch006

Ngugi, J. K., & Goosen, L. (2021c). Computer Science and Information Technology Students' Self-regulated Learning and Knowledge Sharing Behavior as Drivers of Individual Innovative Behavior. Lecture Notes in Networks and Systems, 230, 593-608. doi:10.1007/978-3-030-77442-4_50

Nicholson, P. (2007). A history of e-learning. *Computers & Education*, 1–11.

Njenga, J. K., & Fourie, L. C. (2010). The myths about e-learning in higher education. *British Journal of Educational Technology*, *41*(2), 199–212. doi:10.1111/j.1467-8535.2008.00910.x

Oldham, G. R. (2012). The design of jobs: A strategy for enhancing the positive outcomes of individuals at work. In G. M. Spreitzer & K. S. Cameron (Eds.), *The Oxford Handbook of Positive Organizational Scholarship* (pp. 651–663). Oxford University Press. doi:10.1093/oxfordhb/9780199734610.013.0049

Palys, T., & Lowman, J. (2014). *Protecting research confidentiality: What happens when law and ethics collide*. James Lorimer & Company.

Pampel, F. C. (2000). *Logistic regression: A primer (quantitative applications in the social sciences)*. Sage Publications. doi:10.4135/9781412984805

Pereira, J. M., Dias, R. M., Carvalho, L. M., & Noronha, A. B. (2021). Students' Perceptions About E-Learning Within the Context of the COVID-19 Pandemic: A Study in Brazil and Portugal. In L. C. Carvalho, L. Reis, & C. Silveira (Eds.), *Handbook of Research on Entrepreneurship, Innovation, Sustainability, and ICTs in the Post-COVID-19 Era* (pp. 281–300). IGI Global. doi:10.4018/978-1-7998-6776-0.ch014

Podsakoff, P. M., MacKenzie, S. B., Lee, J. Y., & Podsakoff, N. P. (2003). Common method biases in behavioural research: A critical review of the literature and recommended remedies. *The Journal of Applied Psychology*, *88*(5), 879–903. doi:10.1037/0021-9010.88.5.879 PMID:14516251

Radaelli, G., Lettieri, E., Mura, M., & Spiller, N. (2014). Knowledge sharing and innovative work behaviour in healthcare: A micro-level investigation of direct and indirect effects. *Creativity and Innovation Management*, *23*(4), 400–414. doi:10.1111/caim.12084

Ramayah, T., Yeap, J. A., & Ignatius, J. (2014). Assessing knowledge sharing among academics: A validation of the knowledge sharing behavior scale (KSBS). *Evaluation Review*, *38*(2), 160–187. doi:10.1177/0193841X14539685 PMID:25015259

Rego, A., Sousa, F., Marques, C., & Cunha, M. P. (2012). Authentic leadership promoting employees' psychological capital and creativity. *Journal of Business Research*, *65*(3), 429–437. doi:10.1016/j.jbusres.2011.10.003

Reis, L., Silveira, C., Pires, G., Péricles, C., Carvalho, L. C., & Mata, C. (2021). Integrated Management Platform for Homeless People. In L. C. Carvalho, L. Reis, & C. Silveira (Eds.), *Handbook of Research on Entrepreneurship, Innovation, Sustainability, and ICTs in the Post-COVID-19 Era* (pp. 243–262). IGI Global. doi:10.4018/978-1-7998-6776-0.ch012

Schumacker, R. E., & Lomax, R. G. (2010). *A Beginners Guide to Structural Equation Modeling* (3rd ed.). Lawrence Erlbaum Associates.

Seraphin, K. D., Philippoff, J., Kaupp, L., & Vallin, L. M. (2012). Metacognition as means to increase the effectiveness of inquiry-based science education. *Science Education International*, *23*(4), 366–382.

Shrout, P. E., & Bolger, N. (2002). Mediation in experimental and nonexperimental studies: New procedures and recommendations. *Psychological Methods*, *7*(4), 422–445. doi:10.1037/1082-989X.7.4.422 PMID:12530702

Sim, T. Y., Dewika, M., & Devandran, A. (2014). Improving students engagement through Social Media: A case study of a private university in Malaysia using Facebook. *International Journal of e-Education, e-Business, e-. Management Learning*, *4*(6), 354–396.

Srinivasa Varadhan, D. R. (2021). The Impact of Virtual Learning in the Indian Education System. In L. C. Carvalho, L. Reis, & C. Silveira (Eds.), *Handbook of Research on Entrepreneurship, Innovation, Sustainability, and ICTs in the Post-COVID-19 Era* (pp. 364–380). IGI Global. doi:10.4018/978-1-7998-6776-0.ch018

Sufi, T., & Ahmed, S. (2021). Surviving COVID-19 Crisis by New Business Models: A Case Study of the Indian Restaurant Industry. In L. C. Carvalho, L. Reis, & C. Silveira (Eds.), *Handbook of Research on Entrepreneurship, Innovation, Sustainability, and ICTs in the Post-COVID-19 Era* (pp. 301–316). IGI Global. doi:10.4018/978-1-7998-6776-0.ch015

Thompson, A. A., Strickland, A. J., & Gamble, J. E. (2014). *Crafting and Executing Strategi: The Quest for Competitive Advantage: Concepts and Cases* (19th ed.). McGraw Hill Education.

Thompson, M., & Heron, P. (2006). Relational quality and innovative performance in R&D based science and technology firms. *Human Resource Management Journal, 16*(1), 28–47. doi:10.1111/j.1748-8583.2006.00003.x

Tomar, D., Singh, P., Bhati, J. P., & Tomar, P. (2021). Sustainability of Cloud-Based Smart Society. In P. Tomar (Ed.), Integration and Implementation of the Internet of Things Through Cloud Computing (pp. 113-132). IGI Global. doi:10.4018/978-1-7998-6981-8.ch006

Tresp, V., Overhage, J. M., Bundschus, M., Rabizadeh, S., Fasching, P. A., & Yu, S. (2016). Going digital: A survey on digitalization and large-scale data analytics in healthcare. *Proceedings of the IEEE, 104*(11), 2180–2206. doi:10.1109/JPROC.2016.2615052

Van Heerden, D., & Goosen, L. (2012). Using Vodcasts to Teach Programming in an ODL Environment. *Progressio, 34*(3), 144–160.

Van Heerden, D., & Goosen, L. (2021). Students' Perceptions of e-Assessment in the Context of Covid-19: The Case of UNISA. In M. Qhobela, M. M. Ntsohi, & L. G. Mohafa (Ed.), *Proceedings of the 29th Conference of the Southern African Association for Research in Mathematics, Science and Technology Education (SAARMSTE)* (pp. 291-305). SAARMSTE.

Verma, R., & Kharb, L. (2021). Smart Farming Using Internet of Things: A Solution for Optimal Monitoring. In P. Tomar (Ed.), Integration and Implementation of the Internet of Things Through Cloud Computing (pp. 236-250). IGI Global. doi:10.4018/978-1-7998-6981-8.ch012

Vorster, J., & Goosen, L. (2017). A Framework for University Partnerships Promoting Continued Support of e-Schools. In J. Liebenberg (Ed.), *Proceedings of the 46th Annual Conference of the Southern African Computer Lecturers' Association (SACLA 2017)* (pp. 118 - 126). North-West University.

Wang, Z., Wang, D., Wen, C., Guo, F., & Wang, W. (2021). Push-Based Distributed Economic Dispatch in Smart Grids Over Time-varying Unbalanced Directed Graphs. *IEEE Transactions on Smart Grid, 12*(4), 3185–3199. doi:10.1109/TSG.2021.3063128

World Bank. (2011). *World Development Report 2011–Conflict, Security, and Development.* Washington, DC: World Bank Group. doi:10.1596/978-0-8213-8439-8

Za, S., Spagnoletti, P., & North-Samardzic, A. (2014). Organisational learning as an emerging process: The generative role of digital tools in informal learning practices. *British Journal of Educational Technology, 45*(6), 1023–1035. doi:10.1111/bjet.12211

KEY TERMS AND DEFINITIONS

Class Communications: Refers to the structure means and forms of exchanges in a technology class or project group in seeking answers to ill-structured problems.

Communities of Practice (CoP): Refer to an informal groupings of technology students who voluntary share and communicate similar technological interests and topics.

Methods Autonomy: Refers to the degree of liberty and independence allowable to a student to choose methods and schedules while carrying out a technological assignment.

Personal Interactions: Refer to the reciprocal informal personal communication and engagements with the goal of sharing knowledge.

Problem Solving: Refers to the cognitive engagement of a student in seeking and providing answers to ill-structured questions that have no best answer.

Rehearsal: Refers to the range of cognitive drills and dry runs that a student engages in repeatedly in the process of memorizing information and sequences required to encode technological information and procedures.

Skill Variety: Reflects the array or multifariousness of skill sets a student requires to accomplish a technological project.

Specialization: Refers to the level of advancement in terms of knowledge and task competencies required to carry out a technological piece of work for instance programming skills.

Chapter 11
Diabetes Tracker and Volunteer+ Software Engineering for Sustainability

Joao Torres
Polytechnic Institute of Guarda, Portugal

David Julio
Polytechnic Institute of Guarda, Portugal

Clara Silveira
Polytechnic Institute of Guarda, Portugal

Leonilde Reis
https://orcid.org/0000-0002-4398-8384
Instituto Politécnico de Setúbal, Portugal

ABSTRACT

In a world where sustainability is increasingly important, we must look for ways to promote it; the Sustainable Development Goals (SDGs) fulfill this function. In software engineering, one of the main challenges for the success of a software solution is to achieve sustainability. This chapter introduces the development of two mobile applications on Android: Diabetes Tracker and Volunteer+ that are inspired by the SDGs, incorporating the principles and dimensions of the Karlskrona Manifesto in relation to the software development phases. In this investigation, a customized adaptation of the Scrum agile methodology was used, with a concern to promote software engineering for sustainability. To achieve this end, an iterative approach is used, allowing the principles of the manifesto to be crossed to emphasize the various dimensions of sustainability. The main results can be seen in the applications developed, specifically to facilitate the control of the diabetes disease and promote quality health, as well as enhance the participation of citizens by promoting volunteering.

DOI: 10.4018/978-1-7998-9227-4.ch011

INTRODUCTION

Increasingly, issues underlying Sustainability are being addressed around the world in different areas, as well as some strategies designed to create a new global model to alleviate poverty, promote prosperity and well-being for everyone, protect the environment and fight climate change. The Sustainable Development Goals (SDGs) aim to improve the well-being of Human Beings as well as improve the entire environment that surrounds them, fulfilling the objective of promoting sustainability (UNDP, 2015). The Covid-19 pandemic has a real impact on the achievement of the SDGs, namely on poverty, employment, or inequality. In this sense, it is considered that the Pandemic represents a threat in the fight against poverty and the sustainable development model (Plataforma Portuguesa das ONGD, 2020).

The main motivation to develop this work focuses on the opportunity to present the development of sustainable software solutions that promote the SDGs. These solutions are intended to facilitate the search by citizens for voluntary actions, focused on helping the environment or people in need. On the other hand, volunteering was a great support for health structures during the pandemic, alleviating the pressure on medical professionals (Pickell, Gu, & Williams, 2020). It should be noted that many countries have expanded their health care capacity by mobilizing retired volunteers or health professionals (Aristodemou, Buchhass, & Claringbould, 2021). The Tech4Covid initiative (Almeida, 2020) also brought together volunteers to support healthcare professionals and hospital equipment, healthcare and education services, among others.

Considering the need to integrate sustainability into software development, this chapter presents the development of two mobile Android applications: Diabetes Tracker and Volunteer+ (Júlio, Torres, & Silveira, 2021) that are inspired by the Sustainable Development Goals and include the principles and dimensions of sustainability. The Diabetes Tracker application will allow the senior population to be able to have a platform focused on diabetes monitoring. The Volunteer+ application will enhance the participation of citizens to encourage volunteering and mutual help, promoting sustainability through various SDGs.

The chapter discusses several SDGs in general and, in particular, SDG 3, Good Health, and SDG 17, Partnerships for the goals, whose aim is to promote well-being for everyone, at all ages, as well as to promote solidarity. In this work, a customized adaptation of the agile Scrum methodology was used. This methodology is a way of developing software with great concern in balancing the cost, time, and quality of the product. To promote sustainability in software development, the principles of the Karlskrona Manifesto regarding software development phases were also incorporated. To achieve this end, sustainability concerns have been included from the requirements analysis stage.

This chapter is organized into five sections. The first is the introduction in which the need identified in the context of sustainability is presented, specifying the objective of the chapter. In the second section, the theoretical framework regarding the various themes that are addressed in the chapter is presented. The development of mobile applications is described in the third section in order to present concerns regarding sustainability. The fourth section describes the procedures underlying verification and validation. Finally, in section five, the main conclusions are included and proposals for future work are presented.

BACKGROUND

One of the most relevant themes, currently, on a Global scale is the theme of Sustainability, be it Economic, Environmental, Social, Human or Technical Sustainability. The 17 SDGs (Figure 1) define global priorities and aspirations for 2030 and require global action by governments, businesses, and civil society to eradicate poverty create and a life with dignity and opportunities for all, within the limits of the planet (UNDP, 2015). Indeed, the SDGs can and should be applied to promote the sustainability of information systems, software development processes and contribute to various axes to enhance the use of technologies for people (Silveira & Reis, 2021).

Figure 1. Sustainable development goals
Source: (UNDP, 2015)

SDGs can be divided into different groups:

- People – referring to the eradication of poverty and hunger, the promotion of dignity and equality;
- Planet – focusing on sustainable consumption and production, combating climate change and managing natural resources;
- Prosperity – with regard to personal fulfillment, economic and social progress;
- Peace – peaceful, just and inclusive societies, free from fear and violence;
- Partnerships – regarding transversal integration, interconnection, and joint mobilization in favor of the most vulnerable.

It should be noted that the SDGs cannot be analyzed in isolation, as the improvement of one SDG will have a positive and/or negative impact on other SDGs (Reis, Silveira, Carvalho, & Mata, 2020).

Considering the looming threats of global climate change and environmental degradation, the scientific software community has begun to recognize the need for a transition to sustainability (Becker, et al., 2015; Software Sustainability Institute, 2019; Ovelheiro, Silveira, & Reis, 2021; Reis, Silveira, Carvalho, & Mata, 2020). Sustainability is interdisciplinary (Oyedeji, Seffah, & Penzenstadler, 2017) working on sustainability means working with people from different disciplines, addressing challenges from different perspectives.

An important challenge is to understand user requirements and sustainability factors in a process of finding a creative and sustainable solution (Silveira, Reis, Santos, & Mamede, 2020). The Karlskrona Manifesto serves as a guide to designing and developing more sustainable software systems. The Karlskrona Manifesto for Sustainability Design includes nine principles (Becker et al., 2015), which are presented in Figure 2.

Figure 2. Karlskrona Manifesto – principles
Source: Adapted from (Becker et al., 2015)

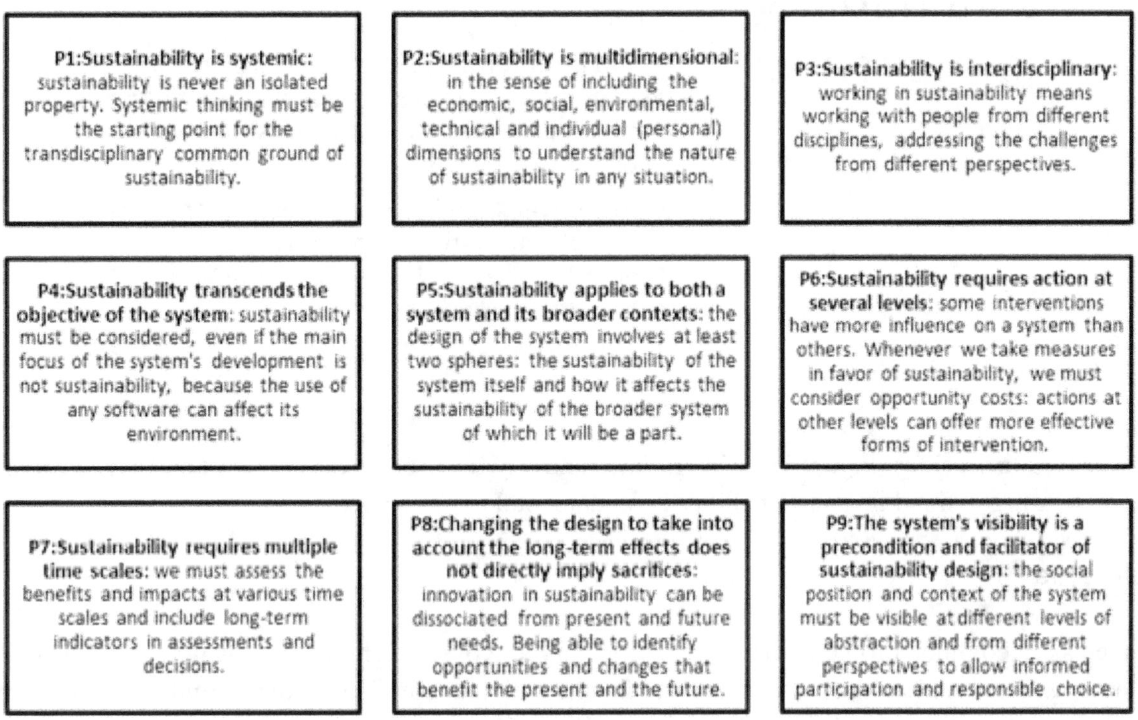

The nine principles of the manifesto are general and abstract but provide the basis for the creation of a reference point that can be applied throughout the software design for different stakeholders. The Manifesto also includes five sustainability dimensions (Becker et al., 2015), described in Figure 3.

Figure 3. Sustainability dimensions
Source: Adapted from (Becker et al., 2015)

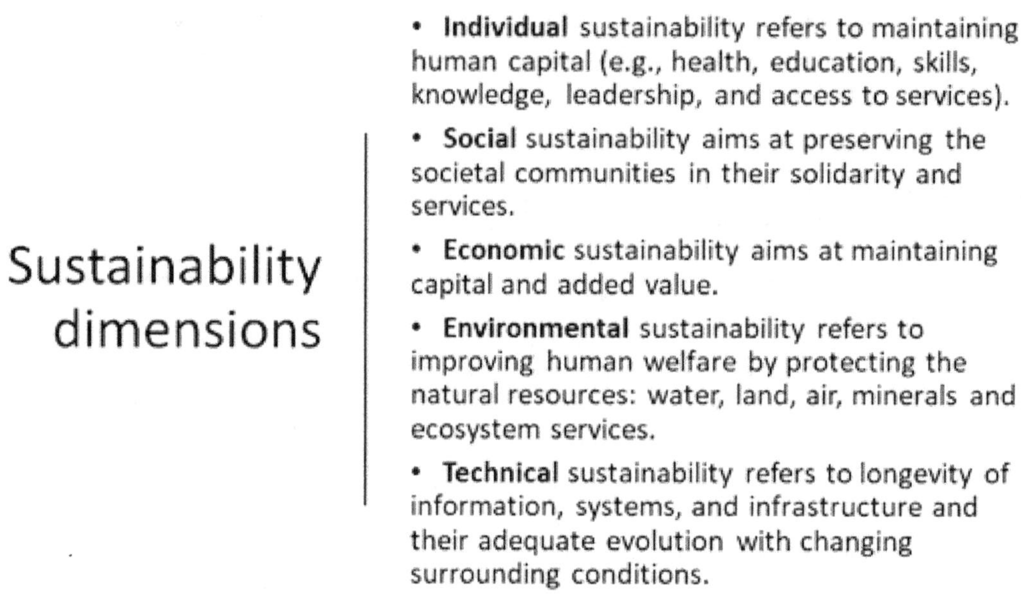

The five dimensions (Figure 3) are interrelated and provide a tool to disaggregate and analyze relevant issues, bearing in mind that sustainability is fundamental to our society.

Diabetes

Diabetes is a common problem, that affects sedentary and overweight or obese people. Monitoring and managing this chronic disease is a challenge for the patients, but also for their families and caregivers since this care is necessary for life (Fonseca, et al., 2015).

This problem needs to be controlled with special attention in the older population. Some of the problems caused by diabetes are in terms of eye damage (MSD Controlar a Diabetes, 2017), and that is why it was thought to create a simple and easy interface for this target audience, taking care to use large font size to facilitate visibility. The chosen theme is associated with SDG 3 – Good Health and Well-Being.

Diabetes is a group of metabolic diseases in which there are high levels of glucose in the blood over a long period – Hyperglycemia. Glucose is a molecule transformed from carbohydrates. It is used by several living beings in the energy production process and is therefore essential. However, when it's found in excess in the body, it can lead to complications such as diabetes (Rede Omnia, 2020).

These complications pose an increased risk to some existing health problems, most of which can be avoided if the blood glucose is on a healthier level, problems such as (MSD Controlar a Diabetes, 2017):

- Heart disease and stroke;
- Kidney injuries;

- Eye Injuries;
- Neurological injuries;
- Foot problems;
- Dental disease;
- Sexual dysfunction.

It is, therefore, necessary to monitor the glucose values and thus control the problems found. In a world where Good Health and Well-Being (SDG 3) must be a priority, it is necessary to have software that facilitates the control of Diabetes in the elderly population. These users have some difficulty using smartphones. In this sense, some applications address these difficulties, for example, BIG Launcher makes smartphones suitable for the elderly, children, and people with eye diseases, motor difficulties, or vision problems (BIGLauncher, 2020); PT MagicContact was designed to take into account the need of users with physical limitations and has a set of features that make mobile devices much older (Pinto, 2016); or even using a simplified user interface on the mobile device to access key features (Donati, 2015); and many others listed in (Ascari, Pereira & Silva, 2018). Therefore, it's considered that accessibility for people with some type of difficulty is very important to ensure social inclusion and promote an independent lifestyle.

In the analysis performed, no applications were found with specific characteristics for the elderly. The applications are shown in Table 1 MySugr (mySugr, 2020), Diabetes: M (Diabetes: M, 2020), BG Monitor Diabetes (BGMonitor, 2020) have innovative characteristics, making a comparison with the proposed objectives for the Diabetes Tracker app.

Table 1. Features of similar existing applications – Diabetes Tracker

Features	MySugr	Diabetes:M	BG Monitor Diabetes	Diabetes Tracker
Authentication	Yes	Yes	Yes	Yes
Insulin Calculator	Yes	Yes	Yes	Yes
Reminders	Yes	Yes	Yes	To be integrated
Meals	Yes	Yes	Yes	Yes
Bluetooth	Yes	No	No	To be integrated
Graphics	Yes	Yes	Yes	No
Measurements	Yes	Yes	Yes	Yes
Type 1 and 2 diabetes	Yes	Yes	Yes	Yes
Interface designed thinking about elderly population	No	No	No	Yes
Email to family member	No	No	No	Yes

After analyzing some of the features in the different applications, it was developed an application (Diabetes Tracker) for the senior population, whose difficulty in using mobile devices is increased.

Functions such as sending the calculus of insulin to be administered to a family member (if the diabetic so desires) allows the monitoring in an age group that sometimes needs help, promoting altruism, and an improvement in life quality. The goal was to develop a simple and appealing interface with large font sizes and buttons, making it easier for those who suffer from some eye problems. Diabetes Tracker will include the most important features for monitoring diabetes, such as managing measurements, managing meals, insulin calculator, among others.

Volunteering

The theme of the other application, Volunteering, was chosen because it fits many of the SDGs and also because volunteering is useful in different situations. Volunteering can be carried out in many ways, whether in actions to protect the planet, or in Actions to help the most disadvantaged, among many others. Therefore, this application helps in the recruitment of volunteers by institutions that need help in the most diverse problems they face. This way, we are contributing to the creation of a sustainable and mutually supportive community, thus being a system that offers social assistance.

The Application of Volunteering will focus heavily on the oceans - SDG 14 – Life Below Water, due to their importance at the Global level as strategic assets for sustainable economic development and human well-being, as well as importance in its preservation and in the preservation of the species (Grilo, Saldanha, & Calado, 2017). The decision to emphasize the oceans in this application is also due to the fact that there are no necessary platforms dedicated mainly to this theme. Despite this, the application will also have other types of actions that encompass other SDGs. The application will have great versatility, as it allows all kinds of volunteer actions, that is: reducing the carbon footprint, raising awareness, and combating global warming, social assistance, combating social inequalities, combating poverty, among others.

Volunteering can be described as an unpaid activity where someone, in this case the volunteer, uses their time to help a particular organization or person. Therefore, volunteering is basically an offer of help in some service or cause, using free time to help others (What Is Volunteering?, 2020). One of the reasons that was a great driver in choosing this project refers to the Preservation of the Oceans, referring to several SDGs. It appears that there are not many options when it comes to Volunteering for this topic. It should also be noted that from the Preservation of the Oceans there is a way of subsistence for millions of people, they are a source of energy and have great preponderance in the world economy. In fact, the oceans sheltered the first forms of life on our planet, 2.5 million years ago and guaranteed the subsistence of man over the centuries (UNITED NATIONS, 2019).

The analyzed apps were: Giving Way (Giving Way, 2020), My Selfless Act (My Selfless Act, 2020), Portugal Voluntário (CASES, 2020), World Packers (Worldpackers Corporation, 2020). Their features will be compared in the Table 2.

Table 2. Features of similar existing applications – Volunteer+

Features	Giving Way	My Selfless Act	Portugal Voluntário	World Packers	Volunteer+
Authentication	Yes	Yes	Yes	Yes	Yes
Access without authentication	No	No	Yes	No	Yes
Social Network inside the app	No	Yes	No	Yes	No
Financial help to the volunteers	No	No	No	Yes	No
Search by Category	Yes	Yes	No	Yes	Yes
Search by Localization	Yes	Yes	No	Yes	Yes

After analyzing these features in each of the applications (Table 2), this project aims to develop an application that is an asset in the area of volunteering, also trying to use good practices and features of the analyzed applications, contributing to a good experience of use and navigation. The Volunteer+ application will have several features such as authentication, search for Volunteer Actions, propose Volunteer Actions, among others. It is expected to contribute to the promotion of the SDGs.

DEVELOPMENT OF THE MOBILE APPLICATIONS

This section aims to present the process and methodology for the development of mobile applications that will allow the implementation and subsequent use on an Android smartphone.

Agile Methodology

This section describes the methodology used during the development of Diabetes Tracker and Volunteer+ mobile applications (Júlio, Torres, & Silveira, 2021). A software development methodology is a tool used to structure, plan and control the software development process. The software development process used in this study was an adaptation of the Scrum methodology. From the perspective of (Jacobson & Seidewitz, 2014), agile software teams are responsible for applying the methods they consider necessary for the project in question, adapting the development process throughout the project as needed. Scrum is an agile methodology framework used in more than half of the agile projects worldwide (CollabNet, 2019), mainly for its simplicity and ease of use and adaptation. As the name implies, agile software development means promoting flexibility and adaptability in the face of requirements that inevitably change during the project.

Scrum is an agile methodology for managing and planning software projects. These projects work into weekly stages – Sprints. A sprint represents a time interval where a set of previously combined tasks must be performed (Rubin, 2013). The Scrum Team is a group of professionals whose objective is to deliver the product successfully. One of the characteristics identified in the team is the high level of communication to ensure that everyone is, focused on the same objective. The Scrum Team is composed of three groups: Product Owner – responsible for making decisions that value and fit with the final vision of the product, Scrum Master – responsible for the Scrum Team, so that it meets the defined objectives and follows the practices of the Scrum methodology, and finally the Development Team – a group of professionals that are in charge of developing the software.

The Sprint Planning occurs when starting a Sprint in this event, the development team meets with the Scrum Master and plans the tasks to be addressed in the following week. These tasks are part of the Sprint Backlog. Every day of a Sprint, the development team meets, preferably in the morning, to transmit the development carried out the day before, identifying problems, solutions, and defining work for the day that will start - Daily Scrum. At the end of each sprint, the team meets again for a Sprint Review, where it presents all the features implemented during the Sprint cycle. Currently there is also the Sprint Retrospective, where the focus is on improvements to help the team plan the next Sprint. The Sprint cycle restarts, and we move on to the next iteration (Rubin, 2013).

This investigation aims to develop two mobile applications that promote awareness of sustainability. In this sense, the principles of the Karlskrona Manifest (listed in Figure 2) were transposed to the agile Scrum methodology. This allows us to cross the Karlskrona Manifest principles with the methodology used to emphasize the various dimensions of sustainability. Figure 4 shows the Karlskrona Manifest Principles included in Product Backlog. It is noteworthy that sustainability is multidimensional and should be considered in the list of Product Backlog features.

Figure 4. Karlskrona Manifest Principles included in Product Backlog
Source: Adapted from (Ovelheiro, Silveira, & Reis, 2021; Oyedeji, Seffah, & Penzenstadler, 2018)

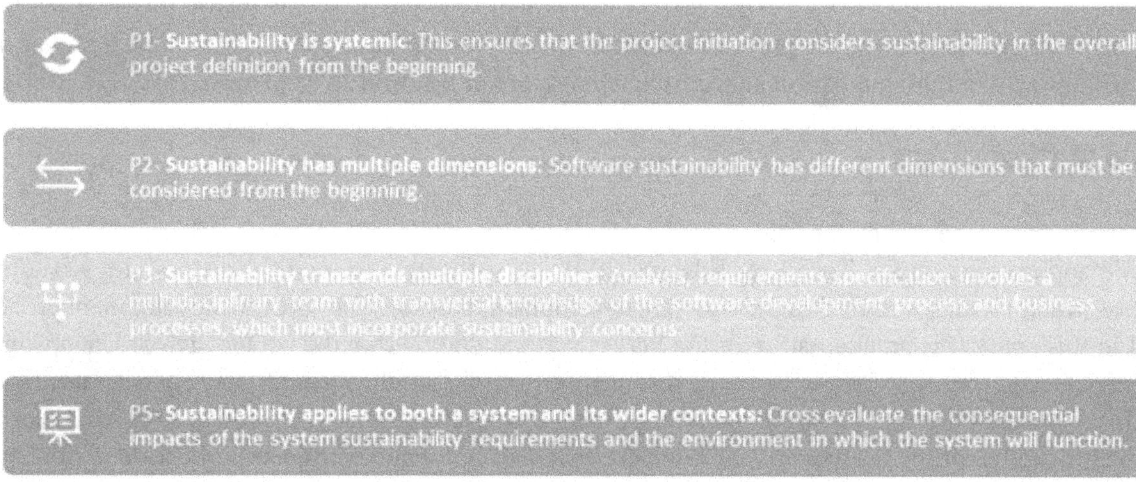

The list of tasks to run in Sprint – Sprint Backlog – should include principles P2, P4 and P6 as illustrated in Figure 5.

Figure 5. Karlskrona Manifest Principles included in Sprint Backlog
Source: Adapted from (Ovelheiro, Silveira, & Reis, 2021; Oyedeji, Seffah, & Penzenstadler, 2018)

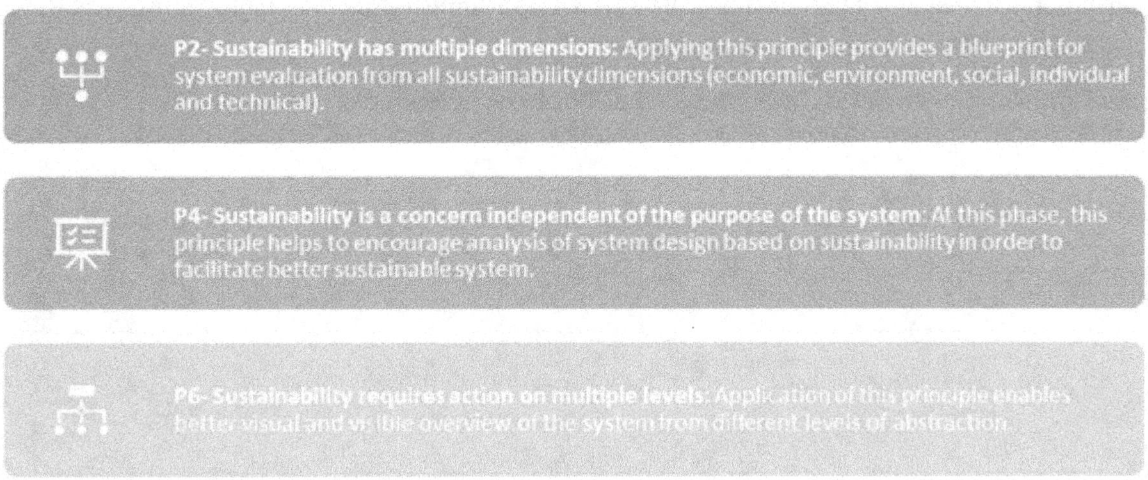

During the Sprint activity, the P2, P4, and P8 principles will be integrated, as shown in Figure 6. Mention the importance of the principle "Sustainability requires long-term thinking", because it will provide a better understanding in selecting the best choices that will help potential users of the system in the present and in the future.

Figure 6. Karlskrona Manifest Principles included in Sprint
Source: Adapted from (Ovelheiro, Silveira, & Reis, 2021; Oyedeji, Seffah, & Penzenstadler, 2018)

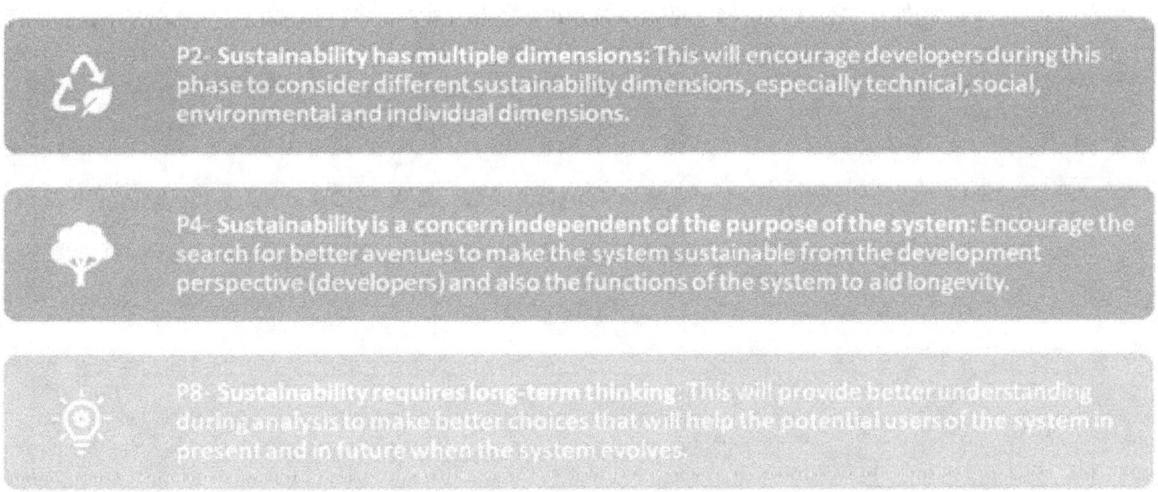

Applying the principle “Sustainability is a concern independent of the purpose of the system” during the “Sprint Review” will help in considering sustainability at this stage, even if the main focus of the system is not sustainability. Figure 7 shows the Karlskrona Manifest Principles included in Sprint Review.

Figure 7. Karlskrona Manifest Principles included in Sprint Review
Source: Adapted from (Ovelheiro, Silveira, & Reis, 2021; Oyedeji, Seffah, & Penzenstadler, 2018)

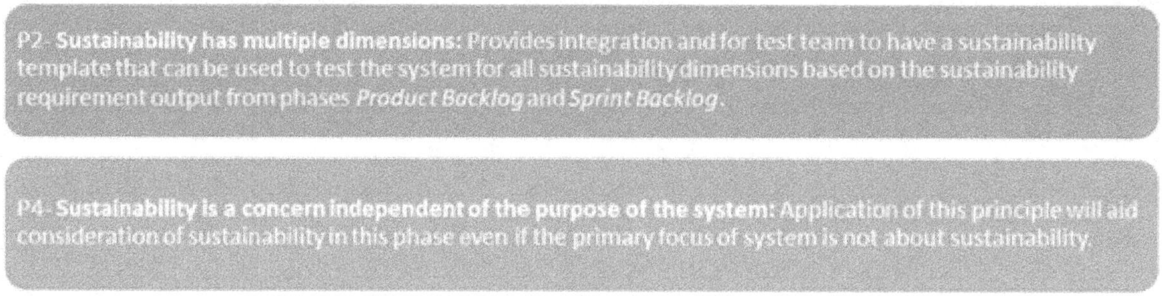

During the “Sprint Retrospective” the principles P5, P7 and P9 are applied (Figure 8). It is important to mention that the application of the principle “It is possible to meet the needs of future generations without sacrificing the prosperity of the current generation”, helps to create awareness so that when the system is in use, there is a continuous assessment of the system’s sustainability and think of ways to optimize and improve sustainability in the five dimensions.

Figure 8. Karlskrona Manifest Principles included in Sprint Retrospective
Source: Adapted from (Ovelheiro, Silveira, & Reis, 2021; Oyedeji, Seffah, & Penzenstadler, 2018)

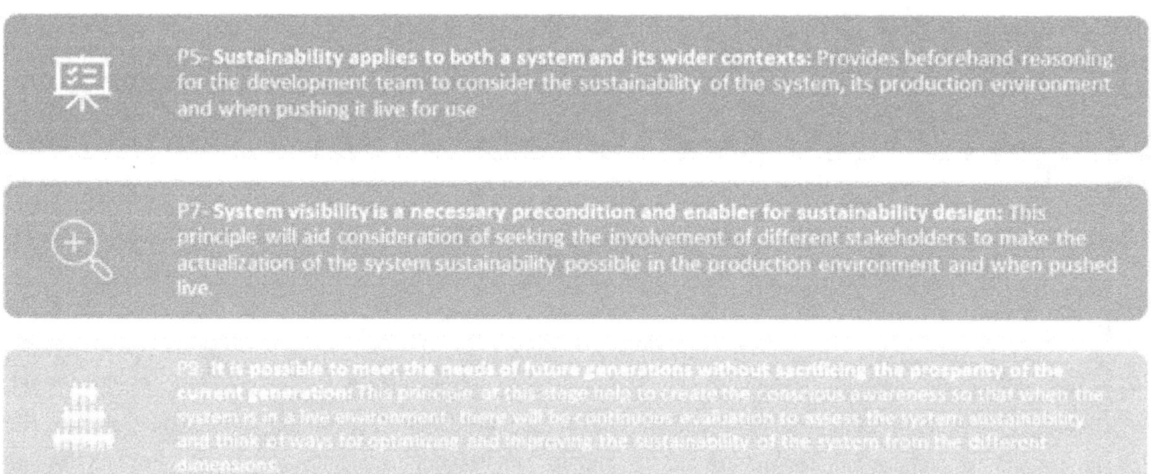

Based on previous experiences (Ovelheiro, Silveira, & Reis, 2021), the use of agile methodology, Scrum, the planning of project tasks with the integration of the principles and commitments of the Karlskrona Manifesto was facilitated.

Figure 9 shows part of the development of the Diabetes Tracker application using the Trello tool (Atlassian, 2020). We can see features already completed, in progress, and to be performed.

Figure 9. Using the Trello Tool (Atlassian, 2020) for Diabetes Tracker

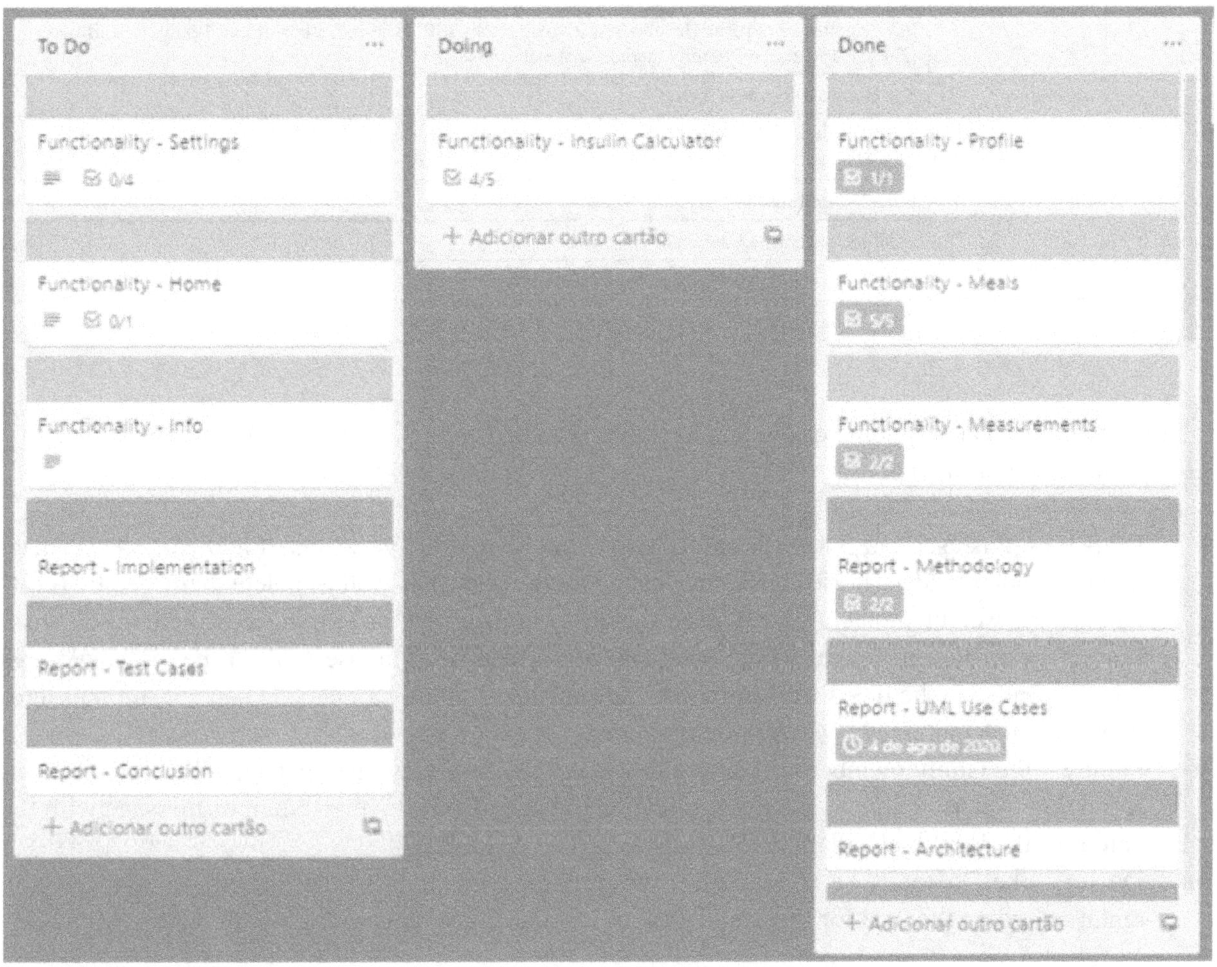

The use of tools such as Trello (Atlassian, 2020) helps developers to have an idea of the work they must do, as well as the work they already developed, helping on managing the time for each task.

Diabetes Tracker

In this section we can see the requirements analysis for the Diabetes Tracker app, showing some diagrams and screenshots. The requirements match the functionalities and restrictions that the app should respect

(Quatrani, 2001). Table 3 shows the list of actors and their respective objectives when using Diabetes Tracker app. These actors are the end-users who interact with the system.

Table 3. System actors table – Diabetes Tracker

Actor	Objectives
Diabetic	View information regarding diabetes.
	See Meal, Insert Meal, Edit Meal, and Delete Meal (CRUD Meals).
	Save data in your Profile (Insulin Sensitivity Factor - ISF, Insulin: Carbohydrates Ratio - ICR, Blood Glucose Target, Save Family member or Doctor email).
	See Body Mass Index (BMI).
	See Measurement, Insert Measurement, Edit Measurement, and Delete Measurement (CRUD Measurement).
	Calculate Insulin.
	Send message from Calculator interface.
Family/Doctor	See family member diabetes measurements.
	Receive message with Insulin Calculation (via email, mobile number, etc.).

In Table 3, we can see some of the features, that the different actors will be able to enjoy. The role of each actor is described below:

- Diabetic – this user can: view the information about diabetes; view, insert and edit meals (meal name, carbohydrates, calories, proteins, fat and attach photo) as well as delete them; see BMI (after entering weight and height); calculate the doses of insulin to be administered and, if you wish, send a pre-written message, with Date/Time of calculation, glucose at the time, carbohydrates ingested and also the doses of insulin to be administered, finally a Diabetic can consult measurements and calculations in Measurements Menu;
- Family – the family member will have a follow-up role and may also manage all the Diabetic information if he is unable to use the application; he can also receive an email or message with the values of the insulin calculation.
- Doctor – the Doctor, if he so wishes, when providing an email to the diabetic, may receive an email regarding the data for the calculation of insulin. This email will allow for better follow-up.

To calculate the insulin doses to be administered, the user must have introduced (Fonseca, et al., 2015): The Insulin Sensitivity Factor - ISF, which indicates how sensitive a person is to insulin; The Insulin: Carbohydrate Ratio – ICR that indicates how many grams of carbohydrates a unit of insulin can cover; Blood glucose – Target which is the value you want to achieve.

Figure 10 presents the actors as well as their use cases in a diagram in Unified Modeling Language notation (Unified Modeling Language, 2020). A use case is a special sequence of transactions carried out, in the form of a dialog, between a user and a system (Jacobson, 2004). Jacobson created a model to describe the system from an external perspective that he called the Use-Case Model, which is a key aspect for all software development activities (Jacobson, 2004; Jacobson et al., 2017). This type of diagram facilitates the visualization of all system features and who will have access to them (Sommerville, 2015).

Figure 10. Use case diagram, Diabetes Tracker

The main user of the application is the actor "Diabetic", he has access to information about diabetes, he can manage his meals (add, view, edit and delete the main components - Carbohydrates, Calories, Fat, and Proteins - of his meals), as well as managing the glucose measurements, he can calculate the insulin doses, and more. To use these features, the actor needs to have a successful login. The "Reminders" use case is said to be out of bounds as it will be a feature in the future.

This application was developed with the health of the elderly population in mind, in which the younger ones often play a major role and can contribute to monitoring their relative's diabetes. The application aims to promote altruism and helping others. It is considered to be a technological innovation that meets the needs of the Human Being, as well as individual well-being.

The role of the family member is represented by the inheritance between actors (arrow between the Family and Diabetic) this means that the Family member will have access to the same features as the Diabetic actor, if the diabetic for some reason is unavailable to use the application, their relative can occupy his place, doing the Diabetes control itself so that it maintains Good Health and Well-Being – SDG 3. In addition to the Family having access to the same features as the Diabetic, they may also receive a message with the date and time, glucose, carbohydrates ingested and the number of insulin doses to administer at the time of calculation (if the Diabetic so wishes). The doctor may also receive these types of messages.

The use case diagram is a useful element for the analysis of system requirements and its cases must be detailed so that later they can be implemented correctly by the programmer. To describe the requirements, in use case format, a template is used with the following fields: Name, Description, Size, Pre-Condition, Main Path, Alternative Paths, and Adornments. The "Main Path" shows the steps the program takes when everything goes well. If something is wrong, it shows the possible failures in the "Alternative Paths". The template also shows a notification in the "Post-Condition" and what is important to test in the "Adornments". Creating additional fields in the use case template, outside of the text describing the main path, containing supplementary information that is useful to associate with use cases, is a good practice taken from the Adornments pattern (Adolph & Bramble, 2003).

Table 4. Use case description – calculate insulin

Name	Calculate Insulin
Description	This use case is intended to describe the process for calculating the insulin doses to administer.
Size	L
Pre-Condition	Valid Login
Main Path	1. The Actor selects the option: "Calculator". 2. The system asks to enter blood sugar levels. 3. The actor fills in the blood glucose value. 4. The system asks to enter the ingested carbohydrates. 5. The actor fills in the carbohydrates and presses "Calculate". 6. The system calculates insulin and displays the doses to be administered. 7. The actor clicks on "Notify Your Family" to send a message. 8. The system automatically saves the measurement, allowing it to be consulted in the "Measurements" menu.
Alternative Paths	1. a) Error - Missing Data, Insert the data in your profile (ISF, ICR, and Blood glucose target). 5. a) Error mandatory fields (glucose or carbohydrates) were not filled in. b) Error invalid carbohydrate values. c) The actor selects a pre-entered meal. 7. a) The actor does not intend to send a message.
Post-Condition	The system sends a message to the family member with the value of glucose, carbohydrates, insulin doses to be administered, and the date and time of the calculation.
Adornments	Test the insulin dose value (Enter invalid values for correcting sugar levels and click "Calculate"; enter invalid values to cover carbohydrates and click "Calculate"); Test message sending. The Interface must be simple and intuitive.

The use case in Table 4 shows the process for calculating insulin. It is important to note that the user must be successfully authenticated (as mentioned in the pre-condition). The system checks if the ISF, ICR, and the Glucose – Target (Fonseca, et al., 2015) values were already entered. Another feature of the application is to notify the family, allowing you to send a message with the insulin calculation information, thus improving monitoring and preventing problems arising from diabetes.

Figure 11 shows the elements that are part of the Diabetes Tracker system architecture. It presents the Firebase Authentication component (Firebase, 2020) to authenticate users; Firebase Realtime Database and Firebase Cloud Storage – database used to store Diabetes Tracker data.

Figure 11. Architecture diagram - Diabetes Tracker

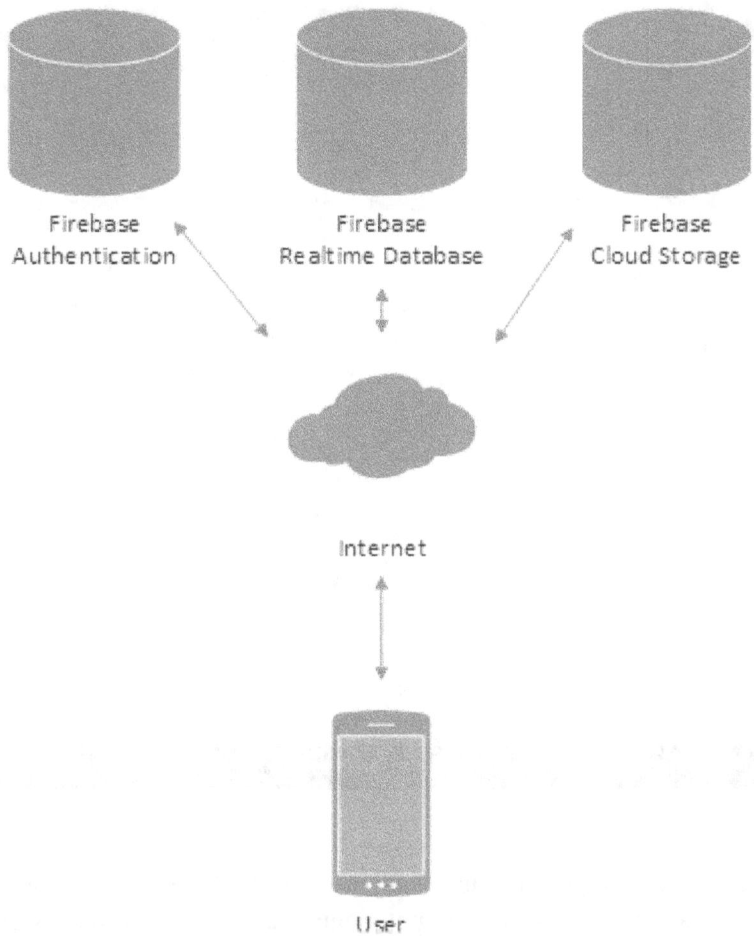

The Diabetic/Family member through, a mobile device has access to the application's features. All code and connections to Firebase were developed using Android Studio (Android Studio 2019).

The Diabetes Tracker, as mentioned above, was developed to facilitate the monitoring of Diabetes for the elderly population since they have more difficulty in keeping up with new technologies, a platform focused on this age group becomes necessary. So, the interface was developed with buttons that provide a better view, with appropriate font size and an appealing appearance. Functions like allowing you to choose a previously entered meal to fill the meal's carbohydrates in the Calculator menu; allowing you to notify your family or your doctor, this feature avoids uncertainty, thus allowing a younger person to support and promote the health of their family member – Good Health and Well-Being, SDG 3.

Figure 12. Intro, create account and navigation drawer - Diabetes Tracker

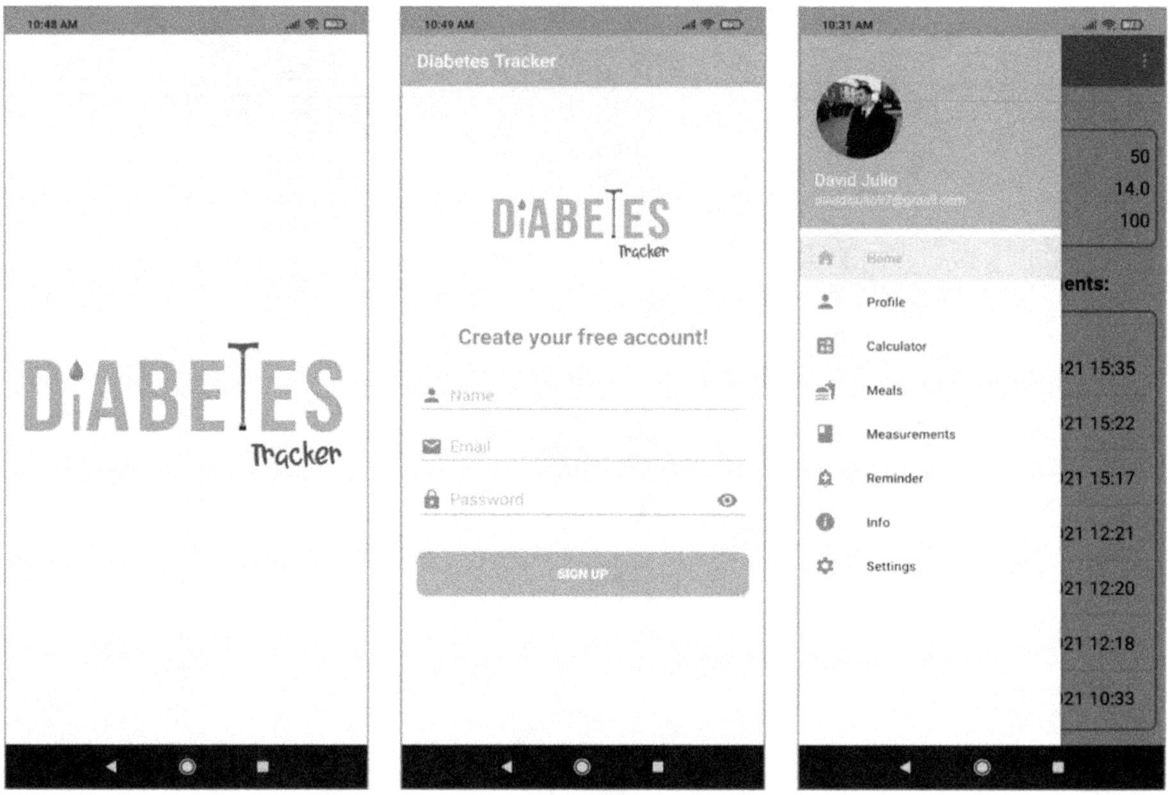

The first image above will appear whenever the user starts the application will show the Diabetes Tracker logo. Next, we can see the Create Account menu where the user after inserting his name a valid email, and a valid password, can create an account in the application. The last image shows the Navigation Drawer, where first the user can see some data from his profile, image name, and email. Next, he can see all the menus provided by Diabetes Tracker.

The Figure 13, shows the menu for entering, editing, and deleting meals (you can also see a pre-entered meal with more detail) into the Firebase Realtime Database, where the Diabetic can enter the name, carbohydrates, calories, fat, and even protein for the corresponding meal. At this point, Firebase Cloud Storage is also used to store a photo associated with the meal.

Figure 13. Add/edit & delete, meals list - Diabetes Tracker

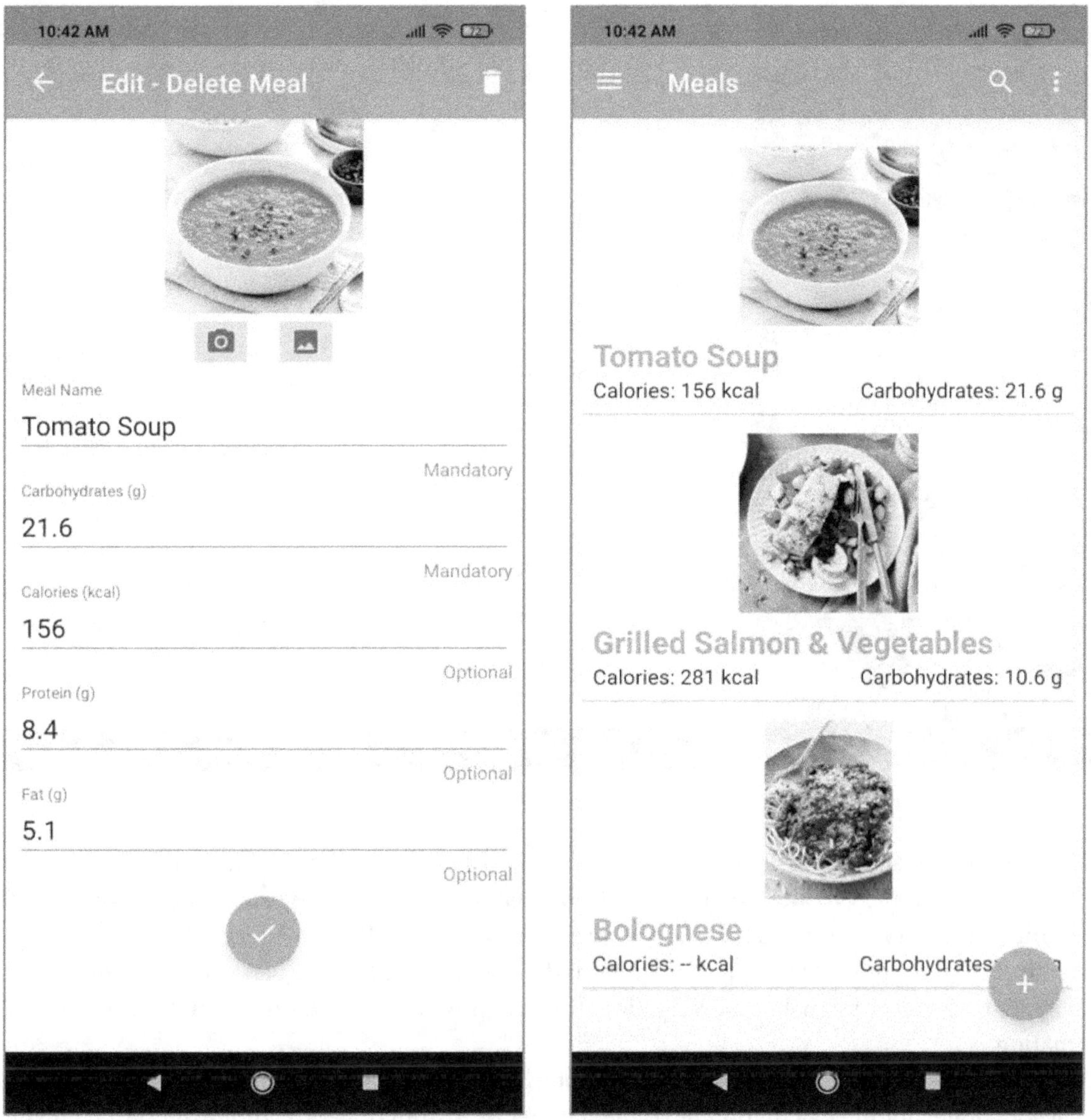

The second image above represents a current list of the Meal Menu, where we can see the meals saved in the Firebase Realtime Database, it is possible to see the name of the meal, the corresponding carbohydrates, and even an optional field – calories.

Figure 14. Warning message, profile menu & calculator menu - Diabetes Tracker

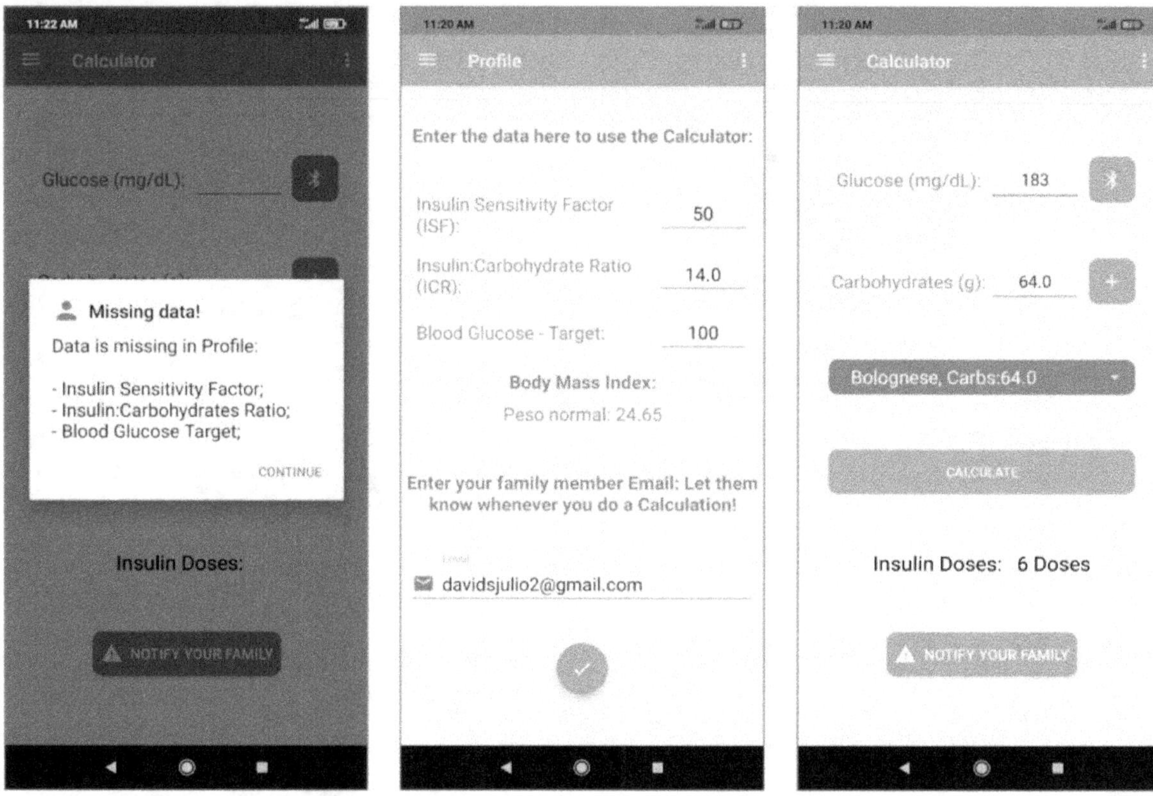

The first image above shows an alert message that lets the user know that is missing data on the profile menu. Next, the Profile Menu image shows that in this menu, the user can enter data related to the Insulin Sensitivity Factor - ISF, Insulin: Carbohydrates Ratio - ICR and Target Blood Glucose these, data are essential for the calculation of insulin, in this menu, the Diabetic can fill in his family member email so that whenever he makes a calculation, this email will be entered if he sends an email with the information.

The last image in Figure 14 is the calculator interface, where the user will enter the value of glucose and carbohydrates for the calculation next, the number of insulin doses to administer will be displayed. The user is allowed to access the Add, Edit-Delete Meal menu – the first image in Figure 14, from the "+" button, or even choose a pre-entered meal so that the carbohydrates are automatically filled. There is also a button that provides the option to send a message (with the result of the insulin calculation) to the family of the Diabetic or his doctor.

Soon, the functionality of integration to measuring devices equipped with Bluetooth functionality will be implemented.

Volunteer+

In this section, some diagrams and screenshots of the Volunter+ app are presented. The Table 5 shows the list of actors for the Volunteer+ app, showing the objectives each user has and how they will interact with the system.

Table 5. System actors table – Volunteer+

Actor	Objective
Volunteer	Create Account; View information about volunteering; View volunteering actions; View old actions.
Institution	Create Account; View volunteering actions; Propose volunteering actions; Change proposed volunteering actions; Terminate volunteering actions; View action results.
System Manager	Add information about volunteering; Edit information about volunteering; Delete information about volunteering; Delete institutions; Delete volunteers.

Each actor has its own roles inside the app, which will be described next:

- Volunteer – final user of this system, who can view information about volunteering and find volunteering actions, both ongoing and old ones.
- Institution – each Institution can propose their own volunteering actions, as well and changing or terminating them.
- System Manager – actor that has access to the whole app to manage it.

The use case diagram shows the app's features, as well has every interaction each actor is going to have with it. The use cases help us with the requirements analysis for the system that is being developed.

Figure 15. Use case diagram, Volunteer+

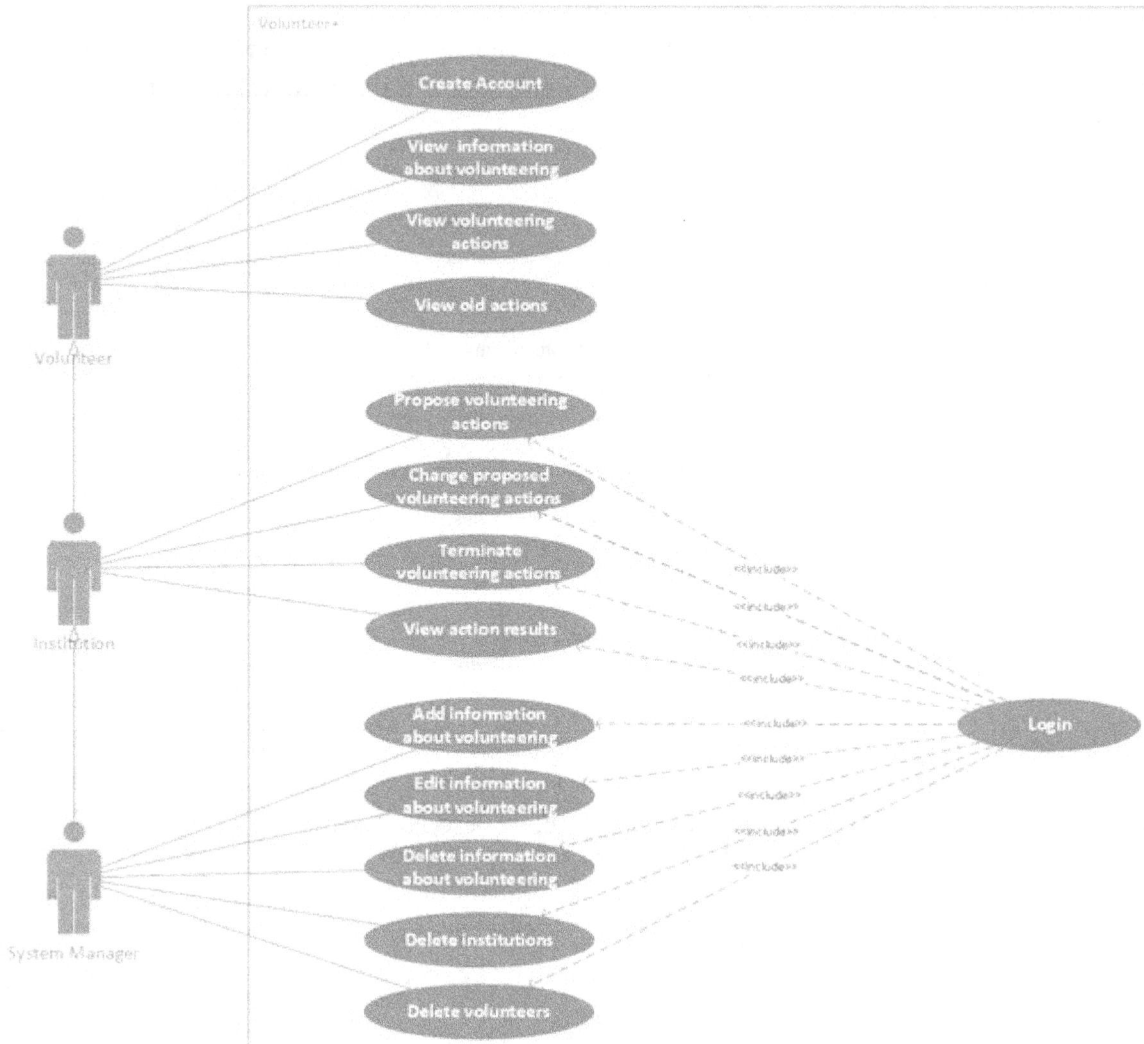

As the Figure 15 shows, there is a heritage between the actors. The actor known as System Manager will inherit the use cases from both the other actors, Volunteer, and Institution, which means he will have access to every functionality in available in the app.

In this section we can visually see how the system works in terms of its architecture, and this is great so we can easily understand how the app works, as well as understanding how the information reaches each one of its users.

Figure 16. Architecture diagram – Volunteer+

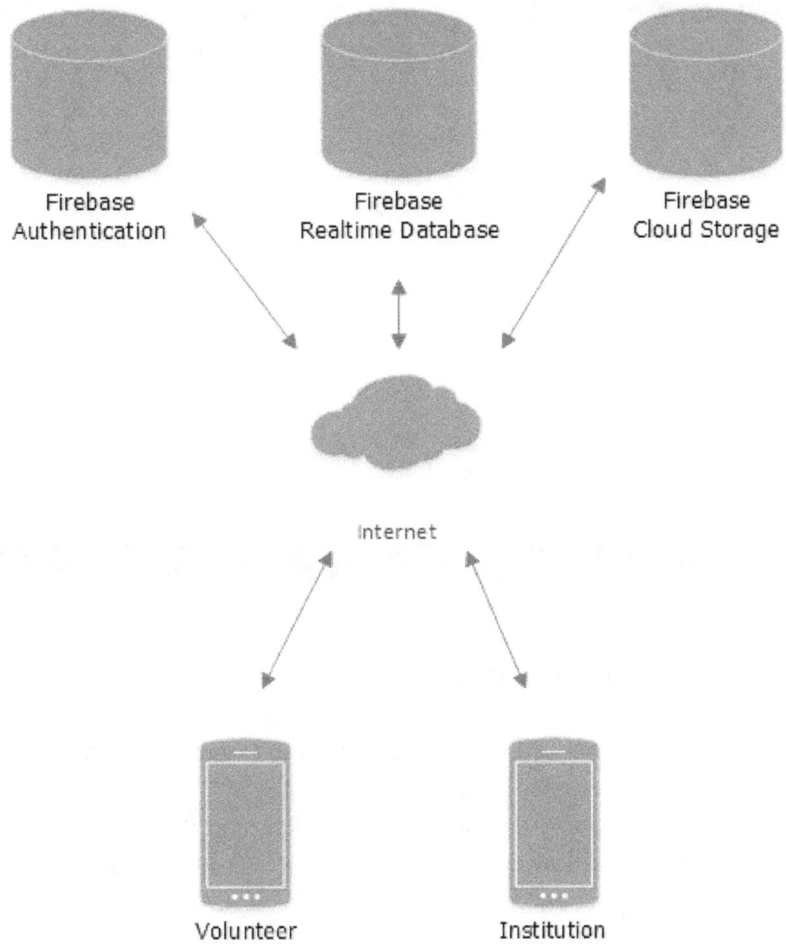

In the Figure 16 we can see that the users access the app through their smartphones, which will contact the database to present the information needed.

The Volunteer+ app is being developed to give a viable option for the search of volunteering actions, offering a platform for Institutions to propose their actions. One this that this app offer is the option to find activities about the Ocean Preservation, since there are not many out there in the market right now. In the following figures will be presented some of the app's menus.

Figure 17. Start screen, login page and registration page

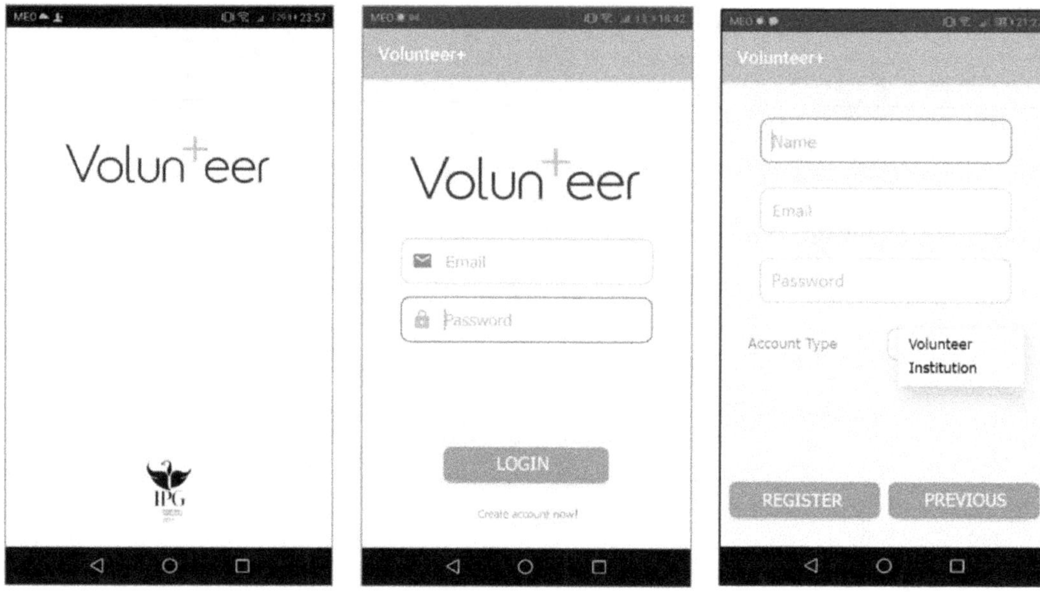

The Figure 17 shows the initial part of the app. The first one shows us the app logo as well as IPG's logo. This page also works as a loading screen, giving the app a few seconds in order to access the database and get all the information needed. We can also see the Login page, where the user will have an option to create an account, in case he doesn't have one yet.

In the registration page the app asks for some information, and it asks the user what account type he wants to create, Volunteer or Institution. This restriction exists just so the app knows which page to show when the user logs in later.

Figure 18. Institution menu, new action and list of actions

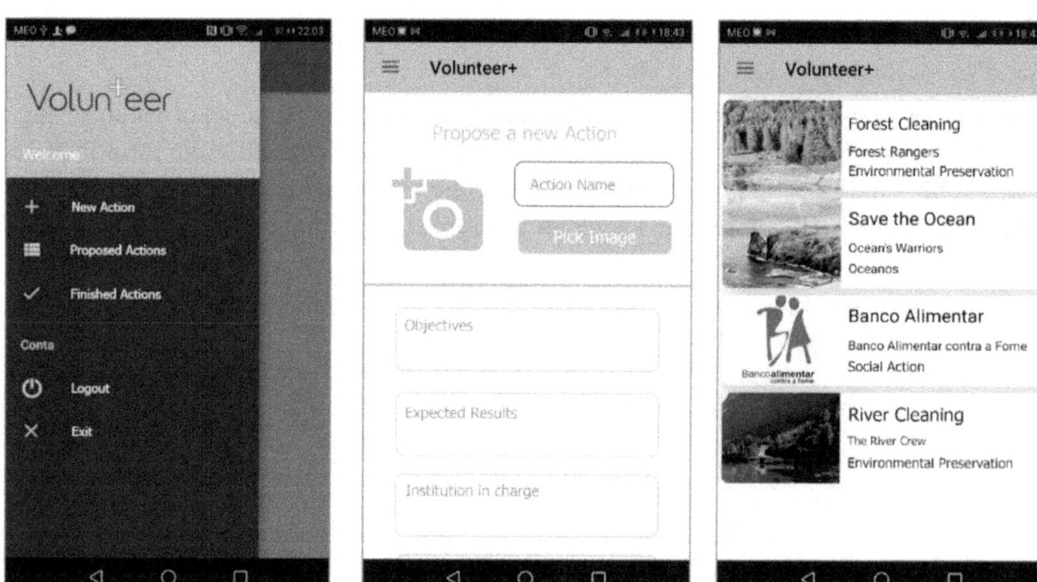

The Figure 18 shows the screen someone who logs in as an Institution will see. The second screen shown shows the form someone needs to fill in to propose a new volunteering action, asking for all the important information regarding said action. The third one shows a list of the actions available in the app. In this, screen, the user can easily search for activities that suit them by writing the key words he wants to search for. The user can search for names, categories, and institutions and then, he can click any action to see more information about it.

Figure 19. Volunteer screen, SDG page and SDG information

The Figure 19 shows the menu someone will see when they log in with a volunteer type account. The user can choose to see ocean related actions, some other different types of actions and the Sustainable Development Goals menu. The other two pictures show us the SDG's part of the app. The user will see a screen with all the Sustainable Development Goals, and in case he wants to know more about one of them, he can just click it and some more information about the clocked item will be shown in the following screen.

RESULTS AND DISCUSSION

On the applications development, some SDGs were focused on, besides promoting the main objective is to combat some of the problems identified. Therefore, the Diabetes Tracker is an app focused on SDG 3 - Good Health and Well-Being. In Figure 20, it is possible to see the app logo and its main objective: Ensure Healthy lives and promote well-being for all of all ages.

Figure 20. Diabetes Tracker in the promotion of SDG 3 "Good Health and Well-Being"

Of the goals to be met in SDG 3, all deal with health, and the one that is most identified with this project, seeks to strengthen the capacity of all countries, particularly developing countries, for early warning, risk reduction, and risk management national and global health (UNDP, 2015). Diabetes Tracker will help to reduce the risk of problems arising from diabetes.

Figure 21. Volunteer+ in the promotion of several SDG's

In what concerns the Volunteer+ app, this one contributes to promoting several SDG's, with the number 14, Life below water, having special attention. In the Figure 21 we can see the application's logo as well as a few examples of the SDG's it helps promoting. Training actions on technological platforms through volunteering can be a driver in the health area (Triana, Gusdorf, Shah, & Horst, 2020), improving literacy and access to medical care to contribute to the well-being of people. A atividade de voluntariado contribui também para realização pessoal dos voluntários uma vez que a sua colaboração potencia a melhoria da qualidade de vida dos cidadãos apoiados pelas diversas iniciativas.

Figure 22. Sustainability dimensions

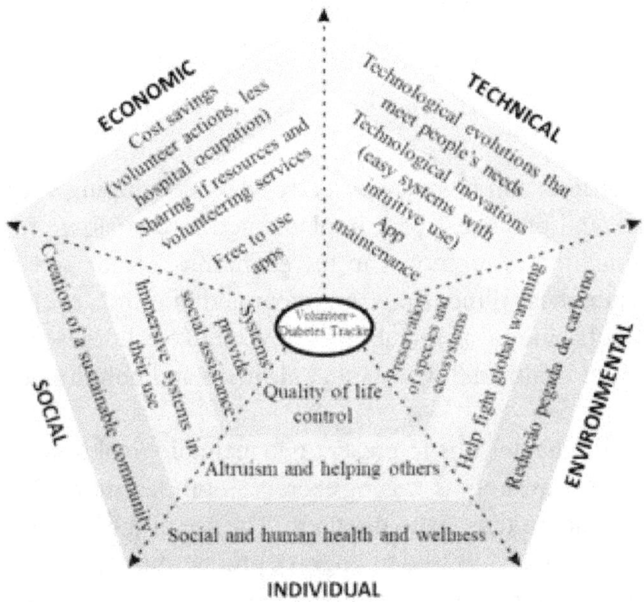

Sustainability is a global approach that considers the environmental, economic, individual, social and technical dimensions, recognizing that all must be considered together for lasting prosperity. Figure 22 shows us the analysis of the impact these two apps regarding the economic, environmental, social, individual, and technical dimensions of the sustainability. This analysis is based in the sustainability investigation about the impact to the environment, society, economy, process, value, and people.

The scheme provides an overview of how the various dimensions of sustainability can influence each other, having as reference the Diabetes Tracker and Volunteer+ apps, specifically:

- Individual Sustainability: the applications were designed to promote the improvement of quality of life, health and well-being, altruism and helping others.
- Environmental Sustainability: it is intended that the applications raise awareness among users in the preservation of species and ecosystems, combating global warming and reducing the carbon footprint by raising awareness with volunteer actions to conserve and sustainably use the oceans.
- In terms of Technical Sustainability, the development of the applications was carried out to allow technological evolutions that meet people's needs, namely ease of use.
- Economic Sustainability: cost reduction boosted by better diabetes control, voluntary actions with the sharing of resources and services, applications free of charge for users.
- Social Sustainability: the development of the Diabetes Tracker and Volunteer + applications include some features to promote the creation of a sustainable community, namely in terms of social assistance.

It is therefore considered that the development of technological platforms fostering volunteering in the sense of implementing solutions of a social nature, considering the development of sustainable software and incorporating concerns in the human, environmental, technical, economic and social dimensions, is of particular importance in the current context pandemic.

CONCLUSION

Sustainability in the field of ICT, and more specifically when developing software, was also one of the concerns. Thus, principles and practices were implemented to contribute to the sustainability of the solution. This way, sustainability is promoted in the economic, social, environmental, technical, and individual dimensions. When these dimensions are integrated into the developed applications, some of the points in which they contribute to sustainability are visualized. In these cases, we can highlight the individual/human dimension: health and well-being, altruism and helping others, allowing for a better quality of life.

The main objective of this chapter was to present two technological implementations inserted in the SDG theme, having served as an awareness-raising exercise for the Sustainable Development Goals, both for those who develop them and for those who use them. The use of the agile development process, more specifically the Scrum methodology, allowed to improve productivity during software development, understanding its agility and understanding its usefulness in work groups. The integration of the principles of the Karlskrona Manifesto in the stages of the SCRUM methodology showed that it is possible to apply the principles of sustainability, the interconnection between dimensions and the promotion of the SDGs.

The main results can be seen in the developed applications, specifically: Diabetes Tracker is a mobile application that facilitates the control of diabetes disease and promotes Quality Health. The application was designed to provide a simple and intuitive interface and allows its users to: manage meals; save measurements; calculate insulin doses to administer; advise your family members of the calculation in order to maintain more effective control; control the body mass index, essential in the senior population, among other features. Volunteer+ is a mutual help platform, in which institutions can seek help in the most diverse scenarios, and volunteers can find volunteer actions that fit what they intend to do, with the option to search for the actions that most interest them. In addition to researching volunteer actions, the Volunteer+ application also provides information on the SDGs.

As perspectives for future work, it is intended to integrate the two applications, as well as development and testing to enhance their applicability, creating a vision of sustainability shared by the various stakeholders. A new integration functionality with a glucose measuring device that is prepared for these functions is also designed. It will allow you to make a Bluetooth connection so that the diabetic can automatically receive the current glucose value in the application, thus preventing insertion errors and facilitating its use. Applications will be tested in charitable organizations. In terms of incorporating the principles and commitments of the Karlskrona Manifesto in the software development process, its continuation in academic projects is envisaged. It is intended to disseminate sustainability practices, contributing to the development and improvement of an approach to sustainable software design (Penzenstadler *et al.*, 2018).

REFERENCES

Adolph, S., & Bramble, P. (2003). *Patterns for Effective Use Cases*. Addison-Wesley Pearson Education.

Alexander, I., & Stevens, R. (2002). *Writing Better Requirements*. Addison-Wesley.

Almeida, F. (2020). The role of tech startups in the fight against COVID-19, *World Journal of Science. Technology and Sustainable Development, 18*(1), 64–75.

Android Studio. (2019). *Android Studio release notes, Android Developers*. Google LLC.

Aristodemou, K., Buchhass, L., & Claringbould, D. (2021). The COVID-19 crisis in the EU: The resilience of healthcare systems, government responses and their socio-economic effects. *Eurasian Econ Rev, 11*(2), 251–281. doi:10.100740822-020-00162-1

Ascari, R., Pereira, R. & Silva, L. (2018). Mobile Interaction for Augmentative and Alternative Communication: a Systematic Mapping, *SBC Journal on 3D Interactive Systems, 9*(2), 105-118.

Atlassian. (2020). *Trello*. https://trello.com/

Becker, C., Betz, S., Chitchyan, R., Duboc, L., Easterbrook, S. M., Penzenstadler, B., Seyff, N., & Venters, C. (2016). Requirements: The Key to Sustainability. *IEEE Software, 33*(1), 56–65. doi:10.1109/MS.2015.158

BGMonitor. (2020). *Diabetes Management for Android*. Gordon Wong.

BIGLauncher. (2020). *BIG Launcher*. Apps Google Play.

CollabNet. (2019). *13th Annual State of Agile Survey*. CollabNet VersionOne Inc.

DeMarco, T., & Lister, T. (2003). Risk Management During Requirements. *IEEE Software, 20*(5), 99–101. doi:10.1109/MS.2003.1231163

DiabetesM. (2020). *Diabetes:M*. www.diabetes-m.com

Donati, M., Fanucci, L., Iacopetti, F., & Vecchio, A. (2015). *A modular suite to support human-smartphone interaction for people with motor skill impairments. 10th International Conference on Design & Technology of Integrated Systems in Nanoscale Era (DTIS)*, Naples, Italy. 10.1109/DTIS.2015.7127385

Firebase. (2020). *Firebase Authentication*. https://firebase.google.com/docs/auth

Fonseca, F., Pichel, F., Albuquerque, I., Afonso, M. J., Baptista, N., & Túbal, V. (2015). *Manual de Contagem de Hidratos de Carbono na Diabetes Mellitus para profissionais de saúde*. Porto: Associação Portuguesa dos Nutricionistas.

Jacobson, I. (2004). Use Cases – Yesterday, Today, and Tomorrow. *Software & Systems Modeling, 3*(3), 210–220. doi:10.100710270-004-0060-3

Jacobson, I., Lawson, B., McMahon, P., & Goedicke, M. (2017). *Software Engineering Essentialized*. www.software-engineering-essentialized.com

Jacobson, I., & Seidewitz, E. (2014). A new software engineering. *Communications of the ACM, 57*(12), 49–54. doi:10.1145/2677034

Júlio, D., Torres, J., & Silveira, C. (2021). Diabetes Tracker & Volunteer+: Implementações Tecnológicas na Promoção dos Objetivos de Desenvolvimento Sustentável. In *V International Forum on Management – IFM2021* (pp. 354-381). Instituto Politécnico de Setúbal.

Kumar, V. S. (2006). Effective requirements management. *PMI® Global Congress 2006—EMEA, Madrid, Spain.* Newtown Square, PA: Project Management Institute.

Maiden, N., & Gizikis, A. (2001). Where Do Requirements Come From? *IEEE Software*, *18*(5), 10–12. doi:10.1109/52.951486

MSD Controlar a Diabetes. (2017). *Entender a Diabetes.* https://controlaradiabetes.pt/entender-a-diabetes/diabetes-mellitus-tipo-1

mySugr. (2020). *mySugr.* www.mysugr.com/en/diabetes-app/

Nunes, M., & O'Neill, H. (2007). *Fundamental de UML* (5th ed.). FCA Editora.

Ovelheiro, B., Silveira, C., & Reis, L. (2021). Sustainability Design Applied to the Digital Signature of Documents. In Handbook of Research on Multidisciplinary Approaches to Entrepreneurship, Innovation, and ICTs (pp. 349-374). IGI Global. http://doi:10.4018/978-1-7998-4099-2.ch016

Oyedeji, S., Seffah, A., & Penzenstadler, B. (2018). A Catalogue Supporting Software Sustainability Design. *Sustainability*, *2018*(10), 2296.

Penzenstadler, B., Betz, S., Venters, C. C., Chitchyan, R., Porras, J., Seyff, N., Duboc, L., & Becker, C. (2018). Everything is Interrelated: Teaching Software Engineering for Sustainability. *IEEE/ACM 40th International Conference on Software Engineering: Software Engineering Education and Training (ICSE-SEET),* 153-162.

Pickell, Z., Gu, K., & Williams, A. (2020). Virtual volunteers: The importance of restructuring medical volunteering during the COVID-19 pandemic. *Medical Humanities*, *46*, 537–540.

Pinto, N. (2016). *PT MagicContact.* Relatório de Projeto Aplicado do Mestrado em Computação Móvel, Escola Superior de Tecnologia e Gestão do Instituto Politécnico da Guarda.

Plataforma Portuguesa das ONGD. (2020). *Impacto da pandemia COVID-19 nos Objetivos de Desenvolvimento Sustentável.* ONGD Plataforma Portuguesa.

Quatrani, T. (2001). *Introduction to the Unified Modeling Language.* IBM Rational.

Reis, L., Silveira, C., Carvalho, L., & Mata, C. (2020). Digitalization as a Key Issue of the Circular Economy to Promote Sustainability: Prototyping Design for Homeless People. In Mapping, Managing, and Crafting Sustainable Business Strategies for the Circular Economy (pp. 111-137). IGI Global. http://doi:10.4018/978-1-5225-9885-5.ch007

Roher, K., & Richardson, D. (2013). Sustainability requirement patterns. *3rd International Workshop on Requirements Patterns (RePa)*, 8-11.

Rubin, K. S. (2013). *Essential Scrum.* Adisson-Wesley.

Silveira, C., & Reis, L. (2021). Sustainability in Information and Communication Technologies. In Handbook of Research on Multidisciplinary Approaches to Entrepreneurship, Innovation, and ICTs (pp. 375-396). IGI Global. doi:10.4018/978-1-7998-4099-2.ch017

Silveira, C., Reis, L., Santos, V., & Mamede, H. (2020). Creativity in Prototypes Design and Sustainability – The case of Social Organizations, Advances in Science. *Technology and Engineering Systems Journal*, *5*(6), 1237–1243. doi:10.25046/aj0506147

Sommerville, I. (2005). Integrated Requirements Engineering: A Tutorial. *IEEE Software*, *22*(1), 16–23.

Sommerville, I. (2015). *Software Engineering* (10th ed.). Addison-Wesley Pearson Education.

SustainAbility. (2018). *Sustainability: Can our society endure?* SustainAbility an ERM Group Company.

Thew, S., & Sutcliffe, A. (2018). Value-based requirements engineering: Method and experience. *Requirements Engineering*, *23*, 443–464.

Triana, A., Gusdorf, R., Shah, K., & Horst, S. (2020). Technology literacy as a barrier to telehealth during COVID-19. *Telemedicine Journal and e-Health*, 1118–1119.

UNDP. (2015). *Sustainable Development Goals*. United Nations Development Programme.

Unified Modeling Language. (2020). *Unified Modeling Language*. Object Management Group, Inc.

KEY TERMS AND DEFINITIONS

Agile Software Development: Software development process that favors direct communication between all stakeholders and simplifies documentation.

Information Systems: Is the organized set of components such as people, processes of collection and transmission of data and material resources, automated or manual. The interaction of components enhances the processing and dissemination of information.

Karlskrona Manifesto: Establishes the principles and dimensions for the design of sustainable software systems.

Requirements Analysis: Iterative process to identify features and restrictions with a view to developing or changing a software product. Usually use cases are used.

Software Systems Development: Set of activities involved in the production of software. These activities are related to each other in an iterative and incremental process.

Sustainability: Ability to sustain life on the planet, considering the five dimensions: individual, social, economic, technical, and environmental.

Chapter 12
The Impact of Information and Communication Technology (ICT) on Hotel Classification Ratings

Tahir Sufi
https://orcid.org/0000-0003-3407-4828
Amity University, Noida, India

Akrivi Vagena
https://orcid.org/0000-0001-9135-9200
University of Patras, Greece

ABSTRACT

There has been increased interest among researchers and industry to generate insights from user-generated data and ratings on account of valuable information such as data carry and its authenticity. Numerous studies offer insight into how traditional hotel classification ratings are influenced by the information and communication technology. However, no such studies that explore the relationship between traditional hotel ratings and the largest online hotel review website, TripAdvisor, could be found. To bridge the gap, the study uses the TripAdvisor hotel rating data from Greek hotels to explore this relationship using Kruskal-Wallis H test. The results show that mean TripAdvisor ratings of hotels are in proportion to the traditional hotel classification ratings.

INTRODUCTION

The traditional hotel classification system is undergoing a rapid transformation because of technological innovations in the business world. The transformation is mainly due to the emergence of the internet that led to establishing online travel agents (OTA's) like TripAdvisor, Expedia, Yelp and many other such companies. These OTA's publish millions of the reviews posted by the travellers who stay in such

DOI: 10.4018/978-1-7998-9227-4.ch012

properties (Aristio, Supardi, Hendrawan & Hidayat, 2019). Professor Andrew McAfee coined the term 'Enterprise 2.0' to highlight the significance of social networking and computing on business organizations, leading the organizations to embrace change and rapid transformation (Lakhani &McAfee, 2015). Hospitality Industry is also transforming because of the emerging 'Enterprise 2.0' paradigm as an important channel for maintaining technological innovations for the hospitality sector to compete and succeed in the market (Büyüközkan, Feyzioğlu & Havle, 2019). Before the advent of the internet, travel used to be private, and experiences were shared with only a small circle of acquaintances characterized by mutual trust. However, with the advent of the internet, guest experiences have converted into global databases of consumer information managed by firms. Further, the process has enabled the user's real-time recording and sharing of experiences. Many studies showings the reasons for motivation for sharing experiences online pointed at altruistic and community-related motivations that include including reason for helping others (Munar and Jacobsen, 2014), emotional and social support (Baym, 2010) and providing advice on practical matters (Munar & Ooi, 2012).

Online travel agents like TripAdvisor also evaluate hotel services using several stars to represent customer satisfaction with hotel services. Such ratings are temporarily sensitive, continually reconfigured, personal and relatively based upon unregulated content (Talwar, Dhir, Kaur & Mäntymäki, 2020). TripAdvisor uses the Popularity Index calculated through algorithms to rank the accommodation. This index incorporates the traveller ratings to determine traveller satisfaction emphasizing the most recent information. The algorithm considers quality, quantity, and the recency of the reviews. The guests rate the properties on a scale of 1-5, where five stands for the best (TripAdvisor, 2021). The hotels are evaluated in terms of service, cleanliness, location, and overall impression of the property. The previous research studies on online hotel ratings focus on an econometric approach (Lee, Xie, Besharat & Tan, 2017; Xie, Zhang & Zhang, 2014), or a survey approach (Filieri, Alguezaui, & McLeay, 2015) using overall ratings, hotel stars, and the number of hotel reviews, as well as responses.

The study by (Hu & Chen 2016) adopted choose few cities for hotel review analysis. However, the study exploring how the relationship between ICT and traditional hotel ratings is yet to be explored. This study, therefore, bridges the gap to understanding the relationship between traditional hotel ratings and online hotel ratings, which are primarily driven by the revolution in ICT. The study's objectives include exploring the relationship between the two different ratings allocated to a sample of hotels in Greece and establishing if the hotels awarded higher star ratings by the traditional classification system (HOTREC) are also rated high by the travellers TripAdvisor. For this purpose, the online and traditional ratings of one hundred fifty hotels of one, two, three, four and five-star hotels in Greece shall be compared using the Kruskal-Wallis test shall be conducted. The results shall explain the relationship between the two hotel ratings- if they are in tandem with each other or have no relationship at all. The results shall explain how the travellers rate the hotels with high star ratings from the traditional rating system.

BACKGROUND

The advent of technology has touched each aspect of travel and tourism. The use of tourism technologies has been pervasive and growing in the last few decades. The term smart tourism, along with the associated technologies, provides access to critical information to travellers that enhance traveller satisfaction. Further, travellers choose a suitable accommodation hotel by browsing the online evaluations of several alternative hotels on several platforms to learn more about these hotels and make decisions based on them (Zhao, Li & Xu, 2021). The Covid-19 crisis has enhanced the use of digital technology in the Hotel Industry.

The researchers also recommend technology as a panacea to COVID-19 driven-needs and offering solutions for re-opening tourism and triggering the economy. While as there is clear evidence that Industry is adopting emerging technology in Robotics, Artificial Intelligence, Big Data, Automation, Virtual & augmented reality in operations (Agrawal, Dutta, Kelly & Millán, 2021), the classification agencies still rely on physical inspection of hotels to evaluate the hotels. The online hotel ratings generated by TripAdvisor are already computed with the help of ICT tools and algorithms. Such a framework for classifying hotels is not compatible with Post Covid-19 world, and there is an urgent need to revisit the framework.

The problems and challenges due to the arrival of the internet are threatening the existence of the traditional hotel classification ratings. The traditional ratings offer incomplete information to the travellers by such ratings- in comparison, the online rating systems are emerging as a more effective source of hotel information. The customers, therefore, find online ratings more informative and reliable. A study by (Torres, Adler, Behnke,2014) explored how hotel review websites and (OTA's) have made the traditional hotel classification redundant. The online ratings provide more candid pictures of the hotel properties that travellers share. The database generated by many customers provides detailed information that helps travellers book-related decisions in a better way (Hashim & Fadhil, 2017).

Such challenges to the traditional classification system and the simultaneous emergence of online ratings are the central theme of this study. While traditional hotel ratings are generated by the manual procedure involving inspection of the hotels by the experts- the online hotel ratings, on the other hand, are generated by the online review of the hotels by the travellers who stay in such properties and rate the hotels after experiencing the services and facilities. As both ratings are available to the travellers to make booking-related decisions, this study analyses the relationship between the hotel ratings generated from two different sources. The findings shall confirm the nature of the relationship between the two ratings.

HOTEL CLASSIFICATION SYSTEMS

United Nations World Tourism Organization (UNWTO) defines a hotel classification system as the ranking of hotels, usually by using nomenclature such as stars or diamonds, with one star donating the basic facilities and standards of comfort and five stars donating the luxury in facilities and services. The purpose of the hotel classification is to inform the intending guests in advance on what can be expected to reduce the gap between expected and experienced facilities and service delivery. The terms 'classification', 'grading', 'rating' refer to the same concept i.e. to rank the hotels by their facilities and standard (UNWTO, 2015).

Further, another term is frequently used apart from 'classification', ' Grading'. Talias (2016) defined both the terms to clear the difference. While classification distinguishes the hotels according to physical features (amenities, facilities, service, and cost), such as the number of guest rooms with bathrooms, etc., the grading evaluates hotels based on service features, for example, 24 hours coffee shop etc. Martin, Fernandez& Marine (2018) explained that the hundred-plus ratings worldwide could be classified into two groups- official and unofficial ratings. While an official rating system is conducted by the Government agencies and followed on a compulsory and regulatory basis, the unofficial rating system is carried out by private organizations such as Hotel Associations, trade bodies, and hotels that participate voluntarily in these ratings.

The hotel classification system, also referred to as the 'hotel-rating system, ' aims to inform travellers about the hotel facilities and services. The system, therefore, reduces the gap between expected and experienced facilities and service delivery. The classification helps evaluate hotels based on features like infrastructure, amenities, and facilities, thereby resulting in the hierarchy of hotels (Holloway and Humphrey's, 2016). The hotel classification system has many advantages from hoteliers and customers' perspectives (Li, 2013). The system offers fair competition between hotels, thereby facilitates hotel marketing and positioning (Federation, 2017). From a hotel point of view, the benefits include offering consumers confidence in purchasing rooms at high rates, offering comparable information through natural symbols like diamonds and stars (UNTWO, 2014). Such symbols help in marketing and promotional tool for hotels (Quo, 2014). Despite many benefits, the classification system suffers from several drawbacks. First, these systems rely on infrastructure and facilities mainly for hotel evaluation. Several research studies have concluded that the hotel rating systems put much stress on quantitative structural factors of evaluation like room size, bed, and furniture instead of the quality of service (Lyu, 2016). The disregard towards evaluating service quality makes such schemes ineffective for customer satisfaction (Baccarani, Ugolini and Bonfanti, 2017).

ONLINE RATING SYSTEM

The traditional ratings provided by the classification system stresses that hotels have all the facilities, amenities, comfort, cleanliness, and security for guest satisfaction. It is a challenge for the hotels to ensure that guests are satisfied with their products and services, including guest handling procedure, pricing, complaint management system, guest requests system, etc. That is where precisely the services of social media, travel-related websites and travel blogs are utilized. With the advent of social media and the internet, guests have access to all these sources of information about the hotels. Such websites have become more popular among travellers and are influencing booking-related decisions. The focus of travellers has shifted from the traditional hotel classification ratings to the hotel feedback provided by travellers on social networking sites and hotel review websites (Nielsen, 2010).

With the continued growth of social media platforms providing guest feedback, the demand for hotel ratings emerging from such feedback has emerged. The social media sites and online travel agents (OTA's) provide rich information to travellers about hotel features, activities, room rates to satisfy traveller's needs and wants. These websites provide actual property pictures or videos in real-time and word-of-mouth, enabling travellers to pay more attention and engage them more effectively. Traveller's use social media during all stages decision-making process, and therefore, there is a need for social media in the tourism industry (Sigala, 2020). The study by (Ye, Law, Gu and Chen, 2011) showed how online ratings could influence online hotel business by up to ten per cent. Considering the importance of online hotel ratings, therefore, integration of online hotel reviews and hotel classification systems under two options are reported – full integration mode and comparative performance mode.

Under the 'full integration mode, hotel star rating can move up or down depending upon the guest perception of its service quality and the ratings generated, therefore. Hotels in Norway have already switched to the full integration category. Under the 'comparative performance' category, the guest review rating is separately displayed without integration. The integration of online and traditional hotel ratings is achieved through an algorithm using a series of formulae. While as under comparative performance mode, the online ratings and traditional ratings are written separately without integrating (UNTWO,

2014). Hotel Review website "'TrustYou' allows the hotel chains to integrate the hotel reviews and rake (TrustYou score) on their websites. Besides hotel review websites providing hotel reviews, hotel chains like Marriott have started their review and rating process. Integrating guest review and hotel classification is recommended on account of helping the hotels in improving services, image and revenue (Anderson, 2011). Based on the discussion, the chapter proposes the following hypothesis

$H_0$1 *There is no significant difference between the TripAdvisor ratings of different star-rated hotels.*

HOTEL CLASSIFICATION SYSTEM POST-COVID-19 PANDEMIC

The COVID-19 crisis is an inflexion point that forced the hospitality industry to take a giant leap which otherwise would have been unthinkable even a few months before the arrival of a pandemic (Foroudi, H. Tabaghdehi & Marvi, 2021). There is a noticeable change in consumer behaviour forcing the hospitality industry to reorganize the traditional operational approach. Technology is seen as a panacea to our COVID-19 driven needs and offering solutions for re-opening tourism and triggering the economy (Sigala, 2020). With the situation beginning to improve, the businesses that prioritize customer safety and experience management thrived during the pandemic. The recent survey during the COVID-19 crisis indicated that only 9% of US consumers rank travel and Hospitality as the innovative Industry(Customer Experience Trends', 2021). The study also identified chatbots, virtual reality (VR), and AI as the most popular technologies to create an exceptional customer experience.

However, the COVID-19 crisis also acted as a catalyst to speed up the hospitality industry's adoption of such technologies. A recent study by (Lau 2020) revealed live-stream promotion and conferencing, 5G network, Wi-Fi 6, event facial check-in services with AI temperature checks, Robots for F&B room services and housekeeping deliveries as survival strategies of the Chinese Hotel Industry during the Covid 19 pandemic. Further, to enhance service quality and safety, AI and Robots are integrated into daily operations. The one popular buzzword in travel is 'seamless'- a term used to represent a set of experiences during a travel journey happening effortlessly and yet customized to the traveller's needs and interests. The Covid-19 crisis has enhanced the importance of 'seamless travel' as coronavirus has exposed the invisible risks associated with physical touchpoints (Zhang, 2020).

Therefore, the goal of a 'hands-free experience' has become paramount for both travellers and brands. The hotel industry is forced to introduce digital concierge bots, digital check-in, digital room keys, in-room voice for customer safety, contactless temperature-check kiosk, digital guest registration system. There is evidence that hotels are eliminating 'touchpoints' in their internal operations by allowing hotel staff to track and schedule the cleanliness of "high foot traffic" areas to provide a safe environment for their staff and guests (Sorrells, 2021). The technology in the form of chatbots, virtual reality (VR), AI, 5G network, Wi-Fi 6, digital check-in, digital room keys, the in-room voice for customer safety, contactless temperature-check kiosk, digital guest registration found useful for Covid-19 pandemic also reflect the requirements of I4.0. The discussion clarifies that the pandemic has geared the momentum of adopting such technologies by the tourism and hospitality industry. In the backdrop of such immense changes taking place in the hospitality industry, the classification agencies also need to gear up to adopt such technologies for evaluating hotels and make efforts to rely less on a physical inspection by the inspectors and adopt the approach of seamless hotel classification.

HOTELSTARS UNION CLASSIFICATION SYSTEMS

Tourism is one of the most critical sectors of the Greek economy and a key pillar of economic growth. Tourism Growth Domestic Product (GDP) accounted for 6.8% of total GVA (Gross value added) in 2017, directly employed 381800 people in 2018(10.0% of total employment). Greek hotels star rating system is under the patronage of HOTREC (The Confederation of National Associations of Hotels, Restaurants, Cafés and Similar Establishments in the European Union and European Economic Area) (OECD, 2020). The stringent measures undertaken by HotelStars Union have helped the system is becoming more acceptable amongst the customers. Scheibel (2014) survey reported an increase in the system's popularity from 26% to 47%. However, the system lags behind personal recommendations (74%) and online reviews 52%.

The HotelStars Union hasclassified10330 hotel properties in Greece (Table 1) based on seven primary criteria-Building/ Room, Furniture equipment, Service, Leisure, Arrangement of the offer and In-house Conference facilities. Table 2 explains how the system allocates the highest grades to Furniture/ Equipment (352), followed by Services/ Facilities (285), Leisure (206), Building Rooms (172), Arrangement of an offer-Service Quality system (59) and In-house Conference Facility (47). Based on this criterion, hotels with a score of 570 and above are rated five-star ratings, 380(four-star), 250(three-star), 170(two-star) and hotels with 90 and above points are allocated with (one-star) ratings (Table 3, Figure 1).

Table 1. Total number of star-rated hotels in Greece

Star Category	Number of Hotels
1	1291
2	3798
3	2851
4	1727
5	663
Total	10330

Table 2. Areas of hotel evaluation and maximum score

Area Of Evaluation	Maximum score
Building Rooms	172
Furniture/ Equipment	352
Services/ Facilities	285
Leisure	206
Arrangement of offer-Service Quality system	59
In-house Conference Facility	47
Total	1121

Table 3. Evaluation of hotels under the HotelStars Union classification system

Star Category	1 -Star	2-Star	3-Star	4-Star	5-Star
Number of points required to qualify	90	170	250	380	570

Figure 1. Points required by hotels for the award of star ratings under HotelStars Union

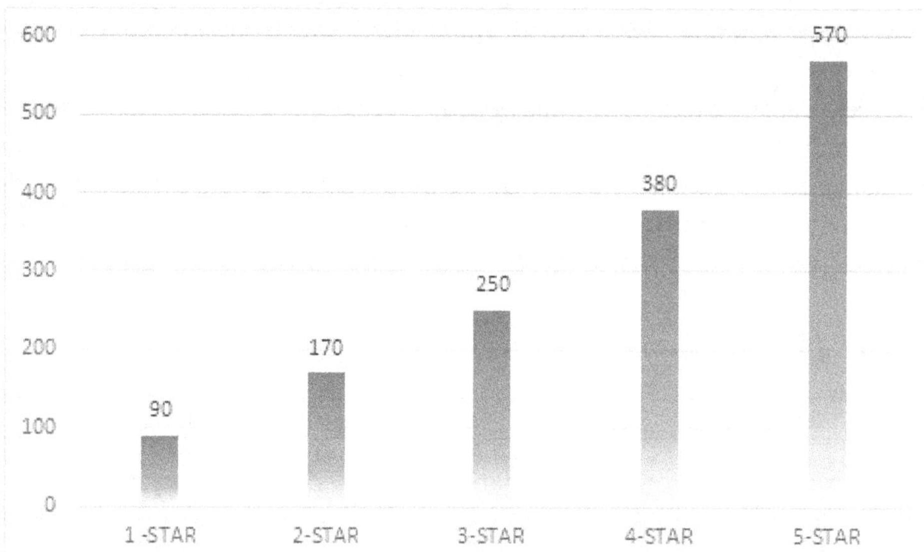

METHODOLOGY

The study's objectives include exploring the relationship between the two different ratings allocated to a sample of hotels in Greece and establishing if the hotels awarded higher star ratings by the traditional classification system (HOTREC) are also rated high by the travellers TripAdvisor. To explore the first objective, a quantitative method is compared to study the relationship between the ratings and the mean score of TripAdvisor ratings of thirty hotels of each star category (five, four, three, two and one). The traditional classification ratings convey hotel service quality through several stars- one star means lowest, and five-star ratings mean highest hotel service quality. The comparison with TripAdvisor ratings shall offer insight into the relationship between the two different hotel rating systems. To address objective two of the chapter, mean ratings of one, two, three, four and five-star hotels shall be compared to establish the statistical difference between such hotels- especially if the higher star rated hotels four and five-stars are highly rated TripAdvisor also. For this purpose, the following hypothesis shall be tested.

$H_0$1 *There is no significant difference between the TripAdvisor ratings of different star-rated hotels.*

The data for the chapter was gathered from the TripAdvisor website. Using the two filters country (Greece) and Star category, the ratings of thirty hotels of each star category five, four, three, two and one) was captured in an excel sheet and using SPSS software, the ratings were analyzed. Among the choice between parametric and non-parametric data tests, the Kruskal-Wallis (non-parametric test) was chosen because the data (TripAdvisor ratings of different hotels) was non-parametric. The test does not assume the normality of the data (Tao, 2020). Therefore, the study uses the Kruskal-Wallis test to compare the mean ratings between hotels of five different star categories of hotels (hypothesis 1). The test investigates whether different samples originated from the same distribution.

Further, the test is an extension of the Mann-Whitney U test used for testing more than two groups. The null hypothesis popularly used for this test is that 'mean ranks of the groups are the same. Since the test is used for non-parametric data, as a substitute for one-way ANOVA, the Kruskal-Wallis test is called one-way ANOVA on ranks. The descriptive statistics of such ratings are computed to compare their standard deviation, mean, median and mode to compare the consistency and robustness.

DATA ANALYSIS

Before applying the Kruskal-Wallis Test, the normality of the data (TripAdvisor hotel ratings) was verified using the Shapiro-Wilk test (Table 4). The significance level of the Shapiro-Wilk test is one-star, ($p = 0.91 > 0.05$), two-star hotels ($p = 0.04 > 0.05$), three-star hotels ($p = 0.00 > 0.05$), four-star hotels ($p = 0.02 > 0.05$) and five-star hotels ($p = 0.00 > 0.05$). The results indicate that the data in all such cases is not normally distributed, and the use of a non-parametric test is justified, therefore.

Table 4. Test of normality

	Kolmogorov-Smirnova			Shapiro-Wilk		
	Statistic	**df**	**Sig.**	**Statistic**	**Df**	**Sig.**
One Star	0.166	30	0.034	0.94	30	0.091
Two Star	0.191	30	0.007	0.888	30	0.004
Three Star	0.243	30	0	0.707	30	0
Four Star	0.247	30	0	0.876	30	0.002
Five Star	0.309	30	0	0.754	30	0
a. Lilliefors Significance						

Table 5. Kruskal Wallis test

	Hotel category
Chi-Square	48.469
df	4
Asymp. Sig.	0

To evaluate the differences between TripAdvisor hotel ratings across five different categories were tested using the Kruskal-Wallis test(Table 5). The test revealed significant difference (Asymp Sig =0) for five different hotel categories (Five-star,n=30;Four-star,n=30; Three-star,n=30; Two-star,n=30 andOne-star,n=30). A Kruskal-Wallis H test showed that there is no statistically significant difference between the five groups H(4)=48, p=0< 0.1, thereby rejecting the null hypothesis set for the study and confirming that there is a significant difference between the TripAdvisor hotel ratings between hotels of different star categories. Therefore, the results reject the first null hypothesis and confirm the alternate hypothesis that there is a significant difference between the TripAdvisor ratings of different star-rated hotels. For the second objective of the chapter, the descriptive statistics of the hotels were computed with SPSS. The median TripAdvisor score of hotels (Table 6) of different star categories indicates that five-star hotels have a very high median score (4) followed by four-star hotels(3), three, two and one-star hotels(1).

Table 6. Median TripAdvisor score

Hotel Star Category	N	Median Trip Advisor Ratings
1	30	1.0000
2	30	1.0000
3	30	1.0000
4	30	3.0000
5	30	4.0000
Total	150	3.0000

Table 7. Descriptive statistics

	N	Minimum	Maximum	Mean	Std. Deviation	Variance
1-Star	30	1.00	4.50	3.2000	.78345	.614
2-Star	30	2.00	4.50	3.7000	.73812	.545
3-Star	30	1.00	4.50	3.5667	1.11211	1.237
4-Star	30	3.50	5.00	4.2000	.42750	.183
5-Star	30	4.00	5.00	4.3333	.30324	.092

Table 7 explores the descriptive statistics of different star category hotel groups. The results indicate the highest mean ratings for five-star hotels (4.33), followed by four-star hotels (4.20), two-star hotels (3.70), three-star hotels (3.56) and one-star hotels (3.20). The results also show that travellers give the highest ratings (5) to four- and a five-star hotel.

DISCUSSION AND CONCLUSION

The TripAdvisor ratings analyzed for a sample of one, two-, three-, four- and five-star Greek Hotels have revealed the significance of online ratings. The data analysis has found similarities in the traveller ratings for hotels and the traditional star ratings allocated to the hotels by HotelStars Union. The highest TripAdvisor mean ratings for five-star hotels convey several messages- first, the TripAdvisor rating system successfully evaluates hotel properties. The travellers can use the traditional star ratings to narrow down the search for each hotel category, allowing them to express their satisfaction with the hotel properties. The results indicate that the traveller's perception about the hotel service quality is in proportion to the level of hotel star rating. The results indicate the importance of both the type of hotel ratings -online hotel ratings and the traditional ratings in each way. While the traditional ratings are commonly used as a filter by the travellers to shortlist hotels of different star categories – the online hotel ratings like the one provided by TripAdvisor help travellers in the making booking related decisions by providing access to the hotel reviews along with pictures of the property shared by the travellers. The literature review also shows how the hotel star ratings mitigate the effect of the negative online hotel reviews posted by travellers. However, the study results can be due to the influence of the ownership pattern of the hotel, as reported by (Ariffin & Maghzi, 2012), explaining how travellers expectations remain primarily unchanged when known chain hotels fail to meet their expectations effectively. Several such mitigating factors can influence the hotel ratings that need to be explored carefully.

SOLUTIONS AND RECOMMENDATIONS

In the backdrop of the study results, the analysis confirms that both ratings agree with each other. The finding establishes the authenticity of traditional hotel ratings, especially in the backdrop of massive criticism in literature especially failing to evaluate hotel service quality. However, as confirmed by (Rhee & Yang, 2015), the traditional ratings still hold considerable significance because of their ability to influence hotel room rates. Therefore, they cannot be written off so quickly. It, therefore, makes sense that the agencies responsible for the traditional classification process take steps to restore the prestige of such ratings by adopting innovative measures in the hotel evaluation process especially adopting the smart tourism techniques based on Information and Communication Technology tools. For example, the traditional hotel rating system does not consider traveller feedback, which is an essential source of information about how hotels are performing.

At present, some classification agencies countries have adopted the online ratings- but for comparative purposes only. Apart from the inspector's report on hotels, the agencies can think about how travellers can be made a part of the rating system so that the creditability of such ratings is enhanced. Further, the concerned agencies must overhaul the traditional rating system by allowing travellers access to comprehensive information and traveller experiences about hotel properties. The lack of information is the most significant area of concern for travellers. The classification agencies at present expect travellers to trust the stars and diamonds exclusively without any supporting evidence. However, the agencies need to adapt to the changing environment, leap out of the pre-internet era, and provide additional information to harness ICT tools and technology. Such an approach shall also take the hotel classification process towards the seamless system and rely less on physical inspection systems. As discussed in Post Covid world- technology should play a significant role in hotel classification also- given the fact that the concept of seamless travel has touched upon all other aspects of travel and tourism.

IMPLICATIONS

The results have indicated that the five-star deluxe hotels have the highest mean guest ratings than any other hotel star category hotel. The better guest ratings of these hotels can be due to various reasons- that include branding. Almost all these hotel chains belong to strong International and national hotel brands. The superior ratings of five-star hotels can result from stringent practices of guest satisfaction, availability of superior workforce, stringent training development, ensuring close monitoring of the guest review and taking measures to improve the same. The results convey that the five-star hotels in Greece can meet the guest expectations better than the other category of the hotels. The HotelStars Union classification system, therefore, accurately represents the guest perceptions about the properties.

The standard operating procedures of those hotel brands are likely to be stringent enough to ensure guest satisfaction and comfort. The award of the higher star ratings by the agency compliments what these hotels stand for. The impressive presence of these hotels compared to three-star, two-star, and one-star hotels on hotel review websites indicate the seriousness of higher star rated hotels towards social media management. The higher category star hotels pay due attention to good ratings on hotel rating websites. These hotels quickly respond to the guest feedback and ensure they improve their services for better guest satisfaction and ratings (Radojevic, Stanisic & Stanic, 2015).

The traveller's ratings on TripAdvisor indicate that the hotels' HotelStar Unions ratings are consistent and statistically representative. In comparison, lower ratings for one, two and three-star hotels can indicate a lack of willingness of such hotels to be listed and improve online guest ratings by a quick response system like higher star rated hotels. The results have further indicated the strong presence of Greek hotels on TripAdvisor.

THEORETICAL CONTRIBUTION

This study contributes to theory as well as practice. The theoretical front attempts to study differences in rating patterns between ratings awarded to hotels in Greece by the HotelStars Union and the ratings awarded by TripAdvisor to such hotels. By exploring such an area, it dovetails the effort to the extent of tourism literature. The findings of this study contribute to the understanding of patterns of hotel ratings from two different agencies. The findings of this study suggest travellers' rating patterns of two different agencies are almost in sync with each other. On the practical front, this study recommends that all hotels continuously monitor their online ratings on different platforms regardless of star ratings. The present study gives the impression that it is mainly the four- and five-star hotels that somehow manage to have good ratings on TripAdvisor. This suggests that to minimize chances of receiving negative ratings, low star category hotels should primarily focus on meeting the traveller expectations. This paper has implications for hotel review websites. As discussed in the literature, the online hotel ratings for five- and four-star hotels could be influenced by hotel branding. Good hotel brands are rated favourably by travellers. Hotel review websites must address the concern to offer travellers real and free of bias information about the hotel to make fairer comparisons between hotels for a well-informed booking decision.

Social media has opportunities for businesses to present information and facts in the most innovative ways leading to the growth of the travel and hospitality industry. Numerous modes of communication are available for businesses-social media and hotel and travel review websites. The first finding of this study is that the higher the star category, the better the guest ratings are among the essential findings. One, two, and three-star categories need to create a system where the guest feedback is recorded, evaluated, improvements are made and exceeds guest expectations. This can happen these hotels acknowledge the role of online ratings. Another important finding is that the online travel companies have a superior mechanism of rating the hotels compared to the official hotel classification system. Whether in Greece or anywhere else, the official classification systems must incorporate the online ratings for guest reference to stay relevant, a practice started by few countries like Norway.

FUTURE RESEARCH DIRECTIONS

The study has several shortcomings that need to be addressed in future studies. First, the study's findings are constrained by the scope of the dataset because it was collected from a single OTA website TripAdvisor. Future studies can collect the online hotel ratings from multiple sources like Expedia, hotels.com, and many such sites to understand better the relationship between online ratings and traditional hotel classification ratings. Second, the restraint of sample size also can be taken into consideration by future studies. The large sample size shall ensure a more accurate picture of the findings. The hotels were not classified into independent or chain, luxury, or budget because of the small sample size. The large sample size shall allow researchers to run parallel tests for such categories of hotels to have a clearer picture of how different types of hotels are influenced by such ratings. The limitation of choosing one geographical region of Greece can be removed by collecting data from multiple cities for comparing the results. A granular country-wise analysis could include representative samples of different hotel categories to ensure better findings. The problems of including such ratings contributed fictitiously by non-bona fide travelers have a potential to distort travelers' perceptions, can interfere with the results. Such possibilities need to be eliminated by proper methods.

REFERENCES

Agrawal, M., Dutta, S., Kelly, R., & Millán, I. (2021). *COVID-19: An inflection point for Industry 4.0.* Retrieved August 1st 2021, from https://www.mckinsey.com/business-functions/operations/our-insights/covid-19-an-inflection-point-for-industry-40#

Anderson, C. K. (2011). Search, OTAs, and Online Booking: An Expanded Analysis of the Billboard Effect. *Cornell Hospitality Report, 11*(8). Retrieved from https://sha.cornell.edu/wp-content/uploads/sites/4/2019/03/christopher-anderson_billboard-effect-still-alive-and-well.pdf

Ariffin, A., & Maghzi, A. (2012). A preliminary study on customer expectations of hotel hospitality: Influences of personal and hotel factors. *International Journal of Hospitality Management, 31*(1), 191–198. doi:10.1016/j.ijhm.2011.04.012

Aristio, A., Supardi, S., Hendrawan, R., & Hidayat, A. (2019). Analysis on Purchase Intention of Indonesian Backpacker in Accommodation Booking through Online Travel Agent. *Procedia Computer Science*, *161*, 885–893. doi:10.1016/j.procs.2019.11.196

Baccarani, C., Marta, U., & Angelo, B. (2015). A Conceptual Service Quality Map:The Value Of A Wide Opened Perspective. *13th Toulon-Verona Conference Excellence in Services.*

Baym, N. K. (2010). *Personal Connections in the Digital Age*. Polity Press.

Büyüközkan, G., Feyzioğlu, O., & Havle, C. (2019). Intuitionistic Fuzzy AHP Based Strategic Analysis of Service Quality in Digital Hospitality Industry. *IFAC-PapersOnLine*, *52*(13), 1687–1692. doi:10.1016/j.ifacol.2019.11.443

Customer Experience Trends in a Post-COVID-19 World | Study. (2021). Retrieved January 6th 2021, from https://www.sitel.com/covid-19-customer-experience-impact-study

Federation of Hong Kong Hotel Owners. (2012). *Proposal to Establish a Hotel Classification System for Hong Kong*. Hong Kong: Federation of Hong Kong Hotel owners. Retrieved August 4th 2021 from http://www.fedhotelowners.com.hk/books/Hotel%20classification%20Jul0300.pdf

Filieri, R., Alguezaui, S., & McLeay, F. (2015). Why do travelers trust TripAdvisor? Antecedents of trust towards consumer-generated media and its influence on recommendation adoption and word of mouth. *Tourism Management*, *51*, 174–185. doi:10.1016/j.tourman.2015.05.007

Foroudi, P. H., Tabaghdehi, S., & Marvi, R. (2021). The gloom of the COVID-19 shock in the hospitality industry: A study of consumer risk perception and adaptive belief in the dark cloud of a pandemic. *International Journal of Hospitality Management*, *92*, 102717. doi:10.1016/j.ijhm.2020.102717

Hashim, K., & Fadhil, N. (2017). Engaging with Customer Using Social Media Platform: A Case Study of Malaysia Hotels. *Procedia Computer Science*, *124*, 4–11. doi:10.1016/j.procs.2017.12.123

Holloway, J., & Humphreys, C. (n.d.). *The business of tourism* (10th ed.). London: Pearson.

Hu, Y., & Chen, K. (2016). Predicting hotel review helpfulness: The impact of review visibility, and interaction between hotel stars and review ratings. *International Journal of Information Management*, *36*(6), 929–944. doi:10.1016/j.ijinfomgt.2016.06.003

Lakhani, K., & Mcafee, A. (2015). *Wikipedia*. Retrieved June 26th 2021, from http://courseware.hbs.edu/public/cases/wikipedia/main.html

Lau, A. (2020). New technologies used in COVID-19 for business survival: Insights from the Hotel Sector in China. *Information Technology & Tourism*, *22*(4), 497–504. doi:10.100740558-020-00193-z

Lee, Y., Xie, K., Besharat, A., & Tan, Y. (2017). Management Responses to Online WOM: Helpful or Detrimental? SSRN *Electronic Journal*. doi:10.2139/ssrn.2919553

Lyu, S. (2016). Which Accessible Travel Products Are People With Disabilities Willing To Pay More. A choice experiment? *Tourism Management*, *59*, 404–412. doi:10.1016/j.tourman.2016.09.002

Li, F., & Ryan, C. (2020). Western guest experiences of a Pyongyang international hotel, North Korea: Satisfaction under conditions of constrained choice. *Tourism Management*, *76*, 103947. doi:10.1016/j.tourman.2019.07.001

Martin-Fuentes, E., Fernandez, C., Mateu, C., & Marine-Roig, E. (2018). Modelling a grading scheme for peer-to-peer accommodation: Stars for Airbnb. *International Journal of Hospitality Management*, *69*, 75–83. doi:10.1016/j.ijhm.2017.10.016

Munar, A., & Jacobsen, J. (2014). Motivations for sharing tourism experiences through social media. *Tourism Management*, *43*, 46–54. doi:10.1016/j.tourman.2014.01.012

Munar, A. M., & Ooi, C.-S. (2012). The truth of the crowds: social media and the heritage experience. In L. Smith, E. Waterton, & S. Watson (Eds.), *The cultural moment in tourism (pp. 255-273)*. Routledge.

OECD Tourism Trends and Policies 2020. (2021). Retrieved June 26th 2021, from https://www.oecd-ilibrary.org/sites/f3180e03-en/index.html?itemId=/content/component/f3180e03

Quo, G. (2014). *Is The Official Hotel Rating System Sinking Into The Past?* 4Hoteliers. Retrieved July 23rd 2014, from http://www.4hoteliers.com/ features/article/7954

Radojevic, T., Stanisic, N., & Stanic, N. (2015). Ensuring positive feedback: Factors that influence customer satisfaction in the contemporary hospitality industry. *Tourism Management*, *51*, 13–21. doi:10.1016/j.tourman.2015.04.002

Rhee, H., & Yang, S. (2015). Does hotel attribute importance differ by hotel? Focusing on hotel star-classifications and customers' overall ratings. *Computers in Human Behavior*, *50*, 576–587. doi:10.1016/j.chb.2015.02.069

Sheibel, K. (2014). *Guests appreciate hotel stars as guidance in the review sky*. http://blog.hotelstars.eu/2014/07/22/ guests-appreciate-hotel-stars-as-guidance-in-the-review-sky/

Sigala, M. (2020). Tourism and COVID-19: Impacts and implications for advancing and resetting IndustryIndustry and research. *Journal of Business Research*, *117*, 312–321. doi:10.1016/j.jbusres.2020.06.015 PMID:32546875

Sorrells, M. (2021). *Touchless tech: How hotels are preparing for a post-COVID guest experience*. PhocusWire. Retrieved January 8th 2021, from https://www.phocuswire.com/contactless-technology-solutions-hotels-covid-19

Talias, M. (2016). Voluntary hotel regulation as a political compromise. *International Journal of Hospitality Management*, *56*, 10–17. doi:10.1016/j.ijhm.2016.04.007

Talwar, S., Dhir, A., Kaur, P., & Mäntymäki, M. (2020). Why do people purchase from online travel agencies (OTAs)? A consumption values perspective. *International Journal of Hospitality Management*, *88*, 102534. doi:10.1016/j.ijhm.2020.102534

Tao, Y. (2020). Progress in molecular biology and translational science. elsevier.com.

Torres, E., Adler, H., & Behnke, C. (2014). Stars, Diamonds, And Other Shiny Things: The Use Of Expert And Consumer Feedback In The Hotel Industry. *Journal of Hospitality and Tourism Management*, *21*, 34–43. doi:10.1016/j.jhtm.2014.04.001

TripAdvisor Popularity Ranking: Key Factors and How to Improve. (2021). Retrieved June 26th 2021, from https://www.tripadvisor.com/TripAdvisorInsights/w722

UNTWO. (2014). Online Guest Reviews and Hotel Classification systems. Madrid, Spain: World Tourism Organization (UNWTO).

Xie, K., Zhang, Z., & Zhang, Z. (2014). The business value of online consumer reviews and management response to hotel performance. *International Journal of Hospitality Management*, *43*, 1–12. doi:10.1016/j.ijhm.2014.07.007

Ye, Q., Law, R., Gu, B., & Chen, W. (2011). The influence of user-generated content on traveler behavior: An empirical investigation on the effects of e-word-of-mouth to hotel online bookings. *Computers in Human Behavior*, *27*(2), 634–639. doi:10.1016/j.chb.2010.04.014

Zhang, J. (2020). Transport Policymaking against COVID-19 and Future Public Health Pandemics: A PASS Approach. SSRN *Electronic Journal*. doi:10.2139/ssrn.3642979

Zhao, M., Li, L., & Xu, Z. (2021). Study on hotel selection method based on integrating online ratings and reviews from multi-websites. *Information Sciences*, *572*, 460–481. doi:10.1016/j.ins.2021.05.042

KEY TERMS AND DEFINITIONS

Algorithms: A finite sequence instructions that are well-defined, implementable for computer instructions aimed at solving specific problems or to perform a computation.

Enterprise 2.0: Integration of Web 2.0 technologies into Intranet, extranet and business processes. Such technologies include blogs, RSS, Social bookmarking, social networking, and wikis.

Hotel Classification System: A system of creating hierarchy of hotels based on the level of service quality, infrastructure, quality of manpower, and other legal aspects.

Official Rating System: Hotel classification system initiated by the Government agencies.

Online Hotel Ratings: Hotel ratings generated by online travel agents and hotel review websites.

Online Travel Agents (OTAs): Internet based travel agency allowing travelers to search and book travel products and services like hotels, cars, flights, tours, etc.

Popularity Index: The index generated by incorporates traveler ratings to determine overall traveler satisfaction using a proprietary algorithm to take into account traveler perceptions about quantity, quality and recency of reviews of products and services.

HotelStars Union: The professional association of hotels, restaurants and cafés in Europe comprising of Austria, Belgium, Czech Republic, Denmark, Estonia, Germany, Greece, Hungary, Latvia, Liechtenstein, Lithuania, Luxembourg, Malta, Netherlands, Slovenia, Sweden, and Switzerland.

Chapter 13
ICT Pandemic Time Adoption and Immersive Technologies:
A Comprehensive Review

Ali Yuce
https://orcid.org/0000-0003-4700-2006
School of Graduate Studies and Tourist Guidance, Cappadocia University, Turkey

ABSTRACT

It was not until recently that we could imagine immersive technology's popularity would be raised and adaptability would reshape almost all businesses in the tourism landscape. Immersive technology has been a transition phenomenon from a traditional marketing strategy to a postmodern approach that encourages, motivates, and satisfies the potential consumers towards a particular tourism product or service. On the other hand, the tourism industry has been the hardest hit and most suffering sector due to the declaration of emergency measures such as travel bans which caused catastrophic consequences in the industry during the coronavirus pandemic. Hence, this chapter intends to present comprehensive reviews about the impact of COVID-19 on the tourism industry through conceptualizing and contextualizing the remarkable aspects of innovation, digitalization, and digital transformation using immersive technologies.

INTRODUCTION

Tourism is a vital economic activity, particularly for emerging economies. Many developed or developing countries depend on tourism revenue to drive their economies. Tourism has grown rapidly and gradually (except the global pandemic COVID-19 period) over the past several decades (Yuce, 2021). Tourism significantly impacts overall economic growth as a major source of foreign exchange earnings that enhances livelihoods and improves citizens' living standards in developing and developed countries (Hidalgo, Martín-Barroso, Nuñez-Serrano, Turrión, & Velázquez, 2022). According to the World Tourism Organization (WTO), tourism is the third-largest industry which accounts for 7% of the global trade while creating a large portion of (one in ten jobs) employment worldwide (UNWTO, 2020). Yet, despite the

DOI: 10.4018/978-1-7998-9227-4.ch013

increasing visiting number and expectations about overall improvement in the tourism industry by 10% during the post-corona era, tourism businesses feel competitive pressures to increase their productivity and efficiency while reducing operational costs.

On the other hand, besides natural disasters and political crises, pandemics and epidemics also negatively impact businesses, individuals, and societies. Suffice it to say that the novel COVID-19 has proved one more time that tourism is a highly sensitive industry, which is hardest hit one, towards the external harmful events such politic, economic crises, and disaster and pandemic (Gretzel et al., 2020; Hidalgo et al., 2022; Zhong, Sun, Law, & Li, 2021). Although the tourism industry faced challenges with the previous numerous disasters and pandemics, COVID-19 has caused more severe challenges due to the uncertain duration, magnitude, speed, and prevalence of the pandemic, particularly in the tourism industry, which relies on the mobilization of its consumers. UNWTO (2020) reports that tourism originated export revenue (between $910 billion and $1.2 Trillion) lost could reduce the global GDP by 1.5% to 2.8% in 2020. The impact of COVID-19 can be assessed by investigating from several dimensions to the tourism industry as a whole and from business, employees, and tourist perspectives. All these aspects are crucial to providing helpful strategies for all the shareholders in the tourism industry.

COVID-19 had a significant negative impact on the tourism industry (Gössling, Scott, & Hall, 2020; Karatepe, Saydam, & Okumus, 2021). One of the first and the most vulnerable effect of the COVID-19 was widespread business closures due to travel restrictions, strict lockdowns, and isolations during the coronavirus pandemics (T. Baum & Hai, 2020; Gössling et al., 2020; Karatepe et al., 2021; Ntounis, Parker, Skinner, Steadman, & Warnaby, 2021; Park, Kim, & Kim, 2020). In particular, as the duration and prevalence of the pandemic last in a longer period, its negative impact also gets more vulnerable to businesses of all sizes. The majority of the current studies report that the tourism industry is also suffering to respond and survive during the COVID-19 pandemics (Mao, He, Morrison, & Andres Coca-Stefaniak, 2020; Sharma, Shin, Santa-María, & Nicolau, 2021). COVID-19 put the businesses, whether small, medium, or large-sized enterprises, viability or sustainability at great risk in terms of mandatory closing the hotels and accommodations restaurants temporarily or permanently. According to recent studies, the consequences of the pandemics have been hurting the tourism-dependent country economies heavily. Hence, one of the most crucial elements that can protect the businesses' long-term survival requires several measures such as solidarity among business owners, tourism employees and their unions, and governmental support. A study suggests that organizations can attract tourists by offering more services with lower fees to ensure that the businesses survive pre and post COVID-19 pandemics (Lai & Wong, 2020; Neuburger & Egger, 2021; Ritchie & Jiang, 2019). Another approach that can help organizations confront economic-related concerns and hardship is transforming the classical business operation into a digital platform where businesses can serve year-round (Dantas et al., 2021).

From the labor perspective, millions of employees and their families have already relied on low and irregular wages have already been suffering from extremely long working hours, living in poor conditions, and lacking labor and social rights. Jiang and Wen (2020) and Hang, Aroean, and Chen (2020) stated that COVID-19 did not only damage traveling at the local, national and international levels, but it also had significant emotional outcomes on an individual level. Some of these detrimental consequences are such as disappointment and anxiety employees owing to the fear of losing being transmitted of virus and losing the loved ones, and other traveling restrictions (Jungmann & Witthöft, 2020; Karatepe et al., 2021; Landi, Pakenham, Boccolini, Grandi, & Tossani, 2020). UNWTO (2020) also asserted that COVID-19 had placed 100 to 120 million direct tourism jobs at risk. This severe impact threads the employees' livelihoods and their psychological well-being in the long term. The Covid-19 pandemic-based stress and uncertainty of the future are closely associated because those mentioned above the escalated high risk of virus transmission threatens the economic affairs in the tourism industry and causes mental health issues of the tourism employees. COVID-19 stress has caused various challenges and dramatic afflictions among individuals and organizations because of the growing fear of uncertainty and lack of efficient diagnosis and treatment procedures in current epidemiology despite available numerous vaccination and other preventive measures (Gretzel et al., 2020; Karatepe et al., 2021; Neuburger & Egger, 2021).

On the other hand, from the consumer perspective, tourism has a significant correlation with the employment rate across the world. In addition to a massive negative impact on organizations' millions of employees, travelers have also suffered and experienced severe traumatic grounded mental health issues due to the socio-economic hardship and uncertain future due to direct or indirect exposure to the most recent pandemic called SARS-2 or COVID-19. According to the Forum (2021), Devastating COVID-19, as one of the most recent disasters, has been jeopardizing the existence and well-being of people while it places all sizes of organizations' survival at a particular risk around the world (Karatepe et al., 2021; Sara A. Cloonan, 2021). People have not traveled since the beginning of these pandemics due to flight cancellations. Besides the negative impacts of coronavirus on various industries, it also undermines people's psychological resources worldwide. COVID-19 has altered tourists' visiting approach and behavior significantly. Unlike previous disasters and crises, the pandemics' duration and vagueness have forced individuals to use alternative strategies such as information communication technologies (Yeh, 2021).

BACKGROUND

COVID-19 and ICT Impact of Digitalization on the Tourism Industry

As noted above, the COVID-19 pandemic halted many businesses, resulting in devastating financial costs around the globe (Dantas et al., 2021). The tourism sector has direct, indirect, and induced benefits on many economies. Besides the business owners of all sizes of the companies, employees also try to cope with the disrupted income sources and livelihood while discovering alternative strategies to recover from the traumatic emotional disorder (Dube, Nhamo, & Chikodzi, 2021; Kapoor, Yadav, Bajpai, & Srivastava, 2021). Moreover, the tourism industry has been experiencing a dramatic down (87%) in 'tourist arrivals numbers in January 2021 compared to 2020 January (UNWTO, 2021). At this point, transforming the tourism services into a digital platform using the right, effective, and adaptable digital mediums can overcome most of these challenges. Within the context of tourism, the expansion of technology plays a key role in creating enormous opportunities for the supply and demand sides of the tourism industry.

The role of information and communication technologies in the tourism area has been significantly changed even quickly during the past several decades, particularly with the emergence of the 4th Industrial Revolution (Gonzalez, Gasco, & Llopis, 2020; Law, Buhalis, & Cobanoglu, 2014). Digitalization has been recognized as one of the greatest opportunities to achieve organizational goals and improve customer satisfaction in the tourism industry landscape (J. Lee, Cameron, & Hassall, 2019). In the rapidly changing travel and hospitality industry, the growth of transportation, logistic, distribution, and promotion of goods and services have been paralleled by the digital transformation. In response to the pandemic-related disruption, businesses have undergone radical changes in the transformation of their infrastructure.

Businesses in almost all industries, especially the service sector, whether they are technology adopted or not, grapple with the delirious effects of COVID-19. However, technology is an effective alternative approach to curb the damaging effects of the pandemics and helps them for economic recovery in the eye of pandemics (Yuce, 2021). As noted earlier, unprecedented COVID-19 negatively and dramatically impacts socio-economic, psychological, and physical well-being and the high risk of business' sustainability (Dube et al., 2021; Karatepe et al., 2021). Although vaccination efforts helped control the speed of COVID-19 among individuals, it continues threading the organizations' viability at great risk due to sole dependency on tourism affairs. ICT has unmeasurable benefits for the business to respond, maintain and revive from the economic failures of this vicious pandemic (Gretzel et al., 2020). Technology helps them by providing adaptable and adaptable approaches, knowledge, and ability to improve the organizations' and employees' productivity and instant and enhanced communication accessibility and creating effective marketing styles to all contemporary workplaces. Technology does not only help organizations to be reborn from unprecedented disasters of any kind, such as pandemics, but it also supports them in maintaining and strengthening their economic existence in the highly competitive tourism industry in a post-COVID-19 era (Abbas, Mubeen, Iorember, Raza, & Mamirkulova, 2021; Islam, 2021; Sharma et al., 2021).

Digital Transformation and Innovation

Digital transformation has begun during Industry 3.0, which refers to the third industrial revolution, and since then, it has been the primary parameter of economic growth and catalyzer for globalization (Adeyeri, 2018). With the development of sophisticated **information and communication technologies (ICT),** digitalization has accelerated postindustrial society's transformation and led to the emergence of digital-age society (Martins et al., 2017). Digitalization's vitality has been recognized and considered as the most important dimension of Industry 4.0 (Ghobakhloo, 2020; Silvestri, Forcina, Introna, Santolamazza, & Cesarotti, 2020), which refers to the fourth industrial revolution and Society 5.0 (Fukuyama, 2018), a human-centered society in which virtual and physical spaces are proximate. Industry 3.0 heavily consisted of an automated process by implementing smart ICT.

In industry 3.0, there has been little room for human involvement in producing services and goods. Apart from Industry 3.0, Industry 4.0 aims to eliminate human intervention due to the comprehensive autonomous integration of Cyber-Physical Systems (CPS) (Pivoto et al., 2021; Zanero, 2017) and highly sophisticated technologies such as Artificial Intelligence (AI) (Lv, Chen, Lou, & Alazab, 2021), machine and deep learning technologies (Neshat, Moayedfar, Rezaee, & Amrollahi Biuki, 2021). The historical and technical aspects of the Society 5.0 and Industry 4.0 are beyond the concept of this study. Therefore, we will focus on the features and role of immersive technologies in the tourism and hospitality landscape in the following sections.

There has been confusion on the definition of digital transformation, digitalization, and digitization terminologies in the extant literature. *Digitization* (Ghobakhloo, 2020) refers to converting analog data or physical objects into digital data sets or digital representation. D*igitalization* (Filipiak, Dylewski, & Kalinowski, 2020) is a process of integrating various and existing technologies in social, private, and workplace platforms. Digitalization presents numerous benefits for companies that adopt and keep up with it to unleash business and employee potential, lowering operational costs while improving customer satisfaction (Filipiak et al., 2020; Sharma et al., 2021). On the other hand, *digital transformation* differs from the antic approaches and systems regarding the solutions they used to produce for business operations and marketing (Yuce, 2021). Digital transformation is a phenomenon that integrates sophisticated digital technologies that present instant and faster information/knowledge to the users/consumers compared to the old-fashioned methods, applications, and tools such as radio, brochures, and newspapers (J. Lee et al., 2019; Parviainen, Tihinen, Kääriäinen, & Teppola, 2017; Schweer & Sahl, 2017). There is no doubt that with the future digitalization-driven innovations, digital representation of tangible and intangible non-digital information and objects will be converted and presented to individuals with more sophisticated technologies at a light speed.

MAIN FOCUS OF THE CHAPTER

Issues, Controversies, and Problems

Many industries have experienced a significant loss; however, as noted above, the tourism industry has been one of the most suffering service sectors during the most recent catastrophic events of COVID-19 epidemics (Hidalgo et al., 2022; Karatepe et al., 2021; Neshat et al., 2021). Despite the devastating toxic effects of COVID-19, some companies that have completed and embraced the digital innovation process using the most recent digital innovative technologies and the knowledgeable employees have provided a safe, healthy, and flexible virtual environment during the increased complexity and uncertainty of the tourism sector (Abbas et al., 2021). While businesses engage with inclusiveness, they strive to embrace technology's unprecedented newer transformational power (Gretzel et al., 2020). Transformational power is one of the most notable features of digitalization since digital transformation allows organizations and societies to form a new model of business and life.

From the traveling perspective, advanced digitalization has been a driving force for business efficiency and sectorial transformation in the landscape of tourism. Digital transformation allowed some tourism organizations such as museums and historical areas to transform their walk-in-based classical business approach to the digitalized business-driven virtual platforms (Errichiello, Micera, Atzeni, & Del Chiappa, 2019; H. Lee, Jung, tom Dieck, & Chung, 2020). Digitalization in a business environment refers to the ability and capability of bringing digital technology into the workplace. Moreover, digitalization creates and offers considerable benefits and helps tourism-depended organizations ensure business stability, sustainability, and growth in a very fragile and highly compatible tourism marketplace (Sharma et al., 2021).

Innovation is another crucial concept that requires public or private organizations, companies, and businesses of all sizes to succeed in their organizational goals and remains compatible in their socio-economic spheres (Sharma et al., 2021). On the one hand, innovation aims to introduce fundamentally new and visional ideas, methods, and approaches that provide novel guidance and solutions to make revolutionary changes and help create or add remarkable value in a private, public, or business environment. In this context, although there is no common agreement on the definition of innovation, it can be defined as 'innovation is an idea that goes beyond renovation process which produces notable and, valuable outcomes for individuals, business and society. On the other hand, technological innovation is a process of implementing either the newest technologies or significantly newer and much superior versions of the current technologies, but displacing the previous ones and making revolutionary changes in the workplace (J. A. C. Baum, 2001). Technology-driven innovation serves as a locomotive for the tourism organization to leverage its business capacity and performance while helping to establish a sustainable development position in the very competitive and fragile travel industry. Technological innovations have enormous potential to help organizations to survive during hard times.

Immersive Technologies: Virtual Reality and Augmented Reality

Immersive technologies have elicited remarkable digital transformations that create novel business operations improvements, lower operational costs, sectoral growth, and consumer satisfaction (Loureiro, Guerreiro, & Ali, 2020; Marasco, Buonincontri, van Niekerk, Orlowski, & Okumus, 2018; Yuce, Arasli, Ozturen, & Daskin, 2020). With the most recent technological innovations, immersive technologies have become integrated with our personal lives and workplaces (Atzeni, Del Chiappa, & Mei Pung, 2021; Beck, Rainoldi, & Egger, 2019). Individuals enjoyed experiencing virtual, real, or mixed environments through immersive technologies. Moreover, businesses have taken significant advantages and benefits by implementing these new innovative technologies to improve business outputs and increase visitor satisfaction with the newest business insights, ideas, and concepts in the tourism industry (van Nuenen & Scarles, 2021; Wortley, 2013). Due to the remarkable similarities and the lack of clarity and familiarity of the immersive technologies, people often confuse the functionality and definition of the VR and AR technologies (Beck et al., 2019). However, there are differences between these two immersive technologies, which integrate the real-world physical environment with the stimulated location using virtual devices and platforms (Beck et al., 2019; Weber-Sabil & Han, 2021).

Virtual Reality and Virtual Tourism and Virtual Workplace

Although modern Virtual Reality (VR), with its mobilized head-mounted displays (HDM) using smartphones, is in its early stage of development, it has become a fundamentally effective marketing tool of the tourism industry for the past several years (Guttentag, 2010; Lu et al., 2021; Yuce, 2021). Virtual Reality has been one of the leading emerging technologies convincing and inspiring potential travelers towards the destinations with its unique features (Flavián, Ibáñez-Sánchez, & Orús, 2021). Virtual Reality has wholly revamped tourism products delivery and turned into a mobilized environment where potential consumers could visit the destinations while sitting on their couches due to the advanced telepresence functionality of the latest VR technology (Lu et al., 2021). As noted above, telepresence or sense of presence is the backbone characteristic of virtual reality technologies. Furthermore, as its implementation has been flourishing, VR's notable impact in developing sustainable tourism has also been discovered over the past few years.

Virtual Reality has been an innovative resource to the tourism industry to transition from a classical marketing approach to the most effective technological solutions. VR enables high-quality 2D or 3D authentic images or real videos to present instant access to a broader population and at speed light. Virtual Reality also provides more significant customer satisfaction than other technologies because of its 'try before you buy option, convenience for accessibility, and interactive engagement with the immersive content (Guttentag, 2010; Yuce et al., 2020). Furthermore, VR changes how tourism works; in a traditional tourism business, consumers must be mobilized from their homes to a destination to experience a tourism product. However, virtual reality technology converts the tourism services and products into a virtual environment which expands the accessibility of these resources to a broader layer of the society by taking the tourism products to the people's homes.

Business owners, authorities, and consumers have been interested in how to experience a depicted environment in which as if they are present virtually during the simulation. Virtual reality is among one of the most used innovative technologies in the past few decades, even though the root of the VR idea goes back to the 1930s. VR technology depends on computer-generated 360-degree simulations through images or videos, creating highly immersive direct and intuitive user interaction (Bricken & Byrne, 1993). With the advent of the invention of VR headsets, the feeling immersed has been increased at a greater level, which led more realistic and exciting experience for the users (Beck et al., 2019; Yuce et al., 2020). Besides VR headsets, developers have also been working on even more cutting-edge innovative technologies and interactive devices such as gloves and bodysuits that stimulate and capture the user at a level that allows the user to feel as if they are in a realistic environment. If we need to give an example, someone can feel like they are in a hot balloon over the antic Cappadocia area while having dinner in another part of the world. This example or type of experience might have sounded futuristic or an unbelievable science fiction before the digital era began. However, immersive technologies create such a sense of presence in a simulated location as real as possible (H. Lee et al., 2020). Hence, the increased telepresence or sense of presence-based experience via immersive technologies makes this technology a unique and more promising digitalized tool for businesses of all sizes in all sectors (Wortley, 2013; Yuce et al., 2020).

Digital Tourism using VR and AR

VR is one of the most effective and promising marketing tools that present numerous benefits, such as entertainment activity for destinations and businesses in boosting their performance, creating more favorable and substitutable destinations, and improving their competitiveness in global tourism commerce (Guttentag, 2010; Lu et al., 2021). As already mentioned, VR is an inclusive technology that removes the accessibility barriers and excludes tourism resources due to the physical, financial, or other challenges individuals encounter. Furthermore, VR offers opportunities to maximize tourism business potential while reducing the cost of supply and demand sides and enabling the accessibility of the tourism contents affordably and conveniently (Flavián et al., 2021; Yuce, 2021). The majority of the studies report a significant positive correlation between VR technology and consumers' perceptions of destinations.

The majority of the current studies also posit the importance of digital transformation in immersive technologies. According to these studies, advanced immersive technology has been a transition phenomenon from a traditional marketing strategy to a postmodern approach that encourages, motivates, and satisfies the potential consumers towards a particular tourism product or service. From the postmodern marketing perspective, digital transformation in tourism changes the production technique, system and delivers value to customers quickly and effectively regardless of the accessibility issues. In this context, with the advent and implementation of VR technology into the tourism industry, many destinations have used VR as a sophisticated marketing substitution device to appeal to the potential visitors' destination preferences and influence their choice attitude. In particular, due to constant advancements in immersive technologies, innovative hardware and software development have played a game changer role in the service and marketing landscape.

Moreover, as innovation in technology advances, most devices, including phones and computers, got smaller and their overall efficiency in speed, performance and usability increased even at a greater level. For example, the integration of mobilized wearable virtual glasses and cellphones using the VR applications through the various online stores helped a significant achievement in the tourism field. Unlike the applicability of VR technology in the context of the tourism industry, characteristics of AR technology does not allow the users to experience the virtual tourism options while people have been lockdown in their houses during the COVID-19 (Gössling et al., 2020; Lu et al., 2021; Sigala, 2020). Nevertheless, AR technology's impact on users' perception and intention to visit a destination and marketing purposes should not be underestimated.

SOLUTIONS AND RECOMMENDATIONS

As a result, immersive technologies have enormous potential and can help organizations revive from the coronavirus pandemic's ashes (Lu et al., 2021). While the socio-economic cost rises due to the coronavirus pandemic, organizations strive to minimize the loss of their human and fiscal resources with a greater investment in technology. However, the most appropriate and cost-effective information community technologies (ICT) can be a key element in recovering from the pandemics' short-term, medium, and long-term harmful effects.

CONCLUSIONS AND FUTURE WORK

ICT has been the major factor that helped world trade, in terms of large firms, remain on track during the COVID-19. Yet, small and medium-sized businesses (SMBs) have not proportionally benefited from the technology-oriented developments in the face of unprecedented COVID-19 (Forum, 2021). Hence, as stated earlier, small businesses need to adopt technologically oriented strategies to overcome the long-term negative effects of pandemics and crises before jeopardizing their business sustainability or survival.

In particular, immersive technologies have vast potential for sectoral growth and present an alternative digitalized tourism environment for all but especially tourism-dependent destinations. Hence, it is essential to understand the immersive technology's epistemological aspect to rip the benefits of the technology-enabled marketing solutions and create alternative tourism approaches. In this context, by implementing advanced immersive technology with cutting-edge and adaptable applications, the tourism sector will effectively confront the crisis, overcome the hardships, and endure the challenges during hard times, such as the unprecedented COVID-19 outbreak. Organizations and entrepreneurs should understand and meet the dynamics and nature of society's constant changes and tourist behavior. They must adapt to the most innovative technologies to enrich their potential and deepen an engaging customer experience. Implementation of VR or AR technology also helps organizations continually transform their business operations according to the consumers' changing behaviors, expectations, attitudes, and motives regardless of how technological transformation can be disruptive and entails unprecedented adaptation challenges. Therefore, this study suggests that investors consider VR and AR technologies that enable postmodern alternative approaches away from classical marketing strategies.

To shed further light on the impact of immersive, innovative technologies developments in the tourism sector, this research reveals that VR-driven innovative technology plays a remarkable transition in transforming and reshaping the entire tourism industry for sustainable, responsible, affordable, accessible, and inclusive tourism development around the globe. Furthermore, unlike the current popular outlook for the benefits of VR technology, this study also put forward some critical aspects of immersive technologies to spur the organizations' short and long-term productivity growth and coping strategies with the growing global challenges the industry faced during the last few years. Finally, in addition to the abovementioned significant benefits, the technology-driven global economy also presents significant opportunities such as conserving the environment, including the historical resources, and the overall business growth for responsible and sustainable tourism development in developed and developing countries worldwide.

REFERENCES

Abbas, J., Mubeen, R., Iorember, P. T., Raza, S., & Mamirkulova, G. (2021). Exploring the impact of COVID-19 on tourism: Transformational potential and implications for a sustainable recovery of the travel and leisure industry. *Current Research in Behavioral Sciences*, *2*, 100033. doi:10.1016/j.crbeha.2021.100033

Adeyeri, M. K. (2018). From Industry 3.0 to Industry 4.0: Smart Predictive Maintenance System as Platform for Leveraging. *Art Journal*, *71*(11), 64–81.

Atzeni, M., Del Chiappa, G., & Mei Pung, J. (2021). Enhancing visit intention in heritage tourism: The role of object-based and existential authenticity in non-immersive virtual reality heritage experiences. *International Journal of Tourism Research*. doi:10.1002/jtr.2497

Baum, J. A. C. (2001). Ecology: Organizations. In N. J. Smelser & P. B. Baltes (Eds.), *International Encyclopedia of the Social & Behavioral Sciences* (pp. 4048–4053). Pergamon. doi:10.1016/B0-08-043076-7/04206-6

Baum, T., & Hai, N. (2020). *Hospitality, tourism, human rights and the impact of COVID-19*. Academic Press.

Beck, J., Rainoldi, M., & Egger, R. (2019). Virtual reality in tourism: A state-of-the-art review. *Tourism Review*, *74*(3), 586–612. doi:10.1108/TR-03-2017-0049

Bricken, M., & Byrne, C. M. (1993). Summer Students in Virtual Reality: A Pilot Study on Educational Applications of Virtual Reality Technology. In A. Wexelblat (Ed.), *Virtual Reality* (pp. 199–217). Academic Press. doi:10.1016/B978-0-12-745045-2.50019-2

Cloonan, Persich, Dailey, & Killgore. (2021). Sleep and Resilience during the COVID-19 Pandemic. *IntechOpen*. doi:0.5772/intechopen.98298

Dantas, C., Mackiewicz, K., Tageo, V., Jacucci, G., Guardado, D., Ortet, S., . . . Vassiliou, C. (2021). Benefits and Hurdles of AI In The Workplace@ What Comes Next? *COVID-19 Cripples Global Restaurant and Hospitality Industry, 24*(11), 1487-1490.

Errichiello, L., Micera, R., Atzeni, M., & Del Chiappa, G. (2019). Exploring the implications of wearable virtual reality technology for museum visitors' experience: A cluster analysis. *International Journal of Tourism Research*, *21*(5), 590–605. doi:10.1002/jtr.2283

Filipiak, B. Z., Dylewski, M., & Kalinowski, M. (2020). Economic development trends in the EU tourism industry. Towards the digitalization process and sustainability. *Quality & Quantity*. Advance online publication. doi:10.100711135-020-01056-9 PMID:33132445

Flavián, C., Ibáñez-Sánchez, S., & Orús, C. (2021). Impacts of technological embodiment through virtual reality on potential guests' emotions and engagement. *Journal of Hospitality Marketing & Management, 30*(1), 1–20. doi:10.1080/19368623.2020.1770146

Forum, W. E. (2021). *For a true economic recovery, small businesses will need more support*. Retrieved from https://www.weforum.org/agenda/2020/12/small-businesses-will-need-more-support-for-covid-recovery/

Fukuyama, M. (2018). Society 5.0: Aiming for a new human-centered society. *Japan Spotlight, 27*, 47–50.

Ghobakhloo, M. (2020). Industry 4.0, digitization, and opportunities for sustainability. *Journal of Cleaner Production, 252*, 119869. doi:10.1016/j.jclepro.2019.119869

Gonzalez, R., Gasco, J., & Llopis, J. (2020). Information and communication technologies and human resources in hospitality and tourism. *International Journal of Contemporary Hospitality Management, 32*(11), 3545–3579. doi:10.1108/IJCHM-04-2020-0272

Gössling, S., Scott, D., & Hall, C. M. (2020). Pandemics, tourism and global change: A rapid assessment of COVID-19. *Journal of Sustainable Tourism, 29*(1), 1–20. doi:10.1080/09669582.2020.1758708

Gretzel, U., Fuchs, M., Baggio, R., Hoepken, W., Law, R., Neidhardt, J., Pesonen, J., Zanker, M., & Xiang, Z. (2020). e-Tourism beyond COVID-19: A call for transformative research. *Información Tecnológica, 22*(2), 187–203. doi:10.100740558-020-00181-3

Guttentag, D. A. (2010). Virtual reality: Applications and implications for tourism. *Tourism Management, 31*(5), 637–651. doi:10.1016/j.tourman.2009.07.003

Hang, H., Aroean, L., & Chen, Z. (2020). Building emotional attachment during COVID-19. *Annals of Tourism Research, 83*, 103006. doi:10.1016/j.annals.2020.103006 PMID:32834221

Hidalgo, A., Martín-Barroso, D., Nuñez-Serrano, J. A., Turrión, J., & Velázquez, F. (2022). Does hotel management matter to overcoming the COVID-19 crisis? The Spanish case. *Tourism Management, 88*, 104395. doi:10.1016/j.tourman.2021.104395 PMID:34720321

Islam, M. (2021). *International tourism during and after COVID-19: The role of digital technology*. Academic Press.

Jiang, Y., & Wen, J. (2020). *Effects of COVID-19 on hotel marketing and management: a perspective article*. Academic Press.

Jungmann, S. M., & Witthöft, M. (2020). Health anxiety, cyberchondria, and coping in the current COVID-19 pandemic: Which factors are related to coronavirus anxiety? *Journal of Anxiety Disorders, 73*, 102239. doi:10.1016/j.janxdis.2020.102239 PMID:32502806

Kapoor, V., Yadav, J., Bajpai, L., & Srivastava, S. (2021). Perceived stress and psychological well-being of working mothers during COVID-19: A mediated moderated roles of teleworking and resilience. *Employee Relations: The International Journal, 43*(6), 1290–1309. doi:10.1108/ER-05-2020-0244

Karatepe, O. M., Saydam, M. B., & Okumus, F. (2021). COVID-19, mental health problems, and their detrimental effects on hotel employees' propensity to be late for work, absenteeism, and life satisfaction. *Current Issues in Tourism, 24*(7), 934–951. doi:10.1080/13683500.2021.1884665

Lai, I. K. W., & Wong, J. (2020). *Comparing crisis management practices in the hotel industry between initial and pandemic stages of COVID-19*. Academic Press.

Landi, G., Pakenham, K. I., Boccolini, G., Grandi, S., & Tossani, E. (2020). *Health anxiety and mental health outcome during COVID-19 lockdown in Italy: the mediating and moderating roles of psychological flexibility*. Academic Press.

Law, R., Buhalis, D., & Cobanoglu, C. (2014). Progress on information and communication technologies in hospitality and tourism. *International Journal of Contemporary Hospitality Management, 26*(5), 727–750. doi:10.1108/IJCHM-08-2013-0367

Lee, H., Jung, T. H., tom Dieck, M. C., & Chung, N. (2020). Experiencing immersive virtual reality in museums. *Information & Management, 57*(5), 103229. doi:10.1016/j.im.2019.103229

Lee, J., Cameron, I., & Hassall, M. (2019). Improving process safety: What roles for Digitalization and Industry 4.0? *Process Safety and Environmental Protection, 132*, 325–339. doi:10.1016/j.psep.2019.10.021

Loureiro, S. M. C., Guerreiro, J., & Ali, F. (2020). 20 years of research on virtual reality and augmented reality in tourism context: A text-mining approach. *Tourism Management, 77*, 104028. doi:10.1016/j.tourman.2019.104028

Lu, J., Xiao, X., Xu, Z., Wang, C., Zhang, M., & Zhou, Y. (2021). The potential of virtual tourism in the recovery of tourism industry during the COVID-19 pandemic. *Current Issues in Tourism*, 1–17. doi:10.1080/13683500.2021.1922363

Lv, Z., Chen, D., Lou, R., & Alazab, A. (2021). Artificial intelligence for securing industrial-based cyber–physical systems. *Future Generation Computer Systems, 117*, 291–298. doi:10.1016/j.future.2020.12.001

Mao, Y., He, J., Morrison, A. M., & Andres Coca-Stefaniak, J. (2020). Effects of tourism CSR on employee psychological capital in the COVID-19 crisis: From the perspective of conservation of resources theory. *Current Issues in Tourism*, 1–19. doi:10.1080/13683500.2020.1770706

Marasco, A., Buonincontri, P., van Niekerk, M., Orlowski, M., & Okumus, F. (2018). Exploring the role of next-generation virtual technologies in destination marketing. *Journal of Destination Marketing & Management, 9*, 138–148. doi:10.1016/j.jdmm.2017.12.002

Neshat, N., Moayedfar, S., Rezaee, K., & Amrollahi Biuki, N. (2021). Sustainable planning of developing tourism destinations after COVID-19 outbreak: A deep learning approach. *Journal of Policy Research in Tourism, Leisure & Events*, 1–21. doi:10.1080/19407963.2021.1970578

Neuburger, L., & Egger, R. (2021). Travel risk perception and travel behaviour during the COVID-19 pandemic 2020: A case study of the DACH region. *Current Issues in Tourism, 24*(7), 1003–1016. doi:10.1080/13683500.2020.1803807

Ntounis, N., Parker, C., Skinner, H., Steadman, C., & Warnaby, G. (2021). Tourism and Hospitality industry resilience during the Covid-19 pandemic: Evidence from England. *Current Issues in Tourism*, 1–14. doi:10.1080/13683500.2021.1883556

Park, E., Kim, W.-H., & Kim, S.-B. (2020). *Tracking tourism and hospitality employees' real-time perceptions and emotions in an online community during the COVID-19 pandemic*. Academic Press.

Parviainen, P., Tihinen, M., Kääriäinen, J., & Teppola, S. (2017). Tackling the digitalization challenge: how to benefit from digitalization in practice. *International Journal of Information Systems Project Management, 5*(1), 63-77.

Pivoto, D. G. S., de Almeida, L. F. F., da Rosa Righi, R., Rodrigues, J. J. P. C., Lugli, A. B., & Alberti, A. M. (2021). Cyber-physical systems architectures for industrial internet of things applications in Industry 4.0: A literature review. *Journal of Manufacturing Systems*, *58*, 176–192. doi:10.1016/j.jmsy.2020.11.017

Ritchie, B. W., & Jiang, Y. (2019). A review of research on tourism risk, crisis and disaster management: Launching the annals of tourism research curated collection on tourism risk, crisis and disaster management. *Annals of Tourism Research*, *79*, 102812. doi:10.1016/j.annals.2019.102812

Schweer, D., & Sahl, J. C. (2017). The digital transformation of industry–the benefit for Germany. In *The drivers of digital transformation* (pp. 23–31). Springer. doi:10.1007/978-3-319-31824-0_3

Sharma, A., Shin, H., Santa-María, M. J., & Nicolau, J. L. (2021). Hotels' COVID-19 innovation and performance. *Annals of Tourism Research*, *88*, 103180. doi:10.1016/j.annals.2021.103180

Sigala, M. (2020). Tourism and COVID-19: Impacts and implications for advancing and resetting industry and research. *Journal of Business Research*, *117*, 312–321. doi:10.1016/j.jbusres.2020.06.015 PMID:32546875

Silvestri, L., Forcina, A., Introna, V., Santolamazza, A., & Cesarotti, V. (2020). Maintenance transformation through Industry 4.0 technologies: A systematic literature review. *Computers in Industry*, *123*, 103335. doi:10.1016/j.compind.2020.103335

UNWTO. (2020). *Tourism and covid-19 – Unprecedented economic impacts*. Retrieved from https://www.unwto.org/tourism-and-covid-19-unprecedented-economic-impacts

UNWTO. (2021). *UN tourism news #23*. Retrieved from https://www.unwto.org/un-tourism-news-23

van Nuenen, T., & Scarles, C. (2021). Advancements in technology and digital media in tourism. *Tourist Studies*, *21*(1), 119–132. doi:10.1177/1468797621990410

Weber-Sabil, J., & Han, D.-I. D. (2021). *Immersive Tourism-State of the Art of Immersive Tourism Realities through XR Technology*. Academic Press.

Wortley, D. (2013). Immersive Technology Strategies. *Simulation & Gaming*, *44*(2-3), 452–465. doi:10.1177/1046878113488850

Yeh, S.-S. (2021). Tourism recovery strategy against COVID-19 pandemic. *Tourism Recreation Research*, *46*(2), 188–194. doi:10.1080/02508281.2020.1805933

Yuce, A. (2021). The Impact of Digital Transformation and Virtual Reality in Tourism Marketing: A Conceptualized Exploration. In Handbook of Research on IoT, Digital Transformation, and the Future of Global Marketing (pp. 1-14). IGI Global. doi:10.4018/978-1-7998-7192-7.ch001

Yuce, A., Arasli, H., Ozturen, A., & Daskin, M. (2020). Feeling the Service Product Closer: Triggering Visit Intention via Virtual Reality. *Sustainability*, *12*(16), 6632. doi:10.3390u12166632

Zanero, S. (2017). Cyber-Physical Systems. *Computer*, *50*(4), 14–16. doi:10.1109/MC.2017.105

Zhong, L., Sun, S., Law, R., & Li, X. (2021). Tourism crisis management: Evidence from COVID-19. *Current Issues in Tourism*, *24*(19), 2671–2682. doi:10.1080/13683500.2021.1901866

Compilation of References

GPP. (2020, June). *TR 22.804 (2Q20/197 p.) – on Automation in Vertical Domains*. Retrieved July 1, 2021, from https://www.tech-invite.com/3m22/tinv-3gpp-22-804.html

Gtango. (2021). *5GTANGO*. Retrieved July 1, 2021, from https://www.5gtango.eu/

VINNI. (2021). *5G-VINNI – 5G Verticals Innovation Infrastructure*. Retrieved July 1, 2021, from https://www.5g-vinni.eu/

Abbas, W. (2019). *Vision to connect entire Gulf with Hyperloop, Abu Dhabi to Riyadh in 48 minutes*. Retrieved June 15, 2021, from https://www.khaleejtimes.com/news/transport/uae-hyperloop-to-reduce-travel-time-to-just-6-minutes--

Abbas, J., Mubeen, R., Iorember, P. T., Raza, S., & Mamirkulova, G. (2021). Exploring the impact of COVID-19 on tourism: Transformational potential and implications for a sustainable recovery of the travel and leisure industry. *Current Research in Behavioral Sciences*, *2*, 100033. doi:10.1016/j.crbeha.2021.100033

Abrar, I., Pottoo, S. N., Masoodi, F. S., & Bamhdi, A. (2021). On IoT and Its Integration With Cloud Computing: Challenges and Open Issues. In P. Tomar (Ed.), Integration and Implementation of the Internet of Things Through Cloud Computing (pp. 37-64). IGI Global. doi:http://doi:10.4018/978-1-7998-6981-8.ch003

Adeyeri, M. K. (2018). From Industry 3.0 to Industry 4.0: Smart Predictive Maintenance System as Platform for Leveraging. *Art Journal*, *71*(11), 64–81.

Adolph, S., & Bramble, P. (2003). *Patterns for Effective Use Cases*. Addison-Wesley Pearson Education.

Agrawal, M., Dutta, S., Kelly, R., & Millán, I. (2021). *COVID-19: An inflection point for Industry 4.0*. Retrieved August 1st 2021, from https://www.mckinsey.com/business-functions/operations/our-insights/covid-19-an-inflection-point-for-industry-40#

Ahmad, T. (2019). The Impact of New IT Adoption on Business Process Management. *Proceedings - International Conference on Research Challenges in Information Science*. 10.1109/RCIS.2019.8877085

Alaiad, A., Alnsour, Y., & Alsharo, M. (2019). Virtual teams: Thematic taxonomy, constructs model, and future research directions. IEEE Transactions on Professional Communication, 62(3), 211–238. doi:10.1109/TPC.2019.2929370

Alexander, I., & Stevens, R. (2002). *Writing Better Requirements*. Addison-Wesley.

Allan, M., & Ali, N. N. (2017). Employing social media websites and its role in determining the target audience for marketing within cloth manufacturing in Jordan. *Innovative Marketing*, *13*(2), 47–55. doi:10.21511/im.13(2).2017.05

Almeida, F. (2020). The role of tech startups in the fight against COVID-19, *World Journal of Science. Technology and Sustainable Development*, *18*(1), 64–75.

Alonso-Garcia, J., Pablo-Martí, F., & Nunez-Barriopedro, E. (2021). *Omnichannel Management in B2B. Complexity-based model. Empirical evidence from a panel of experts based on Fuzzy Cognitive Maps*. Industrial Marketing Management.

Alotaibi, Y., & Liu, F. (2013). Business process modelling towards derive and implement IT goals. *Proceedings of the 2013 IEEE 8th Conference on Industrial Electronics and Applications, ICIEA 2013*. 10.1109/ICIEA.2013.6566649

Alves, A. (2014). *Literacia financeira e comportamento na tomada de decisões financeiras*. Dissertação de Mestrado, Universidade de Aveiro, Departamentode Economia, Gestão e Engenharia Industrial, Obtido de Engenharia Industrial, Aveiro. https://ria.ua.pt/bitstream/10773/15756/1/Literacia%20financeira%20e%20comportamento%20na%20tomada%20de%20decis%C3%B5es%20financeiras.pdf

Amagir, A., Groot, W., & Maassen van den Brinkc, H. (2020). Financial literacy of high school students in the Netherlands: Knowledge, attitudes, self-efficacy, and behavior. *International Review of Economics Education*, *34*(100185), 100185. doi:10.1016/j.iree.2020.100185

Anbima - Associação Brasileira das Entidades dos Mercados Financeiro e de Capitais. (2020). *Raio X do investidor Brasileiro*. https://www.anbima.com.br/pt_br/especial/raio-x-do-investidor-2020.htm

Anderl, E., Schumann, J. H., & Kunz, W. (2016). Helping Firms Reduce Complexity in Multichannel Online Data: A New Taxonomy-Based Approach for Customer Journeys. *Journal of Retailing. New York University*, *92*(2), 185–203. doi:10.1016/j.jretai.2015.10.001

Anderson, C. K. (2011). Search, OTAs, and Online Booking: An Expanded Analysis of the Billboard Effect. *Cornell Hospitality Report, 11*(8). Retrieved from https://sha.cornell.edu/wp-content/uploads/sites/4/2019/03/christopher-anderson_billboard-effect-still-alive-and-well.pdf

Anderson, J. C., & Gerbing, D. W. (1988). Structural equation modelling in practice: A review and recommended two-step approach. *Psychological Bulletin*, *103*(3), 411–423. doi:10.1037/0033-2909.103.3.411

Android Studio. (2019). *Android Studio release notes, Android Developers*. Google LLC.

APED - Associação Portuguesa de Empresas de Distribuição. (2021). *Vendas no retalho com quebra de 1,5% em ano de pandemia Vendas no retalho com quebra de 1,5% em ano de pandemia*. http://aped.pt/2021/03/30/vendas-no-retalho-com-quebra-de-15-em-ano-de-pandemia/

Aprender Valor. (2021). *O que é o programa aprender valor?* https://aprendervalor.caeddigital.net/#!/programa

Aquino, E. M., Silveira, I. H., Pescarini, J. M., Aquino, R., Souza-Filho, J. A. D., Rocha, A. D. S., Ferreira, A., Victor, A., Teixeira, C., Machado, D. B., Paixão, E., Alves, F. J. O., Pilecco, F., Menezes, G., Gabrielli, L., Leite, L., Almeida, M. C. C., Ortelan, N., Fernandes, Q. H. R. F., ... Lima, R. T. D. R. S. (2020). Medidas de distanciamento social no controle da pandemia de COVID-19: Potenciais impactos e desafios no Brasil. *Ciencia & Saude Coletiva*, *25*(suppl 1), 2423–2446. doi:10.1590/1413-81232020256.1.10502020 PMID:32520287

Ariffin, A., & Maghzi, A. (2012). A preliminary study on customer expectations of hotel hospitality: Influences of personal and hotel factors. *International Journal of Hospitality Management*, *31*(1), 191–198. doi:10.1016/j.ijhm.2011.04.012

Aristio, A., Supardi, S., Hendrawan, R., & Hidayat, A. (2019). Analysis on Purchase Intention of Indonesian Backpacker in Accommodation Booking through Online Travel Agent. *Procedia Computer Science*, *161*, 885–893. doi:10.1016/j.procs.2019.11.196

Aristodemou, K., Buchhass, L., & Claringbould, D. (2021). The COVID-19 crisis in the EU: The resilience of healthcare systems, government responses and their socio-economic effects. *Eurasian Econ Rev*, *11*(2), 251–281. doi:10.100740822-020-00162-1

Arsel, Z. (2017). Asking questions with reflexive focus: Atutorial on designing and conducting interviews. *The Journal of Consumer Research*, *44*(4), 939–948. doi:10.1093/jcr/ucx096

Arvidson, M., Lyon, F., McKay, S., & Moro, D. (2010). *The ambitions and challenges of SROI.* Third Sector Research Centre. Available from: http://www.tsrc.ac.uk/LinkClick.aspx?fileticket1/4QwHhaC%2br88Y%3d&tabid1/4762

Arvidsson, A., & Caliandro, A. (2016). Brand public. *The Journal of Consumer Research*, *42*(5), 727–748. doi:10.1093/jcr/ucv053

Ascari, R., Pereira, R. & Silva, L. (2018). Mobile Interaction for Augmentative and Alternative Communication: a Systematic Mapping, *SBC Journal on 3D Interactive Systems, 9*(2), 105-118.

Atalay, A. S., & Meloy, M. G. (2011). Retail therapy: A strategic effort to improve mood. *Psychology and Marketing*, *28*(6), 638–659. doi:10.1002/mar.20404

Atlassian. (2020). *Trello*. https://trello.com/

Atzeni, M., Del Chiappa, G., & Mei Pung, J. (2021). Enhancing visit intention in heritage tourism: The role of object-based and existential authenticity in non-immersive virtual reality heritage experiences. *International Journal of Tourism Research.* doi:10.1002/jtr.2497

Avelino, F., Wittmayer, J., Pel, B., Weaver, P., Dumitru, A., Haxeltine, A., Kemp, R., Jørgensen, M., Bauler, T., Ruijsink, S., & O'Riordan, T. (2019). Transformative social innovation and (dis)empowerment. *Technological Forecasting and Social Change*, *145*, 195–206. doi:10.1016/j.techfore.2017.05.002

Baccarani, C., Marta, U., & Angelo, B. (2015). A Conceptual Service Quality Map:The Value Of A Wide Opened Perspective. *13th Toulon-Verona Conference Excellence in Services.*

Bacen. (2021a). *Banco Central do Brasil. Registrato*. https://www.bcb.gov.br/cidadaniafinanceira/registrato

Bacen. (2021b). *Banco Central do Brasil. Calculadora do Cidadão*. https://www.bcb.gov.br/acessoinformacao/calculadoradocidadao

Bag, S., Gupta, S., & Telukdarie, A. (2018). Importance of Innovation and Flexibility in Configuring Supply Network Sustainability. *Benchmarking*, *25*(9), 3951–3985. doi:10.1108/BIJ-06-2017-0132

Balaji, M. S., & Roy, S. K. (2017). Value co-creation with Internet of things technology in the retail industry. *Journal of Marketing Management*, *33*(1-2), 7–31. doi:10.1080/0267257X.2016.1217914

Baltar, F., & Brunet, I. (2012). Social research 2.0: Virtual snowball sampling method using Facebook. *Internet Research*, *22*(1), 57–74. doi:10.1108/10662241211199960

Banco Central do Brasil. (2021). Estudos Especiais do Banco Central. Fechamento de empresas durante a pandemia. *Relatório de Inflação, 99*. Available at: https://www.bcb.gov.br/conteudo/relatorioinflacao/EstudosEspeciais/EE099_Fechamento_de_empresas_na_pandemia.pdf. Accessed in: Dec. 2021

Banco de Portugal. (2010). *Relatório do Inquérito à Literacia Financeira da População Portuguesa*. https://www.bportugal.pt/sites/default/files/relatorio_do_ inquerito_a_literacia_financeira_da_populacao_portuguesa_2010.pdf

Bardhi, F., & Arnould, E. J. (2005). Thrift shopping: Combining utilitarian thrift and hedonic treat benefits. *Journal of Consumer Behaviour*, *4*(4), 223–233. doi:10.1002/cb.12

Baregheh, A., Rowley, J., & Sambrook, S. (2009). Towards a Multidisciplinary Definition of Innovation. *Management Decision*, *47*(8), 1323–1339. doi:10.1108/00251740910984578

Baron, R. M., & Kenny, D. A. (1986). The moderator-mediator variable distinction in social psychological research: Conceptual, strategic, and statistical considerations. *Journal of Personality and Social Psychology*, *51*(6), 1173–1182. doi:10.1037/0022-3514.51.6.1173 PMID:3806354

Barreta, J. (2012). *O comércio de proximidade – fazer acontecer a regeneração urbana*. Confederação Empresarial de Portugal.

Bates, M. J. (2007). What is browsing - Really? A model drawing from behavioural science research. *Information Research*, *12*(4).

Baum, T., & Hai, N. (2020). *Hospitality, tourism, human rights and the impact of COVID-19*. Academic Press.

Baum, J. A. C. (2001). Ecology: Organizations. In N. J. Smelser & P. B. Baltes (Eds.), *International Encyclopedia of the Social & Behavioral Sciences* (pp. 4048–4053). Pergamon. doi:10.1016/B0-08-043076-7/04206-6

Bawa, K., & Shoemaker, R. W. (1987). The Coupon-Prone Consumer: Some Findings Based on Purchase Behavior Across Product Classes. *Journal of Marketing*, *51*(4), 99–110. doi:10.1177/002224298705100409

Baym, N. K. (2010). *Personal Connections in the Digital Age*. Polity Press.

BdP. (2020). *OCDE emite recomendação sobre literacia financeira*. Obtido de Banco de Portugal: https://clientebancario.bportugal.pt/pt-pt/noticias/ocde-emite-recomendacao-sobre-literacia-financeira

Becker, C., Betz, S., Chitchyan, R., Duboc, L., Easterbrook, S. M., Penzenstadler, B., Seyff, N., & Venters, C. (2016). Requirements: The Key to Sustainability. *IEEE Software*, *33*(1), 56–65. doi:10.1109/MS.2015.158

Beck, J., Rainoldi, M., & Egger, R. (2019). Virtual reality in tourism: A state-of-the-art review. *Tourism Review*, *74*(3), 586–612. doi:10.1108/TR-03-2017-0049

Bednall, T. C., Sanders, K., & Runhaar, P. (2014). Stimulating informal learning activities through perceptions of performance appraisal quality and human resource management system strength: A two-wave study. *Academy of Management Learning & Education*, *13*(1), 45–61. doi:10.5465/amle.2012.0162

Belchior, R., Guerreiro, S., Vasconcelos, A., & Correia, M. (2020). *A survey on business process view integration*. ArXiv.

BEPA (Bureau of European Policy Advisors). (2010). *Empowering people, driving change. Social Innovation in the European Union*. European Commission.

Bertuglia, C. S., Lombardo, S., & Nijkamp, P. (Eds.). (2012). *Innovative behaviour in space and time*. Springer Science & Business Media.

BGMonitor. (2020). *Diabetes Management for Android*. Gordon Wong.

Bhatnagar, A., & Papatla, P. (2016). Increasing online sales by facilitating spillover shopping. *Journal of Retailing and Consumer Services*, *29*, 58–69. doi:10.1016/j.jretconser.2015.11.009

Bianchi, I., & Dinis de Sousa, R. (2015). *Governança de TI em universidades públicas: Proposta de um modelo*. Instituto Universitário de Lisboa (ISCTE-IUL).

Bianconi, F., Catalucci, S., Filippucci, M., Marsili, R., Moretti, M., Rossi, G., & Speranzini, E. (2017). Comparison between two non-contact techniques for art digitalization. *Journal of Physics: Conference Series*, *882*(1), 012005. doi:10.1088/1742-6596/882/1/012005

BIGLauncher. (2020). *BIG Launcher*. Apps Google Play.

Bitterman, A., & Hess, D. B. (n.d.). *Going dark: The post-pandemic transformation of the metropolitan retail landscape*. Academic Press.

Bloch, P. H., Ridgway, N. M., & Sherrell, D. L. (1989). Extending the concept of shopping: An investigation of browsing activity. *Journal of the Academy of Marketing Science*, *17*(1), 13–21. doi:10.1007/BF02726349

Bloch, P. H., Sherrell, D. L., & Ridgway, N. M. (1986). Consumer Search: An Extended Framework. *The Journal of Consumer Research*, *13*(1), 119. doi:10.1086/209052

Bodlaj, M., & Čater, B. (2019). The Impact of Environmental Turbulence on the Perceived Importance of Innovation and Innovativeness in SMEs. *Journal of Small Business Management*, *57*(sup2), 417–435. doi:10.1111/jsbm.12482

Bollen, K. A. (1989). A new incremental fit index for general structural equation models. *Sociological Methods & Research*, *17*(3), 303–316. doi:10.1177/0049124189017003004

Bollen, K., & Lennox, R. (1991). Conventional wisdom on measurement: A structural equation perspective. *Psychological Bulletin*, *110*(2), 305–314. doi:10.1037/0033-2909.110.2.305

Bollweg, L., Lackes, R., Siepermann, M., & Weber, P. (2020). Drivers and barriers of the digitalization of local owner operated retail outlets. *Journal of Small Business and Entrepreneurship*, *32*(2), 173–201. doi:10.1080/08276331.2019.1616256

Bolton, A., Goosen, L., & Kritzinger, E. (2021). An Empirical Study into the Impact on Innovation and Productivity Towards the Post-COVID-19 Era: Digital Transformation of an Automotive Enterprise. In L. C. Carvalho, L. Reis, & C. Silveira (Eds.), *Handbook of Research on Entrepreneurship, Innovation, Sustainability, and ICTs in the Post-COVID-19 Era* (pp. 133–159). IGI Global. doi:10.4018/978-1-7998-6776-0.ch007

Boysen, N., Fedtke, S., & Schwerdfeger, S. (2021). Last-mile delivery concepts: A survey from an operational research perspective. *OR-Spektrum*, *43*(1), 1–58. doi:10.100700291-020-00607-8

Brasil (2021a). *Projeto de educação financeira nas escolas públicas é expandido para todo o país*. Portal Gov.br. Publicado em 31 mai. 2021. https://www.gov.br/pt-br/noticias/financas-impostos-e-gestao-publica/2021/05/projeto-de-educacao-financeira-nas-escolas-publicas-e-expandido-para-todo-o-pais

Brasil. (2021b). *Banco Central oferece ferramentas gratuitas de educação financeira*. Publicado em 15 de março de 2021. https://www.gov.br/pt-br/noticias/financas-impostos-e-gestao-publica/2021/03/banco-central-oferece-ferramentas-gratuitas-de-educacao-financeira

Brasil. (2021c). *Solicitar kits de Educação Financeira do Futuro na Mão* (Educfin). https://www.gov.br/pt-br/servicos/solicitar-kits-de-educacao-financeira-do-futuro-na-mao

Bria, F. (2015). *Growing a digital social ecosystem for Europe*. DSI report, EU Commission. https://www.nesta.org.uk/sites/default/files/dsireport.pdf

Bria, F. (2014). *Digital Social Innovation. Interim Report. A deliverable of the project "Digital Social Innovation*. European Commission, DG Connect.

Bricken, M., & Byrne, C. M. (1993). Summer Students in Virtual Reality: A Pilot Study on Educational Applications of Virtual Reality Technology. In A. Wexelblat (Ed.), *Virtual Reality* (pp. 199–217). Academic Press. doi:10.1016/B978-0-12-745045-2.50019-2

Brown, H. S., de Jong, M., & Levy, D. L. (2009). Building institutions based on information disclosure: Lessons from GRI's sustainability reporting. *Journal of Cleaner Production*, *17*(6), 571–580. doi:10.1016/j.jclepro.2008.12.009

Bruneckiene, J., & Sinkiene, J. (2014), Critical Analysis of Approaches to Smart Economy. *International Scientific Conference Business and Management*. http://www.dx.doi.org/10.3846/bm.2014.106

Bundesnetzagentur. (2019). *5G spectrum fees for local usages*. Retrieved July 1, 2021, from https://www.bundesnetzagentur.de/SharedDocs/Pressemitteilungen/EN/2019/20191031_LokalesBreitband.html

Büyüközkan, G., Feyzioğlu, O., & Havle, C. (2019). Intuitionistic Fuzzy AHP Based Strategic Analysis of Service Quality in Digital Hospitality Industry. *IFAC-PapersOnLine*, *52*(13), 1687–1692. doi:10.1016/j.ifacol.2019.11.443

CAFU. (n.d.). https://www.cafu.com

Cai, Y. J., & Lo, C. K. (2020). Omni-channel management in the new retailing era: A systematic review and future research agenda. *International Journal of Production Economics*, *229*, 107729. doi:10.1016/j.ijpe.2020.107729

Cajaiba-Santana, G. (2014). Social innovation: Moving the field forward: A conceptual framework. *Technological Forecasting and Social Change*, *82*, 42–51. doi:10.1016/j.techfore.2013.05.008

Calle, J. Y. (2020) *Understanding COVID-19's impact on small food retailers in Finland.* Master's Thesis of Master Programme in International Business Development. LAB University of Applied Sciences LTD.

Cangiano, S.; Romano, Z. & Loglio, L. (2017). The growth of digital social innovation in Europe. An Open Design approach to support innovation for the societal good. *The Design Journal, 20*(sup1), 3546-3559.

Cardenas, I., Borbon-Galvez, Y., Verlinden, T., Van de Voorde, E., Vanelslander, T., & Dewulf, W. (2017). City logistics, urban goods distribution and last mile delivery and collection. *Competition and Regulation in Network Industries, 18*(1-2).

Carita, P. (2016). *A importância da literacia financeira nas decisões de investimento.* Dissertação de Mestrado, ISCTE. Obtido de http://hdl.handle.net/10071/13428

Carnevale, J. B., & Hatak, I. (2020). Employee adjustment and well-being in the era of COVID-19: Implications for human resource management. *Journal of Business Research*, *116*, 183–187. doi:10.1016/j.jbusres.2020.05.037 PMID:32501303

Carvalho, L. C., Jeleniewicz, M., Franczak, P., & Vanková, Ž. (2021). Business Models for Digital Economy: Good Practices and Success Stories. Handbook of Research on Multidisciplinary Approaches to Entrepreneurship, Innovation, and ICTs, 1-21.

Carvalho, L. (2017). Entrepreneurial Ecosystems. Lisbon as a Smart Start-up City. In L. Carvalho (Ed.), *Handbook of Research On Entrepreneurial Development and Innovation within Smart Cities* (pp. 1–24). IGI Global. doi:10.4018/978-1-5225-1978-2.ch001

Carvalho, L., & Paiva, T. (2021). Education 4.0 - drivers, challenges, and opportunities. *Journal Advances in Higher Education*, *13*(1), 5–16.

Centennial U. A. E. 2071 - The Official Portal of the UAE Government. (n.d.). https://u.ae/en/about-the-uae/strategies-initiatives-and-awards/federal-governments-strategies-and-plans/uae-centennial-2071

CGD. (2020). *European Money Quiz*. Obtido de CGD: https://www.cgd.pt/Sustentabilidade/Responsabilidade-Social/Pages/European-Money-Quiz.aspx

CGI.BR. (2019). *Pesquisa TIC Domicílios*. Resumo Executivo. Available at: https://cetic.br/media/docs/publicacoes/2/20201123115919/resumo_executivo_tic_dom_2019.pdf

Chakravarti, S. (2021). Ascertaining the Interest of Women to Drive Innovation Through Entrepreneurship Post-Pandemic: A Research Study in the United Arab Emirates (UAE). In Handbook of Research on Entrepreneurship, Innovation, Sustainability, and ICTs in the Post-COVID-19 Era (pp. 341–363). IGI Global.

Chakravarti, S. (2017). Entrepreneurship in the Emirates. *International Journal of Management IT and Engineering*, *7*, 126–138.

Chang, S.-J. S. J., & Rice, R. E. (1993). *Browsing: A multidimensional framework*. Annual Reviews of Information Science and Technology.

Ciasullo, M. V., Fenza, G., Loia, V., Orciuoli, F., Troisi, O., & Herrera-Viedma, E. (2018). Business process outsourcing enhanced by fuzzy linguistic consensus model. *Applied Soft Computing*, *64*, 436–444. doi:10.1016/j.asoc.2017.12.020

Cigref. (2018). *Cigref Nomenclature Information Systems job profiles Framework*. https://www.cigref.fr/cigref-nomenclature-information-systems-job-profiles-framewok-update-2018

Cloonan, Persich, Dailey, & Killgore. (2021). Sleep and Resilience during the COVID-19 Pandemic. *IntechOpen*. doi:0.5772/intechopen.98298

Coleman, L. J., Chandler, K., & Gu, J. (2013). Social media: A moving target. *Journal of Marketing Development and Competitiveness*, *7*(1), 73–77. doi:10.100740139-013-0010-2

CollabNet. (2019). *13th Annual State of Agile Survey*. CollabNet VersionOne Inc.

ColorADD. (2015). *ColorADD*. Retrieved from http://www.coloradd.net/index.asp: http://www.coloradd.net/about.asp

Coman, I. (2020). Art Consumption During COVID-19 Pandemic: Influence upon the Sentiment of Life Fulfilment. *Business Excellence and Management, 10*(SI1), 112-126.

Commission for University Education (CUE). (2016). *Statistics on University Education in Kenya*. CUE.

Conselho Nacional Supervisores Financeiros Banco de Portugal. (2016). *Relatório do Inquérito à Literacia Financeira da População Portuguesa*. https://www.todoscontam.pt/sites/default/files/SiteCollectionDocuments/Relatorio2InqueritoLiteraciaFinanceira.pdf

Cooke, A. D. J., & Zubcsek, P. P. (2017). The Connected Consumer: Connected Devices and the Evolution of Customer Intelligence. *Journal of the Association for Consumer Research*, *2*(2), 164–178. doi:10.1086/690941

Cordeiro, N. J. N., Costa, M. G. V., & da Silva, M. N. (2018). Educação financeira no Brasil: uma perspectiva panorâmica. *Ensino da Matemática em Debate*, *5*(1), 69 – 84.

Costa, C. M., & Miranda, C. J. de. (2013). Educação financeira e taxa de poupança no Brasil. *Revista de Gestão, Finanças e Contabilidade*, *3*(3), 57-74.

Costello, A. B., & Osborne, J. W. (2005). Best practices in exploratory factor analysis: Four recommendations for getting the most from your analysis. *Practical Assessment, Research & Evaluation*, *10*(7), 1–9.

Crespi-Vallbona, M., & Dimitrovski, D. (2016). Food markets visitors: A typology proposal. *British Food Journal*, *118*(4), 840–857. doi:10.1108/BFJ-11-2015-0420

Cunha, M. P. (2020). O mercado financeiro chega à sala de aula: Educação financeira como política pública no Brasil. *Educação e Sociedade, 41*.

Customer Experience Trends in a Post-COVID-19 World | Study. (2021). Retrieved January 6th 2021, from https://www.sitel.com/covid-19-customer-experience-impact-study

CVM. (2018). *CVM lança projeto Precisamos Falar Sobre Dinheiro*. https://www.investidor.gov.br/noticias/2018_11_12.html

CVM. (2021). *Centro CVM de Educação e Letramento Financeiro para a América Latina e Caribe.* https://www.investidor.gov.br/menu/atividades/CentroEducacional/CentroEducacionalCVM_OCDE.html

Dahlgren, A.N, & Wasielewski, A. (2021). Cultures of Digitization: A Historiographic Perspective on Digital Art History. *Visual Resources*, 1-21.

Damanpour, F. (1996). Organizational Complexity and Innovation: Developing and Testing Multiple Contingency Models. *Management Science*, *42*(5), 693–716. doi:10.1287/mnsc.42.5.693

Damanpour, F., & Schneider, M. (2006). Phases of the Adoption of Innovation in Organizations: Effects of Environment, Organization and Top Managers. *British Journal of Management*, *17*(3), 215–236. doi:10.1111/j.1467-8551.2006.00498.x

Dames, H., Hirschfeld, G., Sackmann, T., & Thielsch, M. T. (2019). Searching vs. Browsing—The Influence of Consumers' Goal Directedness on Website Evaluations. *Interacting with Computers*, *31*(1), 95–112. doi:10.1093/iwc/iwz006

Dantas, C., Mackiewicz, K., Tageo, V., Jacucci, G., Guardado, D., Ortet, S., . . . Vassiliou, C. (2021). Benefits and Hurdles of AI In The Workplace@ What Comes Next? *COVID-19 Cripples Global Restaurant and Hospitality Industry, 24*(11), 1487-1490.

Davis-Sramek, B., Ishfaq, R., Gibson, B. J., & Defee, C. (2020). Examining retail business model transformation: A longitudinal study of the transition to omnichannel order fulfillment. *International Journal of Physical Distribution & Logistics Management*, *50*(5), 557–576. doi:10.1108/IJPDLM-02-2019-0055

De Jong, J. P., & Den Hartog, D. N. (2010). Measuring innovative work behaviour. *Creativity and Innovation Management*, *19*(1), 23–36. doi:10.1111/j.1467-8691.2010.00547.x

De Luca, A. (2006). *Le ricerche di mercato. Guida pratica e teorica* (Vol. 622). FrancoAngeli.

de Lucas Ancillo, A., del Val Núñez, M. T., & Gavrila, S. G. (2021). Workplace change within the COVID-19 context: A grounded theory approach. *Economic Research-Ekonomska Istraživanja*, *34*(1), 2297–2316. doi:10.1080/1331677X.2020.1862689

De Silva, C. K., Sano, K., & Hatoyama, K. (2020). Exploring the relationship between urban form and spatial organisation of Amazon fulfilment facilities in the United Kingdom and Japan. *Transportation Research Procedia*, *46*, 46. doi:10.1016/j.trpro.2020.03.175

Dean, C. (2019) *Social Media Strategies used by Owners of Small Retail Businesses.* PhD Thesis. Walden University

DECO. (2020). *Em risco de sobre-endividamento? Peça ajuda à DECO.* https://www.deco.proteste.pt/familia consumo/orcamento-familiar/dossies/como-travar-o-sobre-endividamento-com-a-deco

Deloitte. (2020). *Last Mile Logistics. Challenges and solutions in Spain.* Deloitte.

DeMarco, T., & Lister, T. (2003). Risk Management During Requirements. *IEEE Software*, *20*(5), 99–101. doi:10.1109/MS.2003.1231163

Dessart, L., Veloutsou, C., & Morgan-Thomas, A. (2016). Capturing consumer engagement: Duality, dimensionality and measurement. *Journal of Marketing Management*, *32*(5-6), 399–426. doi:10.1080/0267257X.2015.1130738

DGrade. (n.d.). https://www.dgrade.com

DiabetesM. (2020). *Diabetes:M.* www.diabetes-m.com

Dickinger, A., & Kleinjnen, M. (2008). Coupons going wireless: Determinants of consumer intentions to redeem mobile coupons. *Journal of Interactive Marketing*, *22*(3), 23–39. doi:10.1002/dir.20115

Digital U. A. E. - The Official Portal of the UAE Government. (n.d.). https://u.ae/en/about-the-uae/digital-uae

Donati, M., Fanucci, L., Iacopetti, F., & Vecchio, A. (2015). *A modular suite to support human-smartphone interaction for people with motor skill impairments. 10th International Conference on Design & Technology of Integrated Systems in Nanoscale Era (DTIS)*, Naples, Italy. 10.1109/DTIS.2015.7127385

Dorenbosch, L., Van Engen, M., & Verhagen, M. (2005). On-the-job innovation: The impact of job design and human resource management through production ownership. *Creativity and Innovation Management*, *14*(2), 129–141. doi:10.1111/j.1476-8691.2005.00333.x

Dowbor, L. (2020). *O capitalismo se desloca: novas arquiteturas sociais*. Available at: https://sesc.digital/conteudo/programacao/42778/o-capitalismo-se-desloca-novas-arquiteturas-sociais

Drath, R., & Horch, A. (2014). Industrie 4.0: Hit or Hype? *IEEE Industrial Electronics Magazine*, *8*(2), 56–58. https://doi.org/10.1109/MIE.2014.2312079

Drucker, P. (1985). *Innovation and Entrepreneurship*. Harper Business.

Dumas, M., La Rosa, M., Mendling, J., & Reijers, H. A. (2018a). BPM as an Enterprise Capability. Fundamentals of Business Process Management. doi:10.1007/978-3-662-56509-4_12

Dumas, M., La Rosa, M., Mendling, J., & Reijers, H. A. (2018b). *Fundamentals of Business Process Management*. Springer Berlin Heidelberg. doi:10.1007/978-3-662-56509-4

Dwivedi, Y. K., Hughes, D. L., Coombs, C., Constantiou, I., Duan, Y., Edwards, J. S., Gupta, B., Lal, B., Misra, S., Prashant, P., Raman, R., Rana, N. P., Sharma, S. K., & Upadhyay, N. (2020). Impact of COVID-19 pandemic on information management research and practice: Transforming education, work and life. *International Journal of Information Management*, *55*, 102211. doi:10.1016/j.ijinfomgt.2020.102211

Ebrahimi, A., Ebrahimi, S., & Esfahani, S. A. (2020). How COVID-19 pandemic can lead to promotion of remote medical education and democratization of education? *Journal of Advances in Medical Education & Professionalism*, *8*(3), 144. PMID:32802909

Edosomwan, S., Prakasan, S. K., Kouame, D., Watson, J., & Seymour, T. (2011). The history of social media and its impact on business. *The Journal of Applied Management and Entrepreneurship*, *16*(3), 79–91. doi:10.1007/9781-4419-5725-2_9

Effing, R., & Spil, T. A. (2016). The social strategy cone: Towards a framework for evaluating social media strategies. *International Journal of Information Management*, *36*(1), 1–8. doi:10.1016/j.ijinfomgt.2015.07.009

Elia, G., & Margherita, A. (2021). A conceptual framework for the cognitive enterprise: Pillars, maturity, value drivers. *Technology Analysis and Strategic Management*, 1–13. doi:10.1080/09537325.2021.1901874

Emerson, J., Wachowicz, J., & Chun, S. (1999). *Social return on investment: exploring aspects of value creation in the nonprofit sector. In REDF Box Set* (Vol. 2). Roberts Enterprise Development Foundation.

Encyclopædia Britannica Inc. (n.d.). *Land of the United Arab Emirates*. Encyclopædia Britannica. https://www.britannica.com/place/United-Arab-Emirates/Land

ENDC. (2021). *Escola Nacional de Defesa do Consumidor*. https://www.defesadoconsumidor.gov.br/escolanacional

Endres, H., Stoiber, K., & Wenzl, N. M. (2019). Managing digital transformation through hybrid business models. *The Journal of Business Strategy*, *41*(6), 49–56. doi:10.1108/JBS-07-2019-0142

Engel, J. F., & Roger, D. (1978). Consumer Behavior. The Dryden Press.

Epstein, M. J., & Yuthas, K. (2014). *Measuring and improving social impacts: A guide for nonprofits, companies, and impact investors*. Berrett-Koehler Publishers.

Ergun, K. (2018). Financial literacy among university students: A study in eight European countries. *International Journal of Consumer Studies*, *42*(1), 2–15. doi:10.1111/ijcs.12408

Eriksson, N., & Stenius, M. (2020). Changing Behavioral Patterns in Grocery Shopping in the Initial Phase of the Covid-19 Crisis—A Qualitative Study of News Articles. *Open Journal of Business and Management*, *8*(05), 1946–1961. doi:10.4236/ojbm.2020.85119

Erner, C., Goedde-Menke, M., & Oberste, M. (2016). Financial literacy of high school students: Evidence from Germany. *The Journal of Economic Education*, *47*(2), 95–105. doi:10.1080/00220485.2016.1146102

Erol, S., Schuhmacher, A., & Sihn, W. (2016). Resource Efficiency for Global Competitiveness. In *International Conference on Competitive Manufacturing (COMA)* (pp. 495–500). Retrieved from http://publica.fraunhofer.de/documents/N-382579.html

Errichiello, L., Micera, R., Atzeni, M., & Del Chiappa, G. (2019). Exploring the implications of wearable virtual reality technology for museum visitors' experience: A cluster analysis. *International Journal of Tourism Research*, *21*(5), 590–605. doi:10.1002/jtr.2283

ETSI. (2011). *TR 102 889-2 - V1.1.1 - Electromagnetic compatibility and Radio spectrum Matters (ERM); System Reference Document; Short Range Devices (SRD); Part 2: Technical characteristics for SRD equipment for wireless industrial applications using technologies different from Ultra-Wide Band (UWB)*. Sophia Antipolis Cedex. Retrieved from https://www.etsi.org/deliver/etsi_tr/102800_102899/10288902/01.01.01_60/tr_10288902v010101p.pdf

ETSI. (2015). *TS 103 235 - V1.1.1 - Reconfigurable Radio Systems (RRS); System architecture and high level procedures for operation of Licensed Shared Access (LSA) in the 2 300 MHz - 2 400 MHz band*. Sophia Antipolis Cedex.

ETSI. (2018a). *Reconfigurable Radio Systems (RRS); Feasibility study on temporary spectrum access for local high-quality wireless networks*. Sophia Antipolis Cedex.

ETSI. (2018b). *TR 103 515 - V1.1.1 - Digital Enhanced Cordless Telecommunications (DECT); Study on URLLC use cases of vertical industries for DECT evolution and DECT-2020*. Sophia Antipolis Cedex. Retrieved from https://www.etsi.org/deliver/etsi_tr/103500_103599/103515/01.01.01_60/tr_103515v010101p.pdf

ETSI. (2021). *TS 123 501 - V15.12.0 - 5G; System architecture for the 5G System (5GS) (3GPP TS 23.501 version 15.12.0 Release 15)*. Sophia Antipolis Cedex. Retrieved from https://www.etsi.org/deliver/etsi_ts/123500_123599/123501/15.12.00_60/ts_123501v151200p.pdf

Evans, B. L., Fuse, I., Munekata, N., & Ono, T. (2017). Deployment of an Interactive JavaScript Application to Aid in Understanding the Digitalization of Sound. *Journal of Information Systems Education*, *15*(1), 42–47. doi:10.12937/ejsise.15.42

Fact sheet - The Official Portal of the UAE Government. (n.d.). https://u.ae/en/about-the-uae/fact-sheet

Federation of Hong Kong Hotel Owners. (2012). *Proposal to Establish a Hotel Classification System for Hong Kong*. Hong Kong: Federation of Hong Kong Hotel owners. Retrieved August 4th 2021 from http://www.fedhotelowners.com.hk/books/Hotel%20classification%20Jul0300.pdf

Felix, R., Rauschnabel, P. A., & Hinsch, C. (2017). Elements of strategic social media marketing: A holistic framework. *Journal of Business Research*, *70*, 118–126. doi:10.1016/j.jbusres.2016.05.001

FEP. (2019). *€DUCAR na U.Porto*. Obtido em 17 de 05 de 2021, de Programa de Promoção da Literacia Financeira da U.Porto: https://literaciafinanceira.fep.up.pt/

Fernandes, D. (2011). *Acerca da Literacia Financeira*. Dissertação de Mestrado, ISCTE - Instituto Universitário de Lisboa. https://repositorio.iscte-iul.pt/bitstream/10071/4382/1/Tese%20Acerca%20da%20LF%2

Feroz, A. K., Zo, H., & Chiravuri, A. (2021). Digital transformation and environmental sustainability: A review and research agenda. *Sustainability (Switzerland)*, *13*(3), 1–20. doi:10.3390u13031530

Ferreira, I., Ferreira, S., Silva, C., & Carvalho, J. (2012). Dilemas iniciais na investigação em TSI design science e design research, uma clarificação de conceitos. *Conferência Ibérica de Sistemas y Tecnologias de Informação*. https://repositorium.sdum.uminho.pt/bitstream/1822/21696/1/CISTI 2012.pdf

FGV. (2020). *Relatório sobre os Impactos Econômicos da Covid-19*. Economia Criativa. Available at: https://fgvprojetos.fgv.br/sites/fgvprojetos.fgv.br/files/economiacriativa_formatacaosite.pdf

Filieri, R., Alguezaui, S., & McLeay, F. (2015). Why do travelers trust TripAdvisor? Antecedents of trust towards consumer-generated media and its influence on recommendation adoption and word of mouth. *Tourism Management*, *51*, 174–185. doi:10.1016/j.tourman.2015.05.007

Filipiak, B. Z., Dylewski, M., & Kalinowski, M. (2020). Economic development trends in the EU tourism industry. Towards the digitalization process and sustainability. *Quality & Quantity*. Advance online publication. doi:10.100711135-020-01056-9 PMID:33132445

Firebase. (2020). *Firebase Authentication*. https://firebase.google.com/docs/auth

Firjan. (2014). *Mapeamento da Indústria Criativa no Brasil*. Available at: https://www.firjan.com.br/EconomiaCriativa/downloads/MapeamentoIndustriaCriativa-Firjan2014.pdf

Fischer, M., Imgrund, F., Janiesch, C., & Winkelmann, A. (2020). Strategy archetypes for digital transformation: Defining meta objectives using business process management. *Information & Management*, *57*(5), 103262. doi:10.1016/j.im.2019.103262

Flavián, C., Ibáñez-Sánchez, S., & Orús, C. (2021). Impacts of technological embodiment through virtual reality on potential guests' emotions and engagement. *Journal of Hospitality Marketing & Management*, *30*(1), 1–20. doi:10.1080/19368623.2020.1770146

Fonseca, F., Pichel, F., Albuquerque, I., Afonso, M. J., Baptista, N., & Túbal, V. (2015). *Manual de Contagem de Hidratos de Carbono na Diabetes Mellitus para profissionais de saúde*. Porto: Associação Portuguesa dos Nutricionistas.

Fonseca, M. J. & Rossi, C A. V. (1998). O estudo do envolvimento com o produto em comportamento do consumidor: fundamentos teóricos e proposição de uma escala para aplicação no Brasil. *Anais do Encontro Anual da Anpad*.

Foroudi, P. H., Tabaghdehi, S., & Marvi, R. (2021). The gloom of the COVID-19 shock in the hospitality industry: A study of consumer risk perception and adaptive belief in the dark cloud of a pandemic. *International Journal of Hospitality Management*, *92*, 102717. doi:10.1016/j.ijhm.2020.102717

Forum, W. E. (2021). *For a true economic recovery, small businesses will need more support*. Retrieved from https://www.weforum.org/agenda/2020/12/small-businesses-will-need-more-support-for-covid-recovery/

Fossatti, M., & Gemetto, J. (2011). *Arte joven y cultura digital*. Available at: https://www.articaonline.com/wp-content/uploads/2017/08/Arte-joven-y-cultura-digital.pdf

Franz, H. W., Hochgerner, J., & Howaldt, J. (2012). *Challenge Social Innovation: Potentials for Business, Social Entrepreneurship, Welfare and Civil Society*. Springer. doi:10.1007/978-3-642-32879-4

Fruitbook Magazine. (2020). *Dopo il Covid-19, i dark store potranno davvero essere il futuro del retail?* Fruitbook Magazine Online.

Fukuyama, M. (2018). Society 5.0: Aiming for a new human-centered society. *Japan Spotlight*, *27*, 47–50.

Fundação Ageas. (2020). *Ori€nta-te*. https://www.concursorientate.pt/

Galati, A., Tinervia, S., Crescimanno, M., & Spezia, F. (2017). Social media as a strategic marketing tool in the Sicilian wine industry: Evidence from Facebook. *International Journal of Globalisation and Small Business*, *6*(1), 40–47. doi:10.1016/j.wep.2017.03.003

Galperina, L., Girenko, A., & Mazurenko, V. (2016). The Concept of Smart Economy as the Basis for Sustainable Development of Ukraine. *International Journal of Economics and Financial Issues*, *6*(S8), 307–314.

Garg, R., & Garg, H. (2021). Internet of Things-Enabled Smart Entry System for Telecom Sites. In P. Tomar (Ed.), Integration and Implementation of the Internet of Things Through Cloud Computing (pp. 155-177). IGI Global. doi:10.4018/978-1-7998-6981-8.ch008

Gazzola, P., Pavione, E., Pezzetti, R., & Grechi, D. (2020). Trends in the fashion industry. The perception of sustainability and circular economy: A gender/generation quantitative approach. *Sustainability (Switzerland)*, *12*(7), 1–19. doi:10.3390u12072809

Ghobakhloo, M. (2020). Industry 4.0, digitization, and opportunities for sustainability. *Journal of Cleaner Production*, *252*, 119869. doi:10.1016/j.jclepro.2019.119869

Giaretta, A., Dragoni, N., & Massacci, F. (2019). IoT security configurability with security-by-contract. *Sensors (Basel)*, *19*(19), 4121. https://doi.org/10.3390/s19194121

Giusto, D., Iera, A., Morabito, G., & Atzori, L. (2016). Internet of Things (IoT) – A Technological Analysis and Survey on Vision, Concepts, Challenges, Innovation Directions, Technologies, and Applications. *American Journal of Electrical and Electronic Engineering*, *4*(1), 23–32. http://www.sciepub.com/reference/146416

Godfrey, E. (1983). Structuring Freedom: An Alternative Approach to Post-Graduate Course Design. *Management Education and Development*, *14*(1), 68–81. doi:10.1177/135050768301400110

Goeking, V. (2020). *Brasileiros ligam finanças pessoais a sentimentos ruins e perpetuam tabu sobre dinheiro*. Valor Investe. https://valorinveste.globo.com/educacao-financeira/noticia/2020/11/10/brasileiros-ligam-financas-pessoais-a-sentimentos-ruins-e-perpetuam-tabu-sobre-dinheiro.ghtml

Goelm, A., & Singhal, P. (Eds.). (2016). *Product Innovation Through Knowledge Management and Social Media Strategies*. IGI Global. doi:10.4018/978-1-4666-9607-5

Gonzalez, R., Gasco, J., & Llopis, J. (2020). Information and communication technologies and human resources in hospitality and tourism. *International Journal of Contemporary Hospitality Management*, *32*(11), 3545–3579. doi:10.1108/IJCHM-04-2020-0272

Goosen, L. (2016, February 18). *We don't need no education"? Yes, they DO want e-learning in Basic and Higher Education!* Retrieved from https://uir.unisa.ac.za/handle/10500/20999

Goosen, L., & Ngugi, J. K. (2018). Rethinking Teaching and Learning in the 21st Century: Course Design Characteristics towards Innovative Behaviour. In M. M. Dichaba, & M. A. Sotayo (Ed.), *Proceedings of the South Africa International Conference on Education* (pp. 376 - 394). African Academic Research Forum.

Goosen, L., & Ngugi, J. K. (2019b). Towards Innovative Behaviour For Technology Students. In *Proceedings of the 10th Institute of Science and Technology Education (ISTE) International Conference on Mathematics, Science and Technology Education* (pp. 333 - 342). UNISA. Retrieved from https://uir.unisa.ac.za/handle/10500/26055

Goosen, L., & Van Heerden, D. (2013). Project-Based Assessment Influencing Pass Rates of an ICT Module at an ODL Institution. In E. Ivala (Ed.), *Proceedings of the 8th International Conference on e-Learning*. Cape Town: Academic Conferences and Publishing.

Goosen, L., & Van Heerden, D. (2017). Beyond the Horizon of Learning Programming with Educational Technologies. In U. I. Ogbonnaya, & S. Simelane-Mnisi (Ed.), *Proceedings of the South Africa International Conference on Educational Technologies* (pp. 78 - 90). Pretoria: African Academic Research Forum.

Goosen, L. (2004). *Criteria and Guidelines for the Selection and Implementation of a First Programming Language in High Schools*. Potchefstroom Campus: North West University. Retrieved from http://hdl.handle.net/10394/226

Goosen, L. (2018). Students' Access to an ICT4D MOOC. In S. Kabanda, H. Suleman, & S. Jamieson (Ed.), *Proceedings of the 47th Annual Conference of the Southern African Computer Lectures' Association (SACLA 2018)* (pp. 183 - 201). University of Cape Town.

Goosen, L. (2019). Technology-Supported Teaching and Research Methods for Educators: Case Study of a Massive Open Online Course. In L. Makewa, B. Ngussa, & J. Kuboja (Eds.), *Technology-Supported Teaching and Research Methods for Educators* (pp. 128–148). IGI Global., doi:10.4018/978-1-5225-5915-3.ch007

Goosen, L., Mentz, E., & Nieuwoudt, H. (2007). Choosing the "Best" Programming Language?! In E. Cohen (Ed.), *Proceedings of the 2007 Computer Science and IT Education Conference* (pp. 269-282). Santa Rosa: Informing Science Press.

Goosen, L., & Ngugi, J. K. (2019a). Innovation for Computing Students Matter, of Course! In B. L. Tait & J. H. Kroeze (Eds.), *Proceedings of 48th Annual Conference of the Southern African Computer Lecturers' Association (SACLA 2019)* (pp. 19–36). University of South Africa. Retrieved from http://osprey.unisa.ac.za/sacla2019/SACLA2019%20Proceedings.pdf#page=31

Gössling, S., Scott, D., & Hall, C. M. (2020). Pandemics, tourism and global change: A rapid assessment of COVID-19. *Journal of Sustainable Tourism*, *29*(1), 1–20. doi:10.1080/09669582.2020.1758708

Grant, R. M., & Baden-Fuller, C. O. (2018). *How to Develop Strategic Management Competency: Reconsidering the Learning Goals and Knowledge Requirements of the Core Strategy Course*. Academy of Management Learning and Education. doi:10.5465/amle.2017.0126

Gravemeijer, K., Stephan, M., Julie, C., Lin, F.-L., & Ohtani, M. (2017). What Mathematics Education May Prepare Students for the Society of the Future? *International Journal of Science and Mathematics Education*, *15*(S1, Suppl 1), S105–S123. doi:10.100710763-017-9814-6

Greencred. (2021). *Finanças Pessoais: pesquisa revela que 73% dos brasileiros não guardam dinheiro*. https://greencred.com.br/financas-pessoais-brasileiros-nao-guardam-dinheiro/

Gretzel, U., Fuchs, M., Baggio, R., Hoepken, W., Law, R., Neidhardt, J., Pesonen, J., Zanker, M., & Xiang, Z. (2020). e-Tourism beyond COVID-19: A call for transformative research. *Información Tecnológica*, *22*(2), 187–203. doi:10.100740558-020-00181-3

Gutierrez, G., Garzas, J., De Lena, M. T. G., & Moguerza, J. M. (2019). Self-Managing: An Empirical Study of the Practice in Agile Teams. *IEEE Software, 36*(1), 23–27. Advance online publication. doi:10.1109/MS.2018.2874324

Guttentag, D. A. (2010). Virtual reality: Applications and implications for tourism. *Tourism Management, 31*(5), 637–651. doi:10.1016/j.tourman.2009.07.003

Haider, N., Baig, M. Z., & Imran, M. (2020). Artificial Intelligence and Machine Learning in 5G Network Security: Opportunities, advantages, and future research trends. *Computer Science.*

Hair, J. F., Black, W. C., Babin, B. J., Anderson, R. E., & Tatham, R. L. (2009). *Análise multivariada de dados.* Bookman.

Handayani, S. F., & Er, M. (2019). Antecedent and Business Process Management Non-Technical Capabilities in Social Media Implementation for Micro, Small and Medium Enterprises: A Conceptual Model. *Procedia Computer Science, 161*, 1114–1121. doi:10.1016/j.procs.2019.11.223

Hang, H., Aroean, L., & Chen, Z. (2020). Building emotional attachment during COVID-19. *Annals of Tourism Research, 83*, 103006. doi:10.1016/j.annals.2020.103006 PMID:32834221

Hanson, K. T., & Léautier, F. A. (2011). *Development drivers in Africa: Role of innovation.* ACBF Occasional Paper, 14. Retrieved February 20, 2015, from http://elibrary.acbfpact.org/collect

Hargreaves, T., Longhurst, N., & Seyfang, G. (2013). Up, down, round and round: Connecting regimes and practices in innovation for sustainability. *Environment & Planning, 45*(2), 402–420. doi:10.1068/a45124

Hartjes, B. J. (2010). *Aligning employee competences with organizational innovation strategy: A case study at B.V. Twentsche Kabelfabriek* (Unpublished Master's Thesis). Enschede, The Netherlands: University of Twente. Retrieved March 14, 2015, from http://essay.utwente.nl/59930/1/MA_thesis_B_Hartjes.pdf

Hashim, K., & Fadhil, N. (2017). Engaging with Customer Using Social Media Platform: A Case Study of Malaysia Hotels. *Procedia Computer Science, 124*, 4–11. doi:10.1016/j.procs.2017.12.123

Hassan, M., & Casaló Ariño, L. V. (2016). Consumer devotion to a different height: How consumers are defending the brand within Facebook brand communities. *Internet Research, 26*(4), 963–981. doi:10.1108/IntR-03-2015-0090

Hassan, S., Nadzim, S. Z. A., & Shiratuddin, N. (2015). Strategic use of social media for small business based on the AIDA model. *Procedia: Social and Behavioral Sciences, 172*, 262–269. doi:10.1016/j.sbspro.2015.01.363

Hastings, J., Madrian, B., & Skimmyhorn, W. (2013). Financial literacy, financial education, and economic outcomes. *Annual Review of Economics, 5*(1), 347–373. doi:10.1146/annurev-economics-082312-125807 PMID:23991248

Hauff, J. C., Carlander, A., Garling, T., & Nicolini, G. (2020). Retirement Financial Behaviour: How Important Is Being Financially Literature? *Journal of Consumer Policy, 43*(3), 543–564. doi:10.100710603-019-09444-x

Helbin, T., & Van Looy, A. (2019). Business Process Ambidexterity and its impact on Business-IT alignment. A Systematic Literature Review. *2019 13th International Conference on Research Challenges in Information Science (RCIS)*, 1–12. 10.1109/RCIS.2019.8877073

Hermann, M., Pentek, T., & Otto, B. (2016). Design Principles for Industrie 4.0 Scenarios. In *2016 49th Hawaii International Conference on System Sciences (HICSS)* (pp. 3928–3937). IEEE. doi:10.1109/HICSS.2016.488

Hesmondhalgh. (2002). *The Cultural Industries.* London: Sage.

Hevner, A., March, S., Park, J., & Ram, S. (2004). Design Science in Information Systems Research. *Management Information Systems Quarterly, 28*(1), 75–105. doi:10.2307/25148625

Hidalgo, A., Martín-Barroso, D., Nuñez-Serrano, J. A., Turrión, J., & Velázquez, F. (2022). Does hotel management matter to overcoming the COVID-19 crisis? The Spanish case. *Tourism Management*, *88*, 104395. doi:10.1016/j.tourman.2021.104395 PMID:34720321

Hill, B. M., Helmke, M., & Burger, C. (2009). *The official Ubuntu book*. Pearson Education.

Hjørland, B. (2011). The importance of theories of knowledge: Browsing as an example. *Journal of the American Society for Information Science and Technology*, *62*(3), 594–603. doi:10.1002/asi.21480

Hofacker, C. F., & Belanche, D. (2016). Eight social media challenges for marketing managers. *Spanish Journal of Marketing-ESIC*, *20*(2), 73–80. doi:10.1016/j.sjme.2016.07.003

Holbrook, M. B., & Hirschman, E. C. (1982). The experiential aspects of consumption: Consumer fantasies, feelings, and fun. *The Journal of Consumer Research*, *9*(2), 132–140. doi:10.1086/208906

Holloway, J., & Humphreys, C. (n.d.). *The business of tourism* (10th ed.). London: Pearson.

Howaldt, J., & Kopp, R. (2012). Shaping social innovation by social research. In Challenge Social Innovation. Springer. doi:10.1007/978-3-642-32879-4_3

Howkins, J. (2002). *The creative economy: how people make Money from ideas*. Penguin Global.

Hoyle, R. H. (Ed.). (2012). *Handbook of structural equation modeling*. Guilford Press.

Huang, P., Lurie, N. H., & Mitra, S. (2009). Searching for experience on the web: An empirical examination of consumer behavior for search and experience goods. *Journal of Marketing*, *73*(2), 55–69. doi:10.1509/jmkg.73.2.55

Hübner, A. H., Kuhn, H., Wollenburg, J., Towers, N., & Kotzab, H. (2016). Last mile fulfilment and distribution in omni-channel grocery retailing: A strategic planning framework. *International Journal of Retail & Distribution Management*, *44*(3). Advance online publication. doi:10.1108/IJRDM-11-2014-0154

Hudson, S., Huang, L., Roth, M. S., & Madden, T. J. (2015). The influence of social media interactions on consumer-brand relationships: A three-country study of branch perceptions and marketing behaviors. *International Journal of Research in Marketing*, *33*(1), 27–41. doi:10.1016/j.ijresmar.2015.06.004

Huston, S. (2010). Measuring financial literacy. *The Journal of Consumer Affairs*, *44*(2), 296–316. doi:10.1111/j.1745-6606.2010.01170.x

Hu, Y., & Chen, K. (2016). Predicting hotel review helpfulness: The impact of review visibility, and interaction between hotel stars and review ratings. *International Journal of Information Management*, *36*(6), 929–944. doi:10.1016/j.ijinfomgt.2016.06.003

Hyperloop, V. (n.d.). Retrieved June 15, 2021, from https://virginhyperloop.com/

IEC. (2017). *IEC 62657-2:2017 Industrial communication networks - Wireless communication networks - Part 2: Coexistence management*. Retrieved from https://cdn.standards.iteh.ai/samples/22382/3f887e55ed074e2ba81dd356a18b176f/IEC-62657-2-2017.pdf

Ieva, M., De Canio, F., & Ziliani, C. (2018). Daily deal shoppers: What drives social couponing? *Journal of Retailing and Consumer Services*, *40*, 299–303. doi:10.1016/j.jretconser.2017.03.005

Industrial Internet Consortium. (2013). *Fact Sheet*. Retrieved March 2, 2019, from https://www.iiconsortium.org/docs/IIC_FACT_SHEET.pdf

INFE. (2020). *Oecd.Org. International Gateway For Financial Education - Organisation For Economic Co-Operation And Development*. Https://Www.Oecd.Org/Financial/Education/Oecd-International-Network-On-Financial-Education.Html

Innovation - The Official Portal of the UAE Government. (n.d.). https://u.ae/en/about-the-uae/the-uae-government/government-of-future/innovation-in-the-uae

Innovation and Change During a Global Pandemic. (n.d.). *Knowledge*@Wharton. https://knowledge.wharton.upenn.edu/special-report/innovation-change-global-pandemic/

Islam, M. (2021). *International tourism during and after COVID-19: The role of digital technology*. Academic Press.

Istat. (2020). *Rapporto sul territorio 2020. Appendice*. Le geografie e le classificazioni territoriali usate nel rapporto.

Istat. (2020a). *22 Commercio interno e altri servizi*. Istat, Annuario Statistico Italiano 2020.

Istat. (2021). *Notizie sul commercio al dettaglio*. Sito ufficiale Istat.

Jacobson, I., Lawson, B., McMahon, P., & Goedicke, M. (2017). *Software Engineering Essentialized*. www.software-engineering-essentialized.com

Jacobson, I. (2004). Use Cases – Yesterday, Today, and Tomorrow. *Software & Systems Modeling*, *3*(3), 210–220. doi:10.100710270-004-0060-3

Jacobson, I., & Seidewitz, E. (2014). A new software engineering. *Communications of the ACM*, *57*(12), 49–54. doi:10.1145/2677034

Janjevic, M., & Winkenbach, M. (2020). Characterizing urban last-mile distribution strategies in mature and emerging e-commerce markets. *Transportation Research Part A, Policy and Practice*, *133*, 133. doi:10.1016/j.tra.2020.01.003

Jauhar, J. B., Ghani, A. B., & Islam, R. (2016). Results and data analysis. In *Brain Drain* (pp. 127–158). Springer.

Jiang, Y., & Wen, J. (2020). *Effects of COVID-19 on hotel marketing and management: a perspective article*. Academic Press.

Jilcha, K., Kitaw, D., & Beshah, B. (2016). Workplace innovation influence on occupational safety and health. *African Journal of Science, Technology, Innovation and Development*, *8*(1), 33–42. doi:10.1080/20421338.2015.1128044

Jocevski, M. (2020). Blurring the lines between physical and digital spaces: Business model innovation in retailing. *California Management Review*, *63*(1), 99–117. doi:10.1177/0008125620953639

Johnson, E. J., Moe, W. W., Fader, P. S., Bellman, S., & Lohse, G. L. (2004). On the Depth and Dynamics of Online Search Behavior. *Management Science*, *50*(3), 299–308. doi:10.1287/mnsc.1040.0194

Jørgensen, U. (2012). Mapping and navigating transitions – the multi-level perspective compared with the arenas of development. *Research Policy*, *41*(6), 996–1010. doi:10.1016/j.respol.2012.03.001

Júlio, D., Torres, J., & Silveira, C. (2021). Diabetes Tracker & Volunteer+: Implementações Tecnológicas na Promoção dos Objetivos de Desenvolvimento Sustentável. In *V International Forum on Management – IFM2021* (pp. 354-381). Instituto Politécnico de Setúbal.

Jungmann, S. M., & Witthöft, M. (2020). Health anxiety, cyberchondria, and coping in the current COVID-19 pandemic: Which factors are related to coronavirus anxiety? *Journal of Anxiety Disorders*, *73*, 102239. doi:10.1016/j.janxdis.2020.102239 PMID:32502806

Kagermann, H. (2014). Chancen von Industrie 4.0 nutzen. In *Industrie 4.0 in Produktion, Automatisierung und Logistik* (pp. 603–614). Wiesbaden: Springer Fachmedien Wiesbaden. doi:10.1007/978-3-658-04682-8_31

Kagermann, H., Wahlster, W., Helbig, J., Hellinger, A., Stumpf, M. A. V., & Treugut, L. … Findeklee, U. (2013). *Recommendations for implementing the strategic initiative Industrie 4.0: Final report of the Industrie 4.0*. Retrieved from http://alvarestech.com/temp/tcn/CyberPhysicalSystems-Industrial4-0.pdf

Kajalo, S., & Lindblom, A. (2015). Market orientation, entrepreneurial orientation and business performance among small retailers. *International Journal of Retail & Distribution Management*, *43*(7), 580–596. doi:10.1108/IJRDM-04-2014-0044

Kalina, J. (2021). Managerial Decision Support in the Post-COVID-19 Era: Towards Information-Based Management. In L. C. Carvalho, L. Reis, & C. Silveira (Eds.), *Handbook of Research on Entrepreneurship, Innovation, Sustainability, and ICTs in the Post-COVID-19 Era* (pp. 225–241). IGI Global. doi:10.4018/978-1-7998-6776-0.ch011

Kang, H., Hahn, M., Fortin, D. R., Hyun, Y. J., & Eom, Y. (2006). Effects of Perceived Behavioral Control on the Consumer Usage Intention of E-coupons. *Psychology and Marketing*, *23*(10), 841–864. doi:10.1002/mar.20136

Kapoor, V., Yadav, J., Bajpai, L., & Srivastava, S. (2021). Perceived stress and psychological well-being of working mothers during COVID-19: A mediated moderated roles of teleworking and resilience. *Employee Relations: The International Journal*, *43*(6), 1290–1309. doi:10.1108/ER-05-2020-0244

Karatepe, O. M., Saydam, M. B., & Okumus, F. (2021). COVID-19, mental health problems, and their detrimental effects on hotel employees' propensity to be late for work, absenteeism, and life satisfaction. *Current Issues in Tourism*, *24*(7), 934–951. doi:10.1080/13683500.2021.1884665

Kargas, A., & Varoutas, D. (2020). Industry 4.0 in Cultural Industry. A Review on Digital Visualization for VR and AR Applications. In C. M. Bolognesi & S. Cettina (Eds.), Impact of Industry 4.0 on Architecture and Cultural Heritage (pp. 1–19). IGI Global. https://doi.org/10.4018/978-1-7998-1234-0.CH001.

Kargas, A., Kiriakidis, M., & Zacharakis, E. (2020). Europe's Economic Crisis: Re - Clustering European Economies. *European Journal of Social Science Education and Research*, *7*(1), 41. https://doi.org/10.26417/ejser.v7i1.p41-50

Kasemsap, K. (2017). *Professional and business applications of social media platforms. In Analyzing the strategic role of social networking in firm growth and productivity*. IGI Global. doi:10.4018/978-1-5225-0559-4.ch021

Kaswan, K. S., Dhatterwal, J. S., & Gaur, N. K. (2021). Smart Grid Using Internet of Things. In P. Tomar (Ed.), Integration and Implementation of the Internet of Things Through Cloud Computing (pp. 251-271). IGI Global. doi:10.4018/978-1-7998-6981-8.ch013

Kaswan, K. S., Dhatterwal, J. S., & Kumar, K. (2021). Blockchain of Internet of Things-Based Earthquake Alarming System in Smart Cities. In P. Tomar (Ed.), Integration and Implementation of the Internet of Things Through Cloud Computing (pp. 272-287). IGI Global. doi:10.4018/978-1-7998-6981-8.ch014

Kemp, S. (2021). *Digital 2021: Global Overview Report*. Hootsuite. Available at: https://datareportal.com/reports/digital-2021-singapore

Kempson, E., Collard, S., & Moore, N. (2005). *Financial capability: An exploratory study. Consumer research report 37*. Financial Services Authority.

Kesari, B., & Atulkar, S. (2016). Satisfaction of mall shoppers: A study on perceived utilitarian and hedonic shopping values. *Journal of Retailing and Consumer Services. Elsevier*, *31*, 22–31. doi:10.1016/j.jretconser.2016.03.005

Khan, I., Hollebeek, L. D., Fatma, M., Islam, J. U., & Riivits-Arkonsuo, I. (2020). Customer experience and commitment in retailing: Does customer age matter? *Journal of Retailing and Consumer Services*, *57*, 102219. doi:10.1016/j.jretconser.2020.102219

Kietzmann, J. H., Hermkens, K., McCarthy, I. P., & Silvestre, B. S. (2011). Social media? Get serious! Understanding the functional building blocks of social media. *Business Horizons*, *54*(3), 241–251. doi:10.1016/j.bushor.2011.01.005

Kim, E., & Drumwright, M. (2016). Engaging consumers and building relationships in social media: How social relatedness influences intrinsic vs. extrinsic consumer motivation. *Computers in Human Behavior*, *63*, 970–979. doi:10.1016/j.chb.2016.06.025

Kim, H. Y., & Kim, Y. K. (2008). Shopping enjoyment and store shopping modes: The moderating influence of chronic time pressure. *Journal of Retailing and Consumer Services*, *15*(5), 410–419. doi:10.1016/j.jretconser.2007.10.003

Kir, H., & Erdogan, N. (2021). A knowledge-intensive adaptive business process management framework. *Information Systems*, *95*, 101639. doi:10.1016/j.is.2020.101639

Klepek, M., & Bauerová, R. (2020). Why do retail customers hesitate for shopping grocery online? *Technological and Economic Development of Economy*, *26*(6), 1444–1462. doi:10.3846/tede.2020.13970

Kozinets, R. V., De Valck, K., Wojnicki, A. C., & Wilner, S. J. S. (2010). Networked narratives: Understanding word-of-mouth marketing in online communities. *Journal of Marketing*, *74*(2), 71–89. doi:10.1509/jm.74.2.71

Kozinets, R., Patterson, A., & Ashman, R. (2017). Networks of desire: How technology increases our passion to consume. *The Journal of Consumer Research*, *43*(5), 659–682.

Kubiak, P., & Rass, S. (2018). An Overview of Data-Driven Techniques for IT-Service-Management. *IEEE Access: Practical Innovations, Open Solutions*, *6*, 63664–63688. doi:10.1109/ACCESS.2018.2875975

Kumar, V. S. (2006). Effective requirements management. *PMI® Global Congress 2006—EMEA, Madrid, Spain*. Newtown Square, PA: Project Management Institute.

Kumar, A., Luthra, S., Mangla, S. K., & Kazançoğlu, Y. (2020). COVID-19 impact on sustainable production and operations management. *Sustainable Operations and Computers*, *1*, 1–7. doi:10.1016/j.susoc.2020.06.001

Kunchala, J., Yu, J., Yongchareon, S., & Liu, C. (2020). An approach to merge collaborating processes of an inter-organizational business process for artifact lifecycle synthesis. *Computing*, *102*(4), 951–976. doi:10.100700607-019-00770-z

Kylliäinen, J. (2019, october). *Types of Innovation – The Ultimate Guide with Definitions and Examples*. Retrieved from https://www.viima.com/blog/types-of-innovation

Lai, I. K. W., & Wong, J. (2020). *Comparing crisis management practices in the hotel industry between initial and pandemic stages of COVID-19*. Academic Press.

Laing, A., & Royle, J. (2013). Bookselling online: An examination of consumer behaviour patterns. *Publishing Research Quarterly*, *29*(2), 110–127. doi:10.100712109-013-9318-3

Laitsou, E., Kargas, A., & Varoutas, D. (2020). Digital Competitiveness in the European Union Era: The Greek Case. *Economies*, *8*(4), 85. doi:10.3390/economies8040085

Lakhani, K., & Mcafee, A. (2015). *Wikipedia*. Retrieved June 26th 2021, from http://courseware.hbs.edu/public/cases/wikipedia/main.html

Landi, G., Pakenham, K. I., Boccolini, G., Grandi, S., & Tossani, E. (2020). *Health anxiety and mental health outcome during COVID-19 lockdown in Italy: the mediating and moderating roles of psychological flexibility*. Academic Press.

Landum, M., Moura, M., & Reis, L. (2021). A framework for the alignment of ICT with Green IT. *Advances in Science, Technology and Engineering Systems Journal*, *6*(2).

Lau, A. (2020). New technologies used in COVID-19 for business survival: Insights from the Hotel Sector in China. *Information Technology & Tourism*, *22*(4), 497–504. doi:10.100740558-020-00193-z

Law, R., Buhalis, D., & Cobanoglu, C. (2014). Progress on information and communication technologies in hospitality and tourism. *International Journal of Contemporary Hospitality Management*, *26*(5), 727–750. doi:10.1108/IJCHM-08-2013-0367

Laycock, R. (2021) *Serviços de Streaming mais Populares*. Available at: https://www.finder.com/br/streaming-estatisticas

Lee, E. A. (2008). Cyber Physical Systems: Design Challenges. In *2008 11th IEEE International Symposium on Object and Component-Oriented Real-Time Distributed Computing (ISORC)* (pp. 363–369). IEEE. doi:10.1109/ISORC.2008.25

Lee, J. (2015). Smart Factory Systems. *Informatik-Spektrum, 38*(3), 230–235. doi:10.1007/S00287-015-0891-Z

Lee, Y., Xie, K., Besharat, A., & Tan, Y. (2017). Management Responses to Online WOM: Helpful or Detrimental? SSRN *Electronic Journal*. doi:10.2139/ssrn.2919553

Lee, H., Jung, T. H., tom Dieck, M. C., & Chung, N. (2020). Experiencing immersive virtual reality in museums. *Information & Management*, *57*(5), 103229. doi:10.1016/j.im.2019.103229

Lee, J., Cameron, I., & Hassall, M. (2019). Improving process safety: What roles for Digitalization and Industry 4.0? *Process Safety and Environmental Protection*, *132*, 325–339. doi:10.1016/j.psep.2019.10.021

Lee, K. J. (2016). Sense of calling and career satisfaction of hotel frontline employees: Mediation through knowledge sharing behaviour with organizational members. *International Journal of Contemporary Hospitality Management*, *28*(2), 346–365. doi:10.1108/IJCHM-01-2014-0026

Li, F. (2020). The digital transformation of business models in the creative industries: A holistic framework and emerging trends. *Technovation*, *92*, 102012. doi:10.1016/j.technovation.2017.12.004

Li, F., & Ryan, C. (2020). Western guest experiences of a Pyongyang international hotel, North Korea: Satisfaction under conditions of constrained choice. *Tourism Management*, *76*, 103947. doi:10.1016/j.tourman.2019.07.001

Li, M., & Hsu, C. (2017). Customer participation in services and its effect on employee innovative behavior. *Journal of Hospitality Marketing & Management*, *26*(2), 164–185. doi:10.1080/19368623.2016.1215946

Li, M., & Hsu, C. H. (2016). A review of employee innovative behavior in services. *International Journal of Contemporary Hospitality Management*, *28*(12), 2820–2841. doi:10.1108/IJCHM-04-2015-0214

Lim, S. F. W., Jin, X., & Srai, J. S. (2018). Consumer-driven e-commerce: A literature review, design framework, and research agenda on last-mile logistics models. *International Journal of Physical Distribution & Logistics Management*, *48*(3), 308–332. doi:10.1108/IJPDLM-02-2017-0081

Lim, S. F. W., & Srai, J. S. (2018). Examining the anatomy of last-mile distribution in e- commerce omnichannel retailing. *International Journal of Operations & Production Management*, *38*(9), 1735–1764. doi:10.1108/IJOPM-12-2016-0733

Liscia, R. (2020). *Consorzio Netcomm. Il lockdown triplica i Nuovi Consumatori Online in Italia tra gennaio e maggio*. https://www.consorzionetcomm.it/il-lockdown-triplica-i-nuovi-consumatori-online-in-italia-tra-gennaio-e-maggio

Liu, S., Chou, C., & Liao, H. (2015). An exploratory study of product placement in social media. *Internet Research*, *25*(2), 300–316. doi:10.1108/IntR-12-2013-0267

Löffler, M., & Tschiesner, A. (2013). *The Internet of Things and the Future of Manufacturing*. Retrieved from https://www.ocf.co.uk/uploads/manufacturing_whitepaper.pdf

Loureiro, S. M. C., Guerreiro, J., & Ali, F. (2020). 20 years of research on virtual reality and augmented reality in tourism context: A text-mining approach. *Tourism Management*, *77*, 104028. doi:10.1016/j.tourman.2019.104028

Lu, J., Xiao, X., Xu, Z., Wang, C., Zhang, M., & Zhou, Y. (2021). The potential of virtual tourism in the recovery of tourism industry during the COVID-19 pandemic. *Current Issues in Tourism*, 1–17. doi:10.1080/13683500.2021.1922363

Lukas, N., Gilmore, A., Jay, C., & Yo, Y. (2021). The impact of COVID-19 on digital data practices in museums and art galleries in the UK and the US. *Humanities & Social. Science Communication*, *8*(1). https://www.researchsquare.com/article/rs-535272/v1

Luthans, F., Norman, S. M., Avolio, B. J., & Avey, J. B. (2008). The mediating role of psychological capital in the supportive organizational climate—Employee performance relationship. *Journal of Organizational Behavior*, *29*(2), 219–238. doi:10.1002/job.507

Lv, Z., Chen, D., Lou, R., & Alazab, A. (2021). Artificial intelligence for securing industrial-based cyber–physical systems. *Future Generation Computer Systems*, *117*, 291–298. doi:10.1016/j.future.2020.12.001

Lyu, S. (2016). Which Accessible Travel Products Are People With Disabilities Willing To Pay More. A choice experiment? *Tourism Management*, *59*, 404–412. doi:10.1016/j.tourman.2016.09.002

Mahalle, A., Yong, J., & Tao, X. (2018). ITIL Processes to Control Operational Risk in Cloud Architecture Infrastructure for Banking and Financial Services Industry. *2018 5th International Conference on Behavioral, Economic, and Socio-Cultural Computing (BESC)*, 197–200. 10.1109/BESC.2018.8697294

Maiden, N., & Gizikis, A. (2001). Where Do Requirements Come From? *IEEE Software*, *18*(5), 10–12. doi:10.1109/52.951486

Majchrzak, A., Markus, M. L., & Wareham, J. (2016). Designing for digital transformation: Lessons for information systems research from the study of ICT and societal challenges. *Management Information Systems Quarterly*, *40*(2), 267–277. doi:10.25300/MISQ/2016/40:2.03

Malik, I., & Tarar, S. (2021). Cloud-Based Smart City Using Internet of Things. In P. Tomar (Ed.), Integration and Implementation of the Internet of Things Through Cloud Computing (pp. 133-154). IGI Global. doi:10.4018/978-1-7998-6981-8.ch007

Mandell, L., & Klein, L. (2007). Motivation and financial literacy. *Financial Services Review*, *16*, 105–116.

Mao, Y., He, J., Morrison, A. M., & Andres Coca-Stefaniak, J. (2020). Effects of tourism CSR on employee psychological capital in the COVID-19 crisis: From the perspective of conservation of resources theory. *Current Issues in Tourism*, 1–19. doi:10.1080/13683500.2020.1770706

Marasco, A., Buonincontri, P., van Niekerk, M., Orlowski, M., & Okumus, F. (2018). Exploring the role of next-generation virtual technologies in destination marketing. *Journal of Destination Marketing & Management*, *9*, 138–148. doi:10.1016/j.jdmm.2017.12.002

Marchão, J., Reis, L., & Martins, P. V. (2021). A Framework to Align Business Processes: Identification of the Main Features. *Advances in Science. Technology and Engineering Systems Journal*, *6*(2), 746–753. doi:10.25046/aj060286

Marchão, J., Reis, L., & Ventura, P. (2020). Operation management using ITIL and COBIT framework. *Conference Proceedings (Part of ITEMA Conference Collection)*, 201–207. 10.31410/ITEMA.2020.201

Maree, M., & Mertens, S. (2012). The limits of economic value in measuring the performance of social innovation. In A. Nicholls & A. Murdock (Eds.), *Social innovation: blurring boundaries to reconfigure markets* (pp. 114–136). Palgrave Macmillan. doi:10.1057/9780230367098_5

Markusen, A., Wassall, G., Denatale, D., & Cohen, R. (2008). Defining the Creative Economy: Industry and Occupational Approaches. *Economic Development Quarterly*, *22*(1), 24–45. doi:10.1177/0891242407311862

Márquez, P., Reficco, E., & Berger, G. (2010). *Socially inclusive business: Engaging the poor through market initiatives in Iberoamerica*. Harvard University Press.

Martin-Fuentes, E., Fernandez, C., Mateu, C., & Marine-Roig, E. (2018). Modelling a grading scheme for peer-to-peer accommodation: Stars for Airbnb. *International Journal of Hospitality Management*, *69*, 75–83. doi:10.1016/j.ijhm.2017.10.016

Mason, A. N., Narcum, J., & Mason, K. (2021). Social media marketing gains importance after Covid-19. *Cogent Business & Management*, *8*(1), 1–17. doi:10.1080/23311975.2020.1870797

Masrek, M. N., Yusof, N. I., Noordin, S. A., & Johare, R. (2013). Exploring the relationship between job design and knowledge productivity: A conceptual framework in the context of Malaysian administrative and diplomatic officers. *Journal of Organizational Knowledge*, 1-8. doi:10.5171/2013.128970

Mathwick, C., & Rigdon, E. (2004). Play, Flow, and the Online Search Experience. *The Journal of Consumer Research*, *31*(2), 324–332. doi:10.1086/422111

Mattei, L., & Heinen, V. L. (2020). Impacts of the COVID-19 crisis on the Brazilian labor market. *Brazilian Journal of Political Economy*, *40*(4), 647–668. doi:10.1590/0101-31572020-3200

Mazareanu, E. (2020). *Last-mile logistics worldwide: statistics & facts*. Statista.

Mazareanu, E. (2020a). *What are your costumers more important wishes when it comes to last mile delivery?* Statista.

MCE. (2013). *Referencial de Educação Financeira para a Educação Pré-Escolar, o Ensino Básico, o Ensino Secundário e a Educação e Formação de Adultos*. https://dge.mec.pt/sites/default/files/ficheiros/referencial_de_educacao_financeira_final_versao_port.pdf

MCE. (2016a). *Plano Nacional de Formação Financeira 2016-2020*. https://cidadania.dge.mec.pt/literacia-financeira-e-educacao-para-o-consumo/plano-nacional-de-formacao-financeira apresenta os pressupostos no âmbito do Plano supracitado

MCE. (2016b). *Educação para a Cidadania. Literacia Financeira e Educação para o Consumo*. https://cidadania.dge.mec.pt/literacia-financeira-e-educacao-para-o-consumo

McKinley, W., Latham, S., & Braun, M. (2014). Organizational decline and innovation: Turnarounds and downward spirals. *Academy of Management Review*, *39*(1), 88–110. doi:10.5465/amr.2011.0356

McKinsey & Company. (2021, June 29). *Economic conditions outlook, June 2021*. McKinsey & Company. https://www.mckinsey.com/business-functions/strategy-and-corporate-finance/our-insights/economic-conditions-outlook-june-2021

Menglong, L., Shuanghui, Y., Mengmeng, Z., Tao, C., Honghui, C., & Xiaoxue, Z. (2020). A coevolutionary framework of business-IT alignment via the lens of enterprise architecture. *Journal of Systems Engineering and Electronics*, *31*(5), 983–995. doi:10.23919/JSEE.2020.000073

Mentz, E., & Goosen, L. (2007). Are groups working in the Information Technology class? *South African Journal of Education*, *27*(2), 329–343.

Meza-Peralta, K., Gonzalez-Feliu, J., Montoya-Torres, J. R., & Khodadad-Saryazdi, A. (2020, October). A unified typology of urban logistics spaces as interfaces for freight transport: A Systematic Literature Review. In Supply Chain Forum. *International Journal (Toronto, Ont.)*, *21*(4), 274–289.

Minhas, W. A. (2018). *Advancing entrepreneurship in the united arab emirates: Start-up challenges and opportunities (1st* (2018 ed.). Palgrave Macmillan. doi:10.1007/978-3-319-76436-8

Moe, W. W. (2003). Buying, Searching, or Browsing: Differentiating Between Online Shoppers Using In-Store Navigational Clickstream. *Journal of Consumer Psychology*, *13*(1–2), 29–39. doi:10.1207/153276603768344762

Moe, W. W., & Yang, S. (2009). Inertial disruption: The impact of a new competitive entrant on online consumer search. *Journal of Marketing*, *73*(1), 109–121. doi:10.1509/jmkg.73.1.109

Molina-García, A., Florido-Ruiz, B., Valenzuela, M. C. & Diéguez-Soto, J. (2020). The effect of family ownership and generation on financial literacy. *Small Business International Review*, *4*(1), 1-15.

Moorthy, S., Ratchford, B. T., & Talukdar, D. (1997). Consumer Information Search Revisited: Theory and Empirical Analysis. *The Journal of Consumer Research*, *23*(4), 263–277. doi:10.1086/209482

Morgan-Thomas, A., & Veloutsou, C. (2013). Beyond technology acceptance: Brand relationships and online brand experience. *Journal of Business Research*, *66*(1), 21–27. doi:10.1016/j.jbusres.2011.07.019

Morgeson, F., & Humphrey, S. (2006). The Work Design Questionnaire (WDQ): Developing and validating a comprehensive measure for assessing job design and the nature of work. *The Journal of Applied Psychology*, *91*(6), 1321–1339. doi:10.1037/0021-9010.91.6.1321 PMID:17100487

Moulaert, F. (Ed.). (2013). *The International Handbook on Social Innovation; Collective Action, Social Learning and Transdisciplinary Research*. Edward Elgar.

MSD Controlar a Diabetes. (2017). *Entender a Diabetes*. https://controlaradiabetes.pt/entender-a-diabetes/diabetes-mellitus-tipo-1

Mulgan, G. (2010). Measuring social value. *Stanford Social Innovation Review*, *8*(3), 38–43.

Mullis, K., & Kim, M. (2011). Factors determining inshopping in rural US communities: Consumers' and retailers' perceptions. *International Journal of Retail & Distribution Management*, *39*(5), 326–345. doi:10.1108/09590551111130757

Munar, A. M., & Ooi, C.-S. (2012). The truth of the crowds: social media and the heritage experience. In L. Smith, E. Waterton, & S. Watson (Eds.), *The cultural moment in tourism (pp. 255-273)*. Routledge.

Munar, A., & Jacobsen, J. (2014). Motivations for sharing tourism experiences through social media. *Tourism Management*, *43*, 46–54. doi:10.1016/j.tourman.2014.01.012

Murray, R., Caulier-Grice, J., & Mulgar, G. (2010). *The open book of social innovation*. Young Foundation/NESTA.

mySugr. (2020). *mySugr*. www.mysugr.com/en/diabetes-app/

Nasiriasayesh, H., & Yari, A. (2019). A Model for Policy-Aware Execution of Business Process in Federated Clouds. *9th International Symposium on Telecommunication: With Emphasis on Information and Communication Technology, IST 2018*, 700–704. 10.1109/ISTEL.2018.8661051

National Strategy for Advanced Innovation - The Official Portal of the UAE Government. (n.d.). https://u.ae/en/about-the-uae/strategies-initiatives-and-awards/federal-governments-strategies-and-plans/national-strategy-for-advanced-innovation

Nault, B. R., & Rahman, M. S. (2019). Proximity to a traditional physical store: The effects of mitigating online disutility costs. *Production and Operations Management*, *28*(4), 1033–1051. doi:10.1111/poms.12957

Naylor, R. W., Lamberton, C. P., & West, P. M. (2012). Beyond the "like" button: The impact of mere virtual presence on brand evaluations and purchase intentions in social media settings. *Journal of Marketing*, *76*(6), 105–120. doi:10.1509/jm.11.0105

Neiva, M. (2020). *ColorADD*. Retrieved from http://www.coloradd.net/index.asp: http://www.coloradd.net/why.asp

Neiva, M. (2020, October). *Covid-19 numa pandemia de semáforos quem não distingue cores enfrenta desafios*. Retrieved from https://observador.pt/2020/10/26/covid-19- numa-pandemia-de-semaforos-quem-nao-distingue-cores-enfrenta-desafios/

Neshat, N., Moayedfar, S., Rezaee, K., & Amrollahi Biuki, N. (2021). Sustainable planning of developing tourism destinations after COVID-19 outbreak: A deep learning approach. *Journal of Policy Research in Tourism, Leisure & Events*, 1–21. doi:10.1080/19407963.2021.1970578

Netcomm Forum Live. (2020). *La spesa alimentare online si consolida come abitudine dei consumatori italiani. Consorzio Netcomm - Il Commercio Digitale Italiano Nielsen e Politecnico di Milano (2020). Osservatorio Multicanalità. Politecnico di Milano*. School of Management.

Neuburger, L., & Egger, R. (2021). Travel risk perception and travel behaviour during the COVID-19 pandemic 2020: A case study of the DACH region. *Current Issues in Tourism*, *24*(7), 1003–1016. doi:10.1080/13683500.2020.1803807

Neumann, A., Wisniewski, L., Ganesan, R. S., Rost, P., & Jasperneite, J. (2018). Towards integration of Industrial Ethernet with 5G mobile networks. In *14th IEEE International Workshop on Factory Communication Systems - Proceedings, WFCS* (pp. 1–4). Institute of Electrical and Electronics Engineers Inc. doi:10.1109/WFCS.2018.8402373

Ngugi, J. K., & Goosen, L. (2021c). Computer Science and Information Technology Students' Self-regulated Learning and Knowledge Sharing Behavior as Drivers of Individual Innovative Behavior. Lecture Notes in Networks and Systems, 230, 593-608. doi:10.1007/978-3-030-77442-4_50

Ngugi, J., & Goosen, L. (2019, October 25). Towards Smart Innovation for Information Systems and Technology Students: Modelling Motivation, Metacognition and Affective Aspects of Learning. Smart Innovation, Systems and Technologies, 111, 90-99. doi:10.1007/978-3-030-03577-8_11

Ngugi, J. K., & Goosen, L. (2021a). Knowledge Sharing Mediating Information Technology Student Innovation. In M. Khosrow-Pour (Ed.), *Handbook of Research on Modern Educational Technologies, Applications, and Management* (Vol. 2, pp. 645–663). IGI Global. doi:10.4018/978-1-7998-3476-2.ch040

Ngugi, J. K., & Goosen, L. (2021b). Innovation, Entrepreneurship, and Sustainability for ICT Students Towards the Post-COVID-19 Era. In L. C. Carvalho, L. Reis, & C. Silveira (Eds.), *Handbook of Research on Entrepreneurship, Innovation, Sustainability, and ICTs in the Post-COVID-19 Era* (pp. 110–131). IGI Global. doi:10.4018/978-1-7998-6776-0.ch006

Ngugi, J., & Goosen, L. (2017). The Effects of Course Design Characteristics, Self-Regulated Learning and Knowledge Sharing in Facilitating the Development of Innovative Behaviour among Technology Students at Universities. In *Proceedings of the Institute of Science and Technology Education (ISTE) Conference on Mathematics, Science and Technology Education* (pp. 80-86). UNISA Press.

Ngugi, J., & Goosen, L. (2018). Modelling Course-Design Characteristics, Self-Regulated Learning and the Mediating Effect of Knowledge-Sharing Behavior as Drivers of Individual Innovative Behavior. *Eurasia Journal of Mathematics, Science and Technology Education, 14*(8). Advance online publication. doi:10.29333/ejmste/92087

Nicholls, A. (2009). 'We do good things, don't we?': 'blended value accounting' in social entrepreneurship. *Accounting, Organizations and Society*, *34*(6–7), 755–769. doi:10.1016/j.aos.2009.04.008

Nicholson, P. (2007). A history of e-learning. *Computers & Education*, 1–11.

NielsenIQ. (2021). *Evolução dos Canais de Retalho*. Author.

Njenga, J. K., & Fourie, L. C. (2010). The myths about e-learning in higher education. *British Journal of Educational Technology*, *41*(2), 199–212. doi:10.1111/j.1467-8535.2008.00910.x

Nobre, G. (2020). *Creative Economy and Covid-19, Technology, Automation and the New Economy*. Available at: http://www. researchgate.net/profile/Guilherme_Nobre/publication/340438912_Creative_Economy_and_Covid19_technology_automation_and_the_new_economy/links/5e8a71f4299bf130797ffc1e/Creative-Economy-and-Covid-19-technology-automation-and-the-new-economy.pdf

Nokia. (2017, April 18). *Nokia studies outline business return-on-investment from 5G services*. Retrieved July 22, 2021, from https://www.nokia.com/about-us/news/releases/2017/04/18/nokia-studies-outline-business-return-on-investment-from-5g-services/

Novobanco. (2020). *Programa de Literacia Financeira*. https://www.novobanco.pt/site/cms.aspx?labelid=literaciafinanceira

Ntounis, N., Parker, C., Skinner, H., Steadman, C., & Warnaby, G. (2021). Tourism and Hospitality industry resilience during the Covid-19 pandemic: Evidence from England. *Current Issues in Tourism*, 1–14. doi:10.1080/13683500.2021.1883556

Nunes, M., & O'Neill, H. (2007). *Fundamental de UML* (5th ed.). FCA Editora.

OCG. (2007). *The official Introdution to ITIL Service Lifecycle*. Stationery Office.

OECD Tourism Trends and Policies 2020. (2021). Retrieved June 26th 2021, from https://www.oecd-ilibrary.org/sites/f3180e03-en/index.html?itemId=/content/component/f3180e03

OECD. (2015). *OECD / INFE Toolkit for measuring financial literacy and financial inclusion*. OECD.

OECD. (2019). *Digital Innovation: Seizing Policy Opportunities*. OECD Publishing. doi:10.1787/a298dc87-

OECD. (2020). *OECD Recommendation on Financial Literacy*. Obtido de OECD: https://www.oecd.org/finance/OECD-Recommendation-on-Financial-Literacy.html

OECD. (2020). *OECD/INFE 2020 International Survey of Adult Financial Literacy*. www.oecd.org/financial/education/launchoftheoecdinfeglobalfinancialliteracysurveyreport.htm

OECD/Eurostat. (2018). Oslo Manual 2018: Guidelines for collecting, reporting and using data on innovation (4th ed.). OECD.

Ogbeibu, S., Chiappetta Jabbour, C. J., Burgess, J., Gaskin, J., & Renwick, D. W. S. (2021). Green talent management and turnover intention: The roles of leader STARA competence and digital task interdependence. *Journal of Intellectual Capital*. Advance online publication. doi:10.1108/JIC-01-2021-0016

Oldham, G. R. (2012). The design of jobs: A strategy for enhancing the positive outcomes of individuals at work. In G. M. Spreitzer & K. S. Cameron (Eds.), *The Oxford Handbook of Positive Organizational Scholarship* (pp. 651 663). Oxford University Press. doi:10.1093/oxfordhb/9780199734610.013.0049

Oliveira, E., Cremonezi, G., Casagrande, J., & Souto, A. (2021). Marketing Strategies: Innovation in retail during the restriction and social measures caused by Covid-19 pandemic. *Brazilian Journal of Development*, *7*(7), 67155–67173. doi:10.34117/bjdv7n7-135

Ono, A., Nakamura, A., Okuno, A., & Sumikawa, M. (2012). Consumer Motivations in Browsing Online Stores with Mobile Devices. *International Journal of Electronic Commerce, 16*(4), 153–178. doi:10.2753/JEC1086-4415160406

Orton, L. (2007). *Financial Literacy: Lessons from International Experience.* http://cprn3.library.carleton.ca/documents/48647_EN.pdf

Osman, C.-C. C., & Ghiran, A.-M. M. (2019). When Industry 4.0 meets Process Mining. *Procedia Computer Science, 159*, 2130–2136. doi:10.1016/j.procs.2019.09.386

Ovelheiro, B., Silveira, C., & Reis, L. (2021). Sustainability Design Applied to the Digital Signature of Documents. In Handbook of Research on Multidisciplinary Approaches to Entrepreneurship, Innovation, and ICTs (pp. 349-374). IGI Global. http://doi:10.4018/978-1-7998-4099-2.ch016

Oyedeji, S., Seffah, A., & Penzenstadler, B. (2018). A Catalogue Supporting Software Sustainability Design. *Sustainability, 2018*(10), 2296.

Ozkara, B. Y., Ozmen, M., & Kim, J. W. (2016). Exploring the relationship between information satisfaction and flow in the context of consumers' online search. Computers in Human Behavior, 63, 844–859. doi:10.1016/j.chb.2016.06.038

Pace, S. (2004). A grounded theory of the flow experiences of web users. *International Journal of Human-Computer Studies, 60*(3), 327–363. doi:10.1016/j.ijhcs.2003.08.005

Pais, E. (2021). *Sob ataque de Bolsonaro, Cultura defende seu impacto na economia com receita de 170 bilhões de reais*. Available at: https://brasil.elpais.com/cultura/2019-12-27/sob-ataque-de-bolsonaro-cultura-defende-seu-impacto-na-economia-com-receita-de-170-bilhoes-de-reais.html

Palys, T., & Lowman, J. (2014). *Protecting research confidentiality: What happens when law and ethics collide.* James Lorimer & Company.

Pampel, F. C. (2000). *Logistic regression: A primer (quantitative applications in the social sciences).* Sage Publications. doi:10.4135/9781412984805

Pandya, J. (2014). Importance of emotional intelligence, creativity and innovation in vuca environment. *Sansmaran Research Journal, 4*(1), 14-17. http://ezproxy.hct.ac.ae/login?url=https://www-proquest-com.ezproxy.hct.ac.ae/scholarly-journals/importance-emotional-intelligence-creativityand/docview/1960232569/se-2?accountid=1215

Pardal, P., Xara-Brasil, D., Carvalho, L., & Cordeiro, J. (2021). O uso da metodologia de focus group na construção de uma análise swot aplicada ao mercado do livramento - Setúbal. In *Book of Proceedings – Full Papers, V International Forum on Management (IFM) "Connected in a Multipolar World: Everything Becomes Smart and Digital"*. Setúbal: Instituto Politécnico de Setúbal.

Park, E., Kim, W.-H., & Kim, S.-B. (2020). *Tracking tourism and hospitality employees' real-time perceptions and emotions in an online community during the COVID-19 pandemic*. Academic Press.

Park, E. J., Kim, E. Y., Funches, V. M., & Foxx, W. (2012). Apparel product attributes, web browsing, and e-impulse buying on shopping websites. *Journal of Business Research. Elsevier Inc., 65*(11), 1583–1589. doi:10.1016/j.jbusres.2011.02.043

Parviainen, P., Tihinen, M., Kääriäinen, J., & Teppola, S. (2017). Tackling the digitalization challenge: how to benefit from digitalization in practice. *International Journal of Information Systems Project Management, 5*(1), 63-77.

Payaro, A., & Papa, A. R. (2021). Online Grocery Brick and Mortar Retailers. State of the Art in Italy, But Is It a Profitable Strategy? *Management, 9*(1), 14–23.

Peffers, K., Tuunanen, T., Rothenberger, M., & Chatterjee, S., (2007). A Design Science Research Methodology for Information Systems Research. *Journal of Management Information Systems*, *24*(3), 45-78.

Pegoraro, M., Uysal, M. S., & van der Aalst, W. M. P. (2021). Conformance checking over uncertain event data. *Information Systems*, *102*, 101810. doi:10.1016/j.is.2021.101810

Pennington, A., & Eltham, B. (2021). *Creativity in crisis: Rebooting Australia's arts and entertainment sector after COVID*. Academic Press.

Penzenstadler, B., Betz, S., Venters, C. C., Chitchyan, R., Porras, J., Seyff, N., Duboc, L., & Becker, C. (2018). Everything is Interrelated: Teaching Software Engineering for Sustainability. *IEEE/ACM 40th International Conference on Software Engineering: Software Engineering Education and Training (ICSE-SEET),* 153-162.

Pereira, D. S. (2018). *Instituto de Apoio e Desenvolvimento*. Retrieved from http://www.itad.pt/daltonismo/

Pereira, J. M., Dias, R. M., Carvalho, L. M., & Noronha, A. B. (2021). Students' Perceptions About E-Learning Within the Context of the COVID-19 Pandemic: A Study in Brazil and Portugal. In L. C. Carvalho, L. Reis, & C. Silveira (Eds.), *Handbook of Research on Entrepreneurship, Innovation, Sustainability, and ICTs in the Post-COVID-19 Era* (pp. 281–300). IGI Global. doi:10.4018/978-1-7998-6776-0.ch014

Pereshybkina, A., Conde, M. E. C., Kalyesubula, T., & Kirner, E. (2017). *Industry 4.0 Scenario Planning. How will the industry 4.0 transformations affect SMEs in Germany by 2030?* Retrieved from https://opus.hs-furtwangen.de/frontdoor/deliver/index/docId/2467/file/Project+A_Scenario+Industry+4.0+and+SMEs_EK2.pdf

Persse, J. (2012). The ITIL Process Manual - Key Processes and their Application. *The ITIL Process Manual*, 55.

Petrelli, D. (2017). Industry 4.0: Is It Time for Interaction Design Craftsmanship? *The Design Journal, 20*, 2735–2745. doi:10.1080/14606925.2017.1352785

Pickell, Z., Gu, K., & Williams, A. (2020). Virtual volunteers: The importance of restructuring medical volunteering during the COVID-19 pandemic. *Medical Humanities*, *46*, 537–540.

Pinheiro, A., & Macêdo, M. E. (2021) Marketing Digital: Estratégias de Vendas com o Varejo Digital na Pandemia do Covid-19. *Revista Multidisciplinar e de Psicologia, 15*(55), 194-205. https://idonline.emnuvens.com.br/id

Pinto, N. (2016). *PT MagicContact*. Relatório de Projeto Aplicado do Mestrado em Computação Móvel, Escola Superior de Tecnologia e Gestão do Instituto Politécnico da Guarda.

Pivoto, D. G. S., de Almeida, L. F. F., da Rosa Righi, R., Rodrigues, J. J. P. C., Lugli, A. B., & Alberti, A. M. (2021). Cyber-physical systems architectures for industrial internet of things applications in Industry 4.0: A literature review. *Journal of Manufacturing Systems*, *58*, 176–192. doi:10.1016/j.jmsy.2020.11.017

Plataforma Portuguesa das ONGD. (2020). *Impacto da pandemia COVID-19 nos Objetivos de Desenvolvimento Sustentável*. ONGD Plataforma Portuguesa.

Podsakoff, P. M., MacKenzie, S. B., Lee, J. Y., & Podsakoff, N. P. (2003). Common method biases in behavioural research: A critical review of the literature and recommended remedies. *The Journal of Applied Psychology*, *88*(5), 879–903. doi:10.1037/0021-9010.88.5.879 PMID:14516251

Portales, L. (2017). De la RSE a la atención de problemas sociales por medio de modelos de negocio con propósito. In E. Raufflet, L. Portales, C. García de la Torre, J. F. Lozano Aguilar, & E. Barrera Duque (Eds.), Responsabilidad, ética y sostenibilidad empresarial (pp. 203–216). Cd. de México: Pearson.

Portales, L. (2019). *Social Innovation and Social Entrepreneurship Fundamentals, Concepts, and Tools*. Palgrave Macmillan. doi:10.1007/978-3-030-13456-3

Prakash, R. (2019, May 30). *Transforming enterprise and industry with 5G private networks*. Retrieved July 22, 2021, from https://www.qualcomm.com/media/documents/files/the-role-of-5g-in-private-networks-for-industrial-iot.pdf

Prasetyo, H. N., Sarno, R., Budiraharjo, R., & Sungkono, K. R. (2021). The Effect of Duration Heteroscedasticity to the Bottleneck in Business Process Discovered by Inductive Miner Algorithm. *Proceedings - 2021 IEEE Asia Pacific Conference on Wireless and Mobile, APWiMob 2021*, 52–58. 10.1109/APWiMob51111.2021.9435199

Premebida, E. A. (2021). E-commerce in 2020, a scenario of opportunities amid a pandemic. *Research. Social Development*, *10*(2).

Pricewaterhouse Coopers. (2016). *Industry 4.0: Building the digital enterprise*. Retrieved from https://www.pwc.com/gx/en/industries/industries-4.0/landing-page/industry-4.0-building-your-digital-enterprise-april-2016.pdf

Psyrris, A., Kargas, A., & Varoutas, D. (2020). 5G networks' implementation and development of smart sustainable cities evidence and key issues. *13th CMI Conference on Cybersecurity and Privacy - Digital Transformation - Potentials and Challenges, CMI 2020*. doi:10.1109/CMI51275.2020.9322717

Quatrani, T. (2001). *Introduction to the Unified Modeling Language*. IBM Rational.

Quester, P., & Lin Lim, A. (2003). Product involvement/brand loyalty: Is there a link? *Journal of Product and Brand Management*, *12*(1), 22–38. doi:10.1108/10610420310463117

Quo, G. (2014). *Is The Official Hotel Rating System Sinking Into The Past?* 4Hoteliers. Retrieved July 23rd 2014, from http://www.4hoteliers.com/ features/article/7954

Radaelli, G., Lettieri, E., Mura, M., & Spiller, N. (2014). Knowledge sharing and innovative work behaviour in healthcare: A micro-level investigation of direct and indirect effects. *Creativity and Innovation Management*, *23*(4), 400–414. doi:10.1111/caim.12084

Radermecker, A. S. V. (2021). Art and Culture in the COVID-19 era: For a Consumer-oriented Approach. *SN Business & Economics*, *1*(1), 1–14. doi:10.100743546-020-00003-y PMID:34778811

Radio Spectrum Policy Group. (2016). *A Spectrum Roadmap for IoT. Opinion on the Spectrum Aspects of the Internet-of-things (IoT) including M2M FINAL 2 A Spectrum Roadmap for IoT Opinion on the Spectrum Aspects of the Internet-of-things (IoT) including M2M Background and scope of work*. Retrieved from https://circabc.europa.eu/sd/a/a0faa1a5-ca41-42c3-83d5-561b197419b0/RSPG17-006-Final_IoT_Opinion.pdf

Radojevic, T., Stanisic, N., & Stanic, N. (2015). Ensuring positive feedback: Factors that influence customer satisfaction in the contemporary hospitality industry. *Tourism Management*, *51*, 13–21. doi:10.1016/j.tourman.2015.04.002

Ramayah, T., Yeap, J. A., & Ignatius, J. (2014). Assessing knowledge sharing among academics: A validation of the knowledge sharing behavior scale (KSBS). *Evaluation Review*, *38*(2), 160–187. doi:10.1177/0193841X14539685 PMID:25015259

Rambe, P. (2017). Social media marketing and business competitiveness: Evidence from South African tourism. *Problems and Perspectives in Management*, *15*(2), 411–423. doi:10.21511/ppm.15(2-2).2017.10

Rego, A., Sousa, F., Marques, C., & Cunha, M. P. (2012). Authentic leadership promoting employees' psychological capital and creativity. *Journal of Business Research*, *65*(3), 429–437. doi:10.1016/j.jbusres.2011.10.003

Reis, L., Silveira, C., Carvalho, L., & Mata, C. (2020). Digitalization as a Key Issue of the Circular Economy to Promote Sustainability: Prototyping Design for Homeless People. In Mapping, Managing, and Crafting Sustainable Business Strategies for the Circular Economy (pp. 111-137). IGI Global. http://doi:10.4018/978-1-5225-9885-5.ch007

Reis, L., Silveira, C., Pires, G., Péricles, C., Carvalho, L. C., & Mata, C. (2021). Integrated Management Platform for Homeless People. In L. C. Carvalho, L. Reis, & C. Silveira (Eds.), *Handbook of Research on Entrepreneurship, Innovation, Sustainability, and ICTs in the Post-COVID-19 Era* (pp. 243–262). IGI Global. doi:10.4018/978-1-7998-6776-0.ch012

Renn, O., Beier, G., & Schweizer, P. J. (2021). The opportunities and risks of digitalisation for sustain able development: A systemic perspective. *Gaia (Heidelberg)*, *30*(1), 23–28. doi:10.14512/gaia.30.1.6

Respin, E. (2018). No Ghost, Just a Shell. In *Art in the Age of the Internet: 1989 to Today* (pp. 13–40). Yale University Press.

Rhee, H., & Yang, S. (2015). Does hotel attribute importance differ by hotel? Focusing on hotel star-classifications and customers' overall ratings. *Computers in Human Behavior*, *50*, 576–587. doi:10.1016/j.chb.2015.02.069

Rick, S. I., Pereira, B., & Burson, K. A. (2014). The benefits of retail therapy: Making purchase decisions reduces residual sadness. *Journal of Consumer Psychology*, *24*(3), 373–380. doi:10.1016/j.jcps.2013.12.004

Ritchie, B. W., & Jiang, Y. (2019). A review of research on tourism risk, crisis and disaster management: Launching the annals of tourism research curated collection on tourism risk, crisis and disaster management. *Annals of Tourism Research*, *79*, 102812. doi:10.1016/j.annals.2019.102812

Rodrigues, E. (2020). *63% dos brasileiros não investem por falta de conhecimento*. Capital Research. https://cantarino-brasileiro.com.br/blog/63-dos-brasileiros-nao-investem-por-falta-de-conhecimento/

Roggeveen, A. L., & Sethuraman, R. (2020). How the COVID-19 pandemic may change the world of retailing. *Journal of Retailing*, *96*(2), 169–171. doi:10.1016/j.jretai.2020.04.002

Roher, K., & Richardson, D. (2013). Sustainability requirement patterns. *3rd International Workshop on Requirements Patterns (RePa)*, 8-11.

Roquete, M. M. F. (2018). *Modelo de maturidade para apoio à implementação de uma filosofia de gestão orientada a processos numa organização*. Academic Press.

Rostami, A. (2019). Private 5G networks for vertical industries: Deployment and operation models. In *IEEE 5G World Forum, 5GWF 2019 - Conference Proceedings* (pp. 433–439). Institute of Electrical and Electronics Engineers Inc. doi:10.1109/5GWF.2019.8911687

Rowley, J. (2001). "Window" shopping and browsing opportunities in cyberspace. *Journal of Consumer Behaviour*, *1*(4), 369–378. doi:10.1002/cb.81

Rubin, K. S. (2013). *Essential Scrum*. Adisson-Wesley.

Ryder, B. N. (2020). *Cultural Institutions' Digital Responses To COVID-19 Temporary Closures*. Available at: https://stars.library.ucf.edu/honorstheses/820

Saghiri, S., Wilding, R., Mena, C., & Bourlakis, M. (2017). Toward a three-dimensional framework for omni-channel. *Journal of Business Research*, *77*, 53–67. doi:10.1016/j.jbusres.2017.03.025

Salvador, E., Navarrete, T., & Srakar, A. (Eds.). (2021). *Cultural Industries and the Covid-19 Pandemic: A European Focus*. Routledge. doi:10.4324/9781003128274

Sandes, F. S., Komarova, Y., & Botelho, D. (2020). Consumer Online Browsing: distinctive consumer behavior in marketing literature. *American Marketing Association Summer Conference*.

Santiago, A. (2015). A Educação Financeira Escolar Em Portugal. *Boletim GEPEM*, 20-30.

Santos, A. (2015). *Literacia Financeira: O caso dos alunos dos cursos da área financeira da Escola Superior de Ciências Empresariais (ESCE) do Instituto Politécnico de Setúbal (IPS)*. Dissertação de Mestrado.

Saputra, D. A., Nugroho, W. S., & Ranti, B. (2019). Benefits Analysis of IT Investment in Business Support System (BSS) Projects Using Ranti's Generic IS/IT Business Values: Case Studies of the Indonesian Telecommunication Company. *2019 International Conference on Advanced Computer Science and Information Systems (ICACSIS)*, 331–336. 10.1109/ICACSIS47736.2019.8979945

Sbrana, R., & Gandolfo, A. (2007). *Contemporary retailing. Il governo dell'impresa commerciale moderna* (Vol. 1). Giappichelli.

Schindler, R. (1989). The excitement of getting a bargain: Some hypotheses concerning the origins and effects of smart-shopper feelings. *Advances in Consumer Research. Association for Consumer Research (U. S.)*, *16*(2), 447–453. doi:10.100710603-011-9158-5

Schröder, C. (2016). *The Challenges of Industry 4.0 for Small and Medium-sized Enterprises*. Bonn. Retrieved from www.fes-2017plus.de

Schuh, G., Potente, T., Varandani, R., & Schmitz, T. (2014). Global Footprint Design based on genetic algorithms – An "Industry 4.0" perspective. *CIRP Annals*, *63*(1), 433–436. https://doi.org/10.1016/J.CIRP.2014.03.121

Schumacher, A., Erol, S., & Sihn, W. (2016). A Maturity Model for Assessing Industry 4.0 Readiness and Maturity of Manufacturing Enterprises. *Procedia CIRP*, *52*, 161–166. https://doi.org/10.1016/J.PROCIR.2016.07.040

Schumacker, R. E., & Lomax, R. G. (2010). *A Beginners Guide to Structural Equation Modeling* (3rd ed.). Lawrence Erlbaum Associates.

Schweer, D., & Sahl, J. C. (2017). The digital transformation of industry–the benefit for Germany. In *The drivers of digital transformation* (pp. 23–31). Springer. doi:10.1007/978-3-319-31824-0_3

SECUREIoT. (2021). *SECUREIoT Project*. Retrieved October 8, 2021, from https://secureiot.eu/

Seitz, C., Pokrivčák, J., Tóth, M., & Plevný, M. (2017). Online grocery retailing in Germany: An explorative analysis. *Journal of Business Economics and Management*, *18*(6), 1243–1263. doi:10.3846/16111699.2017.1410218

Seraphin, K. D., Philippoff, J., Kaupp, L., & Vallin, L. M. (2012). Metacognition as means to increase the effectiveness of inquiry-based science education. *Science Education International*, *23*(4), 366–382.

Serkal, M. M. A. (2021, June 7). *Revealed: The top 25 tech innovations used in UAE government departments in 2021*. Government – Gulf News. https://gulfnews.com/uae/government/revealed-the-top-25-tech-innovations-used-in-uae-government-departments-in-2021-1.1616051339585

Sharma, A., Shin, H., Santa-María, M. J., & Nicolau, J. L. (2021). Hotels' COVID-19 innovation and performance. *Annals of Tourism Research*, *88*, 103180. doi:10.1016/j.annals.2021.103180

Sheibel, K. (2014). *Guests appreciate hotel stars as guidance in the review sky*. http://blog.hotelstars.eu/2014/07/22/guests-appreciate-hotel-stars-as-guidance-in-the-review-sky/

Shinn, S. A., & Lunz, V. A. (2015). Managing Cost, schedule, and technical performance through a sustained change framework. *IEEE Aerospace Conference Proceedings*. 10.1109/AERO.2015.7119116

Shrout, P. E., & Bolger, N. (2002). Mediation in experimental and nonexperimental studies: New procedures and recommendations. *Psychological Methods*, *7*(4), 422–445. doi:10.1037/1082-989X.7.4.422 PMID:12530702

Sigala, M. (2020). Tourism and COVID-19: Impacts and implications for advancing and resetting IndustryIndustry and research. *Journal of Business Research*, *117*, 312–321. doi:10.1016/j.jbusres.2020.06.015 PMID:32546875

Silva, R. (2021). *Um ano depois do início da pandemia, plataformas de streaming contabilizam ganhos.* Available at: https://forbes.com.br/forbes-money/2021/03/um-ano-depois-do-inicio-da-pandemia-plataformas-de-streaming-contabilizam-ganhos/

Silva, P., & Torres, C. (2010). *Gestão e Liderança* (F. C. A. Editora, Ed.). Lidel Edições.

Silveira, C., & Reis, L. (2021). Sustainability in Information and Communication Technologies. In Handbook of Research on Multidisciplinary Approaches to Entrepreneurship, Innovation, and ICTs (pp. 375-396). IGI Global. doi:10.4018/978-1-7998-4099-2.ch017

Silveira, C., Reis, L., Santos, V., & Mamede, H. (2020). Creativity in Prototypes Design and Sustainability – The case of Social Organizations, Advances in Science. *Technology and Engineering Systems Journal*, *5*(6), 1237–1243. doi:10.25046/aj0506147

Silvestri, L., Forcina, A., Introna, V., Santolamazza, A., & Cesarotti, V. (2020). Maintenance transformation through Industry 4.0 technologies: A systematic literature review. *Computers in Industry*, *123*, 103335. doi:10.1016/j.compind.2020.103335

Sim, T. Y., Dewika, M., & Devandran, A. (2014). Improving students engagement through Social Media: A case study of a private university in Malaysia using Facebook. *International Journal of e-Education, e-Business, e-. Management Learning*, *4*(6), 354–396.

Siriwardhana, Y., Porambage, P., Liyanage, M., Walia, J. S., Matinmikko-Blue, M., & Ylianttila, M. (2019). Micro-Operator driven Local 5G Network Architecture for Industrial Internet. In *IEEE Wireless Communications and Networking Conference, WCNC* (Vol. 2019-April, pp. 1–8). Institute of Electrical and Electronics Engineers Inc. doi:10.1109/WCNC.2019.8885900

Siriwardhana, Y., Porambage, P., Ylianttila, M., & Liyanage, M. (2020). Performance Analysis of Local 5G Operator Architectures for Industrial Internet. *IEEE Internet of Things Journal*, *7*(12), 11559–11575. doi:10.1109/JIOT.2020.3024875

Sismeiro, C., & Bucklin, R. E. (2004). Modeling purchase behavior at an E-commerce Web site: A task-completion approach. *JMR, Journal of Marketing Research*, *41*(3), 306–323. doi:10.1509/jmkr.41.3.306.35985

Skallerud, K., & Wien, A. H. (2019). Preference for local food as a matter of helping behaviour. *Insights from Norway*, *67*(January), 79–88. doi:10.1016/j.jrurstud.2019.02.020

Sogabe, M. (2016). Arte pós-digital. *Proceedings of International Meeting of Art and Technology*. Available at: https://files.cercomp.ufg.br/weby/up/779/o/milton_sogabe.pdf

Sommerville, I. (2005). Integrated Requirements Engineering: A Tutorial. *IEEE Software*, *22*(1), 16–23.

Sommerville, I. (2015). *Software Engineering* (10th ed.). Addison-Wesley Pearson Education.

Sorrells, M. (2021). *Touchless tech: How hotels are preparing for a post-COVID guest experience*. PhocusWire. Retrieved January 8th 2021, from https://www.phocuswire.com/contactless-technology-solutions-hotels-covid-19

Sousa, R., Horta, C., Ribeiro, R., & Rabinovich, E. (2020). How to serve online consumers in rural markets: Evidence-based recommendations. *Business Horizons*, *63*(3), 351–362. doi:10.1016/j.bushor.2020.01.007

Srinivasa Varadhan, D. R. (2021). The Impact of Virtual Learning in the Indian Education System. In L. C. Carvalho, L. Reis, & C. Silveira (Eds.), *Handbook of Research on Entrepreneurship, Innovation, Sustainability, and ICTs in the Post-COVID-19 Era* (pp. 364–380). IGI Global. doi:10.4018/978-1-7998-6776-0.ch018

Srivastava, S. C., & Shainesh, G. (2015). Bridging the service divide through digitally enabled service innovations: Evidence from Indian Healthcare Service Providers. *Management Information Systems Quarterly*, *39*(1), 245–268. doi:10.25300/MISQ/2015/39.1.11

Stolper, O., & Walter, A. (2017). Financial literacy, financial advice, and financial behavior. *Journal of Business Economics*, *87*(5), 581–643. doi:10.100711573-017-0853-9

Stravinskiene, I., & Serafinas, D. (2020). The Link between Business Process Management and Quality Management. *Journal of Risk and Financial Management*, *13*(10), 225. doi:10.3390/jrfm13100225

Strufe, M., Gundall, M., Schotten, H. D., Markwart, C., Ganesan, R. S., & Aleksy, M. (2019). Design of a 5G Ready and Reliable Architecture for the Smart Factory of the Future. *Computer Science*.

Sufi, T., & Ahmed, S. (2021). Surviving COVID-19 Crisis by New Business Models: A Case Study of the Indian Restaurant Industry. In L. C. Carvalho, L. Reis, & C. Silveira (Eds.), *Handbook of Research on Entrepreneurship, Innovation, Sustainability, and ICTs in the Post-COVID-19 Era* (pp. 301–316). IGI Global. doi:10.4018/978-1-7998-6776-0.ch015

Sushil. (2017). Does flexibility mitigate or enhance risk? *Global Journal of Flexible Systems Management, 18*(3), 169-171.

SustainAbility. (2018). *Sustainability: Can our society endure?* SustainAbility an ERM Group Company.

Sustainability. (n.d.). Retrieved June 15, 2021, from https://masdar.ae/en/forasustainablefuture?utm_source=googleutm_medium

Talias, M. (2016). Voluntary hotel regulation as a political compromise. *International Journal of Hospitality Management*, *56*, 10–17. doi:10.1016/j.ijhm.2016.04.007

Talwar, S., Dhir, A., Kaur, P., & Mäntymäki, M. (2020). Why do people purchase from online travel agencies (OTAs)? A consumption values perspective. *International Journal of Hospitality Management*, *88*, 102534. doi:10.1016/j.ijhm.2020.102534

Tao, Y. (2020). Progress in molecular biology and translational science. elsevier.com.

Tenderd. (n.d.). https://www.tenderd.com/ae/about

The Economist Newspaper. (n.d.). *India's economy is suffering from long covid.* The Economist. https://www.economist.com/asia/2021/07/18/indias-economy-is-suffering-from-long-covid

The Economist Newspaper. (n.d.). *Our coverage of the coronavirus.* The Economist. https://www.economist.com/coronavirus-pandemic

The UAE Digital Government Strategy 2025 - The Official Portal of the UAE Government. (n.d.). https://u.ae/en/about-the-uae/digital-uae/uae-national-digital-government-strategy

The UAE's Fourth Industrial Revolution (4IR) Strategy - The Official Portal of the UAE Government. (n.d.). https://u.ae/en/about-the-uae/strategies-initiatives-and-awards/federal-governments-strategies-and-plans/the-uae-strategy-for-the-fourth-industrial-revolution

The Young Foundation. (2012). Social innovation overview: A deliverable of the project. In J. Caulier-Grice, A. Davies, R. Patrick, & W. Norman (Eds.), *The theoretical, empirical and policy foundations for building social innovation in Europe*. European Commission.

Thew, S., & Sutcliffe, A. (2018). Value-based requirements engineering: Method and experience. *Requirements Engineering*, *23*, 443–464.

Thomas, S., Vatavwala, S., & Sinha, P. K. (2017). *BigBasket. com: Redefining the Business Model*. Indian Institute of Management Ahmedabad.

Thompson, D. (2021, June 28). World War II's Lesson for After the Pandemic. *The Atlantic*. https://www.theatlantic.com/ideas/archive/2021/06/covid-19-pandemic-golden-age-innovation/619300/

Thompson, A. A., Strickland, A. J., & Gamble, J. E. (2014). *Crafting and Executing Strategi: The Quest for Competitive Advantage: Concepts and Cases* (19th ed.). McGraw Hill Education.

Thompson, C. J., Locander, W. B., & Pollio, H. R. (1989). Putting consumer experience back into consumer research: The philosophy and method of existential-phenomenology. *The Journal of Consumer Research*, *16*(2), 133–146. doi:10.1086/209203

Thompson, M., & Heron, P. (2006). Relational quality and innovative performance in R&D based science and technology firms. *Human Resource Management Journal*, *16*(1), 28–47. doi:10.1111/j.1748-8583.2006.00003.x

Thota, S. (2018). Social media: A conceptual model of the why's, when's and how's of consumer usage of social media and implications on business strategies. *Academy of Marketing Studies Journal*, *22*(3), 1–12.

Tomar, D., Singh, P., Bhati, J. P., & Tomar, P. (2021). Sustainability of Cloud-Based Smart Society. In P. Tomar (Ed.), Integration and Implementation of the Internet of Things Through Cloud Computing (pp. 113-132). IGI Global. doi:10.4018/978-1-7998-6981-8.ch006

Tongiani, M. G., Carfora, J., & Reut, A. (2019). Digital Marketing and Grocery Retailing Evidence From a Large Retailer in Italy and Belarus. In *Global Campaigning Initiatives for Socio-Economic Development* (pp. 168–189). IGI Global. doi:10.4018/978-1-5225-7937-3.ch010

Torres, E., Adler, H., & Behnke, C. (2014). Stars, Diamonds, And Other Shiny Things: The Use Of Expert And Consumer Feedback In The Hotel Industry. *Journal of Hospitality and Tourism Management*, *21*, 34–43. doi:10.1016/j.jhtm.2014.04.001

Trauth, E., Joshi, K. D., & Yarger, L. K. (2018). ISJ editorial. *Information Systems Journal*, *28*(6), 989–994. doi:10.1111/isj.12201

Tresp, V., Overhage, J. M., Bundschus, M., Rabizadeh, S., Fasching, P. A., & Yu, S. (2016). Going digital: A survey on digitalization and large-scale data analytics in healthcare. *Proceedings of the IEEE*, *104*(11), 2180–2206. doi:10.1109/JPROC.2016.2615052

Trevinal, A. M., & Stenger, T. (2014). Toward a conceptualization of the online shopping experience. *Journal of Retailing and Consumer Services*, *21*(3), 314–326. doi:10.1016/j.jretconser.2014.02.009

Triana, A., Gusdorf, R., Shah, K., & Horst, S. (2020). Technology literacy as a barrier to telehealth during COVID-19. *Telemedicine Journal and e-Health*, 1118–1119.

TripAdvisor Popularity Ranking: Key Factors and How to Improve. (2021). Retrieved June 26th 2021, from https://www.tripadvisor.com/TripAdvisorInsights/w722

UAE 1st among Arab countries in Global Innovation Index 2020. (n.d.). *Gulf Today*. https://www.gulftoday.ae/business/2020/09/03/uae-1st-among-arab-countries--in-global-innovation-index-2020

UAE mGovernment Initiative - The Official Portal of the UAE Government. (n.d.). https://u.ae/en/about-the-uae/digital-uae/uae-mgovernment-initiative

UAE. A Global Hub for Innovation. (2021, February 11). *UAE & USA: United for a Better Future*. https://www.uae-usaunited.com/story/uae-global-hub-innovation/

UNDP. (2015). *Sustainable Development Goals*. United Nations Development Programme.

UNEP. (2011). *Towards a Green Economy: Pathways to Sustainable Development and Poverty Eradication. A Synthesis for Policy Makers*. UNEP.

UNESCO. (2021). *UNESCO e Banco Mundial lançam marco de ação para recuperação, desenvolvimento e crescimento econômico das cidades criativas*. Available at: https://pt.unesco.org/news/unesco-e-banco-mundial-lancam-marco-acao-recuperacao-desenvolvimento-e-crescimento-economico

Unified Modeling Language. (2020). *Unified Modeling Language*. Object Management Group, Inc.

United Nations. (n.d.). *Transforming our world: the 2030 Agenda for Sustainable Development | Department of Economic and Social Affairs*. United Nations. https://sdgs.un.org/2030agenda

United Nations. (n.d.). *UNSDG | UN in Action - United Arab Emirates*. United Nations. https://unsdg.un.org/un-in-action/united-arab-emirates

UNTWO. (2014). Online Guest Reviews and Hotel Classification systems. Madrid, Spain: World Tourism Organization (UNWTO).

UNWTO. (2020). *Tourism and covid-19 – Unprecedented economic impacts*. Retrieved from https://www.unwto.org/tourism-and-covid-19-unprecedented-economic-impacts

UNWTO. (2021). *UN tourism news #23*. Retrieved from https://www.unwto.org/un-tourism-news-23

USA Today. (2017). *Seafood markets around the world*. https://eu.usatoday.com/picture-gallery/travel/experience/food-and-wine/2017/08/17/seafood-markets-around-the-world/104695964/

Vadlamudi, S., & De, S. (2021). A Novel Approach in Cyber Security for securing the Workplace of the Future in large Industry Setups. *2021 International Conference on Intelligent Technologies (CONIT)*, 1–6. 10.1109/CONIT51480.2021.9498468

Valtanen, K., Backman, J., & Yrjola, S. (2019). Blockchain-Powered Value Creation in the 5G and Smart Grid Use Cases. *IEEE Access: Practical Innovations, Open Solutions*, *7*, 25690–25707. https://doi.org/10.1109/ACCESS.2019.2900514

Van Heerden, D., & Goosen, L. (2021). Students' Perceptions of e-Assessment in the Context of Covid-19: The Case of UNISA. In M. Qhobela, M. M. Ntsohi, & L. G. Mohafa (Ed.), *Proceedings of the 29th Conference of the Southern African Association for Research in Mathematics, Science and Technology Education (SAARMSTE)* (pp. 291-305). SAARMSTE.

Van Heerden, D., & Goosen, L. (2012). Using Vodcasts to Teach Programming in an ODL Environment. *Progressio*, *34*(3), 144–160.

van Nuenen, T., & Scarles, C. (2021). Advancements in technology and digital media in tourism. *Tourist Studies*, *21*(1), 119–132. doi:10.1177/1468797621990410

Van Rooij, M., Lusardi, A., & Alessie, R. (2011). Financial Literacy and Stock Market Participation. *Journal of Financial Economics*, *101*(2), 449–472. doi:10.1016/j.jfineco.2011.03.006

Verhoef, P. C. (2021). Omni-channel retailing: Some reflections. *Journal of Strategic Marketing*, *29*(7), 608–616. doi:10.1080/0965254X.2021.1892163

Verma, R., & Kharb, L. (2021). Smart Farming Using Internet of Things: A Solution for Optimal Monitoring. In P. Tomar (Ed.), Integration and Implementation of the Internet of Things Through Cloud Computing (pp. 236-250). IGI Global. doi:10.4018/978-1-7998-6981-8.ch012

Verma, S., & Gustafsson, A. (2020). Investigating the emerging COVID-19 research trends in the field of business and management: A bibliometric analysis approach. *Journal of Business Research*, *118*, 253–261. doi:10.1016/j.jbusres.2020.06.057 PMID:32834211

Veronica & Debora. (2018). Information technology service performance management using COBIT and an ITIL framework: A systematic literature review. *Proceedings of 2017 International Conference on Information Management and Technology, ICIMTech 2017*. doi:10.1109/ICIMTech.2017.8273528

Villasante Marcos, C. (2022). Artificial Intelligence Edge Applications in 5G Networks. In Proceedings of Sixth International Congress on Information and Communication Technology (pp. 269–279). Springer. https://doi.org/10.1007/978-981-16-2380-6_24.

Vorster, J., & Goosen, L. (2017). A Framework for University Partnerships Promoting Continued Support of e-Schools. In J. Liebenberg (Ed.), *Proceedings of the 46th Annual Conference of the Southern African Computer Lecturers' Association (SACLA 2017)* (pp. 118 - 126). North-West University.

Wahlster, W. (2013). Industry 4.0: The Semantic Product Memory as a Basis for Cyber-Physical Production Systems. In *Recent Trends in Artificial Intelligence and Cognitive Science*. Zuruch: SGAICO Forum.

Walstad, W., Rebeck, K. K., & MacDonald, R. A. (2010). The Effects of Financial Education on the Financial Knowledge of High School Students. *The Journal of Consumer Affairs*, *44*(2), 336–357. doi:10.1111/j.1745-6606.2010.01172.x

Wang, Z., Wang, D., Wen, C., Guo, F., & Wang, W. (2021). Push-Based Distributed Economic Dispatch in Smart Grids Over Time-varying Unbalanced Directed Graphs. *IEEE Transactions on Smart Grid*, *12*(4), 3185–3199. doi:10.1109/TSG.2021.3063128

Weber-Sabil, J., & Han, D.-I. D. (2021). *Immersive Tourism-State of the Art of Immersive Tourism Realities through XR Technology*. Academic Press.

Wiener, M., Hoßbach, N., & Saunders, C. (2018). Omnichannel businesses in the publishing and retailing industries: Synergies and tensions between coexisting online and offline business models. *Decision Support Systems*, *109*, 15–26. doi:10.1016/j.dss.2018.01.008

Willard, T., & Halder, M. (2003). *The information society and sustainable development*. International Institute for Sustainable Development (IISD), Winnipeg, Canada. http://www. iisd. org/PUBLICATIONS/pub.aspx

Willis, L. (2008). Against Financial Literacy Education. *Iowa Law Review*.

Wilson, T. D. (2002). Information behaviour: An interdisciplinary perspective. *Information Processing & Management*. Advance online publication. doi:10.1016/S0306-4573(97)00028-9

Wolfinbarger, M., & Gilly, M. C. (2001). Shopping Online for Freedom, Control, and Fun. *California Management Review*, *43*(2), 33–55. https://www.csulb.edu/~mwolfin. doi:10.2307/41166074

World Bank. (2011). *World Development Report 2011–Conflict, Security, and Development*. Washington, DC: World Bank Group. doi:10.1596/978-0-8213-8439-8

World Economic Forum. (2019). *Fourth Industrial Revolution: Beacons of Technology and Innovation in Manufacturing*. Retrieved from https://www3.weforum.org/docs/WEF_4IR_Beacons_of_Technology_and_Innovation_in_Manufacturing_report_2019.pdf

World Economic Forum. (2021). *Understanding the impact of digitalization on society*. Retrieved from https://reports.weforum.org/digital-transformation/understanding-the-impact-of-digitalization-on-society/

Wortley, D. (2013). Immersive Technology Strategies. *Simulation & Gaming*, *44*(2-3), 452–465. doi:10.1177/1046878113488850

Xara-Brasil, D., Pardal, P., Cordeiro, J., & Carvalho, L. (2021). A compra de produtos locais: mercados municipais versus moderna distribuição. In *Book of Proceedings – Full Papers, V International Forum on Management (IFM) "Connected in a Multipolar World: Everything Becomes Smart and Digital"*. Setúbal: Instituto Politécnico de Setúbal.

Xie, K., Zhang, Z., & Zhang, Z. (2014). The business value of online consumer reviews and management response to hotel performance. *International Journal of Hospitality Management*, *43*, 1–12. doi:10.1016/j.ijhm.2014.07.007

Yeh, S.-S. (2021). Tourism recovery strategy against COVID-19 pandemic. *Tourism Recreation Research*, *46*(2), 188–194. doi:10.1080/02508281.2020.1805933

Ye, Q., Law, R., Gu, B., & Chen, W. (2011). The influence of user-generated content on traveler behavior: An empirical investigation on the effects of e-word-of-mouth to hotel online bookings. *Computers in Human Behavior*, *27*(2), 634–639. doi:10.1016/j.chb.2010.04.014

Youn, S., & Jin, S. V. (2017). Reconnecting with the past in social media: The moderating role of social influence in nostalgia marketing on Pinterest. *Journal of Consumer Behaviour*, *16*(6), 565–576. doi:10.1002/cb.1655

Yuce, A. (2021). The Impact of Digital Transformation and Virtual Reality in Tourism Marketing: A Conceptualized Exploration. In Handbook of Research on IoT, Digital Transformation, and the Future of Global Marketing (pp. 1-14). IGI Global. doi:10.4018/978-1-7998-7192-7.ch001

Yuce, A., Arasli, H., Ozturen, A., & Daskin, M. (2020). Feeling the Service Product Closer: Triggering Visit Intention via Virtual Reality. *Sustainability*, *12*(16), 6632. doi:10.3390u12166632

Zanero, S. (2017). Cyber-Physical Systems. *Computer*, *50*(4), 14–16. doi:10.1109/MC.2017.105

Za, S., Spagnoletti, P., & North-Samardzic, A. (2014). Organisational learning as an emerging process: The generative role of digital tools in informal learning practices. *British Journal of Educational Technology*, *45*(6), 1023–1035. doi:10.1111/bjet.12211

Zhang, J. (2020). Transport Policymaking against COVID-19 and Future Public Health Pandemics: A PASS Approach. SSRN *Electronic Journal*. doi:10.2139/ssrn.3642979

Zhao, M., Li, L., & Xu, Z. (2021). Study on hotel selection method based on integrating online ratings and reviews from multi-websites. *Information Sciences*, *572*, 460–481. doi:10.1016/j.ins.2021.05.042

Zheng, X., Men, J., Yang, F., & Gong, X. (2019). Understanding impulse buying in mobile commerce: An investigation into hedonic and utilitarian browsing. *International Journal of Information Management. Elsevier*, *48*(February), 151–160. doi:10.1016/j.ijinfomgt.2019.02.010

Zhong, L., Sun, S., Law, R., & Li, X. (2021). Tourism crisis management: Evidence from COVID-19. *Current Issues in Tourism*, *24*(19), 2671–2682. doi:10.1080/13683500.2021.1901866

Zwanka, R. J., & Buff, C. (2021). COVID-19 generation: A conceptual framework of the consumer behavioral shifts to be caused by the COVID-19 pandemic. *Journal of International Consumer Marketing*, *33*(1), 58–67. doi:10.1080/08961530.2020.1771646

About the Contributors

Leonilde Reis is Coordinator Professor with Aggregation at the School of Business and Administration (ESCE) of the Polytechnic Institute of Setúbal (IPS). The activities of teaching in higher education were developed since 1992 in the field of "Information Systems" and focused on undergraduate, master's and doctoral courses. Aggregation in Information Sciences, Fernando Pessoa University; PhD in Systems Information and Technologies, Minho University; Master's in management informatics, Católica University. Author of several publications in national and international journals, books and book chapters.

Luísa Cagica Carvalho held a PhD in Management in University of Évora – Portugal. Professor of Management on Department of Economics and Management, Institute Polytecnic of Setubal– Portugal. Guest professor in international universities teaches in courses of master and PhDs programs. Researcher at CEFAGE (Center for Advanced Studies in Management and Economics) University of Evora – Portugal. Author of several publications in national and international journals, books and book chapters.

Clara Silveira Coordinator Professor at the School of Technology and Management (ESTG) of the Polytechnic Institute of Guarda (IPG), having 30 years of experience teaching "Software Engineering" in the Computer Science Engineering degree, and 8 years experience leading the management team of ESTG. She holds a PhD in Electrical and Computer Engineering from the Faculty of Engineering, University of Porto (FEUP); Master in Electrical and Computer Engineering, specializing in Industrial Informatics at FEUP; and completed the Training Program on Public Management (FORGEP) by INA. Director of the Software Engineering and Information Systems field. Member of the Polytechnic Institute of Guarda Ethical Committee.

* * *

Adriana Alaimo is living in Agrigento (Italy) she received a B.A. in Business Administration from University of Pisa in 2021 Her graduate dissertation and actual research interests are on Retailing and grocery smaller retailer in Italy.

Conceição Aleixo is Assistent at the School of Business and Administration (ESCE) of the Polytechnic Institute of Setúbal (IPS). The activities of teaching in higher education were developed since 2001 in the field of "Accounting and Finance" and focused on undergraduate and master's courses. Master's in Accounting and Auditing, Évora University; Gradute´s in Business Management, Polytechnic Institute of Beja (IPBeja). Author of some publications in national and international scientific events, national and international journals and book chapters.

Josmar Andrade teaches Marketing at Universidade de S Paulo, Brazil. His areas of interest are related to Marketing Communications, Ethics, Innovation, Entrepreneurship and Creative Economy.

Duarte Xara Brasil has a PhD in Management in University of Évora – Portugal. Professor of Marketing at Institute Polytecnic of Setubal– Portugal, where he teaches subjects mainly related with branding. Author of several publications in national and international journals, books and book chapters. Teaching and research activities gave been developed with a systematic international participation in academic events and courses in several countries, In Europe, Africa, Asia and America.

Giovanna Boava is an undergraduate marketing student at Universidade de Sao Paulo.

Sriya Chakravarti is an education luminary who has led ground breaking roles in building better models of applied education through digitization and entrepreneurship. She is the H.O.D of Business Studies at a federal institution in UAE and holds a Doctor of Education degree from the University of San Francisco, USA. Dr. Chakravarti has worked on various educational projects for the United Nations fraternity and has researched, developed, taught, and led educational initiatives in the USA, UAE, UK, India, Germany, Malaysia, Mexico, Thailand, Vietnam, Laos, and Cambodia. She believes in quality education for all and retains a strong leadership and community development perspective. She has authored peer-reviewed research papers, chapters, and books for various publication houses and has been a juror for national and international education related competitions. Her academic career is decorated with several reputed awards and funding. She is a Life Fellow of the Royal Asiatic Society (FRAS, UK); Fellow of Royal Society for the Encouragement of Arts, Manufacturers, and Commerce (FRSA, UK), and a Principal Fellow of Higher Education (PFHEA, UK). She holds a chartered membership status (MCIPD, UK) with The Chartered Institute of Personnel and Development and is a member of the Royal Institute of International Affairs (Chatham House, UK).

Margarida Cristina graduated in marketing from Institute Polytechnic of Setúbal in 2021.

Sofia Cristina graduated in marketing from Institute Polytechnic of Setúbal in 2021.

Eva Ferrari is living in Mantova (Italy) she received a B.A. in Businees Adminitration and Marketing from University of Modena and Reggio in 2019 and a M.A. in Marketing and Market Research from University of Pisa in 2021. Her graduate dissertation and actual research interests are on Retailing and grocery smaller retailer in Italy.

Geraldo Filho is a Doctorate in Administration from the Federal University of Lavras – UFLA.

Leila Goosen is a full professor in the Department of Science and Technology Education of the University of South Africa. Prof. Goosen was an Associate Professor in the School of Computing, and the module leader and head designer of the fully online signature module for the College for Science, Engineering and Technology, rolled out to over 92,000 registered students since the first semester of

2013. She also supervises ten Masters and Doctoral students, and has successfully completed supervision of 43 students at postgraduate level. Previously, she was a Deputy Director at the South African national Department of Education. In this capacity, she was required to develop ICT strategies for implementation. She also promoted, coordinated, managed, monitored and evaluated ICT policies and strategies, and drove the research agenda in this area. Before that, she had been a lecturer of Information Technology (IT) in the Department for Science, Mathematics and Technology Education in the Faculty of Education of the University of Pretoria. Her research interests have included cooperative work in IT, effective teaching and learning of programming and teacher professional development.

David Júlio has a bachelor's degree in Computer Science Engineering at the School of Technology and Management (ESTG) of the Polytechnic Institute of Guarda (IPG) in Guarda, Portugal. Respectful, open to help, good teamwork, hardworker and always trying to improve his skills.

Ismael Junior is a teacher of Basic and Technological Education (IFNMG). Doctoral Student in Information Science (PGCIN/UFSC). Master in Social Development (PPGDS/Unimontes). Teaching in Professional and Technological Education Specialist (CEAD/IFNMG). Accounting Management and Controllership Specialist (Unimontes). Bachelor of Administration (Unimontes).

Antonios D. Kargas holds a bachelor's degree in economics from National and Kapodistrian University of Athens, as well as a master's degree and a Ph.D. degree from the Department of Informatics and Telecommunications in the same University. His research interests include managerial issues related with technological implementation and digital transformation, as well as cost benefit analysis, technoeconomic analysis, applied economics for the telecommunication sector. He has more than 30 publications in peer reviewed journals / conferences in the field and more than 160 citations, while he serves as reviewer and co-editor in several international editions. Since 2007 he has worked as a research associate for the University of Athens, participating in more than 20 National and European funded projects. He holds significant experience as Economist / Financial Expert, responsible for conducting Cost – Benefit Analysis in several international projects. In 2009 he co-founded "Win to Win, Business Consultants", working in Business Consulting and Evaluating several investment projects. In 2013 he co – founded "Content Management in Culture P.C." (Comic), a private company activated in the field of IT services and serious games' solutions.

Joaquina Marchão has been working in ICT domain since 1990 in different domains and functions, in software development, project management, ICT management control and IT service desk management. In 2015 began teaching activity in Polytecnic higher education, at the School of Business and Administration (ESCE) in Polytecnic Institute of Setúbal (IPS), teaching ICT curricular units. Currently a doctoral student at the University of Algarve, holds a Master's degree in Organizational Information Systems at ESCE-IPS, and a degree in Management and Administration at Moderna University of Setúbal (UM).

Tongiani Maria Giovanna is a Researcher in the Economy and Management of Companies at Department of Econony and Management of University of Pisa. Her primary teaching areas are undergraduate Economy and management of retailing and wholesaling firms and graduate Economy management and strategy of retailing firms. Her research interests include small firms and distribution channel, retailing and wholesaling management and strategy, business process management and the business value and adoption of e-business, shopper Marketing, and in store marketing.

Anabela Marques is IT specialist at the Portuguese Tax and Customs Authority (AT), works as a computer systems designer and analyst (since 2017). Also worked as business manager/project manager in several projects within the organization (2005-2017). Appointed project team coordinator for the tax revenue accounting system of the General Directorate of Taxes - DGCI (2009). Project leader at the General Directorate of Treasury and Finance (DGTF) (1997-2005). Responsible for the accounting of the courses related to the trainers' training and environmental framework, at the Institute for Environmental Promotion (IPAMB) of the Ministry of Environment (1995-1997). Certified by APOGEP IPMA Level D: Certified Project Management Associate and Certified Agile Associate. Master in Organizational IT Systems by the College of Business Administration (ESCE) of Polytechnic Institute of Setúbal (IPS). Degree in Computer Science and Business Management (IGE) from University Institute of Lisbon - ISCTE. Extracurricular course in Tax. Author of papers in international conferences.

Paula Martins is an assistant professor of Electronics and Computers Engineering department of Faculty of Sciences and Technology of Algarve, and a member of the research center for Tourism, Sustainability and Well-being (CinTurs), has a PhD in Computer Science and Engineering from the "Instituto Superior Técnico da Universidade Técnica de Lisboa" (IST/ULT). In 2000 sh got the Master´s in Computer Science and Engeneering from "Faculdade de Ciencias e Tecnologia de Universidade Nova de Lisboa" (FCT/UNL). Personal interests in Software Process Improvement, software development process, domain specific languages, modelling languages and business process modelling.

James Ngugi is an Accreditation Officer at Commission for University Education, Kenya.

Alexandros Psyrris is a PhD candidate in National and Kapodistrrian University of Athens for "Technoeconomic analysis of 5G systems" covering topics such as technology enablers, business models development, smart and sustainable cities, Industry 4.0.

Julia Ramos is an undergraduate student of marketing at Universidade de São Paulo.

Fábio Shimabukuro Sandes is an Assistant Professor of Marketing at Universidade Lusófona and he has complete his Ph.D. in 2020 in Marketing at Fundação Getulio Vargas EAESP, a Brazilian leading business school with triple-crown international accreditation (AACSB, EFMD, AMBA). Fabio also holds a MSc in Marketing at the same school. He was a visiting Ph.D. student at Fordham University in New York during his thesis research.He has worked as a Marketing practitioner for 15 years, working in multinational companies like The LYCRA® company and Vicunha Textiles, consolidating an executive career in the fashion industry. He has published papers in international peer-reviewed journals and presented papers in the most relevant international conferences in Marketing, such as EMAC, ACR, SCP, and AMA. He is a consumer behavior researcher and uses both qualitative and quantitative research methods. He is particularly interested in online consumer behavior and sustainable consumption practices. Due to his background in the Fashion industry, Fabio is also working with advancing the knowledge of the role of Marketing in this market.

Tahir Sufi is working as Professor and Deputy Director with Amity School of Hospitality, Amity University, Noida, India. He has over two decades of work experience with leading academic Institutions and International Hotel brands like Le Meridian, Hilton and Best Western. He is Ph.d in Business Administration and Masters in Hospitality Management from Sheffield Hallam University, UK. He has been the head of various Hospitality Schools in India.

João Torres has a bachelor's degree in Computer Science Engineering at the School of Technology and Management (ESTG) of the Polytechnic Institute of Guarda (IPG) in Guarda, Portugal. Friendly, communicative and a helpful person. Good teamwork and social skills, always willing to learn new things.

Leonor Vacas de Carvalho is an Assistant Professor in the Business Department at Universidade de Évora, Portugal, where she teaches marketing management, brand management and marketing communications. She is a researcher at CEFAGE. Her research interests include brand identity, brand image, social media branding and services branding. Her previous work has been published in the Journal of Business Research, The Journal of Marketing Management, the Journal of Brand Management and the Journal of Product and Brand Management, as well as presented at conferences.

Akrivi Vagena is a senior faculty at Professional Training Institutes in Athens and teaches in departments of Tourism Administration and Hotel Studies. She has also taught at the Higher Technological Institute of Piraeus in the Department of Tourism Business Administration. She is a Ph.D. Candidate of the University of Patras in the Department of Business Administration, and her thesis is about creating a new model for hotel classification in star categories.

Dimitris Varoutas (SM'11, M'98) holds a Physics degree and M.Sc. and Ph.D diplomas in communications and technoeconomics from the University of Athens. He serves as an assistant professor in the Department of Informatics and Telecommunications at the University of Athens. He has been participating in numerous European R&D projects in the RACE I &II, ACTS, Telematics, RISI and IST frameworks in the areas of telecommunications and technoeconomics. He actively participates in several technoeconomic activities for telecommunications, networks and services such the ICT-OMEGA and the CELTIC/CINEMA projects, as well as the Conferences on Telecommunications TechnoEconomics. He also participates in or manages related national activities for technoeconomic evaluation of broadband strategies, telecommunications demand forecasting, price modelling etc. His research interests span design of optical and wireless communications systems to technoeconomic evaluation of network architectures and services. He has published more than 90 publications in refereed journals and conferences in the area of telecommunications, optoelectronics and technoeconomics, including leading IEEE Journals and conferences. He is a Senior Member of Photonics (former LEOS), Communications, Education and Engineering Management Societies of IEEE and serves as reviewer in several including IEEE journals and conferences. Since 2007, he is Member of BOG of ADAE, the National Authority for Communications Security and Privacy and since May 2013 is a BoD member of KEPE, the Center of Planning and Economic Research.

Ali Yuce is born and grew up in Turkey. After working independently for his business, he changed his life dramatically and radically to pursue his passion for academia. After receiving his Bachelor's degree from DePaul University, he obtained his Master's and Doctoral Degrees from Eastern Mediterranean

University. Prior to graduation from the Ph.D. program, he is the author of several articles and book chapters in international journals along with numerous congress papers about the impact of technology on the landscape of tourism, education, and marketing. On the other side, he is a lifelong learner who loves conveying every bit of knowledge that he learns for others. He enjoys swimming, cooking, jogging, reading about history, technology, tourism; he also loves animals and nature.

Index

E

F

G

H

I

K

L

M

O

P

www.ingramcontent.com/pod-product-compliance
Lightning Source LLC
LaVergne TN
LVHW060425300926
849162LV00006B/1524